CRUCIAL ISSUES IN EDUCATION

CRUCIAL ISSUES IN EDUCATION

FOURTH EDITION

EDITED BY *Henry J. Ehlers*

UNIVERSITY OF MINNESOTA, DULUTH

Holt, Rinehart and Winston, Inc.

NEW YORK CHICAGO SAN FRANCISCO
ATLANTA DALLAS
MONTREAL TORONTO LONDON SYDNEY

Library of Congress Catalog Card Number: 74-75920
SBN: 03-077350-4
Printed in the United States of America
1 2 3 4 5 6 7 8 9

Preface

THERE HAS BEEN MUCH THINKING and critical comment about education during the past decade. Some of the criticism reflects misunderstanding about the changes taking place in the schools (for example, about programmed learning). In such cases this anthology gives much more space to the new than to the old and familiar; for until the newer developments are understood, rational discussion about them is impossible. Other criticism merely projects the fears of disturbed and unbalanced minds and may be ignored. But, on the whole, recent criticism of education has been stimulating, constructive, and helpful, and illustrates the vitality as well as the volatility of contemporary educational thought.

In handling controversial issues, this anthology attempts to present opposing viewpoints as fairly as possible. If some selections seem dogmatic and intolerant, the reader should recognize the limitations of language and human nature. Actually, all statements should be considered as hypotheses, that is, as suggestions or proposals to be examined. Were it not for the stylistic problems involved, would it not be well if all our assertions could be made in the form of questions? Should not the reader be encouraged to subject every paragraph, every sentence, to critical examination? Should he not constantly inquire: "Is this true? Is this sound? Is this adequate? Is this practical?" Even if the reader holds a nondemocratic outlook (according to the criteria set forth in some selections), is not this one of his "rights" in a liberal society? If democracy means shared thinking, is not the person who *fails* to think, rather than the one who *differs* from the majority, the least democratic in his basic attitude?

Within such limits as space allows, this anthology allows proponents of opposing viewpoints to speak for themselves. Not only does this procedure help avoid misrepresentation, but, as the editors of *The New Yorker* once noted, "an author so little moved by a controversy that he can present both sides fairly is not likely to burn any holes in the paper." It is not the function of this anthology to provide clearcut answers to any of the problems raised, or to decide the "right side" or the "wrong side" of a disputed area. Rather, each chapter presents claims and counterclaims, assertions and denials, proofs and disproofs, conflicting values and rival hypotheses. Such an approach may tend to unsettle the immature mind—sometimes to the point of confusion and bewilderment—but it also unsettles the habit of dismissing great issues in terms of verbal generalities and stereotypes. And we should always remember that the human mind is like a parachute: useless until open.

Why should we read *both* (or *several*) sides of a disputed issue? The reason is clear. We are so comfortable with ourselves and with the prejudices we now hold that we are loath to read anything that might upset these cherished beliefs. As scholars, however, we must abide by the Socratic maxim, "The unexamined life is not worth human living." This may also be translated, "The unexamined belief is not worth human holding." A careful study of opposing viewpoints will generally clarify an issue. It will help replace emotional outbursts by rational discussion, and it should help remove unreasoned prejudices, misleading clichés, and half-truths. The net result is a restructuring of our original beliefs, making them more comprehensive and precise, as well as an increase in our personal esteem and self-confidence, since our beliefs (and the personality they reflect) are now maintained with understanding and integrity.

An open society is progressive and dynamic precisely because different individuals and organizations are permitted to defend their opposing viewpoints with passionate intensity before the court of public opinion. Hopefully, these controversial issues will be resolved in a manner reasonably satisfactory to all, but the process of arriving at a viable position is one of tension, not rest. For, as Ralph Waldo Emerson wrote in his essay on "Intellect,"

> God offers to every mind its choice between truth and repose. Take what you please—you can never have both. Between them, as a pendulum, man oscillates. He in whom the love of repose predominates will accept the first creed, the first philosophy, the first political party he meets—most likely his father's. He gets rest, commodity and reputation: but he shuts the door of truth. He in whom the love of truth predominates will keep himself aloof from all moorings, and afloat. He will abstain from dogmatism, and recognize all the opposite negations between which, as walls, his being is swung. He submits to the inconveniences of suspense and imperfect opinion, but he is a candidate for truth, as the other is not, and respects the highest law of his being.

Each chapter may be viewed as a dialogue between some of the outstanding minds of our time. To gain the most from this anthology, the student himself must somehow participate in the dialogue. For, in the words of Robert Maynard Hutchins: "Education is a kind of continuing dialogue, and a dialogue assumes, in the nature of the case, different points of view."*

Not every issue in this anthology will seem equally crucial to every reader. Accordingly, you, the reader, should ask yourself at the very start "What issues are most crucial to *me*?" Peruse the book hurriedly, study the general contents carefully, and decide which topics you would like to study in greatest detail. What issues would you add to—or drop from—this anthology? What criteria may be used to determine whether an issue is significant or trivial, whether a discussion is constructive, or merely a form of emotional release (for example, name calling)? The book demands that you exercise your critical faculties, and you are encouraged to exercise them, first of all, on the anthology itself.†

Now some words of thanks. This anthology would not be possible were it not for generous permissions to reprint selections of many authors and publishers. Acknowledgements of these are made in the accompanying footnotes. Many colleagues, students, and friends have contributed to one or another of the anthology's revisions, and for reading one or more chapters of the manuscript to this fourth edition I am indebted to a dozen Minnesota colleagues—especially to Dr. Gerhard von Glahn (Political Science), Dr. Dean Crawford (Education), and Miss Frances Skinner (Sociology)—and to Professor R. Freeman Butts, Teachers College, Columbia University. Gratitude is also expressed to many helpful librarians, to numerous students, to my typist, Mrs. Jo Ann Larson, and to my wife.

Although Dr. Gordon C. Lee's new post as Chief of Party, TCCU/AID Team, Kabul, Afghanistan, has taken him out of the country, and thus prevented his participation in this fourth edition, I remain much indebted for his help in giving form and content to the two previous editions of this anthology.

HENRY EHLERS

Duluth, Minnesota
June 1969

* Robert M. Hutchins, cited (with exact reference) by Justice Felix Frankfurter, in *Wieman v. Updegraff*, 344 U.S. 183 (1952).

† Perusal of related books and anthologies is also recommended—books such as *Controversy in American Education*, Harold Full, ed., New York: Crowell-Collier and Macmillan, 1967, or *Patterns of Power: Social Foundations of Education*, Thomas E. Linton and Jack L. Nelson, eds. New York: Pitman, 1968. An annotated bibliography may be found on pp. 585–591 of the Linton-Nelson anthology.

Contents

Chapter 1
PUBLIC EDUCATION AND NATIONAL UNITY

Conflicting Interests in a Free Society

1.1 INTRODUCTION: THE BALANCING OF CONFLICTING INTERESTS

"Martha, methinks the whole world is queer except thou and me," said the old Quaker to his wife, "and sometimes, Martha, methinks even thou art a bit peculiar." Every person, every group, is more or less like this. We all tend to become narrow, provincial, and so set in our own patterns of belief that we cannot tolerate others. The extreme form of fanaticism or narrow-mindedness was parodied by Lord Macaulay:

> I am in the right and you are in the wrong. When you are stronger, you ought to tolerate me, for it is your duty to tolerate truth. But when I am the stronger, I shall persecute you, for it is my duty to persecute error.[1]

To see democracy in action is to see hundreds of zealous minorities clamoring for power, each sure of its own truth and righteousness.

With so many conflicting ideas, how can we decide which shall prevail? We all agree that society must have unity—"order is heaven's first law"—and the power to manage must ultimately rest in someone's hands. Otherwise we find ourselves like Stephen Leacock's horseman, riding not one horse but many horses, each one galloping wildly in a different direction. To prevent such chaos, democracy accepts majority rule as a working principle.

To prevent the ruling majority from becoming tyrannical, democracy guarantees two fundamental liberties: First, the rulers themselves must be subject to replacement according to the changing attitudes of the people who elect them. Second, there must be genuine freedom for such attitudes to change by allowing lone thinkers and minority groups the right to challenge prevailing beliefs. For a democratic society to remain stable, minority groups must not be compelled to feel that they are *fixed and permanent* minorities. Unless all groups have full rights to speak and to organize,

[1] Attributed to Thomas Babington Macaulay by David Spitz, in *Patterns of Anti-Democratic Thought,* New York: Crowell-Collier and Macmillan Inc., 1949, p. 283. Compare "Holy Willie's Prayer," by Robert Burns.

majority rule will degenerate into rule by force, and enlightenment will be lost to prejudice. The whole strength of reason, and of government based on reason, depends on the condition that reason can be set right when it is wrong—that people hear all sides of an issue. Otherwise errors harden into prejudices; the will of the strong overcomes the judgment of the wise (who may be weak); those in power close the avenues of communication so that rulers cannot be replaced; and there is no protection for minority groups to inquire, criticize, and organize.

When we think of freedom, we generally think only in terms of personal freedom. Yet freedom is also a *social* value, and if there are no social controls, individual liberties will be destroyed. Carried to excess, individual liberty leads to its own destruction, for it then permits the enemies of liberty to gain power. This historical fact is known as "the paradox of freedom"[2]: Complete absence of restraint ultimately leads to the greatest of all restraints; for it permits the bully to enslave the meek, and allows the intolerant to destroy both the tolerant and tolerance itself. The intolerant by nature tend to be active and aggressive, whereas the tolerant may be passive, or even indifferent. Thus a state that permits the intolerant to behave without restraint will thereby be permitting tolerant groups or impotent minorities to be abused. Hence to be truly neutral, a state must be actively tolerant and extend its protection to all citizens by being, to some extent, intolerant of intolerant activities. Only thus can our nation embody its motto—*E pluribus unum*—out of many, one.

In any social group, different individuals will cherish different values; and in the resulting conflict of values, some type of social control is inevitable. Even the freedoms guaranteed by our Bill of Rights have never been absolutes—that is, values which could be pursued with no limitations whatsoever. For example, the constitutional guarantee of freedom of assembly may be restricted if its abuse leads to riots or to other serious disturbances of peace and order:

> It is one thing to say that the police cannot be used as an instrument for the suppression of unpopular views, and another to say that, when . . . the speaker passes the bounds of argument and persuasion and undertakes incitement of riot, they are powerless to prevent a breach of peace.[3]

Again, the constitutional guarantees of free speech and press do not include the obscene, the profane, the libelous, or insulting words which incite an immediate breach of peace:

---

[2] Carried to extremes, both freedom and repression lead to paradoxes. The paradox of freedom has been well stated by Karl R. Popper in *The Open Society and Its Enemies*, Princeton, N.J.: Princeton University Press, 1950, pp. 348–350, 546–547; London: Routledge & Kegan Paul, Ltd., 1945, I: 265–266, II: 160–162. The paradox of repression is less subtle: It is simply a case of throwing out the baby with the bathwater.

[3] *Feiner v. New York*, 340 U.S. 315 (1951).

> Resort to epithets or personal abuse is not in any proper sense communication of information or opinion safeguarded by the Constitution, and its punishment as a criminal act would raise no question under that instrument.[4]

Likewise, in cases involving freedom of religion, our courts have traditionally steered a middle course between unlimited freedom (on the part of individuals or groups of individuals) on the one hand, and complete state control on the other. In the Oregon case, an oft-quoted passage reads:

> The fundamental liberty under which all governments in this Union repose excludes any general power of the State to standardize its children by forcing them to accept instruction from public teachers only. The child is not the mere creature of the State; those who nurture him and direct his destiny have the right, coupled with the high duty, to recognize and prepare him for additional obligations.[5]

But a prior passage in the same Oregon decision reads:

> No question is raised concerning the power of the State reasonably to regulate *all* schools, to inspect, supervise and examine them, their teachers and pupils; to require that all children of proper age attend *some* school, that teachers shall be of good moral character and patriotic disposition, that certain studies plainly essential to good citizenship must be taught, and that nothing be taught which is manifestly inimical to public welfare.

Underlying these court opinions are the following general principles:

> . . . in all freedom of expression cases it [the Court] must grapple with fundamental policy questions as it seeks to balance two significant interests —the public interest in preventing the supposed evil and the public interest in preserving freedom of expression. In each such case the Court must decide whether the seriousness of the evil, and the probability that the utterance under attack may cause or substantially contribute to that evil, are sufficiently great to justify the interference with freedom of expression in this particular case and the resulting suppression of freedom of expression in similar situations.[6]

---

[4] *Cantwell v. Connecticut*, 310 U.S. 296, 310 (1940); *Chaplinsky v. New Hampshire*, 315 U.S. 568, 571 (1942). In *Roth v. United States*, 364 U.S. 467 (1957), the Court reaffirmed this viewpoint: The intent of the First and Fourteenth Amendments was

> . . . to assure unfettered interchange of ideas for the bringing about of political and social changes desired by the people. . . . All ideas having even the slightest redeeming social importance—unorthodox ideas, controversial ideas, even ideas hateful to the prevailing climate of opinion—have the full protection of the [constitutional] guarantees. . . . But implicit in the First Amendment is the rejection of obscenity as utterly without redeeming social importance.

[5] *Pierce v. Society of Sisters*, 268 U.S. 510 (1925).

[6] William B. Lockhart and Robert C. McClure, "Literature, the Law of Obscenity, and the Constitution," 38 *Minnesota Law Review* 295: 295–422 at 368, March 1954.

Realistic democracy provides a middle-of-the-road solution for problems which arise from conflicts among interests or pressure groups. Its method is give-and-take. Its normal solutions are compromises. Extreme solutions are rare. . . . The American democratic faith is a system of checks and balances in the realm of ideas. It asserts the possibility of a balance between liberty and authority, between the self-expression of the free individual and the necessary coercion of the organized group. The democratic faith is, then, in essence, a philosophy of the mean.[7]

1.2 FREE PUBLIC SCHOOLS—A KEY TO NATIONAL UNITY*

Henry Steele Commager

No other people ever demanded so much of schools and of education as have the American. None other was ever so well served by its schools and its educators.

From the very beginning of our national existence, education has had very special tasks to perform in America. Democracy could not work without an enlightened electorate. The States and sections could not achieve unity without a sentiment of nationalism. The nation could not absorb tens of millions of immigrants from all parts of the globe without rapid and effective Americanization. Economic and social distinctions and privileges, severe enough to corrode democracy itself, had to be overcome. To schools went the momentous responsibility of inculcating democracy, nationalism, and equalitarianism.

The passion for education goes back to the beginnings of the Massa-

---

[7] Ralph Henry Gabriel, *The Course of American Democratic Thought,* New York: The Ronald Press Company, 1940, p. 418.

This anthology assumes that American teachers should not only understand some major problems facing education but also should comprehend the differences that separate our society from others. As a backdrop for later issues in this anthology, Chapter 1 studies the manner in which social changes are effected in our society.

* From pp. 546–548 from LIVING IDEAS IN AMERICA edited by Henry Steele Commager. Copyright © 1951, 1964 by Henry Steele Commager. By permission of Harper & Row, Publishers, Incorporated. Adapted from a longer article "Our Schools Have Kept Us Free," *Life* 29: 46–47, October 16, 1950.

Author of many books, Henry Steele Commager was for many years professor of history at Columbia University, and later at Amherst College.

This article summarizes the remarkable achievement of our public schools in amalgamating European immigrants into a common culture and a new nation. The question remains whether—or how—our schools today can do as well for groups whose racial and cultural origins are much more diverse.

chusetts Bay Colony; the Law of 1647, for all its inadequacy, set up the first even partially successful system of public education anywhere in the world. Only three universities in Britain antedate those of America, and by the time of independence America boasted more colleges than did the mother country, while the State Universities of the early national period represented something new under the sun.

From the first, then, education was the American religion. It was—and is—in education that we put our faith; it is our schools and colleges that are the peculiar objects of public largess and private benefaction; even in architecture we proclaim our devotion, building schools like cathedrals.

Has this faith been justified? A case might be made out for justification on purely scholarly grounds, for after all the highest of our schools of higher learning are as high as any in the world. But this is a somewhat narrow test. Let us look rather to the specific historical tasks which were imposed upon our schools and which they have fulfilled. The first and most urgent task was to provide an enlightend citizenry in order that self-government might work. It is well to remember that democracy, which we take for granted, was an experiment—and largely an American experiment. It could not succeed with a people either corrupt or uninformed. People everywhere—as Jefferson and the spokesmen of the Age of Reason believed—were naturally good, but they were not naturally enlightened. To enlighten the people was the first duty of a democracy, and an enlightened people, in turn, saw to it that "schools and the means of education" were forever encouraged.

The second great task imposed upon education and on the schools was the creation of national unity. In 1789 no one could take for granted that the new nation, spread as it was over a continental domain, would hold together. Yet Americans did manage to create unity out of diversity. Powerful material forces sped this achievement: the westward movement, canals and railroads, a liberal land policy, immigration, and so forth. No less important were intellectual and emotional factors—what Lincoln called those "mystic chords of memory stretching from every battlefield and patriot grave to every living heart and hearthstone." These—the contributions of poets and novelists, naturalists and explorers, orators and painters—were transmitted to each generation anew through the schools.

The third task imposed on schools was that which we call Americanization. Each decade after 1840 saw from two to eight million immigrants pour into America. No other people had ever absorbed such large and varied racial stocks so rapidly or so successfully. It was the public school which proved itself the most efficacious of all agencies of Americanization—Americanization not only of the children but, through them, of the parents as well.

A fourth major service that the schools have rendered democracy is that of overcoming divisive forces in society and advancing understanding and equality. The most heterogeneous of modern societies—heterogeneous in race, language, color, religion, background—America might well have been a prey to ruinous class and religious divisions. The divisive forces did not, however, prevail, and one reason that they did not prevail is that the public school overcame them. In the classroom the nation's children learned and lived equality. On the playground and the athletic field the same code obtained, with rewards and applause going to achievements to which all could aspire equally, without regard to name, race, or wealth. . . .[8]

1.3 THE FLAG IS A SYMBOL OF OUR NATIONAL UNITY*

Felix Frankfurter

National unity is the basis of national security. . . . The ultimate foundation of a free society is the binding tie of cohesive sentiment. Such a sentiment is fostered by all those agencies of the mind and spirit which may serve to gather up the traditions of a people, transmit them from genera-

---

[8] Editor's note: During the period when our public schools were making good citizens out of immigrants, the industrial revolution made greater and greater demands on education, until today, in the words of Peter F. Drucker:

> . . . the highly educated man has become the central resource of today's society, the supply of such men the true measure of its economic, its military and even its political potential. . . . The man who works exclusively or primarily with his hands is the one who is increasingly unproductive. Productive work in today's society and economy is work that applies vision, knowledge and concepts—work that is based on the mind rather than on the hand. . . . [From this arises the need for educating *all* members of our society.] On the one hand, education has become the central capital investment, the highly educated people the central productive resources in such society. On the other hand, education, while "higher" and perhaps "highest," can no longer be limited to an elite, but must be general education.
>
> —Peter F. Drucker, *Landmarks of Tomorrow*, New York: Harper & Row, Publishers, Inc., 1959, pp. 114–125. By permission.

The change from an agrarian to an industrial society is a root cause of most of the issues of this anthology.

* The first two paragraphs of Selection 1.3 are from Justice Frankfurter's opinion, written for an 8:1 majority, in *Minersville v. Gobitis*, 310 U.S. 585 (1939). The remaining paragraphs are from his lone dissent in *West Virginia v. Barnette*, 319 U.S. 624 (1942).

As the Commager article (Selection 1.2) implied, the American public school has been an important factor in developing national unity. But the question arises: To what extent can a free society *compel* unity? More specifically, can schools require a compulsory flag salute? Selections 1.3 and 1.5 deal with this question.

tion to generation, and thereby create that continuity of a treasured common life which constitutes a civilization. "We live by symbols." The flag is the symbol of our national unity, transcending all internal differences, however large, within the framework of the Constitution. This Court has had occasion to say that ". . . the flag is the symbol of the Nation's power, the emblem of freedom in its truest, best sense. . . . it signifies government resting on the consent of the governed; liberty regulated by law; the protection of the weak against the strong; security against the exercise of arbitrary power; and absolute safety for free institutions against foreign aggression." . . .

Great diversity of psychological and ethical opinion exists among us concerning the best way to train children for their place in society. . . . The precise issue, then, for us to decide is whether the legislatures of the various states and the authorities in a thousand counties and school districts of this country are barred from determining the appropriateness of various means to evoke that unifying sentiment without which there can ultimately be no liberties, civil or religious. . . .

[In an American public school, a compulsory flag salute is not an] attempt by the State to punish disobedient children or visit penal consequences on their parents. All that is in question is the right of the State to compel participation in this exercise by those who choose to attend the public schools. . . .

The great leaders of the American Revolution were determined to remove political support from every religious establishment. They put on an equality the different religious sects—Episcopalians, Presbyterians, Catholics, Baptists, Methodists, Quakers, Huguenots—which, as dissenters, had been under the heel of the various orthodoxies that prevailed in different colonies. So far as the state was concerned, there was to be neither orthodoxy nor heterodoxy. . . . [But this] constitutional protection of religious freedom . . . gave religious equality, not civil immunity. Its essence is freedom from conformity to religious dogma, not freedom from conformity to law because of religious dogma. . . . Otherwise each individual could set up his own censor against obedience to laws conscientiously deemed for the public good by those whose business it is to make laws. . . .

The essence of the religious freedom guaranteed by our Constitution is therefore this: no religion shall either receive the state's support or incur its hostility. Religion is outside the sphere of political government. This does not mean that all matters on which religious organizations or beliefs may pronounce are outside the sphere of government. Were this so, instead of the separation of church and state, there would be the subordination of the state on any matter deemed within the sovereignty of the religious conscience. . . . The validity of secular laws cannot be measured by their conformity to religious doctrines. It is only in a theocratic state that ecclesiastical doctrines measure legal right or wrong.

An act compelling profession of allegiance to a religion, no matter how subtly or tenuously promoted, is bad. But an act promoting good citizenship and national allegiance is within the domain of governmental authority. . . . Saluting the flag suppresses no belief nor curbs it. Children and their parents may believe what they please, avow their belief and practice it. It is not even remotely suggested that the requirement for saluting the flag involves the slightest restriction against the fullest opportunity on the part both of the children and of their parents to disavow as publicly as they choose to do so the meaning that others attach to the gesture of salute. All channels of affirmative free expression are open to both children and parents.

The Primacy of the Individual

1.4 INTRODUCTION

If democracy is to survive, it will do so because its people maintain for themselves the ultimate powers of decision. Carl Sandburg[9] explains the spirit of democracy in terms of an old Moslem legend. According to this legend, the people greatly revered a prophet named Hadji, and eagerly awaited his message to them. When the prophet arrived, he began his sermon with a question "O true believers, do you know what I am going to say to you?" The congregation answered, "No," and Hadji replied, "Then truly there is no use in my speaking to you."

Some time later Hadji came again to address the congregation, and once more he began his message with the question, "O true believers, do you know what I am going to say to you?" The congregation responded in one voice, "We know! We know!" Then the prophet left the pulpit, saying, "Truly, since you know, why should I take the trouble of telling you?"

Then for the third and last time the prophet came to preach, and the people made extensive preparations for the occasion. When Hadji faced the congregation he again asked the same question, "O true believers, do you know what I am going to say to you?" From the congregation came shouts and cries, "Some of us know and some of us do not know." Then the prophet replied, "It is well in the sight of Allah, O true believers, that some of you know what I am going to say to you and some of you do not. Truly, therefore, let those who know tell those who do not know."

What is the lesson of this ancient fable? According to Carl Sandburg, it is this: How wonderful it might be if we could sift out those who know from those who don't know. But there is no way to do this. Hence we must rely on free communication, on uncensored education, on open debate and public discussion, on the maintenance of an equilibrium between all the great forces and interests in our society, both within the government

[9] Carl Sandburg, *Remembrance Rock*, New York: Harcourt, Brace & World, Inc., 1948, pp. 885–886.

—and education—and outside. For the emergence of any one group, whether it represents many or few, as the dominant force, sooner or later spells the end of freedom to all. In an open society one church may criticize another church. The CIO may differ from the NAM. But the government stands aloof from such controversy unless public peace, order, or welfare is seriously endangered. Free men believe that truth is best found, not by submission, but by the exercise of independent judgment; indeed, it is only by the exercise of such thought and freedom that man gains his true dignity and his fullest self-realization.

There are those who are annoyed by debate and controversy. They look upon issues as crises, as causes for alarm. But we look upon them as opportunities, as occasions for rejoicing. For it is a fundamental faith of our democracy that free debate and open discussion not only help to establish justice but also have a therapeutic value for the participants. Even as a bedcover that was exposed to germs may be purified by exposure to sunlight, so the conflicts and tensions that seem to bedevil an open society may be resolved, provided they can be brought out of the dark recesses of prejudice into the open light of discussion and debate.

Here we should note, with Daniel Boorstein, that

> Dissent is not disagreement. . . . People who disagree have an argument, but people who dissent have a quarrel. . . . A liberal society thrives on disagreement but is killed by dissension. Disagreement is the lifeblood of democracy, dissension is its cancer. A debate is an orderly exploration of a common problem that presupposes that the debaters are worried by the same question. It brings to life new facts and new arguments which make possible a better solution. But dissension means discord. . . . [It] is marked by a break in friendly relations. It is an expression not of a common concern but of hostile feelings. And this distinction is crucial. Disagreement is specific and programmatic, dissent is formless and unfocused. Disagreement is concerned with policy, dissenters are concerned with identity, which usually means themselves.[10]

There are times, it must be admitted, when disagreement leads to dissension, and when controversy generates only heat, and no light. It is for this reason that freedom of thought and expression necessarily involves risk. But, as the Committee on Academic Freedom of the American Association of University Professors once wrote:

> A free society cannot avoid an element of risk. It will search in vain for absolute security. It is based on the assumption that people can be trusted to be free, that a majority of them will not in the long run persist in acting

[10] Daniel J. Boorstein, "Dissent, Dissension and the News," an address reprinted in *Current*, January 1968, pp. 27–31. Unfortunately, as Boorstein said to his audience of newsmen, "It is an easier job to make a news story of men who are fighting with one another than it is to describe their peaceful living together."

to their own disadvantage, that, given freedom to think, to act, and to influence each other, they will on the whole do better for themselves than if their direction were entrusted to a few, however wise, not subject to popular control. This is the traditional faith at the heart of our political society.[11]

The two selections that follow are classic statements of the American tradition that governments derive their just powers from the consent of the people, and that the leaders of a free society are the servants of the people, not their masters.

1.5 PUBLIC SCHOOLS MAY NOT COMPEL DECLARATIONS OF BELIEF*

Robert H. Jackson

. . . The [Jehovah's] Witnesses [hold] that the obligation imposed by law of God is superior to that of laws enacted by temporal government. . . . [They consider the U.S. flag a "graven image" which they dare not "bow down" to, according to Exodus 20:4, 5.] For this reason they refuse to salute it. . . .

As the present Chief Justice [Harlan Stone] said in dissent in the *Gobitis* case, the state may "require teaching by instruction and study of all in our history and in the structure and organization of our government, including the guaranties of civil liberty, which tend to inspire patriotism and love of country." 310 U.S. at 604 (1939). . . . Here, however,

[11] American Association of University Professors, Committee on Academic Freedom and Tenure, William T. LaPrade, Chairman, "Report," *AAUP Bulletin* 37: 72–91, Spring 1951. By permission.

* Majority opinion, *West Virginia . . . v. Barnette* 319 U.S. 624 (1942).

Editor's Note: In the Gobitis case (Selection 1.3) the Court recognized, but did not consider, the issue of religious freedom. It based its decision on the judgment that a state has a constitutional right to set up and demand certain acts to encourage patriotism and to help foster national unity, whereas in the Barnette case (Selection 1.4), the Court squarely faced the religious issue, holding that the state has no constitutional right to invade "the sphere of intellect and spirit which it is the purpose of the First Amendment of our Constitution to reserve from all official control."

Although these two decisions may seem to contradict one another, such is not strictly the case; for the American flag *is* a symbol of national unity precisely *because* it invites loyalty *only* on the basis of free consent, never by force or compulsion.

This decision has some relevance to the Regent's Prayer Case (Selection 3.4); for if a state, under our Constitution, may not compel any student to salute the American flag, how can it require students to recite a prayer?

we are dealing with a compulsion of students to declare a belief. They are not merely made acquainted with the flag salute so that they may be informed as to what it is or even what it means. The issue here is whether this slow and easily neglected route [i.e., presenting information about historical foundations of the American way of life] to arouse loyalties constitutionally may be short-cut by substituting a compulsory salute and slogan. . . .

There is no doubt that, in connection with the pledges, the flag salute is a form of utterance. Symbolism is a primitive but effective way of communicating ideas. The use of an emblem or flag to symbolize some system, idea, institution, or personality, is a short cut from mind to mind. Causes and nations, political parties, lodges and ecclesiastical groups seek to knit the loyalty of their followings to a flag or banner, a color or design. The state announces rank, function, and authority through crowns and maces, uniforms and black robes; the church speaks through the Cross, the Crucifix, the altar and shrine, and clerical raiment. Symbols of state often convey political ideas just as religious symbols come to convey theological ones. Associated with many of these symbols are appropriate gestures of acceptance or respect: a salute, a bowed or bared head, a bended knee. A person gets from a symbol the meaning he puts into it, and what is one man's comfort and inspiration is another's jest and scorn. . . .

Over a decade ago Chief Justice Hughes led this Court in holding that the display of a red flag as a symbol of opposition by peaceful and legal means to organized government was protected by the free speech guaranties of the Constitution. *Stromberg v. California* 283 U.S. 359 (1931). . . . Here it is the state that employs a flag as a symbol of adherence to government as presently organized. It requires the individual to communicate by word and sign his acceptance of the political ideas it thus bespeaks. Objection to this form of communication when coerced is an old one, well known to the framers of the Bill of Rights. . . . The question which underlies the flag salute controversy is whether such a ceremony so touching matters of opinion and political attitude may be imposed upon the individual by official authority. . . .

It was said that the flag-salute controversy confronted the Court with "the problem which Lincoln cast in memorable dilemma: 'Must a government of necessity be too *strong* for the liberties of its people, or too *weak* to maintain its own existence?' " and that the answer must be in favor of strength. . . . [Our answer is that] Government of limited power need not be anemic government. Assurance that rights are secure tends to diminish fear and jealousy of strong government, and by making us feel safe to live under it makes for its better support. Without promise of a limiting Bill of Rights it is doubtful if our Constitution could have mustered enough strength to enable its ratification. To enforce those rights today is not to choose weak government over strong government. It is only to adhere as a means of strength to individual freedom of mind in preference to officially disciplined uniformity for which history indicates a disappointing and disastrous end. . . .

The very purpose of a Bill of Rights was to withdraw certain subjects from the vicissitudes of political controversy, to place them beyond the reach of majorities and officials and to establish them as legal principles to be applied by the courts. One's right to life, liberty, and property, to free speech, a free press, freedom of worship and assembly, and other fundamental rights may not be submitted to vote; they depend on the outcome of no election. . . .

National unity as an end which officials may foster by persuasion and example is not in question. The problem is whether under our Constitution compulsion as here employed is a permissible means for its achievement. . . . As governmental pressure toward unity becomes greater, so strife becomes more bitter as to whose unity it shall be. Probably no deeper division of our people could proceed from any provocation than from finding it necessary to choose what doctrine and whose program public educational officials shall compel youth to unite in embracing. Ultimate futility of such attempts to compel coherence is the lesson of every such effort from the Roman drive to stamp out Christianity as a disturber of its pagan unity, the Inquisition as a means to religious and dynastic unity, the Siberian exiles as a means to Russian unity, down to the fast failing efforts of our present totalitarian enemies. Those who begin coercive elimination of dissent soon find themselves exterminating dissentors. Compulsory unification of opinion achieves only the unanimity of the graveyard.

It seems trite but necessary to say that the First Amendment of our Constitution was designed to avoid these ends by avoiding these beginnings. There is no mysticism in the American concept of the state or of the nature or origin of its authority. We set up government by consent of the governed, and the Bill of Rights denies those in power any legal opportunity to coerce that consent. Authority here is to be controlled by public opinion, not public opinion by authority. . . .

To believe that patriotism will not flourish if patriotic ceremonies are voluntary and spontaneous instead of a compulsory routine is to make an unflattering estimate of the appeal of our institutions to free minds. We can have intellectual individualism and the rich cultural diversities that we owe to exceptional minds only at the price of occasional eccentricity and abnormal attitudes. When they are so harmless to others or to the state as those we deal with here, the price is not too great. But freedom to differ is not limited to things that do not matter much. That would be a mere shadow of freedom. The test of its substance is the right to differ as to things that touch the heart of the existing order.

If there is any fixed star in our constitutional constellation, it is that no official, high or petty, can prescribe what shall be orthodox in politics, nationalism, religion, or other matters of opinion or force citizens to confess by word or act their faith therein.

1.6 TO MAKE MEN FREE*

Archibald MacLeish

Freedom, in American usage, means the freedom of the individual human being to think for himself and to come to the truth by the light of his own mind and conscience. It is the freedom defined by the American Constitution. Congress is forbidden to make any law abridging the freedom of speech. There is to be no establishment of religious authority or supervision. There is to be no meddling, in other words, by state or by church with a man's thoughts or what he chooses to say about them. When it comes to thoughts, when it comes to ideas, when it comes to opinions and their expression, a man is free. His freedom is guaranteed by the fundamental law of the Republic. The opinions of others are not to be imposed upon him, no matter whose opinions they may be—the opinions of a church or the opinions of the government or the opinions of his fellow citizens—even the opinions of a majority of his fellow citizens.

A man's freedom to believe, that is to say, does not depend on *what* he believes. It does not depend on his being "right" as others see the right, no matter how numerous they may be or how well entrenched or how powerful. Right and wrong as others judge the right and wrong are irrelevant to the American conception of freedom to think and believe and say. That, of course, is the nub of the whole matter, and the essential distinction between freedom as we mean it and freedom as it is meant in certain other quarters of the earth. In the American conception of freedom, the man and his conscience come first and the established opinions, the accepted verities, the official views come after.

---

* Achibald MacLeish, "Freedom is the Right to Choose," by permission of Houghton Mifflin Company. Under the title "To Make Men Free," this article appeared in the *Atlantic* 188: 27–30, November 1951.

Archibald MacLeish has been a Pulitzer Prize winner in poetry, Librarian of Congress, Assistant Secretary of State, Assistant Director of the Office of War Information, a member of the executive board of UNESCO, and Boylston Professor of Rhetoric and Oratory at Harvard. He is author of numerous poems, plays, essays, and books. Selections 3.16 and 4.12 are also by Archibald MacLeish.

The pressure which the word freedom has been under in the past few years is a pressure of this character: a pressure from those who have never really accepted or wholly understood the meaning of the word in its American use. There are some, of course, who deliberately reject the American meaning—who would destroy it if they could, replacing it with an interpretation more amenable to their own beliefs—but they are not numerous as yet. The real danger to freedom in the United States—to the word and to the thing—is the danger of the impairment of the American usage by negligence and default. Unless we can maintain the pure traditional meaning of the word—unless we can understand in common and as a nation that the only opinion established in this country by the American Constitution is the opinion that a man is free to hold *any* opinion—unless we can agree among ourselves that by freedom we mean precisely *freedom*, we may end by finding ourselves "free" in the sense in which the Russians now find themselves "democratic." . . .

The American Proposition is the proposition, advanced at the beginning of the Republic and enacted into law when the Constitution was adopted, that a man's freedom to be a man, and to find and speak the truth that is in him, is more important than the protection of any accepted belief, any official verity, against criticism, against challenge, against dissent. More important not only to that man but to all men, to the society which all men compose, to the nation, to the world, to life itself. It is a proposition, in other words, which rests upon an act of faith, the most courageous of all earthly acts of faith—an act of faith in man and in the God whom man, in the freedom of his conscience and his thought, can find.

When it was first enacted into law the American Proposition was new. It is still new: the one wholly new and revolutionary idea the modern world has produced, for all its triumphs in science and technique—an idea so new and so revolutionary in its literal and explicit meaning that half the patriotic societies which celebrate their attachment to the American Revolution have yet to understand it or accept it. But it is new and revolutionary, not solely because it proclaims human liberty, nor solely because it founds its conception of human liberty on the freedom of the individual human mind, defending that freedom in the most explicit and peremptory terms against the tyranny of organized opinion. It is new and revolutionary because of the act of faith which it expresses.

Our reliance in this country is on the inquiring, individual human mind. Our strength is founded there: our resilience, our ability to face an ever-changing future and to master it. We are not frozen into the backward-facing impotence of those societies, fixed in the rigidness of an official dogma, to which the future is the mirror of the past. We are free to make the future for ourselves. And we are free because it is the man who counts in this country: always and at every moment and in any situation, the man.

Not the Truth but the man: not the truth as the state sees the truth or as the church sees the truth or as the majority sees the truth or as the mob sees the truth, but the truth as the man sees it, as the man finds it, for himself as man. Our faith is in the infinite variety of human beings and in the God who made them various and of many minds; in their singularity, their uniqueness, the creativeness of the differences between them. Our faith, in simple, sober truth, is in the human Being, the human spirit, the hungers and the longings that lead it toward its images of truth, its perceptions of the beauty of the world.

Those who launched the great human adventure which this Republic is, dared to put their trust in the individual man, the man alone, the man thinking for himself. They dared to believe in a *people,* which is a nation of individual men constituting among themselves a society; for a people is not what the totalitarians call "the masses"; a people is an agreement of many alone to make together a world in which each one of them can live as himself. The founders of the American Republic believed in a people. They not only provided no censors for the thoughts of those who were to come after them: they prohibited censors. They not only provided no moral or intellectual or religious authority to govern the beliefs of their successors: they rejected forever the establishment of any such authority. They trusted men.

It is in that trust that the Republic can still be defended. Indeed it is only in that trust that it can be defended as the kind of country it is. To attempt to defend it otherwise—to attempt, above all, to defend it by debasing the coinage of meaning in which its nature is expressed—is to lose both the country itself and the struggle against Communism which is cited as justification of the fraud. If freedom can come to mean something less than freedom in the general mind, it can come to mean the opposite of freedom. If freedom ceases to express the American faith in man and in man's unqualified right to find the truth for himself, it will shortly express a faith in established truth, in the rightness of official opinion. When that happens we shall have lost both the American Proposition and the fight against Communism. For the one idea that can triumph over the police-state notion that the truth is already known, once for all, and that the truth is therefore entitled to impose itself by force, is the American Proposition that a man is free to find the truth for himself. It is the one idea that can triumph because, as long as it is held, man himself is the cause of those who hold it. And against that cause no enemy has prevailed for long.

Civil Disobedience and Protesting Demonstrators

1.7 INTRODUCTION: LAW, MORALITY, AND CIVIL DISOBEDIENCE

In the American tradition, tensions arise when social practices become severely disconsonant with democratic ideals—or when the achieved reality falls far short of what might reasonably be expected. The labor movement is a story of workers' strikes and picketing in protest against company management. A large part of American history tells of the rise of political parties and of social change, accompanied not only by soapbox oratory but often by physical violence as well.

The past decade has witnessed far more social conflict than have previous decades. In protest against the 1954 Supreme Court school antisegregation decision in the case of *Brown v. Board of Education,* many parents in Virginia withdrew their children from the public schools, causing some of them to close for several years. In other cases, parades, demonstrations, and sit-ins have been used to bring about open housing, increased voting privileges, or more equitable job opportunities. Sometimes such changes occurred peaceably, sometimes not. At various times during 1966, 1967, and 1968 bloody riots brought terror to Watts, Detroit, Newark, Cleveland, and other American urban communities. Even within academic communities, there has been an increased emphasis on student rights and faculty prerogatives, and in 1967 the president of the New York teachers union served a jail sentence for leading teachers in an "unlawful" strike. A year later the entire academic community at Columbia University in New York City was thrown into chaos as a result of student protests.

Such examples could be multiplied. But here we are not so much interested in the issues themselves as we are in the methods used to help resolve them. In particular, we will examine the method of civil disobedience, as set forth by the late Dr. Martin Luther King, Jr.

From Socrates (in Plato's *Crito*) to modern times, the essential characteristic of civil disobedience is (a) belief in the necessity of law, coupled with (b) a strong belief (moral or religious) that a particular law is immoral. Civil disobedience claims exemption from the obligation to obey particular laws on moral grounds, but (because of belief in the necessity of law) does not claim or ask for immunity from *punishment* for violating a partciular law, which it protests as being unjust.

The problem of civil disobedience has many philosophical ramifications and it has deep historic roots. The Old Testament distinction between "the law" and "the prophets" is based on the ract that laws, unless rewritten or reinterpreted to fit the needs of the times, tend to become rigid, inhumane, and "legalistic." The New Testament, likewise, is filled with statements such as, "Be not conformed to this world, but be transformed by the renewing of your mind" (*Romans* 12:2)—which is an open invitation not to be satisfied with the *status quo*, but to become part of "the Church militant" striving for higher social morality.

American history is filled with examples of civil disobedience. The Boston Tea Party was not a revolt against *all* law and order. It was rather a protest against a specific practice—the practice of "taxation without representation," which seemed to deny to the colonists one of the rights of Englishmen. In the early nineteenth century "the great awakening," the "transcendentalist movement," and a multiplicity of "utopias" all held to the view that "there is a higher law than the Constitution"; and the illegal antebellum slave traffic was only one of many examples of civil disobedience. Disobedience of the law was deliberately practiced again in the twentieth century "bootlegging" violations of the Volstead Act; and such violations helped bring about the repeal of the prohibition amendment. Many other similar examples could be cited; but today's headlines are about sit-ins and protest demonstrations. Since these protests are directed largely against racial inequality, the concluding three selections of Chapter 1 serve also as a prelude to Chapter 2.

1.8 MARTIN LUTHER KING, JR.'S CIVIL DISOBEDIENCE*

Indiana Law Journal Note

In the early 1960's the American Negro's struggle for civil rights underwent a fundamental transformation. The long-used procedure of seeking

* "Note: Contemporary Civil Disobedience," 41 *Indiana Law Journal* 477–505, Spring 1966. By permission.

This article summarizes civil disobedience theories from Plato to Sidney Hook.

progress through judicial decision and legislative action, while not abandoned, was overshadowed by the more direct and dramatic method of challenging discrimination through calculated acts of civil disobedience. This use of civil disobedience raises once again the perennial jurisprudential issue of a citizen's duty to obey enacted law, and perhaps the issue has not been so clearly raised since the post-War reflection on Hitler's reign of terror. . . .

CHARACTERISTICS OF CONTEMPORARY CIVIL DISOBEDIENCE

It is erroneous to look upon the Civil Rights Movement as a monolithic, well-disciplined organization, for the Movement ranges from the radical separationism of the Black Muslims, through the activist, but essentially conciliatory Southern Christian Leadership Conference of Martin Luther King, Jr., to the more conservative and legally oriented National Association for the Advancement of Colored People. Therefore, any generalizations valid for all civil rights groups must of necessity be limited to such banalities as "interest in improving the Negro's status" or "opposition to the present social and economic structure." In order to avoid the problem created by this lack of coherence, this note will concentrate on the "middle group" of civil rights organizations—the Southern Christian Leadership Conference, Students' Non-violent Coordinating Committee, and the Congress on Racial Equality. This group of organizations best fits the purposes of this note, because these organizations have been primarily responsible for the promotion of civil disobedience as a tool in the civil rights struggle, whereas the Muslims seek to become "in but not of the society," while the NAACP has concentrated on legalism. [This categorizing of the organizations of course is not absolute, for the NAACP does assist the demonstrators, and both the "middle group" and the Black Muslims do not hesitate to avail themselves of the courts.] Further, the statements of Martin Luther King, Jr., will be used to show the ideological and philosophical basis of this civil disobedience, for King is probably the best known leader of the "middle group," and an articulate defender of civil disobedience as a legitimate instrument of the Civil Rights Movement. . . .

Perhaps [King's] best known statement on civil disobedience is contained in his "Letter from a Birmingham Jail," written in April, 1963:

> . . . there are two types of laws: just and unjust. I would be the first to advocate obeying just laws. One has not only a legal but a moral responsibility to obey just laws. Conversely, one has a moral responsibility to

disobey unjust laws. I would agree with St. Augustine that "an unjust law is no law at all."[12]. . . .

An unjust law is a code that a numerical or power majority group compels a minority group to obey but does not make binding on itself. . . a just law is a code that a majority compels a minority to follow and that it is willing to follow itself. . . .

. . . A law is unjust if it is inflicted on a minority that, as a result of being denied the right to vote, had no part in enacting or devising the law. . . .

In no sense do I advocate evading or defying the law, as would the rabid segregationist. That would lead to anarchy. One who breaks an unjust law must do so openly, lovingly, and with a willingness to accept the penalty. [An individual who does this] to arouse the conscience of the community over its injustice, is in reality expressing the highest respect for law.[13]

Thus in 1963, King limited his justification of civil disobedience to unjust laws; however, in 1965 he was willing to extend this defense to include defiance under certain circumstances of laws not unjust in themselves. In a question and answer period following an address before the Association of the Bar of the City of New York, April 21, 1965, King was asked: "Does your concept of civil disobedience include such tactics as obstructing sites where Negroes are not employed, where those who use such means . . . are not quarreling with the justice of any law?" King answered:

. . . [A]ll civil disobedience must be centered on something. . . the goals must be clearly stated. . . . [T]here are instances wherein the process of frustration with the structure of things, people find themselves in positions of not quite being able to see the unjust law. But they see injustice in a very large sense existing. Consequently, they feel the need to engage

[12] Editor's Note: Compare Martin Luther King, Jr., *Strides Toward Freedom: The Montgomery Story*, New York: Harper & Row, Publishers, Inc., 1958, pp. 101–107. Here King interprets nonviolence as Christian

love-in-action. . . . seeking to preserve and create community. . . . The aftermath of nonviolence is the creation of the beloved community, while the aftermath of violence is tragic bitterness. . . . [Nonviolence is based on the religious] conviction that the universe is on the side of justice. Consequently, the believer in nonviolence has deep faith in the future. This faith is another reason why the nonviolent resister can accept suffering without retaliation. For he knows that in his struggle for justice he has cosmic companionship.

[13] Editor's Note: On July 31, 1967, the Urban Coalition, of which King was a member, declared:

It is the Government's duty to maintain law and order. But all must understand that law and order is not an excuse for oppression. If law and order is to be accepted by the minorities, the majority must clearly and positively demonstrate its belief that justice, social progress, and equality are the rights of every citizen.

in civil disobedience to call attention to overall injustice. At that point they are not protesting against an unjust law. [Where communities do not work to remove injustice] men of conscience and men of good will have no alternative but to engage in some kind of civil disobedience in order to call attention to the injustice so that the society will seek to rid itself of that overall injustice. Again. . . there must be a willingness to accept the penalty. . . .

[The civil disobedience] Movement, as visualized by King, aims at open defiance of certain unjust laws without violence, while professing respect for all other law, and thus [aims to] "arouse the conscience of the community over [their] injustice." In contrast to a general assault on the whole legal system, this approach seems calculated to keep disorder within narrow limits. . . . its avowed objective is not the destruction of American society, but rather, full participation in it. Unlike the French Revolutionaries who sought to crush the *ancien régime*, the civil rights leaders desire to fulfill the American Way of Life by allowing Negroes to become full participants in it. Their aim is to eradicate patterns of discrimination which they believe prevent this full participation, and while one may argue that the methods employed, or even the eradication itself, will radically alter this Way of Life, the fact remains that the expressed goal is fulfillment, not destruction, of American ideals.[14]

---

[14] Editor's Note: Inasmuch as Martin Luther King, Jr., justified his program of civil disobedience on the basis of nonviolence, it may be well to read what another author says concerning the meaning of *nonviolence*:

> Nonviolence is perhaps the most exacting of all forms of struggle, not only because it demands first of all that one be ready to suffer evil and even face the threat of death without violent retaliation, but because it excludes mere transient self-interest from its considerations. In a very real sense, he who practices nonviolent resistance must commit himself not to the defense of his own interests or even those of a particular group: he must commit himself to the defense of objective truth and right and above all of *man*. His aim is then not simply to "prevail" or to prove that he is right and the adversary wrong, or to make the adversary give in and yield what is demanded of him. . . .
>
> The nonviolent resister is not fighting simply for "his" truth or for "his" pure conscience, or for the right that is in "his side." On the contrary, both his strength and his weakness come from the fact that he is fighting for *the* truth, common to him and to the adversary, *the* right which is objective and universal. He is fighting for *everybody*. . . .
>
> The realism of nonviolence must be made evident by humility and self-restraint which clearly show frankness and open-mindedness and invite the adversary to serious and reasonable discussion. . . . All it seeks is the openness of free exchange in which reason and love have freedom of action. In such a situation the future will take care of itself. . . .
>
> Instead of trying to use the adversary as leverage for one's own effort to realize an ideal, nonviolence seeks only to enter into a dialogue with him in order to attain, together with him, the common good of *man*. . . . In such a confrontation between conflicting parties, on the level of personality, intelligence and freedom, instead of with massive weapons or with trickery and deceit, a fully human solution becomes possible.

1.9 FREE SPEECH AND PUBLIC DEMONSTRATIONS*

Jerome A. Barron

[Let us begin with a classic statement concerning the meaning of the First Amendment:]

But when men have realized that time has upset many fighting faiths, they may come to believe even more than they believe the very foundations of their own conduct that the ultimate good desired is better reached by free trade in ideas—that the best test of truth is the power of thought to get itself accepted in the competition of the market, and that truth is the only ground upon which their wishes safely can be carried out. That at any rate is the theory of our Constitution.[15]

The assumption apparent in this excerpt is that, without government intervention, there is a free market mechanism for ideas. . . .

[However in *Whitney v. California* (1927) Justice Brandeis] stressed the intimacy of the relationship between the goals of a respect for public order and the assurance of free expression. For Brandeis one of the assumptions implicit in the guarantee of free expression is that "it is hazardous to discourage thought, hope and imagination; that fear breeds repression; that repression breeds hate; that hate menaces stable government; that the path of safety lies in the opportunity to discuss freely supposed grievances and proposed remedies. . . ." I would suggest that the contemporary challenge to this "path of safety" has roots in the lack of opportunity for

---

—Thomas Merton (Trappist monk), "Blessed are the Meek: The Roots of Nonviolence," *Fellowship* 33: 18–22, May 1967. See also Thomas Merton, *Disputed Questions*, New York: Farrar, Straus & Giroux, Inc., 1960, pp. 130–137. For a brief summary of Mahatma Gandhi's theory of nonviolence, see E. A. Burtt, *Man Seeks the Divine*, New York: Harper & Row, Publishers, 1964, pp. 454–460.

It should be obvious that nonviolence is much more difficult to practice in situations where there is no genuine community. A statement of Reinhold Niebuhr bears repeating here: "Technical civilizations create great urban centers in which the individual is in danger of losing his identity in the crowd, gathered together by technics, but lacking the virtues of genuine community."—Reinhold Niebuhr, *Pious and Secular America*, New York: Charles Scribner's Sons, 1958, p. 7. See also Paul Goodman, "A Message to the Military-Industrial," *The New York Review of Books* 9: 14–20, November 13, 1967.

* J. A. Barron, "Access to the Press—A New First Amendment Right," 80 *Harvard Law Review* 1641–1678, June 1967. Copyright © 1967 by The Harvard Law Review Association. By permission.

Jerome A. Barron is Associate Professor of Law, George Washington Law School.

[15] Justice Holmes, *Abrams v. United States*, 250 U.S. 616 at 630 (1919).

the disadvantaged and the dissatisfied of our society to discuss supposed grievances effectively.

The "sit-in" demonstrates that the safety valve value of free expression in preserving public order is lost when access to the communication media is foreclosed to dissident groups. It is a measure of the jaded and warped standards of the media that ideas which normally would never be granted a forum are given serious network coverage if they become sufficiently enmeshed in mass demonstration or riot and violence. Ideas are denied admission into media until they are first disseminated in a way that challenges and disrupts the social order. They then may be discussed and given notice. But is it not the assumption of a constitutional guarantee of freedom of expression that the process ought to work just the other way—that the idea be given currency first so that its proponents will not conclude that unrest and violence alone will suffice to capture public attention?. . . .

[Any realistic interpretation of the First Amendment must attempt] to be responsive to the diverse natures of differing modes of communication. . . . [But if Marshall McLuhan is correct, the] new modes of communication engage us by their form rather than by their content; what captivates us is the television screen itself. In his view the electronic media which have eclipsed the typographical age entail a high degree of nonintellectual and emotional participation and involvement. We have become mesmerized by the new forms of communication to the point of indifference to their content and to the content of the older media. . . . For McLuhan it is the technology or form of television itself, rather than the message, which attracts public attention. Hence the media owners are anxious that media content not get enmeshed with unpopular views which will undermine the attraction which the media enjoy by virtue of their form alone:

"Thus the commercial interests who think to render media universally acceptable, invariably settle for 'entertainment' as a strategy of neutrality. A more spectacular mode of the ostrich-head-in-sand could not be devised, for it ensures maximum pervasiveness for any medium whatever."[16]

The first amendment implications of this phenomenon are very great indeed. In the Supreme Court decisions we find a theory of knowledge which revolves around an outmoded conception of decision making: Information is distributed by advocates of various points of view and, after assimilation and reflection, the citizen makes his judgment. But, according to McLuhan, the media defeat this step-ladder approach to decision making: "As the speed of information increases, the tendency is for politics

---

[16] H. M. McLuhan, *Understanding Media,* New York: McGraw-Hill, Inc., 1964, pp. 173, 305. For a criticism of McLuhan's views, read Anthony Quinton, "Salvation through McLuhan," *The New York Review of Books* 9: 6–13, November 13, 1967.

to move away from representation and delegation of constituents toward immediate involvement of the entire community in the central acts of decision. Slower speeds of information make delegation and representation mandatory."[17]

[The first amendment may be viewed as] the constitutional recognition that is given to the necessity of inhibiting "the occasional tyrannies of governing majorities" from throttling opportunities for discussion. But is it such a large constitutional step to take the approach to nongoverning minorities who control the machinery of communication? Is it too bold to suggest that it is necessary to ensure access to the mass media for unorthodox ideas in order to make effective the guarantee against repression?

If [in *Ginzburg* (1966)] dissemination of books can be prohibited and punished when the dissemination is not for any "saving intellectual content" but for "commercial exploitation," it would seem that the mass communications industry, no less animated by motives of "commercial exploitation," could be legally obliged to host competing opinions and points of view. If the mass media are essentially business enterprises and their commercial nature makes it difficult to give a full and effective hearing to a wide spectrum of opinion, a theory of the first amendment is unrealistic if it prevents courts or legislatures from requiring the media to do that which, for commercial reasons, they would be otherwise unlikely to do. . . .

It is not that the mass communication industry is pushing certain ideas and rejecting others, but rather that it is using the free speech and press guarantee to avoid opinions instead of acting as a sounding board for their expression. . . .

The failures of existing media are revealed by the development of new media to convey unorthodox, unpopular, and new ideas. Sit-ins and demonstrations testify to the inadequacy of the old media as instruments to afford full and effective hearing for all points of view. Demonstrations, it has been said, are "the free press of the movement to win justice for Negroes. . ." But like an inadequate underground press, it is a communications medium by default, a statement of the inability to secure access to the conventional means of reaching and changing public opinion. By the bizarre and unsettling nature of his technique the demonstrator hopes to arrest and divert attention long enough to compel the public to ponder his message. But attention-getting devices so abound in the modern world that new ones soon become tiresome. The dissenter must look for ever more unsettling assaults on the mass mind if he is to have continuing impact. Thus, as critics of protest are eager and in a sense correct to say, the prayer-singing student demonstration is the prelude to Watts. But the

[17] McLuhan, p. 204.

difficulty with this criticism is that it wishes to throttle protest rather than to recognize that protest has taken these forms because it has had nowhere else to go. . . .

CONCLUSION

The changing nature of the communications process has made it imperative that the law show concern for the public interest in effective utilization of media for the expression of diverse points of view. Confrontation of ideas, a topic of eloquent affection in contemporary decisions, demands some recognition of a right to be heard as a constitutional principle. . . . With the development of private restraints on free expression, the idea of a free marketplace where ideas can compete on their merits has become just as unrealistic in the twentieth century as the economic theory of perfect competition. The world in which an essentially rationalist philosophy of the first amendment was born has vanished and what was rationalism is now romance. . . . Today's ideas reach the millions to the extent they are permitted entry into the great metropolitan dailies, news magazines, and broadcasting networks. The soap box is no longer an adequate forum for public discussion.[18]

[18] Editor's Note: Compare the following statement by Walter Lippmann:

> Freedom of speech has become a central concern of the Western society because of the discovery among the Greeks that dialectic, as demonstrated in the Socratic dialogues, is a principal method of attaining truth, and particularly a method of attaining moral and political truth. "The ability to raise searching difficulties on both sides of a subject will," said Aristotle, "make us detect more easily the truth and error about the several points that arise." The right to speak freely is one of the necessary means to the attainment of the truth. That, and not the subjective pleasure of utterance, is why freedom is a necessity in the good society. . . .
>
> The method of dialectics is to confront ideas with opposing ideas in order that the pro and con of the dispute will lead to true ideas. But the dispute must not be treated as a trial of strength. It must be a means of elucidation. In a Socratic dialogue the disputants are arguing cooperatively in order to acquire more wisdom than either of them had when he began. . . .
>
> In our times the application of these fundamental principles poses many unsolved problems. For the modern media of mass communication do not lend themselves easily to a confrontation of opinions. . . . Rarely, and on very few public issues, does the mass audience have the benefit of the process by which truth is sifted from error—the dialectic of debate in which there is immediate challenge, reply, cross-examination, and rebuttal. The men who regularly broadcast the news and comment upon the news cannot—like a speaker in the Senate or in the House of Commons—be challenged by one of his listeners and compelled then and there to verify their statements of fact and to re-argue their inferences from the facts.
>
> Yet when genuine debate is lacking, freedom of speech does not work as it is meant to work. It has lost the principle which regulates it and justifies it—that is to say, dialectic conducted according to logic and rules of evidence. . . .
>
> —Walter Lippmann, *The Public Philosophy*, Boston: Little, Brown & Company, pp. 124–131, Copyright 1955, by Walter Lippmann. By permission of the publisher.

1.10 SUMMARY: ARE PROTESTING DEMONSTRATIONS "SPEECH" OR "ACTION"?

This essay will contrast some of the opinions of Justice Black[19] with those of Justices Fortas and Harlan. The questions at issue are these: May sit-ins and other protesting demonstrations be classified as "symbolic speech and expression"—and thus given the protection of the First Amendment? Or should they be classified as "action"—and thus fall outside the coverage of the First Amendment? On these questions the Supreme Court is now divided, often by a vote of 5 to 4.

In the first great sit-in case, *Garner v. Louisiana* (1961), Mr. Justice Harlan, concurring in a 5 to 4 majority opinion, interpreted the sit-in gesture as a form of symbolic speech:

> There was more to the conduct of those petitioners than a bare desire to remain at the "white" lunch counter and their refusal of a police request to move from the counter. We would surely have to be blind not to recognize that these petitioners were sitting at those counters, where they knew they would not be served, in order to demonstrate that their race was being segregated in dining facilities in this part of the country.
>
> Such a demonstration in the circumstances . . . is as much a part of the "free trade in ideas," *Abrams v. United States*, as is verbal expression, more commonly thought of as "speech." It, like speech, appeals to good sense and to the "power of reason as applied through public discussion," *Whitney v. California*, . . . just as much as, if not more than, a public oration delivered from a soapbox at a street corner. . . .

By such reasoning Justice Harlan would extend the First Amendment to protect sit-ins who battle against a variety of Southern breach of peace and trespass statutes.

In *Cox v. Louisiana* (1965), Justice Black's dissenting opinion insisted upon the rule of law even when its application works a restraint upon groups seeking goals which he regards benevolently; and he warned minority groups that their only sure road to progress lies within the constitutional rule of law:

> And minority groups, I venture to suggest, are the ones who always have suffered and always will suffer most when street multitudes are allowed to substitute their pressures for the less glamorous but more dependable and temperate processes of the law. Experience demonstrates

[19] See "Mr. Justice Black: Thirty Years in Retrospect," 14 *UCLA Law Review*, 397–552, January 1967. From this tribute to Justice Black we have borrowed especially from the essays by Harry Kalven, Jr. (pp. 428–453), and Charles E. Rice (pp. 454–466).

that it is not a far step from what to many seems the earnest, honest, patriotic, kind-spirited multitude of today, to the fanatical, threatening, lawless mob of tomorrow. And the crowds that press in the streets for noble goals today can be supplanted tomorrow by street mobs pressuring the courts for precisely opposite ends. Government under law as ordained by our Constitution is too precious, too sacred, to be jeopardized by subjecting the courts to intimidatory practices that have been fatal to individual liberty and minority rights wherever and whenever such practices have been allowed to poison the streams of justice.

Perhaps the most dramatic collision of views came in *Brown v. Louisiana* (1966), the so-called *Library Sit-In Case.* Here, in a 5 to 4 decision, the majority, speaking through Mr. Justice Fortas, reversed breach of peace convictions of five Negroes who, after being asked to leave, sat in a public library in order to protest the segregation of library facilities. Justice Fortas found no evidence of a breach of peace and hence found the convictions a violation of due process, and he went on to say:

> We are here dealing with an aspect of a basic constitutional right—the right under the First and Fourteenth Amendments guaranteeing freedom of speech and assembly, and freedom to petition the Government for a redress of grievances. . . . As this Court has repeatedly stated, these rights are not confined to verbal expression. They embrace appropriate types of action which certainly include the right in a peaceable and orderly manner to protest by silent and reproachful presence, in a place where the protestant has every right to be, the unconstitutional segregation of public facilities. . . .

By this 5 to 4 decision, the sit-in as symbolic speech might seem to have acquired constitutional status. But 5 to 4 decisions are notoriously unstable, and the opinion of the four-man dissent, written by Justice Black, deserves repeating. After noting that the First Amendment was for him the very heart of free government, Black added:

> But I have never thought and do not now think that the First Amendment can sustain the startling doctrine the prevailing opinion here creates. The First Amendment, I think, protects speech, writings, and expression of views in any manner in which they can be legitimately and validly communicated. But I have never believed that it gives any person or group of persons the constitutional right to go wherever they want, whenever they please, without regard to the rights of private or public property or to state law. . . .
>
> It is high time to challenge the assumption in which too many people have too long acquiesced, that groups that think they have been mistreated or that have actually been mistreated have a constitutional right to use the public streets, buildings, and property to protest whatever, wherever, whenever they want, without regard to whom it may disturb. . . . It is an

> unhappy circumstance in my judgment that the group, which more than any other has needed a government of equal laws and equal justice, is now encouraged to believe that the best way for it to advance its cause, which is a worthy one, is by taking the law into its own hands from place to place and from time to time. Governments like ours were formed to substitute the rule of law for the rule of force. Illustrations may be given where crowds have gathered together peaceably by reason of extraordinary good discipline reinforced by vigilant officers. "Demonstrations" have taken place without any manifestations of force at the time. But I say once more that the crowd moved by noble ideals today can become the mob ruled by hate and passion and greed and violence tomorrow. . . .

In another 5 to 4 decision, *Brown v. Louisiana* (1966), the majority opinion seems to imply that the demonstrators' speech and conduct would enjoy an immunity only so long as they were orderly and not boisterous; and the prevailing opinion in *Brown* regarded the demonstrators' conduct as sufficiently orderly and silent to be insulated from punishment.

Justice Black, on the other hand, found it irrelevant to a proper construction of the Louisiana statute whether the demonstrators "who do not want library service stay there an unusually long time after being ordered to leave, make a big noise, use some bad language, engage in fighting, try to provoke a fight, or in some other way become boisterous." Rather, the Black opinion relied upon that portion of the Louisiana statute which, in his words, "makes it an offense to disturb the peace by congregating in a public building over the protest of a person rightfully in charge of the building."

The two opposing viewpoints are summarized in the following statement by Francis A. Allen, Professor of Law and Dean of the Law School, University of Michigan.

> There can be no doubt that the problems of conflict between the exercise of state power and the conscience of citizens are among the most difficult and sensitive of those confronting any society whose values include the worth of individual human personality. No such society can afford to take lightly any instance of the exercise of official authority that is genuinely offensive to the moral convictions of any of its members. All such cases involve the society in costs, and such costs may quickly become exorbitant. . . [Furthermore] an intelligent concern for the scruples of individuals is often required, not only in the interests of decency and compassion, but to secure in the most effective and economical fashion the purposes for which [the legal] measure was enacted. . . .
>
> To me the theoretical defense of civil disobedience by the civil rights leadership reflects a quite deliberate judgment that the dynamics of the movement require it to be viewed by its adherents, above all, as an appeal to morality, conscience, and religious belief. This commitment is seen as

transcending all secondary values, including that of legality, however infrequently legality and conscience have in fact been at war in the movement. . . .

The case for the rule of law requires no more elaborate defense than does the case for civilization. Indeed, the two are inextricably intertwined. . . . There is nothing in the theory of democracy that requires the majority to embrace the tenets of philosophical anarchy. . . . If the children of light are privileged to resist particular laws on grounds of conscience, can the children of darkness be denied a similar privilege? Surely it cannot be doubted that a bad cause may evoke its full quota of conscientious adherents. If there are no "neutral" principles in law or morals to distinguish the two classes of offenders, is there not serious danger that the quantum of law violation may reach levels inconsistent with the maintenance of public order, at least within the assumptions of a free society? Some of these concerns are reflected in an observation of as distinguished and sympathetic a friend of the civil rights movement as Mr. Burke Marshall: "If the decision to break the law really turned on individual conscience, it is hard to see in law how Dr. King is better off than former Governor Ross Barnett of Mississippi, who also believed deeply in his cause and was willing to go to jail [for it]." . . .

My conclusion is . . . that a widespread campaign of civil disobedience and the reactions produced by it could create conditions incompatible with the proper functioning of the legal order and prove destructive of basic democratic procedures. Even if such drastic and dramatic consequences are avoided, the loss of civility in the conduct of public controversies may, and already has, taken a serious toll. Civility is not simply a matter of etiquette; it is part of the essential strategy of the democratic way of life.[20]

---

[20] Francis A. Allen, "Civil Disobedience and the Legal Order," 36 *University of Cincinnati Law Review* 1–38 and 175–195, Winter and Spring 1967, at 15, 7, 14, 28, and 37. By permission of Cin. L. Rev. Compare the following "ACLU Statement on Civil Disobedience":

> . . . Freedom to say what one believes, not to do what one wishes, is what is protected by the First Amendment. A democratic society is as much in need of compliance by citizens with laws with which they disagree as it [is to] provide the freedom to criticize and the means to change such laws by the democratic process. High motivation and deep-felt conscience may be, and often are, the moving force of those who practice civil disobedience. But this does not mean that those who disobey laws for baser principles or less altruistic motives should be convicted while those who deliberately disobey laws for better-motivated reasons should be acquitted. To make this type of distinction would be to change a nation governed by law to one governed by motivation alone. Indeed, conscience can lead men to good or evil—assuming society is able to distinguish between conscience and baser motivations.
>
> —*Civil Liberties*, No. 254, March–April 1968, p. 4.

See also Lewis F. Powell, "Civil Disobedience: Prelude to Revolution?" *U.S. News* 63: 66–69, October 30, 1967.

TOPICS FOR FURTHER STUDY

DEMOCRACY AND CIVIL DISOBEDIENCE: PROS AND CONS[21]

A. Americans like to think of themselves as a peace-loving people, yet violence is and always has been an important and sometimes indispensable instrument of social, economic and political change. . . . In our national history violence was the ultimate instrument in our conquest of the lands on the North American continent that now comprise the nation. Violence freed the American colonists from British rule and later insured freedom of the seas (1812–1815). Violence abolished slavery, established the bargaining rights of labor, twice put down threatening tyrannies in Europe and once in the Asian Pacific. In the present day, violence is the unintended instrument of black citizens to break through oppressive discrimination in housing, employment, education and political rights. . . .

There is substantial agreement among legal and political thinkers that nonviolent challenges to the policies and laws of civil authority are an indispensable mechanism of corrective change in a democratic society. Insofar as possible, procedures for challenge which may involve open and deliberate disobedience should be built into the laws and policies of the system, for such procedures give the system a quality of resilience and flexibility, the capacity to absorb constructive attack from within.

As George Lakay has pointed out, one great strength of democratic institutions is that they build a degree of conflict into the decision-making structure just so that conflicts can be resolved publicly and without violence. Adequately designed democratic institutions deliberately reflect shifting views and power relations of interest groups and the normal workings of compromise and settlement, and equilibrium is usually maintained. Civil disobedience, and other forms of civil protest, are resorted to when political adversaries exhaust means of compromise in the political arena. Then the less powerful of the adversaries is forced to carry his challenge into a legal procedure or to the public in a show of protest. . . . In the United States, the rage felt by Negroes (increasingly manifested in ghetto riots) is based on centuries of oppression, and in latter times on discriminatory practices that frustrate equal opportunity to social, economic and political goals. . . .

[Thus] violence . . . will remain as indispensable a corrective ingredient in our system as peaceful acts of civil disobedience. The sole qualification

[21] These and other "Pros and Cons" are intended to help review some of the issues dealt with (or implicit) in the longer selections of the chapter. Read each statement carefully. Then try to decide in what respects or under what circumstances that statement is justified—or not justified. Teachers may find these "Pros and Cons" useful springboards to class discussion and debate.

is that all other avenues of legitimate and peaceful change first be substantially closed, exhausted or ineffective.

When an aggrieved segment of the population finds it necessary to resist, riot, or commit deliberate acts of insurrection, the government must respond firmly to enforce the law, to protect people and property from the consequences of violence, but it must, with equal energy and dedication, seek out the causes of the outbursts and move speedily to rectify any injustices that are found at the root of the trouble.[22]

B. Most of the [contemporary American college] students and some of the junior faculty share with their fellows elsewhere in the world an insatiable eagerness to make this world a little safer to live in and a little more generous to live through. They are generally better-educated and more intelligent than preceding student generations. They are less conforming, less disciplined, less respectful of mere authority, and more openly critical of anyone or any group that diminishes (in their judgment) the possibilities of improving the human condition.

They hate the war in Vietnam; they hate malfeasance in high office; they hate social and economic inequities; they hate compromise or expediency and deferral of payment on any moral debt. They believe that the world can be made better now, and are convinced that they could do the job, if they were better educated—but they feel that they have been victims of pedagogical malpractice. They have abundant and heavily documented evidence.

The students feel that society deliberately prolongs their adolescence in order to withhold from them as long as possible even the option of sharing in the management of their affairs and the world's. They are noisy, articulate, and sometimes rude. . . . Each student in his own way is a social protestant. . . .

It is almost irresistible to suggest that the causes of student unrest at the Sorbonne are generically related to those at Columbia—high academic pressures to meet the scholarly demands of "irrelevant" courses, overcrowded classrooms, unresponsive administrators, antiquated and inappropriate rules and regulations, and, of course, the demand for "participatory democracy." . . . .

Both American and French students are clearly reacting against a profound malaise in their countries. The French student sees his government wasting its substance in attempting, quixotically, to become a significant nuclear power, at an intolerable cost to the quality of life in France. The

---

[22] Ralph W. Conant, "Rioting, Insurrection and Civil Disobedience," *The American Scholar* 37: 420–433, Summer 1968. Copyright © 1968 by the United Chapters of Phi Beta Kappa. By permission of the publishers.

Ralph W. Conant is on the faculty at Brandeis University and is associate director of the Lemberg Center for the Study of Violence.

Compare the following: "You cannot have progress without some order—but you cannot have order without making it progressive."—James Perkins, president of Cornell University, cited in "Universities: Of Reason and Revolution," *Time* 91: 42, June 21, 1968.

American student, with the unavoidable evidence of the Vietnam war always before him, and with the so-called war on poverty faltering on every front because of what he sees as wrongly diverted funds, is in a savage rage against his government. At this particular time [Spring 1968], that rage is heightened by the loss of military deferment by graduate students. Most markedly, however, it is a reaction against the orderly violence of war, and the hysterical violence in the city streets. . . . [plus] the continual threat of a technological violence more meaningless, absurd, total, and unpremeditated than any ever imagined before.[23]

C. *Declaration of Confidence:* . . . [We express] confidence in the orderly process of change in American universities as well as in the larger society of which universities are a part.

Organized protest is an eminently allowable activity, protected by the Constitution itself against interference by public agencies. Within independent universities like Columbia it is sanctioned by long practice and deep intellectual conviction of its worth. The permissible means of expressing disagreement with existing laws or policies are not, however, limitless. The limits are overstepped when protesters seize buildings or physically restrain the freedom of personal movement, in order to manifest dissatisfaction.

We do not assert that every act of "civil disobedience" is reprehensible. One way to challenge the validity of a statute is to ignore its commands, undergo arrest and prosecution, and then argue that the law is unconstitutional.

We recognize, too, that in rare instances persons whose voices might otherwise not be heard at all may engage in concerted violation of an admittedly constitutional law in order to proclaim their disapproval of it. In that situation, the violators are prepared to pay the penalty for their disobedience, hoping thus to dramatize opposition to the operative policies. Having in mind the difficulties sometimes experienced in drawing attention to public issues and to dissenting views, we cannot condemn this form of civil disobedience in every conceivable circumstance.

The Columbia episodes at the outset did not involve civil disobedience, but an effort to impose opinions by force. Without ascertaining whether other students shared their thoughts about academic and social issues, a relatively small group of students sought to immobilize the University until their conceptions of sound policy were adopted. Tactics like these have nothing in common with principled opposition or with democratic processes. They represented attempted intimidation.

The force of reason rather than the force of massed bodies must be the reliance of those who wish to influence a community guided by intelligence, as is Columbia. Disrupting institutional proceedings is an imper-

---

[23] Frank G. Jennings, "The Savage Rage of Youth," *Saturday Review* 51: 65–67, 80–81, June 15, 1968. Copyright Saturday Review, Inc., 1968. By permission.

Frank G. Jennings is an Education Consultant for the New World Foundation, and is Editor-at-Large for the *Saturday Review*.

missible substitute for rational persuasion. Using muscles instead of minds to express dissent has no place in the academic setting.

We are confident that American students will themselves recognize the unwisdom of attempting to gain goals by illegal force. Violence begets violence. It beclouds rather than illumines issues. No problem that confronts Columbia or other American universities is beyond the capabilities of men who use the tools education has given them. . . .

We strongly endorse the view that student opinions, whatever may be their tenor, should be known and properly considered. The efficacy of available means of assuring that consideration is now under intensive study.

We are confident that Columbia can and will find ways of strengthening decisional processes without converting them into perpetual mass meetings in which the loudest, not necessarily the wisest, counsels may prevail.[24]

D. In the library sit-in case the protestors violated a segregation ordinance. This ordinance was [ruled by the U.S. Supreme Court to be] unconstitutional and its violation could not be constitutionally punished. But if the law violated by the sit-in had been a lawful and reasonable regulation of library hours, the outcome might well have been different. . . .

Despite the limits which the requirements of an ordered society impose, the [constitutionally] protected weapons of protest, dissent, criticism, and peaceable assembly are enormously powerful. . . . The events of the last few years in this nation dramatically illustrate the power of the ordinary citizen, armed with the great rights to speak, to organize, to demonstrate. It would be difficult to find many situations in history where so much has been accomplished by those who, in cold realism, were divorced from the conventional instruments of power. Negroes and the youth-generation held no office. They did not control political machines. They did not own vast newspapers or magazines or radio or television stations. But they have caused great events to occur. They have triggered a social revolution which has projected this nation, and perhaps the world, to a new plateau in the human adventure. They have forced upon the frontier of a new land—a land in which it is possible that the rights and opportunities of our society may be available to all, not just to some; in which the objectives of our Constitution may be fully realized by all; in which the passion and determination of youth may be brought

[24] May 17, 1968, "Declaration of Confidence" by 35 members of the Columbia University Law School Faculty, *The New York Times,* May 17, 1968, pp. 1, 41. © 1968 by the New York Times Company. Reprinted by permission.

There is no better way to understand the democratic process than to study the *U.S. Reports* (or the *Law Records*), which include minority as well as majority opinions; or to read books summarizing them—books such as Thomas I. Emerson and David Haber, eds., *Political and Civil Rights in the United States,* 3rd ed., Boston: Little, Brown & Company, 1968; Milton R. Konvitz, *First Amendment Freedoms: Selected Cases,* Ithaca, New York: Cornell University Press, 1963. See also William Ebenstein, *Today's Isms,* Englewood Cliffs, N.J.: Prentice-Hall, Inc., 1953, 1958, 1964; David Spitz, *Patterns of Anti-Democratic Thought,* New York: Crowell-Collier and Macmillan, Inc., 1949; Frank H. Way, Jr., *Liberty in Balance: Current Issues in Civil Liberties,* New York: McGraw-Hill, Inc., 1964 (paperback).

to the aid of our pursuit of the marvelous ideals that our heritage provides.

How wonderful it is that freedom's instruments—the rights to speak, to publish, the protest, to assemble peaceably and to participate in the electoral process—have so demonstrated their power and vitality! These are our alternatives to violence; and so long as they are used forcefully but prudently, we shall continue as a vital, free society.[25]

E. The French in their immortal division talked of liberty, equality, and fraternity. . . . Liberty means one thing if you are already in the top place and something very different if you are low on the scale. . . . And the society which pretends that it gives liberty to all without being concerned with equality and fraternity is a sham. . . . [It is because of] the concern that the young have about our total order . . . that the young and the Negro are allied, and this is not pure sentimentalism. It is an awareness that in our civilization the litmus paper is black.[26]

Open Book Exam

Here, and at the end of each chapter in the anthology, is a set of problems or questions suitable for the open-book type of examination, which means that you are permitted, indeed encouraged, to make use of your notes, books, and other relevant materials as you see fit. These questions may also be used as topics for oral reports, or for debate topics.

1. The theory of *balance of power* or *balance of conflicting interests* is usually applied only to (a) the legislative, executive, and judicial branches of government, or to (b) national, state, and local units of government. Show how this theory may also be applied to (c) public and private agencies, economic and educational organizations, to (d) secular and ecclesiastical interests, and to (e) conservative (social inertia maintaining

[25] Abe Fortas (Associate Justice, U.S. Supreme Court), *Concerning Civil Disobedience*, New York: Signet Books, 1968, pages 16–19. This 64 page essay is one of the classics of our generation. It is highly recommended as a supplement to Chapters 1 and 2.

See also Mulford Q. Sibley, "Nonviolence and Revolution," *The Humanist* 27: 3–6, November–December 1968; Robert Hessen, "Campus or Battleground?", *Barron's National Business and Financial Weekly* 48: 1 f., May 20, 1968; Irving Howe (editor of *Dissent* magazine) in Jeremy Larner and Irving Howe, eds., *Poverty: Views from the Left*, New York: William Morrow & Company, Inc., 1968, pages 294–306; Harry S. Ashmore, "The Return of a Native," *Center Magazine* 1: 2–13, May 1968; G. Kerry Smith, ed., *Stress and Campus Response*, especially pages 75–76 by Robert Van Waes, Washington, D.C.: American Association for Higher Education (NEA), 1968.

[26] Charles E. Wyzanski, Jr., "A Federal Judge Digs the Young," *Saturday Review* 51: 14–16, 62, July 20, 1968.

See also Kenneth Keniston, "Youth, Change and Violence," *The American Scholar* 37: 227–245, Spring 1968; Harvey Wheeler, "A Moral Equivalent for Riots," *Saturday Review* 51: 19–22, 51 f, May 11, 1968, versus Samuel Eliot Morison's reply to Harvey Wheeler, "Letter to the Editor," *Saturday Review* 51: 19, June 15, 1968. For a worldwide perspective of the problem, read D. W. Brogan and others, "Student Revolt," *Encounter* 31: 20–44, July 1968. See also in this anthology the concluding portion of Selection 2.10 by Robert J. Havighurst.

the *status quo*) and liberal (revolt and reform, replacing new ideas by old ones) movements. Give specific examples illustrating (b), (c), (d), and (e) in education.

2. Which, if any, of the following practices denies human freedom: compulsory vaccination; compulsory school attendance; prescribed courses of study; the right of a majority to impose its policies on a minority; the right of the majority to suppress minority speech, writing, or assembly, and thus to prevent minority viewpoints from ever becoming those of the majority? Be prepared to defend your answers.

3. John H. Hallowell explains the meaning of majority rule as follows:

> Majority rule . . . presupposes widespread discussion and deliberation and presupposes that the discussion will be conducted in the most reasonable manner possible, to the end that policy may be framed in the interests of the common good. . . . It is the reasoned judgment of the majority that obligates our compliance with its decision, not the will of the majority as such. To the extent, therefore, that the rule of the majority becomes more an expression of will and less an expression of reasoned judgment, to that degree does it become less democratic and more tyrannical.[27]

   From American history, try to find one or two examples that illustrate Hallowell's viewpoint. Try to find one or two examples that ignored this ideal.

4. Clarify and distinguish the meanings of the following pairs of terms: *teach* and *teach about*; *reform* and *revolution*; *conspiracy* and *heresy*; *conspiring to overthrow democracy* and *trying to overthrow the party in power*; *communism* and *socialism*.

5. In what respects is it the proper function of our schools (a) to maintain the present social order, (b) to inform the students as to alternative types of society, (c) to encourage students to forsake present practice in favor of new social goals?

6. Discuss the "beatniks," "hippies," and other "protest groups" in terms of the three types of teaching mentioned in Question 5. (A bibliography on this topic may be found in footnote 30 to Selection 2.10.)

7. Discuss the validity of student disruption of the academic process, and the pros and cons of forcible demonstrations versus due process in achieving academic reforms. If possible, provide a specific example of a type of demonstration you would *favor*, and an example of a type you would *disapprove*.

---

[27] John H. Hallowell, "The Meaning of Majority Rule," *Commonweal* 56: 167–169, May 23, 1952. See also H. S. Commager, ed., *Living Ideas in America*, New York: Harper & Row, Publishers, Inc., 1951, Chapter 5 "Democracy: Majority Rule *and* Minority Rights."

(Questions 8, 9, 10, 11, and 12 may be deferred until the end of Chapter 6.)

8. Define *academic freedom*. Is it absolute and unlimited, or does it vary according to the level of development of students, according to national and local climates of opinion? Should academic freedom be limited to the higher levels of education, to utterances inside the classroom, to the area in which a teacher has special training and competence?

9. What action would you (as a teacher) consider to be an abridgment of your academic freedom? Under what circumstances would you accept such abridgment? Who should judge whether or not a teacher's freedom has been abridged, by what standards?

10. To what extent is the practical application of freedom in education governed by the necessity or desirability of "shielding," or protecting, young people from some unpleasant facts of life? To what extent do you feel that such censorship promotes (or hinders) the mental health and emotional stability of children? Illustrate and defend your position. Do radio and television change the traditional meaning attached to the phrase *in loco parentis*? If so, how?

11. Consider the proposition that academic freedom should be extended to protect the teacher who, while competent in his field, is:
    a. strongly anti-Semitic; or who is
    b. an extreme religious fundamentalist; or who is
    c. a staunch advocate of white supremacy; or who is
    d. a conscientious objector; or who is
    e. an avowed social and moral nonconformist.

    With respect to those of the above cases in which you would advocate restriction of the freedom of teaching (for example, refusal to employ as teachers, or restriction of the scope of teaching, as when a conscientious objector may be permitted to teach mathematics, but not permitted to teach social studies), justify or defend your stand.

12. Defend one or the other—or both—of the following:

> (A) [American] school boards and trustees of colleges and universities have a heavy responsibility. They must see to it that among our teachers there is an adequate supply of "Communists," of able, fearless, outspoken advocates of the unpopular view. It must be arranged by the authorities [so] that both sides of fundamental issues shall be represented by teachers who believe in them. Under the actual conditions of democratic life the practical question is not, "Shall we have any Communists on our faculties?" but rather, "How can we get enough Communists to give proper expression of views which run counter to the general trend of habit, emotion, interest of the community at large?" We must provide for the criticism of our institutions as well as for their advocacy.[28]

[28] Alexander Mieklejohn, "Teachers and Controversial Questions," *Harper's*, 177: 15–22, June 1938.

(B) Academic freedom does not demand that we protect those who, wrapped in the cloak of freedom, employ this freedom to destroy the very types of society that guarantee such freedom.

In (A) for *Communist*, you may substitute *pacifist*, *Black Muslim*, *conscientious objector*, *racist*, or any other such term.

Chapter 2
RACE, POVERTY, AND SEGREGATION

2.1 INTRODUCTION: RACIAL SEGREGATION AND THE DEMOCRATIC IDEAL

Democracy is a form of society whereby men and women may gain confidence in themselves and in their fellow humans, and thereby move from force to persuasion, from restriction to liberty, from blind obedience to creative effort. Unlike dictatorial forms of government, democracy has everything to gain and nothing to lose from the intelligence of its citizens. In the words of James Madison:

> A popular government without popular information or the means of acquiring it, is but a Prologue to a Farce or a Tragedy, or, perhaps both. Knowledge will forever govern ignorance; and a people who mean to be their own Governors must arm themselves with the power which knowledge gives.[1]

In any society progress depends on developed leadership. True leadership must be renewed from the ranks of the unknown, not from the small group of families already famous and powerful. If one class possesses all the wealth and education while the laboring class remains both poor and ignorant, labor will inevitably be servile to capital, and our society will be divided into distinctive, permanent classes. But if education is widely and equally diffused according to ability rather than wealth, children of all classes may attain their maximum potential, and society as a whole will gain from the fuller use of its human resources.

Democracy holds that there is no safe repository of the ultimate powers of society except in the people themselves. If the people make mistakes, the remedy is not to take the power away from them, but to help them in forming their judgment through better education and more open communication. In his First Inaugural Address, Abraham Lincoln expressed democracy's faith in the people as follows:

[1] James Madison, Letter to W. T. Barry, Aug. 4, 1822, in *The Complete Madison: His Basic Writings*, Saul K. Padover, ed., New York: Harper & Row, Publishers, 1953, p. 337.

> Why should there not be a patient confidence in the ultimate justice of the people? Is there any better or equal hope in the world? . . . Truth and justice will surely prevail by the judgment of the great tribunal of the American people.

Democratic education should develop citizens who are "easy to lead, but difficult to drive; easy to govern, but impossible to enslave."[2] It should make them easy to lead by bringing out latent talent and leadership, conceived in cooperative terms. It should make them impossible to enslave—and, we would add, intolerant of enslavement—because their education will have emphasized individual self-reliance, free expression, and unthwarted communication.

The democratic citizen will admit that, in specialized areas, there are authorities whose technical knowledge may greatly influence decisions concerning public policy. But in a free society, the citizen should never relinquish his personal freedom, autonomy, and moral dignity. External guidance may be a means, but self-direction is an end in itself. The mature man wants self-confidence, courage to face all difficulties, and the consciousness of being man in the fullest sense of the word.

> Such a man is possessed by the wish to see the same inner strength develop in others. As he himself abhors alien rule, neither does he wish to rule over others. He is pleased to see life unfolding itself free and strong in his fellow humans. He finds himself happiest in a circle of equals, not surrounded by slaves. In education, his aim is not to exact submissive obedience, but to foster young individuals who in due course will themselves be able to form their own lives with freedom and responsibility.[3]

Such is the democratic ideal that moved our schools in the effort to mold immigrants from various European nationality groups into one American culture. Selection 1.2 by Henry Steele Commager, reviewed this inspiring story.

But this story contains one tragic omission, for the American Negro has not yet been accorded a full and honored place in the American community. The early American colonists, desperately in need of labor, imported many indentured servants, or "bondsmen," who, after serving their new masters for a period usually of seven years, were released from further bondage. The first Negroes to come to America in 1619 are believed to have come as indentured servants, not as slaves.[4] But the status of the

---

[2] Lord Henry Peter Broughton, Speech in House of Commons, January 29, 1828.

[3] Alf Ross, *Why Democracy?* Cambridge, Mass.: Harvard University Press, 1952, p. 104. By permission. Compare Harry A. Overstreet, *The Mature Mind*, New York: W. W. Norton & Company, Inc., 1949.

[4] Eric Lincoln, "From African Civilization to the Present," in *Poverty, Education and Race Relations*, W. C. Kvaraceus and others, eds., Boston: Allyn and Bacon, Inc., 1967, pp. 75–112.

Negro declined, and in the nineteenth century men bought and sold Negroes as chattel property; men honestly affirmed that dark-skinned people had neither souls nor intellect; men openly asserted that Negroes were incapable of rational thought, intellectual achievement, or moral action. So today we face such questions as the following:

How effectively, how genuinely does our democratic idealism extend to peoples of non-Western and non-Caucasian cultural and ethnic backgrounds? How readily, warmly, and completely do we welcome into full citizenship the nonwhite American, especially the Negro? And how can our schools reduce or eliminate present educational inequalities due to racial prejudice?

In *The American Dilemma,* his monumental study of the problem of race relations in the United States, Gunnar Myrdal presents a "white man's rank order of discrimination"—a charting of the discrimination patterns, as he discerned them, in the order of their importance to the white American, North (though somewhat less sharply) as well as South.

Rank 1. Highest in this order stands the bar against intermarriage and sexual intercourse involving white women.

Rank 2. Next comes the several etiquettes and discriminations, which specifically concern behavior in personal relations. These are the barriers against dancing, bathing, eating, drinking together, and social intercourse generally; peculiar rules as to handshaking, hat lifting, use of titles, house entrance to be used, social forms when meeting on streets and in work, and so forth. These patterns are sometimes referred to as the denial of *social equality* in the narrow meaning of the term.

Rank 3. Thereafter follow the segregations and discriminations in use of public facilities such as schools, churches, and means of conveyance.

Rank 4. Next comes political disfranchisement.

Rank 5. Thereafter come discriminations in law courts, by the police, and by other public servants.

Rank 6. Finally come the discriminations in securing land, credit, jobs, or other means of earning a living, and discriminations in public relief and other social welfare activities.[5]

---

[5] Gunnar Myrdal, *The American Dilemma,* New York: Harper & Row, Publishers, 1944, Vol. I, pp. 60–61. By permission.

In the concluding chapter of his great 1944 classic, Myrdal observed that the Negro problem was not only America's greatest failure, "but also America's incomparably great opportunity for the future." The great American dilemma, he thought, arose from the gap between what we profess to be right—Myrdal called it the American creed—and what we actually think and do. This point of view is reflected in a more recent classic: *The Negro American,* by Talcott Parsons and Kenneth B. Clark, Boston: The Beacon Press, 1967. Members of this school of thought (including the editor of *Crucial Issues in Education*) have faith in the American commitment to principles of justice and equality, and they recognize that change is badly needed. But they believe that peaceful

The significance of this for the future of integration is crucial. It is apparent that segregation in education is neither the most nor the least important bastion in the defense of "racial integrity." Education seems to stand about midway between the area of most extreme intolerance (marriage and sexual relations) and the area of greatest tolerance (employment and social welfare). It would seem unwise and naive to expect the realization of school desegregation (Rank 3) in states which have not yet accorded to the Negro full political rights (Rank 4). Thus the desegregation of our public schools is but a single part of a larger social revolution. This social revolution came to a climax on May 17, 1954, when the United States Supreme Court, in what many would regard as its most important twentieth-century decision, outlawed the practice of compulsory racial segregation in public schools. Few judgments from our highest court have dealt so squarely with a basic question of social tradition, with a conflict between opposed mores and values. Probably no Supreme Court case has been watched as closely by the rest of the world, and its significance for American relations with other countries can hardly be overestimated. Gandhi was once asked by an American visiting India: What can the United States do that would make the greatest contribution to the improvement of the lot of the peoples of the Eastern nations? Gandhi's answer was unequivocal: "Solve your own race problem."

The heart of the decision on school segregation, a judgment prepared and presented by Chief Justice Earl Warren on behalf of a unanimous Court, is contained in the following passage:

> . . . Does segregation of children in public schools solely on the basis of race, even though the physical facilities and other "tangible" factors may be equal, deprive the children of the minority group of equal educational opportunities? We believe that it does.
>
> . . . To separate [children in grade and high schools] from others of similar age and qualifications solely because of their race generates a feeling of inferiority as to their status in the community that may affect their hearts and minds in a way unlikely ever to be undone. The effect of this separation on their educational opportunities was well stated by a finding in the Kansas cases by a [lower] court which neverthless felt compelled to rule against the Negro plaintiffs:
>
> Segregation of white and colored children in public schools has a detrimental effect upon the colored children. The impact is greater

---

change within the existing political system is the surest method, whereas revolutionary violence will thwart rather than aid the goals of justice and equality for all Americans.

In a democratic society, political rights are perhaps even more important than economic opportunities. Indeed, as William Stringfellow has expressed it, "The representation of the poor in politics and in the law measures the maturity and health of society. By that assessment, contemporary America is profoundly decadent."—William Stringfellow, "The Representation of the Poor in American Society," 31 *Law and Contemporary Problems* 142–151, Winter 1966.

> when it has the sanction of the law; for the policy of separating the races is usually interpreted as denoting the inferiority of the Negro group. A sense of inferiority affects the motivation of a child to learn. Segregation with the sanction of law, therefore, has a tendency to retard the educational and mental development of Negro children and to deprive them of some of the benefits they would receive in a racial[ly] integrated school system.
>
> We conclude that in the field of public education the doctrine of "separate but equal" has no place. Separate educational facilities are inherently unequal. . . . Such segregation is a denial of the equal protection of the laws.[6]

The contention that this finding was sudden, unannounced, and therefore unexpected belies the antecedent history. This rejection of the famous "separate but equal" doctrine[7] was the logical and inescapable product of changing times and a changing outlook, and an awakened consciousness that racial segregation is incompatible with democracy's basic ideals. Thus, in rejecting the longstanding "separate but equal" doctrine, the 1954 Supreme Court decision compelled many Americans to reexamine their beliefs and prejudices in the light of democratic ideals. The process has not been easy, as the selections in this chapter will show. But we may recall the lines of Kipling:

> It is not learning, grace nor gear,
> Nor easy meat nor drink,
> But bitter pinch of pain or fear
> That makes creation think.[8]

---

[6] *Brown v. Board of Education of Topeka*, 347 U.S. 483 (1954).

[7] In *Plessy v. Ferguson*, 163 U.S. 537 (1896), the U.S. Supreme Court sustained a Louisiana law requiring separate but equal railroad accommodations. The Court held that

> If one race be inferior to the other socially, the Constitution of the United States cannot put them on the same plane. . . . [If] the enforced separation of the two races stamps the colored race with a badge of inferiority . . . it is not by reason of anything found in the [Louisiana] act, but solely because the colored race chooses to put that construction upon it.

Justice Harlan, in a noteworthy dissent, insisted

> [I]n view of the Constitution, in the eye of the law, there is in this country no superior, dominant ruling class of citizens. There is no caste system here. Our Constitution is color blind, and neither knows nor tolerates classes among citizens. . . . The law regards man as man, and takes no account of his surroundings or of his color when his civil rights guaranteed by the supreme law of the land are involved.

[8] Rudyard Kipling, "The Benefactors," Stanza 3, in Bartlett's *Familiar Quotation*. Kipling's lines are particularly applicable to those who retain the nineteenth century belief in "the white man's burden" and whose attitude toward non-Europeans—perhaps the attitude of Kipling himself—is one of pity or contempt.

It should be obvious that we are in the midst of a great social revolution—one whose patterns and forms change with each passing year. Yet the over-all movement seems to be toward the democratic ideal. Thus, in April, 1968, shortly after the assassination of Dr. Martin Luther King, Jr., President Johnson

> signed the 1968 Civil Rights Act, opening some 80 per cent of all the nation's housing to Negroes. . . . The measure contained other titles—two anti-riot clauses and language safeguarding the constitutional rights of American Indians—but its crucial provision was for open housing, which will eventually help turn the lock to release Negroes from their imprisoning urban ghettos. Like other recent civil rights bills, the 1968 act carries the danger of promising too much and delivering too little. . . . [Nevertheless] For the first time by federal law, a Negro in the U.S. is as entitled as any white—or more accurately, four-fifths are entitled—to buy or rent any house or apartment that he can afford.[9]

In conclusion, we should remind ourselves that the desegregation issue in our nation is but one small part of a great worldwide social revolution in which "the have-nots" across the face of the globe are determined to join "the haves." Even in our own affluent society some 20 to 40 million Americans are trapped and nearly helpless in deep fissures of economic and educational impoverishment. In this social revolution, the school is a powerful force for building personality, for helping the deprived change their self-images, for creating in them hope and aspiration, and for building a society whose citizens gain freedom through excellence and excellence through freedom.

---

[9] *Time* 91: 20–21, April 19, 1968.

From Slavery to Citizenship

2.2 RACE: THE AMERICAN DILEMMA*

Henry J. Abraham

A GLANCE AT HISTORY

Although the Declaration of Independence had stipulated, as a self-evident truth, that "all men are created equal," it soon became obvious that, in the pithy comment of George Orwell, "some men are created more equal than others." The second section of the first article of the Constitution clearly recognized the existence of slavery in the United States by directing the inclusion of "three-fifths of all other persons," i.e., the slaves, in the enumeration which was to form the basis for representative apportionment and taxation. True, Section 9 of Article I did make it possible to stop the "migration of importation" of slaves after 1808, provided Congress chose to do so then, and the Thirteenth Amendment was designed to settle the matter by outlawing slavery in 1865. But it was not really until the ratification of the Fourteenth Amendment in 1868, five years after Lincoln's Emancipation Proclamation, that the white-supremacy concept inherent in Article I was removed from the Constitution. In the language of the Amendment's second section:

> Representatives shall be apportioned among the several States according to their respective numbers, *counting the whole number of persons* in each State, excluding Indians not taxed. . . .

Yet despite these enactments . . . [which] seemed to assure to the Negro the privilege of the ballot, neither the myth of white supremacy nor the

---

* Abridged from *Freedom and the Court: Civil Rights and Liberties in the United States*, by Henry J. Abraham. The exact page and line excerpts are: 245:30—248:20; 248:29–30; 249:11–13; 249:27—250:12; 250:35—251:21; 270:13—271:2; 271:10–19; 272:14—273:1; 273:7–25; 274:11–13; 274:37—276:4; 277:19–26; 278:1–8; 278:25—279:30; 294:13—295:21; 295:34—296:22; 297:7–14; 298:22—300:9.

Henry J. Abraham is Professor of Political Science, University of Pennsylvania.

fact of color prejudice was wiped out. Section 1 of the Fourteenth Amendment, now so significant but then so ineffective, would have to wait more than eight decades for its triumphs on behalf of the Negro:

> *All persons born or naturalized in the United States, and subject to the jurisdiction thereof, are citizens of the United States and of the State wherein they reside. No State shall make or enforce* any law which shall abridge the privileges or immunities of citizens of the United States; *nor shall any State deprive* any person of life, liberty, or property, without due process of law; *nor deny to any person within its jurisdiction the equal protection of the laws.*

The Emancipation Proclamation and these three Civil War amendments intended, above all, to ameliorate the lot of the Negro by attacking the constitutional silence on federal protection of civil rights, a protection which had, until then, been left wholly to the several states. They proved to be but paper tigers. True, Reconstruction briefly shot the Negro's star skyward; Southern Negroes went to Congress and two of them became United States senators from Mississippi. True also that in the decade following the passage of the Thirteenth Amendment Congress enacted five major civil-rights statutes, [including the Anti-K.K.K. Act of 1871 and the Public Accommodations Act of 1875] spelling out the rights of the new Negro freedmen and providing penalties for their denial. But the South proved itself equal to the challenge of restoring the *status quo ante* through a host of ingenious and ingenuous devices. By 1910 every former Confederate state, for example, had succeeded in disfranchising the Negro either by state statute—e.g., the "white primary" and the "grandfather clause"; by state constitutional amendment; or with the aid of such United States Supreme Court decisions as those in the *Slaughterhouse Cases* and the *Civil Rights Cases*.[10] The Court's position . . . was that the Fourteenth

[10] Editor's Note: In *Barron v. Baltimore*, 8 Peters 243 (1833), Chief Justice John Marshall wrote for a unanimous Court that "The Constitution was ordained and established by the people of the United States for themselves, for their own government, and not for the government of the individual states. . . . [The Bill of Rights] contains no expression indicating an intention to apply them to the state governments."

The *Slaughterhouse* cases, 16 Wallace, 36 (1873), went further than *Barron* by ruling that the "privileges and immunities" clause of the Fourteenth Amendment ("No State shall make or enforce any law which shall abridge the privileges of citizens of the United States") was not intended to protect the rights of *federal* citizenship, but solely that of *state* citizenship. This 5 to 4 majority decision declared: "It is quite clear, then, that there is a citizenship of the United States, and a citizenship of a state, which are distinct from each other, and which depend upon different characteristics or circumstances in the individual."

In short, the majority's decision meant that the "privileges and immunities" clause of the Fourteenth Amendment really meant nothing at all insofar as the states were concerned.

These points are discussed at considerable length in Abraham's book, pp. 26–78 and 252–265.

Amendment did not place under federal protection "the entire domain of civil rights heretofore belonging exclusively to the states," and that the protection offered by the Fourteenth and Fifteenth Amendments was *against state action only*, not against private action. And in 1896 the Court upheld the convenient discriminatory concept of "separate but equal" in the famous case of *Plessy v. Ferguson.* To all intents and purposes the Negro's lot was at the mercy of the states. Until World War II the federal government assumed at most a limited role in the protection of civil rights on the state level.

In 1900 almost 90 percent of America's Negroes lived in the South [a figure that had declined to 53 per cent by 1967], and the heart of racial discrimination naturally beat there. Racial discrimination occurred on both the public and the private level. Thus, *public* authorities at the state and local levels, usually under the guise of the Court-upheld "separate but equal" concept, enacted measures [sometimes taking the form of a constitutional provision] *permitting* or even *requiring* segregation of busses, streetcars, taxicabs, railroads, waiting rooms, comfort stations, drinking fountains, state and local schools, state colleges and universities, hospitals, jails, sports, beaches, bath houses, swimming pools, parks, golf-courses, courthouse cafeterias, libraries, housing, theaters, hotels, restaurants, and other similar facilities—be these public, quasi-public, or private in nature. Private individuals and groups, on their own initiative, and not infrequently encouraged by state authorities, acted to deny Negroes, and often other non-Caucasians as well, access to social clubs, fraternities and sororities, private schools, colleges, and universities, churches, hospitals, hotels, housing, restaurants, movies, bowling alleys, swimming pools, bath houses, sporting events, comfort stations, drinking fountains, barber and beauty shops, employment agencies, and employment itself. There was nothing particularly secretive about either public or private discrimination; it was simply an accepted way of life—accepted by many Negroes as well as by almost all whites. . . .

WINDS OF CHANGE

. . . [The] onset of World War II prompted the federal government to take notice of the problem. [In 1939] President Franklin D. Roosevelt created a Civil Liberties Unit in the Criminal Division of the Department of Justice . . . [and in 1941] he established by executive order the first Committee on Fair Employment Practices [F.E.P.C.]. . . . [However] Congress managed to abolish the Committee in 1946. . . .

With Congress unwilling or unable to make progress on the race problem, President Harry S Truman . . . [in 1946] appointed the 15-member blue ribbon committee, charging it specifically with the careful investigation of the need for legislative and other procedures designed to further and protect civil rights and liberties. One year later, the Committee reported that although civil rights were indeed better and more broadly protected than ever before, there were still alarmingly widespread violations. In its widely distributed report, *To Secure These Rights,* the Committee made numerous recommendations designed to ensure that every violation of a civil right by private persons could be treated as a criminal offense. Were these recommendations to be followed, the enforcement of civil rights would become a new and vigorous government activity on a very much extended scale. Specifically, the Committee's proposals included federal laws to forbid lynching and discrimination in voting requirements; to create a permanent Fair Employment Practices Commission and a permanent Commission on Civil Rights; and to expand into a Civil Rights Division the small, undermanned Civil Rights Section in the Department of Justice. . . .

Alas, like all proposals for the extension of government activities, these became quickly a political issue. . . . [Nevertheless], President Eisenhower, on attaining office in 1953, continued President Truman's civil rights policies . . . [and by executive order] created the President's Committee on Government Contracts . . . [and empowered this committee] to receive complaints alleging discrimination by government contractors, and to cancel contracts if necessary. . . .

THE WATERSHED

These activities were of course not lost on the several states. A good many Northern states turned to F.E.P.C. and similar devices to combat discrimination, and the air was filled with the beginnings of change. Yet the South was determined not to budge. And in Congress it had a seemingly eternal ally. President Eisenhower did not recommend any new civil rights legislation until his Administration's Civil Rights Act of 1956. That measure failed of enactment then, but the ice was broken for Congress to pass a modified version in the Civil Rights Act of 1957, the first major piece of civil rights legislation since Reconstruction. It is fair to say, however, that it would never have become law had not the leader of the third branch of the United States Government, the Supreme Court, swung into the fray with its monumentally significant decision in the *Public School Segregation Cases* on May 17, 1954.[11]

[A year later in Brown II, the Supreme Court] mandated the *local federal courts* to direct and oversee the transition to a racially non-discriminatory system of public school primary and secondary education "with all delib-

[11] Editor's Note: See Selection 2.1 of this anthology.

erate speed." It directed these courts to order a "prompt and reasonable start," but clearly left the door ajar for consideration of the manifold peculiar local problems involved. In fact, "wide open door" may be a more appropriate description of the *initial* judicial attitude, compared to what would be a much stiffer attitude as the fifties turned into sixties. Inevitably the "child of its time," the Court had carefully separated the principle of integration—a word that appears nowhere in the decisions involved—from its actual implementation. Just as the Supreme Court reflected the sociopolitical realities of a new day and age in Brown I, so did it reflect the judicial-limitation realities in Brown II. As the ensuing months and years would prove only too well, the Court can be a leader and the conscience of its land, but in the political process of which, after all, it is a part, it has only "the power to persuade: purse and sword are in other hands," as Alexander Hamilton truly stated.

Thus, no matter how "deliberate" the "speed" [and there was more deliberation than speed in compliance!], the Court would need immediate help from the executive branch. Overt or covert defiance became the rule rather than the exception in a good many sectors of the land, predictably chiefly in the Deep South. . . . as, for example, the closing of all public schools in Prince Edward County, Virginia. . . . Public feeling ran high, indeed, over what the majority of the white population in the affected sectors regarded as a threat to their way of life and the right of the states to govern themselves, the latter more often than not being a camouflage for the former. Some two hundred state segregation statutes would be enacted in the decade following the implementation decision! Customs that have stood for generations do not easily die. . . . [In 1957] President Eisenhower felt compelled to . . . dispatch federal troops to re-establish law and order and allow desegregation to proceed as directed [at Little Rock, Arkansas]. Five years later . . . John F. Kennedy deployed 25,000 federal troops to overcome the opposition of Mississippi, led by its governor, Ross R. Barnett, to the federal court-ordered admission of Negro James Meredith to the University of Mississippi at Oxford. A bloody all-night battle was fought on and near the campus of "Ole Miss," with many wounded and two lives lost. Eight months later, President Kennedy again had to use troops, this time mobilizing the Alabama National Guard in order to overcome Governor George C. Wallace's defiance of the federal court-ordered admission of Negroes Vivian Malone and James Hood to the University of Alabama at Tuscaloosa.

Although even token integration was often resisted, especially in the "black belt" sections of the Deep South, mixed classes eventually became a reality on all levels of the public school system. "Mixed," of course, sometimes meant the presence of only one colored student in an otherwise all-white classroom, but the principle was being established. . . . [and]

on August 14, 1964, Mississippi became the *last* state to desegregate at least one school district when the Biloxi District bowed to the inevitability of a federal court order decreeing the desegregation of its first-grade classes. Less than six months later, in January 1965, the Greenville, Mississippi, School Board, facing the loss of $272,000 in federal aid-to-education funds if it failed to comply with the provisions of the Civil Rights Act of 1964 affecting such federal aid, voted unanimously to prepare a desegregation plan. Providing the first instance of non-court-ordered compliance by that state's authorities, Greenville's Mayor Pat Dunne endorsed the Board's action, pointing out that there was no alternative: "Repugnant as the law is to all of us, it's a Federal law and it's either a case of comply or close the schools."

"Separate but equal" died *legally* on May 17, 1954; it died *practically* only after many a ground-giving battle as the years rolled by. The decision in *Brown v. Board* was but a beginning, of course. It triggered an evolving socio-political conflict reflecting new realities of power, of which the end is not yet in sight. What *is* gone is the concept of "separate but equal.". . . .

By far the most important *legislative* [measures] of the Eisenhower Administration in civil rights . . . [were] the *Civil Rights* [*Acts* of 1957 and]. . . . of 1960. No longer did the Southern members of Congress have the necessary number of votes and allies to block. . . . [legislation, which] promised to safeguard the Negro's right to vote freely and without arbitrary discrimination. . . . [These laws] enabled the federal Department of Justice to file suit to bring about this desired result. More than fifteen times as many suits were subsequently brought during its first three years of life than had been brought during any similar span of time under the previous statute.

Still, Negro leaders and other civil rights spokesmen regarded the Act of 1960 as too slow, too costly to administer, and too cumbersome. Negro restlessness and impatience—assuredly understandable if not inevitably justifiable in all instances—was intensified; the year 1963 saw the peak of visible public protest movements. Repeating over and over their "loss of faith in the white power structure," Negroes took to the streets in ever increasing numbers throughout the United States. The summer of 1963 became known as the "long, hot summer," culminating late in August in a massive, peaceful, interracial march by some 200,000 in Washington, D.C., billed as the "March on Washington for Jobs and Freedom." Other demonstrations were not as peaceful and orderly, especially some of those that took place in scattered cities in the Deep South where feelings ran high and hostility was rampant. Although not necessarily directly connected with the demonstrations, reprisals by white extremists resulted in 44 violent deaths during 1963, 1964, and 1965. The Negro riots in Northern cities in the summer of 1966 led to a score more. Against this background of mounting anger, threats, and sporadic violence, President Kennedy asked Congress in February and again in June of 1963 for new, strong, and expanded civil rights legislation. President Johnson again asked for it when he first addressed Congress as the nation's new Chief Executive following the tragic assassination of President Kennedy on November 22. Late in June of the following year the *Civil Rights Act of* 1964 passed Congress. . . .

Understandably, the two most controversial provisions of the Civil Rights Act of 1964 . . . [were] those dealing with Fair Employment Practices and with Public Accommodations. For here the basic issue of individual rights and of societal obligations were patently joined. . . . One of the steadfast, bitter-end opponents [of the 1964 Civil Rights Act] was the future Republican Presidential nominee, Senator Barry M. Goldwater of Arizona, whose recorded "no" votes, both on cloture and on passage of the bill, probably cost him what little Negro support he might have had. Not only did Senator Goldwater oppose the bill in general, and the fair employment and public accommodations sections in particular, but he denounced the entire measure as "unconstitutional" and declared that it would lead to a "police state.". . . . [In reply, Senator] Dirksen tolled a long list of social and economic legislation that had been similarly called unconstitutional when first proposed. "Today they are accepted," he underscored, "because they were a forward thrust in the whole effort of mankind. There is latitude enough in the Constitution to embrace within its four corners these advances." Evidently, country and Court agreed: Yet there remain many, among them people of good will as well as confirmed bigots, who are not at all convinced that a democratic government should have the power to do what it did in those two provisos. It has been a hard line to draw between competing values.

Yet still more legislation was to come, legislation replete with provisions that promised to cause lively debate in and out of Congress. While conceding that the fruits of the 1964 Act—and the Voting Rights Act of 1965—were already "impressively apparent," President Johnson sent Congress his third civil rights bill in three years in the spring of 1966, declaring that discriminatory practices "still exist in many American communities." Going beyond its predecessors, the 1966 Civil Rights Act would have rendered the murder of a civil rights worker, or the slaying of anyone else exercising certain fundamental rights, such as voting or seeking to attend school, a federal crime with a maximum penalty of life imprisonment. It would also have instituted procedures for eliminating racial discrimination in federal juries, and would have empowered *federal* as well as state courts to halt trial in state courts when evidence of juror discrimination is present; and the bill would have enabled the U.S. Attorney-General to take independent legal action to compel desegregation of schools and other public facilities without having to wait to receive a formal complaint. But the 1966 bill's most contentious provision would have outlawed discrimination on either racial or religious grounds in the "purchase, rental, lease, financing, use and occupancy" of *all housing*. Chiefly because of the so-called open housing provision, the bill, although it had passed the House in a watered-down version by a vote of 259:157, died on the floor of the Senate in September 1966—against a backdrop of Negro riots and demonstrations in cities throughout the land, particularly in the North, and the rise of resentment to the new "black power" slogan that began to characterize much of the civil rights activity of that year. . . .

This growing militancy on the parts of thousands of Negroes—and a good many white supporters—has not abated and is not likely to do so for some time, despite some serious excesses and despite some questionable tactics. The initiative for change has demonstrably shifted from a relatively few professional desegregationists, in such traditional organizations as the NAACP and the Urban League, to large numbers of average citizens who concluded somewhere along the line that they had no choice but to do battle against "The System" by direct action "in the streets." This development both stemmed from and gave rise to a coterie of new and formally organized protest groups, particularly the Southern Christian Leadership Conference [SCLC], created under the leadership of Dr. Martin Luther King, Jr., in 1956–57; the Congress of Racial Equality [CORE], established in 1943 but not really coming to the fore until the 1950's; and the Student Non-Violent Co-ordinating Committee [SNCC], the youngest "action group" founded in 1960. While SCLC under Dr. King's guidance steadfastly maintained its dedication to non-violence, CORE and especially SNCC—despite "Non-Violent" in its name—proved to be not averse to violent action, as demonstrated in 1965 and 1966 under the direction of such fiery, young, and new leaders as CORE's Floyd McKissick and SNCC's Stokely Carmichael.

The "sit-in" movement of 1960 first illustrated the belief that only *action* would obtain results, a belief which became a religious conviction of these groups and their followers—action as a supplement or complement to the educational and legal means heretofore employed predominantly. For Dr. King and other protest movement leaders and the vast number of Negroes, while the educational and especially the legal tools had produced significant results since World War II, they were nevertheless too slow in producing change. In certain communities, not even a gradualist approach was acceptable to the white "power structure." Turning then to "action," the Negro leadership rapidly discovered that the development of community "crisis situations," such as economic boycotts, by the Negro protest movements, was usually at least partly successful simply because the crises demanded a speedy resolution by the community decision-makers. Yet "activism" was certain to raise serious problems in and for society—problems of the limits of civil disobedience—problems, once again, of where to draw the line.

ILLUSTRATIONS OF NEW TACTICS

Of course, some "action" had accompanied the movement even prior to the days of Greensboro [1960]; there were sporadic rallies, marches, boycotts, and picket lines. Almost none really attained major significance. . . .

But the Montgomery, Alabama, bus boycott [which lasted a full year from 1955 to 1956]. . . . set a precedent for similar boycotts and demonstrations in cities throughout the South, extending to retail stores, produce markets, and a host of other sales and service facilities.

Yet a boycott destined to be far more militant and far more controversial began on February 1, 1960, when four Negro boys, all freshmen at North Carolina Agricultural and Technical College, began what at first was a spontaneous "sit-in" demonstration at the lunch counter of Woolworth's dime store in Greensboro. They had asked for cups of coffee, and had done so politely, but were refused service. They then simply continued to sit at the counter in protest—notwithstanding cursing, pushing, spitting, and catsup-throwing by their white neighbors. Ultimately, the four filed out, formed a tight circle on the sidewalk, and recited the Lord's Prayer. Then another group took over for them inside.

This example of non-violent protest spread to six other North Carolina cities and seven other Southern states within four weeks. Not only did the Greensboro sit-in set a precedent, it led directly to the organization of the Student Non-Violent Co-ordinating Committee. SNCC quickly began to serve both in the South and in the North as an organizer and backer for "sit-ins" and a large variety of other "ins," such as "stand-ins," "read-ins," "pray-ins," "wade-ins," "sleep-ins," and "lie-ins." Thousands who had never before taken an active part in the protest movement now joined. [The Southern Regional Council estimated that from February 1, 1960, to March 27, 1961, the total number of demonstrators was 74,350, the total number of arrests, 3,585.]

Other participants in "ins" movements, mounted largely by CORE, were so-called freedom riders. The chief target of these riders was transportation, supposedly desegregated for some time. The "rides" not only pinpointed but actually tested, often at the cost of imprisonment and violence, the still prevalent segregation practices in almost all interstate travel and terminal facilities in the Deep South. In general, these rides accomplished their purpose: the exposure of continued, rampant violation of what was now the law of the land. . . .

[The Birmingham, Alabama, demonstration of April, 1963, was followed by almost 800 other racial demonstrations.] They culminated in the mammoth, orderly Washington march of August 1963, in which, as we have noted, more than 200,000 Negroes and whites participated. Racial demonstrations continued during the summers of 1963, 1964, 1965 and 1966 in such Northern cities as New York, Philadelphia, Chicago, Newark, Rochester, St. Louis, Cleveland, San Francisco, Los Angeles (the bloody Watts riots) . . . and Jersey City. Not even the new federal civil rights and voting statutes would lessen the now determined, often militant and impatient drive for Negro equality. It had obtained results! For most Southerners, adaptation to change had become a fact of daily life for state and local governments; racial incidents had to be avoided; and resistance to federal authority was, in the long run, futile. Still, the Southern leadership was allowed to move slowly and, with some exceptions, to do nothing more than the bare minimum. "Tokenism" was the word of the day.

This attitude, however understandable it might be in terms of the practices and traditions of generations, continued to incite militancy on the part of the increasingly restive Negroes—and now particularly those in the ghettos of the Northern cities. They were tired of waiting, tired of gradualism, tired of tokenism. In effect, they demanded what was patently impossible; full equality "here and now"—and if that meant "favored treatment," so be it! But Negro poverty, both of means and of opportunity, and prejudice—always prejudice—could not so quickly be eradicated. The resultant frustration frequently generated an excessive belligerency, often referred to by the participants as "direct action," which did more harm than good to the Negro cause, and . . . provided a serious split in the Supreme Court[12] which had been supporting civil rights causes with unanimity.

QUESTIONABLE AND TRAGIC TACTICS

The continuing actions were less "demonstrations" than they were "community harassment," and they usually occurred in the large urban Northern centers. Thus, for example, the prostrate bodies of Negroes and white supporters halted traffic during rush hours on such vital arteries as the Brooklyn Bridge; there was deliberate stalling of automobiles on the highways to the World's Fair and to baseball games; in Cleveland demonstrators lay down in the path of bulldozers on construction projects, resulting in the tragic death of a white minister who was run over; in Philadelphia a private school was picketed and harassed daily for months, necessitating the employment of a large additional police detail at great expense to the city; there were sit-ins in the offices of governors [e.g., Rockefeller and Scranton] and of mayors [e.g., Wagner and Tate]. These

[12] Editor's Note: See, among others, *Bell v. Maryland,* 378 U.S. 226 (1964); *Hamm v. City of Rock Hill,* 370 U.S. 306; *Elton v. Cox,* 379 U.S. 536 (1965); *Brown v. Louisiana,* 383 U.S. 131 (1966); and *Adderly v. Florida,* 385 U.S. 39 (1966). See also the concluding selections of Chapter 1 in this anthology.

and similar disruptive tactics raised serious questions of both their legality and regard for the rights of others.

Worse, of course, was the wave of wanton riots that swept many Northern cities in 1965 and 1966. There could be no excuse for the looting, the burning, the destruction, the loss of lives—the reckless dedication to licentious manifestations of hate. As a result, at the end of 1966 there was mounting fear among civil rights leaders and supporters that the days of wide national support for civil rights had come to an end, at least temporarily. Indeed there were those who felt that the now mounting Northern white disaffection could lead to such a setback that it would be years before the movement, and the Negro masses, would recover. The failure of Congress to pass the 1966 Civil Rights bill was a case in point. As President Johnson told a group of visiting bishops from the all-Negro African Methodist Episcopal Church in October of that year:

> We have entered a new phase. . . . What if the cry for freedom becomes the sound of a brick cracking through a store window, turning over an automobile in the street, or the sound of the mob? If that sound should drown out the voices of reason, frustration will replace progress and all of our best work will be undone. . . .

2.3 THE ROCKY ROAD TO CITIZENSHIP*

W. A. Low

THE NEGRO'S HISTORIC LOYALTY AND DEVOTION TO AMERICANISM

The story of the American education of the Negro begins with the modern African slave trade. It ends with the education of the Negro as an Ameri-

* W. A. Low, "The Education of Negroes Viewed Historically," Chap. I of *Negro Education in America: Sixteenth Yearbook of the John Dewey Society*, edited by Virgil A. Clift, Archibald W. Anderson, and H. Gordon Hullfish, New York: Harper & Row, Publishers, 1962, pages 27–59. Reprinted by permission of Harper & Row, Publishers. W. A. Low is Professor of History, Maryland State College.

Some authorities dispute Low's thesis, arguing that there were some Negroes who did *not* come to America as slaves, that there were quite a number of free and indentured Negroes in colonial times and in the early nineteenth century, and that racism and Jim Crowism came later. This viewpoint may be found in Arnold and Caroline Rose, *America Divided*, New York: Alfred A. Knopf, Inc., 1948, Chap. 2 (bibliography), and C. Vann Woodward, *The Strange Career of Jim Crow*, New York: Oxford University Press, 1955, rev. ed., 1966, (bibliography).

can. From beginning to end, the story raises the fundamental question of the extent and quality of cultural integration in time—the question, in this instance, of the education and Americanization of the Negro in his transition from slave to citizen. . . .

[Slavery] denied him the right to perpetuate an African culture and homeland; but it did not acknowledge him as an American. Rather, the implication was that the Negro lived in America by sufferance as a caste in a somewhat cultural purgatory, a timeless, nebulous, no-man's land somewhere between Africa and America.

Thus, by an acquiescence enforced upon him, the transplanted Negro in continental America was to lose his spiritual and meaningful orientation to Africa, the meaning of old gods and languages, myths, and legends. Whatever meaningful residues of African cultures were to survive, the remnants were to live in remote patterns and problems of anthropology and sociology. They did not survive as vital, cogent forces in the stream of consciousness of Negro history. *Africa became irretrievably lost; yet this loss, paradoxically, opened the way through the enforced denial of Africa, for the acceptance of America.* . . . The student of history looks in vain for serious manifestations and expressions of any kind of African Zionism or Pan-Africanism in the history of the American Negro. . . . *Herein lies the paradox of the American Negro's life; a historic devotion, allegiance, and loyalty to America in spite of the intense harshness with which he was often treated here.* . . .[13]

[Skipping 150 years of history, we learn that] The Morrill Act of 1890 . . .

[13] Editor's Note: With respect to cultural assimilation, the contrast between the American Negro and some American Indians is quite significant. In an article on "The Right not to Assimilate" (*Social Science Review* 35: 135–143, June 1961, by permission of the University of Chicago Press and of the Phelps-Stokes Fund) Alexander Lesser shows that accommodations and adjustments to our industrial society by many Indian communities is not accompanied by correlated changes in their basic Indian attitudes of mind and personality: ". . . They choose principally what we call material culture and technology and little of our sentiments and values and our philosophy of life. . . . [Many Indians] want and need the freedom to be Indians within the framework of America. . . . The disappearance of our Indian communities by assimilation has a crucial finality that assimilation can never have for other American minorities. Irish, or German, or Scandinavian, or Italian immigrants who become assimilated can still look toward a homeland from which they came, a viable tradition and culture which dignifies their origins. For the Indian, the tribal community is the only carrier of his tradition; if it disintegrates and disappears, his tradition becomes a matter of history, and he loses part of his identity. We are coming to know the importance of this sense of identification with a viable tradition in the meaning of Israel for many American Jews, or of the emergence of free African nations for many American Negroes. . . . [The white man's policy toward the Indians should be] to stop hampering their efforts to work out their own destiny, and especially to stop trying to make them give up their Indian identity. In a world which may be moving toward greater internationalism, in which we hope that peoples, however diverse, will choose the way of democracy, we cannot avoid the responsibility for a democratic resolution of the American Indian situation. Our attitude toward the Indians, the stubbornest non-conformists among us, may be the touchstone of our tolerance of diversity anywhere."

was designed to prevent the expenditure of land-grant funds in any state where "a distinction of race or color is made." [However, a 1911 report on federal land-grant institutions revealed] that Negro colleges not infrequently gave instruction on a "grade as low as the 4th or 5th of the public schools." . . .

[In 1895] Booker T. Washington, in a memorable speech, gave permissive sanction to the course of Southern sectionalism in the new South [and the "separate but equal" doctrine]. . . . Looking upon questions of social equality as the "extremist folly," he advised Southern Negroes to "Cast down your buckets where you are," educating the "head, hand, and heart" through "the shop, the field, the skilled hand, habits of thrift, and economy, by way of the industrial school and college." . . . [This policy, called the "Atlanta Compromise"] was also written into law. . . .[14]

Despite the sanction of the law, however, some Negro leaders openly opposed the Compromise as a retreat from the principle that Negroes should be educated as free men. . . . The quest for equality, in large measure, represents a reassertion by the Negro of the legal rights granted during Reconstruction. A "new" Negro, far less docile than the post-Reconstruction generation, while aware of his status in contemporary life, sought adjustment through the courts, remembering that he, too, lived within the organic framework of the American democratic heritage. Perhaps in no area of Negro life was the quest more dramatic and significant than in the field of public education, particularly higher education. . . .

Thus in the Gaines' case (1938) the Supreme Court held that the State was bound to furnish "within its borders facilities for legal education substantially equal to those . . . afforded for persons of the white race, whether or not other Negroes sought the same privileges." [And this was but one of a long series of judgments leading straight to Brown.]

There can be little doubt that the acceleration of legal attacks upon the system of caste in organized education was helpful in securing increased appropriations and some equalization of teacher salaries, as well as encouraging experiments at regional education and limited legal integration or "mixing" in some public schools, notably in the state of Indiana. The impact of World War II, with the subsequent integration of the armed forces was an important factor, also. Finally, the unanimous decision of the Supreme Court on May 17, 1954, gave legal force and sanction to the educational theory of integration, as opposed to the old doctrine of "separate but equal," reaffirming the living ideas of the American Dream. This decision was the capstone of the Negro's legal attack. Here was another milestone in the larger and the academic education of the Negro in his transition from slave to citizen.

[14] Editor's Note: See *Plessy v. Ferguson,* in Selection 2.1.

REALIZING THE AMERICAN DREAM

[This transition—the Negro's Dream—was based on] . . . preponderant values in the Western heritage: the classical and Christian concepts of the worth of the individual; the Reformation concepts emphasizing the equality of all men in the sight of God; the Enlightenment concept that by the application of intelligence man can make progress toward the betterment of himself and society.

Behind the Dream also lay the real experience of the Negro in the American environment, his larger education and integration into the stream of American life. This experience is itself a study of the scope and quality of the Americanization of the Negro. The historic steps in the process, applicable to the Negro's academic education as well, may be summarized as follows:

1. The early decision to give Christian instruction to slaves; the decision was acted upon despite opposition.
2. The instruction of Negroes through religious, civic, and benevolent groups, both before and after manumission.
3. The restraints placed upon the Negro and his education by the slave power of the cotton South, notably after Nat Turner's insurrection [1831].
4. The right of Negroes to be educated as free men, established after the military and political collapse of the slave power in the South.
5. The religious and Northern influence in the establishment and support of Negro institutions during and following the period of Reconstruction.
6. The program of industrial education as symbolized and popularized by by Booker T. Washington in the Atlanta Compromise.
7. The advent of public support, premised somewhat upon the principles of the Compromise, wherein segregated institutions and systems eventually flourished and expanded, notably by the time of World War II, under the legal fiction of "separate but equal."
8. The legal protest of the "new" Negro, determined either to make the legal fiction of "separate but equal" more nearly a reality or to replace the fiction altogether with integrated schools. The result, of course, was the May 17, 1954, decision of the Supreme Court against segregation.

It is well to keep in mind that these historic steps in the experience of the Negro took place within the moral order peculiar to the Western heritage, especially colored by the concepts of American democracy. *It may be seen that in each step there was, on one hand, the question of the existence of American ideals; while, on the other hand, there was the question of the existence of specific situations in which the ideals were in some part, if not fully, denied. Herein lies the historic moral dilemma surrounding the existence of the Negro in American life.* If there is to be a "solution" to the so-called Negro "problem" in America, this dilemma has to be resolved; the gap between ideals and practices has to be closed.

The problem is an American one and history has revealed a trend toward its solution, despite the resistance of anti-democratic forces. For example, the question in 1700 of the Christianization of slaves no longer existed in 1800. Again, the question of the abolition of slavery, already on the horizon in 1800, had disappeared by 1900. Further, the question of the education of the Negro as a free man, an anti-climax in 1900, was hardly a grave one for the nation at the time of the decision against segregation in May of 1954.

Thus, inasmuch as the crux of the problem is moral in nature, solutions are to be sought within the moral confines of American democracy, of conduct in American life which results in bringing undemocratic practices into harmony with democratic ideals. This hope has been the essence of the Negro's thinking, feeling, and being, even the very gospel of his religion. The Negro, along with other Americans, has held the faith and hope that democracy would become progressively a more living and meaningful reality for all. This has been his continuing dream, despite the necessary compromises dictated by adverse political, economic, and social conditions. The devotion of the Negro to this aspiration constitutes a tribute to his moral stamina.

2.4 RIGHTS IMPLY RESPONSIBILITIES*

John Fischer

What follows may sound offensive to a good many Negroes and to some white people. Nevertheless it needs to be said. . . [It has to do with] the genuine integration of Negroes into the normal stream of American

* John Fischer, "What the Negro Needs Most: A First Class Citizens' Council," *Harper's*, 225: 12–19, July 1962. Copyright © 1962, by Harper's Magazine, Inc. Reprinted from the July 1962 issue of *Harper's* magazine, by permission of the author.

John Fischer is Editor in Chief, *Harper's* magazine.

See also Thomas R. Waring, "The Southern Case Against Desegregation," *Harper's*, 212: 39–45, January 1956; *U.S. News and World Report*, 50: 66–71, May 22, 1961; and 51: 86–87, December 4, 1961. Also relevant is the following from Murray Friedman, "The White Liberal's Retreat," *The Atlantic Monthly*, 211: 42–46, January 1963 Copyright © 1962, by the Atlantic Monthly Company, Boston, Mass. Reprinted with permission.

> The heavy exodus of Negroes from the South since World War II has, to a large degree, shifted the center of the race problem to the metropolitan areas of the North and West. The Negro is no longer an abstraction to the white liberal but a concrete reality—in many instances, a potential or actual next-door neighbor, a classmate of his child's, a coworker at office or workbench. This confrontation very often points up the gap between the worlds of the Negro and the liberal white. . . .
>
> Liberal whites are, consequently, caught in the dilemma of believing in equal

life. . . . [When] the average Negro is both willing and able to carry the full responsibility of good citizenship . . . he may be surprised to see how fast white prejudice begins to melt away. . . .

What are these white people afraid of? Why do they begin to move out of a neighborhood as soon as any considerable number of Negroes come in? Why are so many desegregated schools becoming "resegregated," as white parents withdraw their children? . . . . [Why is it that so many white] families with children of school age have either moved to the suburbs in large numbers, or have sent their youngsters to private schools.[15]

A candid, careful investigation would show (I think) that many white people are afraid—with some reason—of four things:

---

rights for Negroes and even of working for them, while at the same time attempting to escape from the real and fancied disadvantages of desegregation. In recent years, they have helped put on the books of many cities and states laws banning discrimination in the sale or rental of housing, yet they themselves have been moving to the farthest reaches of the cities and to the suburbs. They have pushed up the enrollment at private and parochial schools, shut their eyes to the widespread practice of gerry-mandering of school district lines to avoid integration, and helped to create pressures for separating slow from rapid learners in the public schools, a process which often results in keeping middle-class white children apart from Negro and Puerto Rican youngsters. . . . The result is that many liberals, while opposed to color lines, are helping to make these lines stronger and tighter. . . . In other words, to the Negro demand for "now," to which the Deep South has replied "never," many liberal whites are increasingly responding "later." But the Negro will accept nothing short of first-class citizenship, now. It will call for a great deal of patience and understanding among those who make up the civil rights coalition if racial progress is not to be seriously jeopardized.

See also "The Black and the Jew: A Falling Out of Allies," *Time* 93: 55–59, January 31, 1969.

[15] Editor's Note: Although laws may prevent public schools from excluding pupils on the basis of race, laws cannot prevent voluntary (*de facto*) segregation. Indeed, in the big cities of the North and West, the exodus of whites from Negro districts has become so widespread that sociologists have described it in terms of the "tipping mechanism":

The process by which whites of the central cities leave areas of Negro in-migration can be understood as one in the social-psychology of "tipping a neighborhood." The variations are numerous, but the theme is universal. Some white residents will not accept Negroes as neighbors under any conditions. But others, sometimes willingly as a badge of liberality, sometimes with trepidation, will not move if a relatively small number of Negroes move into the same neighborhood, the same block, or the same apartment building. Once the proportion of non-whites exceeds the limits of the neighborhood's tolerance for interracial living (this is the "tip point"), the whites move out. The proportion of Negroes who will be accepted before the tip point is reached varies from city to city and from neighborhood to neighborhood. . . .

In the high school situation in New York City the experience seems to be that, as the percentage of Negroes in the student population approaches 30, the white group starts to withdraw *en masse*. When the white pupils start withdrawing, the better students of the Negro group also leave, so that the school is left with a greatly reduced student body, frequently composed of youngsters with various problems of adjustment. . . . At the neighborhood level, the elementary schools make

1. *Crime.* As the proportion of Negroes in a community increases, the crime rate usually rises sharply. The police chief of the District of Columbia has estimated that Negroes are responsible for 80 percent of the serious crimes there, although they make up only a little over half the population. In Chicago, when Negroes were 17 percent of the population, they accounted for 65 percent of the jail inmates; in Philadelphia, the comparable figures were 21 and 80 percent; in Detroit, 19 and 58. . . .

2. *Neighborhood deterioration.* The commonest fear among white families is that their neighborhood will go downhill if many Negroes move in.

Sometimes this fear is plainly unjustified. A number of my Negro friends are as house-proud as anybody I know; one of them has made his home and garden into a town showplace. Nor is this true merely of the relatively wealthy "black bourgeois." A Negro home I visit fairly often is a single room in a slum district, but it always is spotlessly clean, tidy, and comfortable.

Yet this is not always true. A neighborhood where I once lived in Washington is now occupied almost entirely by Negroes; it has indeed gone downhill, swiftly and unmistakably. In part this is due to overcrowding, and to incomes so low that the owners can't afford to keep their places up properly. But it is also partly due to plain old don't-care. Garbage, broken bottles, and old bedsprings accumulate in many a backyard . . . a loose porch board goes unfixed for weeks, though all it needs is one nail and two licks with a hammer . . . broken window-panes get stuffed with rags. Moreover, the same families that can't find money for a bucket of paint or a pane of glass somehow manage, surprisingly often, to drive fancy cars and buy a fifth of whiskey every weekend. . . .

3. *Civic apathy.* A kindred fear is that Negro newcomers will not pull their weight in the community boat. Few of them seem willing to invest time and effort in the web of civic, political, and voluntary organizations which holds every American community together. . . . Louis Lomax, in his notably outspoken book, *The Negro Revolt* [(1962) wrote:] "One reason why Negro leadership organizations think several times before launching highly publicized voter-registration drives is that they know Negroes simply will not go to the polls and register."

4. *Moral irresponsibility.* White people also are bothered by the casual attitude of many Negroes about sex, and about their family responsibilities.

---

out better. Here proportions of Negroes to whites seem to make little difference up to and well beyond the 50 percent point. Stable and sustained mixed elementary school populations are achieved in most neighborhoods with little difficulty.

—Earl Raab, editor (Morton Grodzins, Dan W. Dodson, and others), *American Race Relations Today; Studies of the Problems Beyond Desegregation,*

Such worries are seldom discussed out loud—maybe because so many whites know that their own morals aren't exactly impeccable. But they do have some statistical justification. About 2 per cent of the white babies born each year are bastards; among Negroes the illegitimacy rate is above 20 percent. And even when they are married, Negro fathers tend to abandon their families with light-hearted frequency. About 8 percent of the white families with children under eighteen are broken homes: for non-whites, the comparable figure is 21 percent.[16]

One result is a heavy burden on the relief rolls, and a growing resentment among white taxpayers; nobody likes to support somebody else's bastards. Another result is that hundreds of thousands of Negro children grow up without a man in the family, to provide discipline and example; which in turn means a steady rise in delinquency. A third is the reluctance of white parents to keep their children in schools with a high proportion of Negroes—not because they are afraid of inter-marriage, but because they worry about the habits and attitudes their youngsters might pick up.

Is this blind prejudice? Can a man who won't support his children call himself a first-class citizen?

To all of these complaints, the traditional Negro leaders have a ready answer. The Negro's shortcomings, they argue, are the inevitable consequence of three hundred years of slavery and discrimination. When you hold a man down for that long, he can't spring upright over-night when the pressure is removed. He won't vote because he doesn't yet really believe that he can have any influence on government. He won't attend civic meetings because he has never been welcomed or listened to—and he is still afraid he will be insulted, or at best ignored. Broken families and promiscuity were forced on the Negro during slavery, and the resulting pattern takes a long time to change.

Crime, so the explanation continues, is largely a result of the Negro's low place on the economic totem pole. "Most Negroes would rather work than steal," as Lomax puts it. "By the same token they would rather steal than starve." And so long as many jobs are closed to them—by their edu-

---

[16] Editor's Note: "Negro girls in slums have an illegitimacy rate about ten times as high as that of Negro girls in middle-class residential communities."—S. K. Weinberg, *Social Problems in Our Time*, Englewood Cliffs, N.J.: Prentice-Hall, Inc., 1960, p. 234.

In an excellent discussion of "The City and the Negro" (*Fortune*, 65: 89–92f., March 1962) Charles E. Silberman points out that approximately twice as many Negro girls as boys go to college. (Among white students this proportion is reversed.)

> Negro women frequently find it easier to get jobs—e.g., as domestics—than Negro men, thus making them the financial center of the family. The inability of Negro men to find jobs that confer status and dignity, together with the servility required of them in the South, have led Negro men to sexual promiscuity, drinking, and violence as means of asserting their masculinity.

In general, a slum boy has no male model to follow, and he has little reason to hope that education will offer a way out of the slum.

cational handicaps, or by union or employer discrimination—those are the stark alternatives. . . . Much Negro crime, as Lomax points out, "has to do with getting back at white people."

These are valid explanations. For white people, they mean that Negroes need a great deal more help than they have yet had, to overcome the cultural lag that has been imposed upon them. They need—and deserve—the same concentration of money, talent, and organization that we are devoting to underdeveloped people in Asia, Africa, and Latin America. Given the best teachers, the best social workers, special attention to vocational education and job placement, an extra share of understanding and patience, most Negroes will be able to close the cultural gap surprisingly fast. The experimental Higher Horizons program in New York City's schools has already demonstrated how quickly they can move ahead, with a little encouragement and special attention.

For the Negroes, however, these same explanations can be dangerous. It is all too easy to use them as an excuse for despair. And they offer no solutions. So long as the Negro blames his plight entirely on circumstances, history, and the white man, he is going to stay in that plight. He will get out of it only when he begins to change his circumstances, make new history, and shoulder a bigger share of responsibility for the fix he is in. . . .

Maybe the answer lies in a parable frequently told by Dr. Benjamin E. Mays, president of Morehouse College in Atlanta. A zoo lion spent years pacing back and forth in his cage. Then one day somebody left the door of his cage open; but the lion still kept pacing back and forth.

. . . [Hence it is important] to convince American Negroes that the door of their cage is at last open—not all the way yet, but wider than most of them realize. And each one who pushes through that door can help open it a little further for those who lag behind. Or, if he doesn't use his new opportunities well, he can make it harder for the next man to get through the door. . . .

Some of the more courageous Negro leaders are at last beginning to speak up—though not yet very loudly or often. The Reverend Martin Luther King has called on his followers "to admit that our standards do often fall short" and to do something about it. "Even the most poverty-stricken among us," he has written, "can purchase a ten-cent bar of soap; even the most uneducated among us can have high morals. . . . By improving our standards here and now we will go a long way toward breaking down the arguments of the segregationist." . . .

Such men are not content just to demand their rights. They insist on carrying their responsibilities too. That's how you get to be a first-class citizen—as Crispus Attucks knew when he marched to his death in the Boston Massacre. The first man to die in the American revolution, he was a Negro who knew that citizenship is earned, not given.

2.5 THE ACHIEVING GHETTO*

Eugene P. Foley

[Today] It is obvious to all what has been going on in almost every major northern American city. The middle class and upper class whites are moving out; Negroes are moving in. For example, between 1950 and 1960, Chicago's central city experienced a net loss of 399,000 whites and a net gain of 320,000 Negroes; Detroit lost 363,000 whites and gained 182,000 Negroes; New York lost 476,000 whites and gained 240,000 Negroes. At the same time this is happening, the industrial jobs are moving to the suburbs. New York lost 204,000 industrial jobs between 1947 and 1964. Between 1960 and 1964 alone, New York lost 8.2 percent of its manufacturing jobs; Philadelphia lost 4 percent; and Pittsburgh lost 5 percent.

The result, of course, is that the unemployment rate for Negroes is going up, the demand for city services is increasing, and the tax resources with which to pay them is decreasing.

According to the 1960 census, 25 percent of the immigrants into New York City during the previous five years had annual family incomes below $4,000, while only 6.5 percent of those who had moved from the city to

---

* Eugene P. Foley, *The Achieving Ghetto*, Washington, D.C.: The National Press, Inc., 1968, pp. 18–20, 48–49. Copyright © 1968 by Eugene P. Foley, The National Press Inc. See also W. H. Ferry, "The Case for a New Federalism," *Saturday Review* 51: 14–17, June 15, 1968.

Eugene P. Foley was Assistant Secretary of Commerce for Economic Development with responsibility for the economic rehabilitation of "depressed areas."

Compare the following statement by Eli Ginsberg:

> Our broad definition of the Negro middle class includes roughly one-third of the 21 million American Negroes—those who have incomes above the poverty level, stability of employment, and reasonable opportunities for education. It is this much-expanded base that lends substance to contemporary discussions about whether the future of the Negro in the United States is to be conceived in terms of the characteristic model of ethnic minorities who, originally despised and harassed, were able, nevertheless, to fight their way into American society. . . .
>
> [Interviews with hundreds of young Negroes within the above category lead to the following conclusion:] These young Negroes do not believe that the whites will lose all of their prejudice or that Negroes will live on terms of intimacy with the white population. Their optimism is more restrained. They look forward to a multiracial democracy in which Negroes will not be inhibited from exercising either their rights or their talents. They look forward to equality with all other Americans who are able and willing to study, to work, and to shape their lives as they see fit. These young men want no more than this opportunity and they are quite sure that they will get it.

—Eli Ginsberg, *The Middle-Class Negro in The White Man's World*, New York: Columbia University Press, 1967, p. 6, 171. See also D. W. Brogan's review of *Beyond the Melting Pot*, by Nathan Glazer and Daniel P. Moynihan, M.I.T. Press, 1963; in *Encounter* 22: 55–60, June 1964.

neighboring suburbs were in that category. . . . This state of affairs not only will continue unless serious efforts are made to overcome it, but more than likely will get worse—very seriously worse. . . .

"Black Power" in 1967 became a major issue on the national civil rights scene. . . . The power the overwhelming body of Negroes seek is not the power of violence or of hate, but the power of constructive pride and group achievement. Black Power means to the vast majority of Negroes what James Farmer says it should mean: "It should preach self-respect and group pride to those who have been without respect and pride."

It is said in international affairs that "a Nation seeks not friends, but mutual interests." The Negroes have arrived at just that degree of political and social sophistication. It is crucial to peaceful race relations that we understand this and understand what directly follows from this; viz., the ghetto is here to stay for a long, long time. . . . [Says St. Clair Drake] "Few Negroes believe that Black Ghettos will disappear within the next two decades despite much talk about 'open occupancy' and 'freedom of residence.' There is an increasing tendency among Negroes to discuss what the quality of life could be within Negro communities as they grow larger and larger." . . .

[Ralph Ellison, author of *The Invisible Man*, told a Senate Subcommittee in September 1966] much the same:

> It is a misunderstanding to assume that Negroes want to break out of Harlem. They want to transform Harlem, the Harlems of their country. These places are precious to them. . . People want Harlem improved, not torn down. They want Harlem to remain as a base, just as people in other sections want their old blocks to remain as home base. . . . [Harlems] are where they [Negroes] have dreamed, where they have lived, where they have loved, where they have worked out their life as they could. . . . Harlem is a place where our folklore is preserved and transformed. It is the place where the body of Negro myth and legend thrives. It is a place where our styles, musical styles, and many styles of Negro life, find continuity and metamorphosis.

This is the world in which the upper classes wince as at an embarrassment, and which race leaders point to as proof that Negroes have been victimized. But for the masses of the ghetto dwellers this is a warm and familiar milieu, preferable to the sanitary coldness of middle-class neighborhoods. . . .

[What] is desperately needed in the ghetto is the creation of success symbols, at the neighborhood and block level, inducing a sense of locally recognized accomplishment and leading thereby to black pride, Negro self-respect and the achieving ghetto. In the American culture, this means jobs. . . . As [the late] Senator Robert Kennedy (D., N.Y.) has said: "Employment is the only true long-run solution; only if Negroes achieve full and equal employment will they be able to support themselves and their families, become active citizens and not passive objects of our action, become contributing members, and not recipients of our charity."[17]

2.6 POVERTY: VIEWS FROM THE LEFT*

Michael Harrington

A small library of books written in recent years has demonstrated the brutal fact that tens of millions of Americans are poor. For convenience, the definitions and figures used here will be those published by the government

[17] Editor's Note: The present status of the Negro in American society has been neatly summarized by Harry L. Miller and Marjorie B. Smiley:

> Negro men fill only 2.5 per cent of professional and technical jobs, only 6 per cent of clerical jobs, only 4 per cent of craftsmen and foremen positions, and only 10 per cent of semiskilled jobs. They make up instead 44 per cent of private household workers, 20 per cent of low-paid service workers, and about 25 per cent of both farm and nonfarm unskilled labor. In whatever category they work, their median earnings for that job are less than whites' in the same category (for example, median earnings of Negro professional and technical workers are $4,563 versus $6,691 for whites).
>
> Education presumably means better jobs, but in 1960 almost 50 per cent of white high-school graduates, but only 20 per cent of Negro graduates, were in clerical jobs. Only 10 per cent of white graduates, but 25 per cent of Negroes, were employed in service occupations. The percentage of the Negro work force unemployed is about double that of the white work force, and recent declines in over-all unemployment rate (in 1965, particularly) has left the Negro rate virtually undisturbed.
>
> There is a positive and high correlation in this country between level of education and income, but if one considers only the group in the upper quarter of intellectual ability, 75 per cent of upper-middle- and upper-class youth finish four years of college, in contrast to 25 per cent of working-class and lower-lower-class youngsters. In 1960, only 6 per cent of the boys from the lower-lower-class entered college, as compared with 40 per cent of their total age group.
>
> Thus, in summarizing the life change of the Negro child one can point to the following probabilities: He will be far more likely to drop out of school before high-school graduation. . . ; no matter how intellectually competent, he is far less likely to go on to college; in the job market, he will be the last hired and first fired; it is unlikely that he will attain occupational status of a high order; and in whatever job, he will be relatively less well paid. In what is becoming an unbroken circle of deep poverty and social dependency, for many families into the third generation, his own children may face the same limited life chance that he did.

—Harry L. Miller and Marjorie B. Smiley, *Education in the Metropolis* (*Readings*), New York: The Free Press (Crowell-Collier and Macmillan, Inc.), 1968, pp. 11–12. Footnote references substantiating these data are here omitted.

* Michael Harrington, "The Politics of Poverty," from *Poverty: Views from the Left,*

in the Economic Reports of 1964 and 1965. We discuss, then, a misery which, in a most cautious and prudent statement, embraces thirty-five million Americans and particularly afflicts the aging, the young, the non-white, and certain categories of workers and farmers. (It should be noted that a recent study of the Social Security Administration is even grimmer than the Economic Reports. It finds "about fifty million Americans, one quarter of the population," who "live within the bleak circle of poverty or at least hover around its edge.")

How can these thirty-five million—or perhaps even fifty million—be given "the opportunity to live in decency and dignity?"

To begin with, one must understand the obsolescence of much of the traditional American wisdom about abolishing poverty. The "old," pre-World War II poor, whose experiences dominate so much of our present thinking, were different kinds of people than the poor of the 1960s and they faced different problems.

The old poor lived at a time when economic opportunity was a trend of the economy itself. They suffered terribly, to be sure, and by statistical indices of living standard and life expectancy many were worse off than the impoverished of 1965. But they also participated in that incredible growth of American capitalism, a development which, in Colin Clark's figures, saw a 4500 per cent increase in the net income from manufacturing between 1860 and 1953. The farmers came to the city in good times to better their luck. They were not driven into the metropolis as bewildered, despairing exiles, which is so often the case today. And the insatiable man-power needs of mass production meant that there were jobs for grade school dropouts and for Eastern European immigrants who could hardly speak English.

There was objective, realistic reason for hope—and the old poor of the cities were hopeful. The immigrants, for instance, often brought a language or a culture with them. The resultant solidarity provided the basis for self-help institutions within the culture of poverty: for political machines, churches, social clubs, and the like. In a good many instances aspiration and hunger for learning became a way of life.

These internal resources of the old poor were used in the creation of the big-city political machines, one of the first welfare systems in the United States. But they also provided the basis for something more than "self-help" and group benevolence. In the 1930s they played a role in a climactic moment of American social history. Millions of the old poor participated in the organization of unions, particularly the CIO, and in the

---

Michael Harrington is the author of *The Other America, The Accidental Century,* and *Towards a Democratic Left.*

political struggle for the New Deal. They—and their ethnic drives and community hopes—became an important constituent of a new political coalition which translated into law many of the reforms advocated by liberals and socialists of an earlier generation—the Wagner Act, Social Security, minimum wage, etc. . . .

Still, the American percentage of the gross national product devoted to direct social benefits has yet to achieve even half the level of the typical European contribution. . . .

Nevertheless, Roosevelt did define the fundamentals of the American welfare state: modest contributions in direct welfare spending, a legal framework for the conflict between labor and management, and a government commitment to stimulate, or brake, the private economy in the interest of orderly growth without depression.

After World War II there was only one amendment in principle to the wisdom of the thirties. It centered around programs for training and retraining. . . .

The training-retraining component was built into a series of laws: Area Redevelopment, Manpower Development and Training, Economic Opportunity, and even the Federal Aid to Education Act of 1965. Some workers, it was acknowledged, were not participating in the general economic advance or were even being expelled from it by automation. They, and a growing number of high school dropouts, were denied economic opportunity because they lacked the right skills. The government was to give them the training, or the retraining, which would change this situation. . . .

The basic reason why the poor of today differ from those of a generation ago, and therefore require radical measures if their poverty is to be abolished, is that the economy has changed much in a generation. In absolute terms and objective indices, the impoverished today are better off than their predecessors in misery; but relatively speaking, in terms of hope and economic opportunity, their plight is much worse. Moreover, this economic fact has all kinds of social and psychological consequences for the poor and it therefore cannot be described in simple, statistical terms. . . .

About half of the families of the poor are headed by an employed worker. These people work long, hard hours in jobs which are not covered by the minimum wage law (17.6 million workers in private industry are not) and in which the minimum wage set by law is lower than the accepted poverty line. They are in the occupations—laundry work, lowly service functions in restaurants, hotels, and hospitals, etc.—which in general are not organized by unions.

The new poor are thus in a different, and much more difficult, position than the old poor. In saying this, I do not want to romanticize the misery and exploitation of the past, or to imply that the poverty-stricken of today somehow just don't possess the spirit of their predecessors and never will.

. . . To the extent that they are demoralized, their attitude derives from an accurate perception of the future as well as from the terrible heritage of the past. . . .

In 1964 the Senate Subcommittee estimated that a young worker needed fourteen years of schooling—two years beyond high school—in order to have a really good chance for economic opportunity. But in 1975, when the skill requirements for the available decent jobs will presumably be much higher, more than one fourth (26.6 per cent) of the workers twenty-five to thirty-four years of age will be without a high school diploma. This society apparently plans for them to be either unemployed or janitors, i.e., poor.

Thus the newness of poverty, and the consequent obsolescence of so much of President Johnson's current program, can be defined in the following way. The decisive factor, the terrible novelty, of impoverishment today is that it takes place in a time of automation. Under such circumstances the systematically undereducated and undertrained (which is another way of saying "the poor") are justifiably pessimistic. Thus far the government has offered them the possibility of further education and training but, at the same time, essentially says that it really doesn't expect to have enough decent jobs for its own graduates. All this reinforces the cynicism and resistance to organization which characterizes poor communities.

The situation is particularly acute for the fifteen million young people who are poor and the even larger number (one in three) who are high-school dropouts in the age of post-high-school technology. This is the "growth potential" of American poverty. . . .

[According to] the 1965 Economic Report. . . . A fifth of the country, but a fourth of the youth, live in the other America. Of the thirty-five million defined as poor by the Council of Economic Advisers, over 40 per cent are young people. And one of the terrible things we have learned about present-day poverty—it was brilliantly documented in a Department of Labor Study of Selective Service Rejectees in 1964—is that it tends to be hereditary. . . .

[This study showed that a] quarter of the young men who take the draft exam fail because they are not educated enough to train as army privates (they are typically in their early twenties when they take the test). And they are, to a depressing degree, the children of the poor.

If all other things remain constant, one could then expect these 25 per cent of the youth who are poor to become heads of families—or, more precisely, heads of large families, for that is one of the patterns of poverty. And this would mean that impoverishment has a great future in this country. However, it is now the express purpose of the Administration not to let all things remain constant. These young people have been made the crux of the Economic Opportunity Act and of federal aid to education. So the question remains: faced by a poverty which is peculiarly corrosive in its impact on individual psychology and the internal resources of various subgroups of the poor, can present government programs provide "economic opportunity" for millions of impoverished youth in a period of automation and cybernation?. . . .

The social investment approach assumes that the gross national product is not an economic fate played out on the free market but a subject for political debate and determination. In the Clark Subcommittee proposals, for instance, if a projected GNP does not fit the nation's social aims, then the government creates a new, more appropriate GNP. A major instrument of such a policy is the expansion of the public sector. There are two arguments for such a tack: the private, goods-producing sector will not create jobs for the poor, so there must be a conscious generation of work in the public sector; in the course of providing the needed quantity of jobs through the public sector, we will be able to transform the quality of American life. . . .

The issue is not simply providing a given quantity of work, important as that is to the new poor. It is also one of providing the right kind of socially useful work. And this will require that new occupational categories be consciously created. The middle class has defined some new pursuits for its children already: the occupation of graduate student as a first career; the foundation industry with its fellowships and consultantships; Peace Corps and VISTA volunteer; and so on. And now, under the impetus of the War on Poverty, there are tentative new definitions of work for the poor themselves.

The "indigenous" neighborhood worker—the slum dweller recruited for paid social work because of his existential training in poverty—is already appearing in various Community Action Programs. Other possibilities are being explored: teacher's aide, community organizer, research assistant. Significantly, these new occupations tend to appear in the public and "human care" sector of the economy. This trend owes at least as much to technological necessity as to the popular conscience. For it is the private and goods-producing part of the economy which automates; and it is in the service, and particularly the public service, sector that new needs and opportunities appear. . . .

In brilliant testimony before the Joint Committee on the Economic Report in February 1965, John Kenneth Galbraith spoke of "reactionary Keynesianism." This is the thesis that one promotes economic growth by expanding private, individual consumption through policies like the tax cut, but not by making planned investments in social consumption.

> I am not quite sure what the advantage is, (Galbraith said) in having a few more dollars to spend if the air is too dirty to breathe, the water

too polluted to drink, the commuters are losing out in the struggle to get in and out of the city, the streets are filthy and the schools so bad that the young perhaps wisely stay away, and hoodlums roll citizens for some of the dollars they saved in the tax cut.[18]

---

[18] Editor's Note: In the same Larner-Howe anthology (pp. 83–93) an essay by Stephan Thernstrom "Is There a New Poor?" presents an opposing point of view:

A specter is haunting the imaginations of commentators upon the contemporary scene, the specter of the "new poor." In days of old (precise time conveniently unspecified), the cliché goes, "the immigrant saw poverty as a *temporary state* and looked forward to the day when he or his children could gain greater access to opportunity and financial resources. The poor of today are more inclined to regard poverty as a *permanent way of life* with little hope for themselves or their children. This change in the outlook of the poor can be explained by changes in the opportunity structure." (From Louis Furman's *Poverty in America.*) You can fill in the rest for yourself easily enough: the poor of old had aspirations; the poor today do not. The poor of old had a culture; the poor today have only a culture of poverty. The poor once had political machines which protected them; now they have only social workers who spy upon them. And the crucial contrast, from which so much else follows: the poor were once on the lowest rungs of a ladder most of them could climb; the poor today are a fixed underclass, a permanent proletariat.

A compelling, dramatic image, this, but is there any evidence that it is *true*? This is not the place for an exhaustive analysis of the data, but I suggest that the answer is negative. . . .

There has been a good deal of heated argument about precisely where to draw the poverty line, but little attention to what seem the two points of greatest significance. One is that wherever the line is drawn—$3000, $4000, or whatever—an ever-smaller fraction of the American population falls below that line. The long-term trend of per capita income in this country is dramatically upward, and the way in which that income is distributed has not shifted abruptly in a direction unfavorable to those on the lower end of the scale. The rich have been getting richer, all right, but the poor have been getting richer at much the same rate. There has been no major increase in the proportion of the national income going to those on the bottom in recent decades—a fact American liberals have been pathetically slow to recognize. But the unpleasant truth that there is no pronounced trend toward more equal distribution of income in this country should not obscure the elementary fact that the disadvantaged are now receiving the same fraction of a pie which has grown substantially larger. Admittedly they *expect* more; in some ways it can be said that they *need* more, but that it *is* more is of considerable consequence, however it might seem to those of us who do not have to worry about the grocery bills. . . .

It is clear that the educational requirements for many desired jobs have been going up steadily, but it also appears that, on the whole, the expansion of educational opportunities has kept pace with, if not outrun, this development. . . .

[However] hard it may be for many people to find steady employment in our society today, it was often still harder in the past. Robert Hunter's 1904 study *Poverty* pulls together a few chilling fragments we might profitably recall. In the year 1900, 44.3 per cent of the unskilled laborers in the United States were unemployed at some time; of a sample of Italian workers in Chicago, for example, 57 per cent had been out of a job some time during the previous year, with the average time unemployed running over seven months! The fact that horror stories like this become increasingly difficult to duplicate as we approach the present, plus the mild but distinct downward trend in the overall unemployment time series since 1900, makes me feel very skeptical about the common assumption that things are getting worse for those on the bottom.

Education for the Disadvantaged

2.7 AMERICA'S DUAL SYSTEM OF EDUCATION*

Peter Schrag

[Today's] city schools are at the crossroads of three revolutions—in civil rights, in technology, and in the style of urban life itself. All three are making fantastic demands upon education, and all three must be accommodated through an awkward political process that has never been efficient, even in the best of circumstances. . . .

The quandary of the concerned—people who passionately believe in public schools but who, nevertheless, send their children elsewhere—defines what may be the greatest tragedy in urban America today. . . .

Urban education is not merely a matter of civil rights, of Negroes, or of academic inequality. It lies at the very heart of the city's agony, constitutes its biggest planning liability, and its greatest debit for the future. Its inadequacies have helped make the city a community of the old, the rich, and the poor. It has contributed to the decay of the public interest and to the concomitant decline of related public facilities, and it has helped turn places like Chicago and New York into renaissance cities, complete with baronial high-rise palaces, private body guards, multiple locks, and, after sundown, vacant streets and vacant parks. The princes of these cities, while publicly decrying the state of their facilities, are able to isolate themselves from the surrounding squalor, to buy the private pleasures, the culture, and the education that should be accessible to all, which, after all, are the reasons for the city's existence, but which are available only to the few. What would happen to the schools of New York, for example, if the editors of the *New York Times*, the managers of the Chase Manhattan Bank, the owners of Macy's, if all the executives and painters and artists

---

* Peter Schrag, *Village School Downtown*, Boston: The Beacon Press, 1967, pp. 154, 168, 173–184. Reprinted by permission of The Beacon Press, © 1967 by Peter Schrag.

Peter Schrag is a free-lance writer and author also of *Voices in the Classroom*, Boston: The Beacon Press, 1966.

and intellectuals, if the admen and the television producers—if all of them *had* to send their children to those schools?. . . .

For most Americans the school (after form 1040) is the prime source of public concern and action. No one has ever moved out of a place because the streets were poorly paved or the water works inadequate, or even because the cops were believed to be corrupt. But they *will* leave if the schools are poor.

In city after city the exodus continues. A few years ago urban planners spoke hopefully of the return to the center, of a migration back to the core city by people who had had enough of car pools and commuting, of mowing lawns and compulsory neighborliness. But although some came back—most of them people whose children had grown and moved away—the tide never turned. Nevertheless the planners continued to produce their schemes, each of them calling for more ambitious programs in transportation, housing, and general redevelopment. Yet none ever focused on the single public service that must constitute the very essence of urban life and renewal—public education. . . .

The schools of the city—and in many other American communities—are still run on a premise of success: failures are implicitly attributed to the child, to the community—to almost anything but the system itself. At the same time the system takes credit for motivating children, for interesting them in normal classroom activities, and for the long list of accomplishments with which history has always complimented public education. By not publishing data on performance—except for the most superficial self-serving statistics—the schools can have it both ways. They can take credit for success and blame failure somewhere else. And by so doing they reinforce the comfortable public notion that nothing is very seriously wrong, that a competent hierarchy is administering its funds wisely, and that limited budgets—while not ample—are generally sufficient to maintain reasonably adequate standards.

The fact is that most of the schools of the city are not urban but village schools; they are organized as if the children they served were scattered thinly across vast geographical areas, and they operate on social, intellectual, and moral premises more characteristic of the nineteenth century than of the twentieth. Most of them are still engaged in attempts to impart information at a time when television, tapes, books, magazines, and other media can communicate most data at least as effectively as the vocal cords of the teacher. They have not really begun to take advantage of the technology of this culture, nor have they recognized that genuine education must now deal more with process than with "facts," more with styles of thought, with ways of asking and answering questions and solving problems, than with bodies of material. . . .

The village schools of the city are, on the whole, rigid, obsolete, and often irrelevant; and their performance, given the urgent cultural insistence on education, is a disaster. . . . [However, rather] than beginning with educational necessity and acting as if the society were sufficiently affluent to meet that necessity, [today's leaders] start—and end—with the paltry resources that absentee ownership and local tax consciousness are willing to grant. Every lake in this wealthy country is jammed with motorboats and waterskiers, every highway lined with automobiles, but the schools are abandoned at three every afternoon, and the parks at dusk, because the public treasury is assertedly too weak to sustain better services.

The resources exist, but they still flow in overwhelming abundance to the private sector and to the communities that least need them. They flow to the suburbs and to the great establishments of private wealth; and every year, despite the apparently increasing programs of public welfare, the inequities become greater. If we really mean to have effective *public* education, then urban and suburban systems can no longer operate as independent enterprises each with its separate and unequal local financial capabilities, its own special, and often limited facilities, its own little circumscribed area of concern. The problems of segregation and financing have already spilled from the city to the suburbs—to New Rochelle and Englewood and Malverne—and it is clear that they will spill more in the future. They are no longer subject to containment. At the same time the educational cripples, the welfare cases, the incompetent, the hostile—they will be with us forever. They do not respect political boundaries and geographic limits. Suburban isolation is but a temporary luxury; ultimately the agony of the city will make itself felt in the periphery as well. There is, moreover, no academic rationale for the maintenance of clusters of hundreds of independent little school districts in a single metropolitan region; what they can do separately in integrating schools, in financing them, in planning and operating programs, they can do far more effectively together. The only educational reason for their separation is the perpetuation of segregation and inequity. At the same time there is no reason why large units cannot be subdivided into smaller districts-within-districts to give local communities a greater measure of control in the determination of individual school programs and policy—why the doors of the school cannot be open to any individual or group in the community, and to any ideas, no matter how revolutionary. Central administrations can provide the expertise, can staff and organize the programs, and can articulate the options available. But the people who are served by the schools are—or should be—more than clients. The schools are theirs, and there is no reason why they should not have the major voice in exercising the educational options available to them. . . .

The state of urban education has gone beyond the point where it is possible to think of particular problems requiring solution. The city schools are not healthy enterprises requiring first aid. They are structurally unsound, because they are too old and rigid to serve their social purpose. Urban education—given what now exists—is essentially a new social function that requires new implementation and that will, in most major cities, involve the abandonment of a major part of the machinery that now passes as public education—buildings, books, administrative routines, and personnel. While it is clearly impossible to scrap all existing resources, there is no logic in reproducing them year after year. . . .

In the past generation we have overhauled our highways, our war machine, our airlines, and airplanes, our downtown office buildings, our very style of life. But we have hardly begun to overhaul our urban schools. Most of the school plant dates back a good generation while educational ideas in the schools have changed hardly at all since the nineteenth century. But where the older America—which shaped public education—provided alternatives to successful formal schooling, modern America does not. The shop, the farm, the open spaces are gone. For better or worse, education now has to do it all. Academic necessity, the ailments of the city, the demands of the technology, the pressures of racial and social change, all demand the kind of candid appraisal that few schools have received. They demand a fundamental restructuring of the system itself, and they require a degree of community involvement and accessibility that is denied to most people in most cities. They demand a totally new approach distinct from the concept of the unitary class in the unitary school, and they demand the utilization of all the urban and technological resources now becoming available.

Ultimately the issue of urban education is also the issue of the morale and life of the city itself. The schools have supplanted the market place as the focus of the community. They, not the subways or the sewer system, tie the city together. If they fail—as they are failing—then the community will disintegrate into a congeries of suburbs and renaissance baronies separated by ghettoes and violence. If they fail, then the public weal will forever be committed to an uneasy division between warfare and welfare, while those sectors of public activity that make life rich and meaningful —the arts, recreation, education, the beauty of the city and country—will become ever more privately glorious and publicly neglected. If they fail, then urban life fails, too.

2.8 DESEGREGATION VIA LARGER SCHOOLS*

U.S. Commission on Civil Rights

In the middle of the 19th century, Horace Mann defined education as the "great equalizer of the conditions of men—the balance wheel of the social machinery." Today, the role of education in the attainment of equal opportunity is even more critical. The U.S. Supreme Court, in its 1954 decision on school desegregation, said of education:

> Today it is a principal instrument in awakening the child to cultural values, in preparing him for later professional training, and in helping him to adjust normally to his environment. In these days, it is doubtful that any child may reasonably be expected to succeed in life if he is denied the opportunity of an education. . . . [Furthermore] Separate educational facilities are inherently unequal.

Twelve years after the Supreme Court's decision, the U.S. Office of Education in its national survey, *Equality of Educational Opportunity* [1966], found that:

> . . . when measured by that yardstick [segregation], American public education remains largely unequal in most regions of the country, including all those where Negroes form any significant proportion of the population.
>
> . . . the great majority of American children attend schools that are largely segregated—that is, almost all of their fellow students are of the same racial background as they are.

Sixty-five percent of all first grade Negro pupils surveyed attend schools that have an enrollment 90 percent or more Negro, while almost 80 percent of all first grade white students surveyed attend schools that are 90 percent or more white. . . .

[A] high degree of racial separation in the schools . . . is found in the North as well as in Southern and border States. In Buffalo, N.Y., for example, 77 percent of the Negro elementary schoolchildren attend schools that are more than 90 percent Negro, while 81 percent of the whites are in nearly all-white schools (90 percent or more white). In Gary, Ind., the figures are 90 percent and 76 percent, respectively. . . . Detroit, Mich., has an elementary school enrollment almost four times as large as Newark, N.J., yet in each city more than 90 percent of the Negro children are in majority-Negro schools. . . . Negroes are only 19 percent of the elementary

* Report of the U.S. Commission on Civil Rights, 1967, Volume I: *Racial Isolation in the Public Schools*, Washington, D.C.: Superintendent of Documents, U.S. Government Printing Office.

school enrollment in Omaha, Nebr., and almost 70 percent of the enrollment in Chester, Pa., yet in both cities at least 80 percent of the Negro children are enrolled in majority-Negro schools. . . .

RACIAL ISOLATION AND POPULATION TRENDS

Since the turn of the century, America has become an urban nation. The change from rural to urban residence, although somewhat more dramatic for Negro Americans than for whites, has been a national phenomenon. In 1960, approximately two-thirds of all Americans—white and Negro—lived in metropolitan areas.

Although white and Negro Americans now reside in metropolitan areas in similar proportions, there has been a change in their pattern of residence within those areas. Sixty-six years ago, little more than half the Negroes in metropolitan areas lived in the central city. By 1960, however, 8 of every 10 Negroes in metropolitan areas resided there. White population trends have not been similar. In 1900, more than 6 of every 10 metropolitan whites lived in the central cities, but by 1960 more than half the metropolitan white population resided in the suburbs.

An examination of recent population increases shows the trend clearly. Between 1940 and 1960 the total population of metropolitan areas increased by 40 million persons. Eighty-four percent of the Negro increase occurred in the central cities and 80 percent of the white increase in the suburbs. . . . By 1960, four out of five nonwhite metropolitan children of school age lived in central cities, while nearly three-fifths of the white children lived in the suburbs.

Thus the growth of the Nation's metropolitan areas has been characterized by an increasing separation of the white and Negro populations. . . . A recent study of residential patterns in 207 central cities shows that residential segregation is rigid and uniform. . . . In metropolitan areas there is a growing separation between the poor and the affluent, between the well educated and the poorly educated, between Negroes and whites. . . .

FISCAL DISPARITIES [BETWEEN LOCAL SCHOOL DISTRICTS]

Education, like many other governmental functions, is financed in large part from property taxes levied by local jurisdictions. Under this system of financing, the adequacy of educational services is heavily dependent on the adequacy of each community's tax base. With the increasing loss of their more affluent white population, central cities also have suffered a pronounced erosion of their fiscal capacity. At the same time the need for city services has increased, particularly in the older and larger cities.

The combination of rising costs and a declining tax base has weakened and cities' capacity to support education at levels comparable to those in the suburbs. As the gap between educational services in the cities and suburbs has widened, more affluent white families have been afforded further inducement to leave the cities, again intensifying racial and economic isolation and further widening the gap. . . .[19]

NONPUBLIC SCHOOLS

Private and parochial school enrollment also is an important factor in the increasing concentration of Negroes in city school systems. . . Nationally, about one-sixth of the total 1960 school enrollment (Grades 1 to 12) was in private schools. In metropolitan areas the proportion is slightly higher, and divided unevenly between city and suburb. Nearly one-third more elementary school students in the cities attend non-public schools than in the suburbs. Almost all of them are white. In the larger metropolitan areas the trend is even more pronounced. . . . Thus nonpublic schools absorb a disproportionately large segment of white school-age population

[19] Editor's Note: The following table lists for some 40 large American cities the proportion of Negro students enrolled in public elementary schools 1965–1966:

City	*Percent Negro*	*City*	*Percent Negro*
Washington, D.C.	90.9	Cincinnati*	40.3
Chester, Pa.	69.3	Pittsburgh*	39.4
Wilmington, Del.	69.3	Buffalo*	34.6
Newark*	69.1	Houston	33.9
New Orleans*	65.6	Flint	33.1
Richmond*	64.7	Indianapolis*	30.8
Baltimore*	64.3	New York City	30.1
East St. Louis	63.4	Boston	28.9
St. Louis*	63.3	San Francisco	28.8
Gary	59.5	Dallas*	27.5
Philadelphia*	58.6	Miami	26.8
Detroit*	55.3	Milwaukee	26.5
Atlanta	54.7	Columbus	26.1
Cleveland*	53.9	Los Angeles	23.4
Memphis	53.2	Oklahoma City	21.2
Chicago*	52.8	Syracuse	19.0
Oakland*	52.1	San Antonio	14.2
Harrisburg*	45.7	Denver	14.0
New Haven*	45.6	San Diego	11.6
Hartford*	43.1	Seattle	10.5
Kansas City*	42.4	Minneapolis	7.2

The asterisks refer to *larger* cities whose total (school and nonschool) population is expected to be over 50 percent Negro by 1985. See *Report of the National Advisory Commission on Civil Disorders,* Washington, D.C.: U.S. Government Printing Office, March 1, 1968, pp. 216, 240.

in central cities, particularly in the larger ones. This poses serious problems for city school systems. In St. Louis, for example, 40 percent of the total white elementary school population attended nonpublic schools in 1965; in Boston, 41 percent; in Philadelphia, more than 60 percent. . . .[20]

In earlier years, city school attendance areas encompassed considerably more territory and a more heterogeneous population. In recent decades, as geographical attendance areas have become smaller and residential segregation has intensified, city schools have become more socially and racially homogeneous. At the same time, the concept of neighborhood has been changing. Greater population mobility and significant changes in the pattern of urban life generally have tended to diffuse traditional neighborhood patterns. . . Indeed, more than one-third (15.5 million) of the nation's public school children rode buses to school during the 1963–64 school year. . . . In city school systems, on the other hand, children attend schools closer to their homes than in the past. Today, geographical school zoning in itself is the basis for persistently high levels of school segregation. . . .

St. Louis is a case in point. There, the school administrators voluntarily complied with the *Brown* decision in 1954 by converting from dual to single attendance school zones over a two-year period. The new attendance zones were established after carefully counting public school children on a block-by-block basis without regard to race. Residential segregation was extensive, however, and relatively few boundary changes were made in converting from dual to single attendance zones. Most of the all-Negro schools remained unchanged. By 1965, 91 percent of the Negro elementary school children attended schools that were nearly all-Negro. . . .

SUMMARY

In many metropolitan areas, racial concentrations in the central city schools have reached the point where solutions are no longer even theoretically possible within the city alone. . . . [When] the neighborhood school is the predominant attendance unit. . . . racial isolation in

[20] Editor's Note: The Kerner Report also states:

Racial isolation . . . is magnified by the fact that a much greater proportion of white than Negro students attend private schools. Studies indicate that, in America's 20 largest cities, approximately four out of 10 white students are enrolled in nonpublic schools, as compared with only one out of 10 Negro pupils. The differential appears to be increasing.

—*Report of the National Advisory Commission on Civil Disorders* (The "Kerner Report"), Washington, D.C.: U.S. Government Printing Office, March 1, 1968, p. 237.

See also Joseph M. Cronin, "Negroes in Catholic Schools," *Commonweal* 85: 13–16, October 4, 1966.

city schools is the inevitable result. In addition, the day-to-day operating decisions of school officials—the location of new school facilities, transfer policies, methods of relieving overcrowded schools, determination of the boundary lines of attendance areas—often have further intensified racial isolation. In the North, where school segregation was not generally compelled by law, these policies and practices have helped to increase racial separation. In the South, where until the *Brown* decision in 1954 school segregation was required by law, similar policies and practices have contributed to its perpetuation. . . .[21]

REMEDY

. . . Faced with a critical yet imperfectly understood problem, school systems generally have taken one of two basic approaches: the institution of *compensatory education* in majority-Negro schools or *school desegregation.* At present there is disagreement over the relative efficacy of these approaches. . . .

COMPENSATORY PROGRAMS IN ISOLATED SCHOOLS

The objectives of compensatory education programs have been summarized by Sloan Wayland, a sociologist:

> Start the child in school earlier; keep him in school more and more months of the year; . . . expect him to learn more and more during this period, in wider and wider areas of human experience, under the guidance of a teacher, who has had more and more training, and who is assisted by more and more specialists, who provide an ever-expanding range of services. . . .

Compensatory education is a term which, as used by educators, may embody one or more of several distinct approaches to improving the quality of education for disadvantaged children. One approach—remedial

[21] Editor's Note: For an account of changes occurring in the South, read Jim Lesson, "The Pace Quickens in the South," *Southern Educational Report* 2: 31–36, April 1967; and John Egerton, "De Facto Segregation: A Tale of Three Cities [Atlanta, Nashville, and Little Rock] *Southern Educational Report* 2: 10–16, September 1967. A more recent, more pessimistic account by the Southern Regional Council on actual progress toward school desegregation in the Southern and border states may be found in *Current,* December 1968, pp. 33–47.

In 1968 almost 90 percent of the school districts in the Deep South were using the so-called "freedom of choice" plan—a plan which tended to delay desegregation because it placed all the burden of change on the Negro child and parents who were "free" to choose to desegregate in the face of hostile white opposition. The court ruling against such delaying tactics may be found in *Charles E. Green et al. v. County School Board of New Kent County* (Virginia) *et al.,* 88 U. S. *Supreme Court Reporter* 1689 (1968).

instruction—is to give more intensive attention to students in academic difficulty. Remedial techniques usually include reduction of the number of students per teacher, provision of extra help to students during and after school, counseling, and use of special teaching materials designed to improve basic skills. Many of these techniques have been used in schools for years and currently are employed in suburban as well as inner-city schools.

Another approach—cultural enrichment—expands activities which schools traditionally have offered to students. Cultural enrichment programs attempt to broaden the horizons of poor children by giving them access to activities which ordinarily might be beyond their reach, such as field trips and visits to museums, concerts, other schools, and colleges. Such programs also commonly are found in middle class schools where they operate to supplement the normal cultural experiences of the pupils.

A third element of many compensatory education programs involves efforts to overcome attitudes which inhibit learning. Many educators have recognized that lack of self-esteem is a major cause of academic failure. A number of compensatory programs attempt to improve self-esteem (through the study of Negro history, for example) and to raise confidence by providing successful academic experiences and recognition. Some programs try to raise the expectations of both students and teachers to overcome negative and defeatist attitudes.

A fourth approach to compensatory education, incorporating many elements of the other approaches, is preschool education. This approach seeks to provide disadvantaged children with training in verbal skills and with cultural enrichment activities before they enter the primary grades. Although the importance of preschool education long has been recognized, such projects recently have become widespread with the support of funds from the Office of Economic Opportunity's Head Start Program. . . .

[But after reviewing more than twenty such compensatory programs, the Commission concluded that] there were no significant differences between students who had been in [these programs] . . . and students who had had no compensatory education. . . . [In contrast, the] Syracuse study found that over the course of a school year, the bused students achieved at a rate more than double that of the achievement rate of the students in the compensatory program.

The Commission's analysis does not suggest that compensatory education is incapable of remedying the effects of poverty on the academic achievement of individual children. There is little question that school programs involving expenditures for cultural enrichment, better teaching, and other needed educational services can be helpful to disadvantaged children. The fact remains, however, that none of the programs appear to have raised significantly the achievement of participating pupils, as a *group*, within the period evaluated by the Commission. . . . [and] that efforts to improve a child's self-esteem cannot be wholly productive in a student environment which seems to deny his worth. . . .

SCHOOL DESEGREGATION

. . . [The Commission thus looks upon the reduction of racial imbalance in schools as the most fruitful approach to the problem, and favors increased emphasis on] supplementary centers and magnet schools, education complexes, and education parks. . . . [Such schools would] offer specialized courses designed to attract white as well as Negro students [and would] constitute a variation of the specialized high schools found in many of the Nation's cities such as Bronx Science in New York and Boston Latin in Boston. . . .

Proposals for educational complexes would broaden attendance areas by grouping existing schools and consolidating their attendance zones. . . The size and fragmentation of school districts within metropolitan areas suggests that there may be a need for consolidation. In the Nation's 212 metropolitan areas in 1962, there were approximately 6,000 independent school districts and 600 dependent school districts, an average of 21 school systems for each metropolitan area. More than one-third of the school districts in metropolitan areas serve less than 300 students. . . . Educators who have examined the problems relating to size and complexity have concluded that education parks, properly planned, could in fact provide higher quality education and even greater individual attention to the needs of all students by permitting advances and innovations in educational techniques which are not now possible in smaller schools. . . .[22]

There is ample [legal precedent] . . . that Congress can enact the laws necessary to eliminate racial isolation and to secure the Negroes equality of opportunity in the public schools. . . . Congress may require the States to provide metropolitan solutions, either through reorganization of school districts or cooperative arrangements among school districts, where racial isolation cannot be corrected within the limits of the central city. . . .[23]

---

[22] Editor's Note: The "Comprehensive High School," which has been recommended for the past decade by Dr. Conant and the American Association of Secondary School Principals, and which has resulted in the consolidations of thousands of rural school districts, may be considered as a prelude to the "Park School" recommended by the U.S. Commission on Civil Rights. See James B. Conant, *The American High School Today*, New York: McGraw-Hill, Inc., 1959, 2nd ed., 1967.

[23] Editor's Note: For further details on this point read Stephen F. Roach, "What the Federal Courts Say about Racial Imbalance in Northern School Systems," *NASSP Bulletin* 49: 41–55, October 1965; "Note: School Desegregation and the Office of Education Guidelines," 55 *Georgetown Law Journal* 325–335; November 1966; and James R. Dunn, "Title VI, The Guidelines and School Desegregation in the South," 52 *Virginia Law Review* 42–88 (1967).

CONCLUSION

. . . As our cities have grown, increasing distances, physical and psychological, have separated the affluent majority from disadvantaged minorities. We have followed practices which exclude racial and economic minorities from large areas of the city and we have created structures, such as our method of financing education, which, by providing more attractive facilities with less tax effort, tend to attract the affluent to the very areas from which minorities are excluded. And the fact of racial and economical separation itself has generated attitudes which make integration increasingly difficult. The lines of separation are now well established, self-perpetuating, and very difficult to reverse. . . . In today's world, all of us, adults and children, are residents of many neighborhoods and communities, large and small. We do not hesitate to bus our children long distances in rural areas, or, in cities, to private schools or to other schools offering special advantages. Thus, the issue is not whether small neighborhood schools are good or busing bad, *per se*, but whether the interests of our children will be served or impaired by particular proposals or solutions. Will our children be held back by being placed in classes with children of other, less advantaged backgrounds? Will the education provided at the end of a trip be as good as, or better than, the education our children presently receive?

While public attention has been focused upon the more dramatic [racial] controversies, many small cities and suburban communities in the Nation have quietly integrated their schools. By a variety of techniques these communities have achieved their goal by substituting community schools for those serving smaller neighborhoods. In most cases the issue has been approached calmly and compassionately, with a view toward improving the quality of education for all children. Steps have been taken to maintain and improve educational standards, to avoid the possibility of interracial frictions, and to provide remedial services for children who need them. And, in most cases, the conclusion has been that advantaged children have not suffered from educational exposure to others not as well off, and that the results have been of benefit to all children, white and Negro alike. . . . Fears of the unknown, therefore, are being refuted by practical experience.[24]

---

[24] Editor's Note: For an account of a community that has been quite successful in achieving racial integration, read Reginald G. Damerell, *Triumph of a White Suburb*, New York: William Morrow & Company, Inc., 1968.

Opposed to "consolidation" is the view that parents should be given a greater voice in education by means of "a liberating decentralization" as "a means of reconnecting the parties at interest so that they can work in concert."—*Reconnection for Learning:*

2.9 CULTURAL FACTORS IN REMEDIATION*

Allison Davis

All human groups and members of groups have a very complex and strongly sanctioned culture-language, child-rearing practices, sexual controls, kinship relationships, parent-child, and Superhuman-human relationships. The *low-income groups*, or *lower classes*, or *economically deprived*, or *slum groups*, or *the poor*, have, in fact, cultural patterns of behavior, values, and learned emotions, which organize all the major areas of behavior mentioned in the preceding sentence. . . . The slum, or lower-class, or low-income, or poor groups are not deprived of a culture; in fact, they have learned as a group, and as individuals, a complex and powerfully motivating culture, which all the efforts of the school have relatively little success in changing, except over generations.

These low-status groups are deprived, then, to speak exactly, of certain skills and values possessed by most middle-class groups. . . . To be explicit, low-status groups are disadvantaged in our economy, in our schools, and in our social system because they have to learn a new cultural pattern of behavior, including: (1) habits of speech and writing, use of books, and other skills; and (2) new modes of sublimating or socializing the sexual, acquisitive, and aggressive drives which middle-class children and adolescents learn in their families. . . .

CULTURAL DISTORTION IN PERCEPTION

Efforts to deal with such pupils' cultural behavior as if it were *stupid*, *immoral*, or *lazy*, or attempts to stigmatize it in other value terms, are certain to fail. The naive do-gooders, the humanitarians untrained in comparative psychology and sociology, and those lacking firsthand knowledge of these children and their families will fail, as the moralistic old-style settlement house or social-work approach failed. A new way of life, of skills and values, cannot be given to or forced upon either children or adolescents. It has to be learned. To help anyone learn, one must analyze that person's present pattern of behavior and values, and always withhold judgment. One must also withhold advice and guidance until one learns to

---

A Community School System for New York City: Report of the Mayor's Advisory Panel on Decentralization of the New York City Schools, New York: The Advisory Panel, 1967; reviewed by Theodore R. Sizer, *Harvard Educational Review* 38: 176–184, Winter 1968.

* Allison Davis, "Cultural Factors in Remediation," in *The Body of Knowledge Unique to the Profession of Education*, Wilma A. Bailey, ed., Washington, D.C.: Pi Lambda Theta, 1966. Footnotes omitted.

Allison Davis, anthropologist, is Professor of Education, University of Chicago.

understand this behavior as influenced by low-income culture, and by the stigmatizing demands of the middle-class teacher, middle-class tests, middle-class curriculum, and middle-class guidance. . . .

There are no miracles in changing a group's culture. We must learn, by face-to-face visiting, participation, and observation in these neighborhoods, how families and children live, are motivated, regard the school and the teachers, and how they *survive*. . . . the bludgeoning attacks from life and society which they have to bear. . . .

It is naive to expect the school bureaucracy, or the social work bureaucracy, or the poverty program bureaucracy to know how to change the culture of the low-status groups, even when these *educated* staffs have the best intentions in the world. In the history of *social uplift* the hell of failure and alienation is paved with good intentions. School staffs, and those of other social agencies, must get down to the bedrock of face-to-face participation with families, churches, and peer groups of children and adolescents. We must learn the present behavior of the pupil, in terms of habits, skills, and values, and start exactly where he is. We must abandon deliberately and finally the prim, sheltered, traditional world of the classroom for nice middle-class children, and start dealing with the strange, harsh, and sometimes frightening realities of the real slum world, and the behavior of the child. Life often *is* hard, cruel, and dirty for these pupils. They cannot be reached by those who want to keep their hands *germ-free* and their minds neatly arranged into the conventional *lesson plans*.

The ominous and disheartening truth about the large-scale *projects* being initiated by federal agencies, private foundations, and school systems is simply this: Virtually none of the people who plan these *projects* has lived among slum groups, nor studied them objectively and intensively. They are *outsiders*, alien to the culture of those masses which they are honestly hoping to change. They have to depend, therefore, upon hearsay and anecdotes, and upon quantitative estimates of retardation, familial disorganization, delinquency, and other indices too gross to afford any insight into the causes, dynamics, and meaning of the lower-status culture and child. Even more destructive to such projects is the fact that probably something like 90 percent of the professional staffs of such projects also have no intensive firsthand knowledge of slum homes and people. They are social workers, or other college graduates, or volunteers, most of whom, like 85 percent of urban teachers, have lived only in middle-class homes, and learned to understand only educated culture and values. . . .

The child of low-status culture usually loses early in school his confidence in his ability and in his future. Since his parents usually do not encourage him to compete in school, he usually lacks the drive for achievement which is the prime incentive taught by middle-class parents to their children.

Moreover, the school itself, including the reading-readiness tests, which will not predict reading achievement a year or two later; the educational-aptitude tests; the primers; the readers; and the curriculum as a whole soon damage severely the confidence and the basic self-esteem of the child from low socio-economic groups. Finally, his low place in society, and that of his parents, friends, and neighbors, tends to weaken his self-esteem. This self-depreciation is typical of all low-status groups, and is the result of their having been severely stigmatized in most relationships with dominant groups. It results in self-depreciation and in hidden self-contempt beneath the facade of hostility and resentment. . . . The so-called *lack* of attention, *lack* of desire to learn, and *lack* of competitive drive in school are expressions of urgent realities of *fear* and feelings of inadequacy, and the consequent resentment toward the teacher and the school tasks.

The chief emphasis in the kindergarten and the primary grades, therefore, should be placed upon the establishment of a strong relationship of trust and mutual acceptance between the teacher and pupil. The first step in education is to train the pupil to trust the teacher. If he trusts the teacher, he will later learn to *respect* the teacher and *will want to win her approval.* The feeling of liking and trusting the teacher develops into respect and the desire to win her approval. It is just this step which is missing in the early school life of most Negro and white children from low socio-economic groups, and which must be developed at the preschool and primary level. The teacher must find enjoyable informal activities, such as story reading and games; she must give the child freedom to tell his *own stories* about his *own* life or fantasies, in whatever words he knows. Free talk, together with songs, dances, and little plays, can establish a bridge between the culture of the teacher and that of the low-status child.

Across this bridge the teacher can lead the child into new learning and new behavior, into a new world of letters, numbers, and writing which now becomes invested with the importance and the feeling which the child attaches to the teacher, and to *whatever she values.* From the good relationships with the teacher comes interest in the school, in the materials, in reading, writing, and working in school. . . .

Therefore we need to bring the Negro and white child from low economic groups into a relationship with such a teacher as early as possible, and we need to structure this relationship so that it will be rewarding to both pupil and teacher. . . .

LEARNING A NEW CULTURE

Many thousands of children and adolescents, born into low-status families, learn enough, chiefly through the school—the educated culture—to obtain white-collar positions later. The proportion of all children born in slum families who learn this new culture is less than 10 per cent, but the numbers are impressive, and the proportion certainly can be doubled by better curricula and more skilled teachers. . . . The best evidence we have concerning the marked effects of acculturation upon the academic behavior of Negro students has been provided by the studies of educational aptitude and achievement tests. . . . by Professor Otto Klineberg on Negro migrant children in New York City, and by Professor Everett S. Lee on Negro migrant children in Philadelphia. . . . [These studies point to the conclusion] that acculturation in northern cities results in an increase in I.Q., which is correlated with the length of time the migrant child has been in the northern city. . . . [Furthermore] the mean I.Q. of Negro children in northern cities has been rising steadily in the past twenty years. . . . In less than one generation, . . . the average I.Q. of Negro children [has risen] by about ten I.Q. points. . . .

CONCLUSION

This marked improvement, over just twenty years, in basic academic problem solving, involving verbal, arithmetical, and other cognitive skills, constitutes most convincing evidence that our largest culturally disadvantaged group, Negro Americans, is rapidly learning the symbol systems and cognitive behavior valued by the school. . . . The average I.Q. for the nation as a whole is 100, and that for Negroes in the cities referred to is 97. In another decade there will be no difference.

Wider participation by Negro Americans in the American culture and economy, with the opening of more skilled jobs, more access to libraries, museums, art galleries, and other such educational institutions (which in the South were not open to Negroes) has been a major force in cultural relearning by Negro children and adolescents. Finally, the stimulation of the more complex industrial urban society and the resultant development of more complex responses and needs, of new cultural aspirations and desires, has been a powerful force in changing their culture . . . [giving] new hope . . . [and a] rebirth of the American dream.[25]

[25] Editor's Note: Hoke Norris has listed some events that are changing the attitudes of (Southern) whites toward Negroes:

> Industrialization, the ease of travel, labor unions, the arrival of many new people from other sections and the departure of many Southerners for other places, the return of Army and Navy veterans who have seen the world, the force of outside opinion, the knowledge that the suppression of a colored race makes poor propaganda for the South and for the nation in a world predominantly colored, the impact of television programs that bring un-Southern voices and un-Southern ways into the very living rooms of the Southerners (the unmistakably white Richie Ashburn shakes hands with the unmistakably black Ernie Banks when he completes a home run circuit, and all the nation sees)—these are the changes, they are preparing the way for changes, they are themselves making changes.

—Hoke Norris, *We Dissent*, New York: St. Martin's Press, Inc., 1962, pp. 192–193.

2.10 THE EDUCATIONALLY DIFFICULT STUDENT*

Robert J. Havighurst

When we are confronted by a baffling phenomenon, our first impulse is to name it. During the past five years, educators have been baffled by a substantial number of pupils who do not learn in spite of instruction by reasonably well-trained teachers in well-equipped schools.

We suppose that these pupils come to school under some kind of handicap that makes it difficult to teach them. We have given them a variety of names—"culturally deprived," "intellectually deprived," or "socially disadvantaged." These names imply our belief that these children are not innately dull, but that they have been denied some experiences that other "normal" children have had. If the schools can discover what these mind-building experiences are, perhaps the schools can compensate for the handicaps which the pupils have suffered. Hence we speak of "compensatory" education.

The title of this paper—the difficult student—gives a different name to the phenomenon and suggests a deeper perspective which can include other types of pupils as well as those with social handicaps.

There are three visible and bothersome groups of "difficult" students which are especially important today. They are: The Socially Disadvantaged, The Mentally Handicapped, [and] The Privatist Non-Conformer.

THE SOCIALLY DISADVANTAGED

The socially disadvantaged pupils may be defined and described in three ways: in terms of certain family characteristics relating directly to the child; in terms of their personal characteristics; or in terms of the social group characteristics of their families.

FAMILY CHARACTERISTICS

Compared with other children whose families give them average or better advantages for getting started in modern urban life, the socially disadvantaged child lacks several of the following:

A family conversation which: answers his questions and encourages him to ask questions; extends his vocabulary with new words and with adjectives

* Excerpt from Robert J. Havighurst, "The Educationally Difficult Student: What the Schools Can Do," *Bulletin of the National Association of Secondary-School Principals,* Washington, D.C.: NEA 49: 110–127, March 1965. By permission.

For many years Robert J. Havighurst has been Professor of Education at the University of Chicago; he is also the author of numerous books and articles.

and adverbs; gives him a right and a need to stand up for and to explain his point of view on the world.

A family environment which: sets an example of reading; provides a variety of toys and play materials with colors, sizes, and objects that challenge his ingenuity with his hands and his mind.

Two parents who: read a good deal; read to him; show him that they believe in the value of education; reward him for good school achievement.

Bernstein[26] has studied the language behavior of families that relate to the intellectual development of their children. He distinguishes between two *forms* or *types* of language. (These language types are statistically related to social class, as will be pointed out later.) One form of language is called *restricted* and the other form is called *elaborated*. . . . A child who has learned a restricted language at home is likely to have difficulty in school, where an *elaborate* language is used and taught by the teacher; and the difficulty of the child is likely to increase as he goes further in school, unless he learns the elaborate language that is expected in the school. On the other hand, the child who had had experience with an elaborate language from his earliest years has a relatively easy time in school, because he must simply go on developing the kind of language and related thinking which he has already started.[27]

---

[26] Basil Bernstein, "Language and Social Class," *British Journal of Sociology* 11: 271–276, 1960; "Social Class and Linguistic Development: A Theory of Learning," in A. H. Halsey, J. Floud, and C. A. Anderson, eds., *Economy, Education and Society*, New York: The Free Press (Crowell-Collier and Macmillan, Inc.), 1961, pp. 288ff.; "Social Class, Linguistic Codes and Grammatical Elements," *Language and Speech* 5: 221–240, October–December 1962. . . .

[27] Editor's Note: Stones summarizes Bernstein's views thus:

> Bernstein considers the language of the . . . [culturally deprived] family a linguistically *restricted code*. He considers that of the middle class an *elaborated code*. He suggests the main attributes of the restricted code are its syntactical crudity, its repetitiveness, its rigid and limited use of adjectives and adverbs, short, grammatically simple, often unfinished sentences, and above all, much of the meaning is implicit and dependent upon a commonly held system of speech habits.
>
> The elaborated code is a much more flexible instrument. It has an accurate grammar and syntax. It employs a range of subordinate clauses unknown to the restricted code. It makes much more widespread and flexible use of conjunctions, prepositions, adjectives, and adverbs. It is much more discriminating and it has a much greater potentiality of abstraction. It also differs from the restricted code in that the pronoun *I* is used frequently, reinforcing the personal and individual nature of the language.
>
> Bernstein illustrates the nature of the restricted code for the learning child. He gives an imaginary example of two conversations on a bus. A mother has a child sitting on her lap.
>
> First conversation: [restricted code]
>
> Mother: Hold on tight.
> Child: Why?

PERSONAL CHARACTERISTICS

The family environment with the characteristics just cited tends to produce children with certain personal deficits. Martin Deutsch[28] has studied such children with techniques of the experimental psychologists, and he finds them to have inferior auditory discrimination, inferior visual discrimination, inferior judgment concerning time, number and other basic concepts. He finds that this inferiority is not due to physical defects of eyes and ears and brain, but is due to inferior *habits* of hearing and seeing and thinking. Presumably, the family environment of these children did not teach them to "pay attention" to what was being said around them, or to the visual scene. Then, when they came to school, their school performance suffered because they had not learned to "listen" to the teacher and other important people or to "see" the things they are shown in the school.

SOCIAL GROUP CHARACTERISTICS

We introduce the social group characteristics of socially disadvantaged children last so as to avoid giving the impression that there is a hard-and-fast relation between socio-economic status, or some other group characteristic, and social disadvantage for the child. While there are statistical relations and very important ones between socio-economic status and social disadvantages of children, there are so many individual exceptions to the

---

Mother: Hold on tight.
Child: Why?
Mother: You'll fall.
Child: Why?
Mother: I told you to hold on tight, didn't I?

Second conversation: [elaborated code]

Mother: Hold on tightly, darling.
Child: Why?
Mother: If you don't you will be thrown forward and you'll fall.
Child: Why?
Mother: Because if the bus suddenly stops you'll jerk forward on to the seat in front.
Child: Why?
Mother: Now darling, hold on tightly and don't make such a fuss.

As can be seen in the restricted code the symbolic function is slight; the words have little more than signal significance. . . . Later, when he enters school, the language of the [culturally disadvantaged] child acts as a filter to restrict what gets through from the teacher (an elaborated code user) to the elements of the restricted code.

Following from this Bernstein concludes that the problems facing a. . . . [culturally deprived] child in a school situation aimed at improving his language skills

---

[28] "The Disadvantaged Child and the Learning Process," in Harry A. Passow, ed., *Education in Depressed Areas*, New York: Bureau of Publications, Teachers College, Columbia University, 1963, pp. 163–180.

statistical generalizations that any educational policy aimed at identifying socially disadvantaged children should avoid reliance upon general socioeconomic characteristics as the decisive criteria.

Above all, it is important to avoid the error of saying that all children of working-class families are socially disadvantaged. Approximately 65 percent of the children of this country are living in working-class homes. That is, their fathers or mothers do manual work for a living. The great majority of these families give their children a fairly good start for life in an urban industrial democratic society. Their children are adequately fed and clothed. They are loved and protected by their parents. They learn to respect teachers and to like school. They do fairly well or better than that in school.

While working-class children as a group are somewhat different from the children of white-collar workers, it would not be reasonable to say that the working-class children are socially disadvantaged or culturally deprived. Working-class children as a group score slightly below children of white-collar families in intelligence tests; they fall slightly below on tests of

---

will be very different from that of a middle-class child. The latter has merely to *develop* his linguistic skills, the former has to *change* them. This makes it extremely difficult for the user of a restricted code to schematize the learning he is asked to make, since it is presented in the unfamiliar forms of the elaborated code.

—E. Stones, *An Introduction to Educational Psychology*, London: Methuen & Company, Ltd., 1966, pp. 186–187. By permission of Methuen & Company, Ltd., London.

E. Stones is Lecturer in Educational Psychology at the University or Birmingham.

Elsewhere, Professor Havighurst has contrasted the values of two different cultures—which he calls the *instrumental* culture (of the dominant, upper- and middle-class American) and the *expressive* culture (of some "culturally deprived" subcultures):

In the instrumental culture, composed of the academic skills and knowledge formally stated as educational objectives, one is exposed to procedures which are to advance his prowess as a reader, speller, or mathematician. Thus, participation in the instrumental culture is to reach goals beyond the activity itself such as being promoted, becoming a mechanic or a good citizen. In contrast, the expressive culture consists of those activities in which pupils and teachers engage for the sake of the participation itself rather than for some distant goal. Popular aspects of the expressive culture include playing games at recess, participating in musical events, taking part in festivals, the celebration of holidays, school parties, and physical education.

The expressive culture is considered best for teaching values because it sustains less severe and unfair competition, thereby allowing more children to succeed. Unfortunately, some schools have policies which deny participation in the expressive culture unless one first succeeds in the instrumental culture. (For example, one cannot be in the band or play football unless he has a "B" average.). . . .

[But, it may well be that the order of value emphasis should be reversed. For by] a creative use of its expressive culture, the average inner-city school can make itself a place of constructive influence in the lives of its pupils, can teach them some of its values, and can find opportunity to help them achieve higher levels in the instrumental culture.

—Robert J. Havighurst and Robert D. Strom, in *The Inner-City Classroom: Teacher Behaviors*, R. D. Strom, ed., Columbus, Ohio: Charles E. Merrill Books, Inc., 1966, pp. 53, 168.

school achievement; they attain somewhat less formal education. But the differences are relatively small, and become even smaller when the socially disadvantaged children are removed and the majority of working-class youth who remain are compared with white-collar children.

Most working-class families participate fully in the American mass or core culture. This is certainly not a culture of deprivation. While the differences between the upper working class and the lower middle class are real and they are interesting, these differences should not be described in terms of social advantage or social disadvantage. The great amount of movement of people across the boundary between these two classes as they grow up is evidence that the differences between these two classes are not fundamental ones.

Who, then, are the socially disadvantaged when we attempt to describe them in terms of observable social groups? They are groups with the following characteristics:

1. They are at the bottom of the American society in terms of income.
2. They [or their parents] have a rural background.
3. They suffer from social and economic discrimination at the hands of the majority of the society.
4. They are widely distributed in the United States. While they are most visible in the big cities, they are present in all except the very high income communities. There are many of them in rural areas, especially in the southern and southwestern states.

In racial and ethnic terms, these groups are about evenly divided between whites and non-whites. They consist mainly of the following: Negroes from the rural south many of whom have migrated recently to the northern industrial cities; Whites from the rural south and the southern mountains many of whom have migrated recently to the northern industrial cities; Puerto Ricans who have migrated to a few northern industrial cities; Mexicans with a rural background who have migrated into the west and middle west, also rural Spanish-Americans in the southwestern states; European immigrants with a rural background, from east and southern Europe.

Altogether, these groups make up about 15 percent of the United States population. Since they tend to have large families, their children make up as much as 20 percent of the child population. Not all socially disadvantaged children come from these groups, but the great majority do. Not all children in these groups are socially disadvantaged, but the great majority are.

HOW MANY ARE SOCIALLY DISADVANTAGED?

There is an infinite gradation of social advantage-disadvantage, and therefore any quantitative estimate of the number of socially disadvantaged children and youth must be a personal rather than a scientific statement.

The writer would place the number of socially disadvantaged children at about 15 per cent of the child population. One basis for this estimate is the proportion of unemployed, out of school youth between the ages of 16 and 20. These young people have been relatively unsuccessful in school and in the labor market. The great majority of them come from the social groups listed above. . . . Since these children and their families tend to concentrate in the large cities, while upper-income people tend to move out from the cities to the suburbs, the socially disadvantaged children are in big cities in larger proportions than 15 percent. Probably *30 percent of the children* in such cities as New York, Chicago, Philadelphia, Washington, Detroit, Cleveland, and Baltimore fall into the socially disadvantaged category.

THE MENTALLY HANDICAPPED

The truly mentally handicapped child is one with inborn mental deficiency, indicated by an IQ below 75 or 80, depending on the definition adopted by the state or the school system. Some of these children have clearly marked physical signs of mental deficiency, but others do not. The number of mentally handicapped children is estimated by various authorities to be about two percent of the age group.

However, it is not an easy matter to distinguish a true mentally handicapped from a socially disadvantaged child. Mental retardation is no longer regarded as a condition easily diagnosed. It appears that a considerable fraction, perhaps as many as half, of the school age children now treated as mentally retarded could have developed normal intelligence if they had expert treatment in their pre-school years.

Thus we may expect to see school programs designed for young children who appear to be mentally retarded with the aim of bringing some of them into the range of normal intelligence.

Bloom has published a study[29] supporting the proposition that variations in the environment can produce changes in human characteristics and that such variations have the greatest effect at the period when the particular characteristic is changing most rapidly. This bears out Hunt's thesis (which was also that of Mme. Montessori) that different age levels are crucial for different kinds of learnings, and that children go through various phases of learning, with each phase lending support to those which follow.

Bloom has also assembled the results of research indicating the extent of educational growth experienced by children at various age levels. Results indicate that at least one-third of the learnings which will determine later levels of school achievement have already taken place by age 6, and at

---

[29] Benjamin Bloom, *Stability and Change in Human Characteristics*, New York: John Wiley & Sons Inc., 1964.

least 75 percent by age 13. These findings point to the most important periods for school programs directed to raising achievement levels of children. Based on the estimate that 33 percent of educational growth takes place before age 6, Bloom suggests that "nursery schools and kindergartens could have far-reaching consequences on the child's general learning pattern." The approximately 17 percent of growth which takes place between ages 6 and 9 suggests that elementary Grades 1 to 3 are also crucial. Tending to support this suggestion in another way are the rather disappointing results now being reported of the Higher Horizons program in New York, which has not attempted to reach any children below the third grade. On the other hand, experimental programs at the prekindergarten level in Baltimore, New York, and elsewhere have already shown gratifying results in better performance on IQ tests and other measures of readiness and achievement. A final quotation from Bloom sums up the situation:

> A conservative estimate of the effect of extreme environments on intelligence is about 20 IQ points. This could mean the difference between a life in an institution for the feeble-minded or a productive life in society. It could mean the difference between a professional career and an occupation which is at the semi-skilled or unskilled level. . . . The implications for public education and social policy are fairly clear. Where significantly lower intelligence can be clearly attributed to the effects of environmental deprivations, steps must be taken to ameliorate these conditions as early in the individual's development as education and other social forces can be utilized. . . .

THE PRIVATIST NON-CONFORMER

An entirely different kind of "educationally difficult student" [—different than the "culturally deprived" or the "intellectually deprived"—] is found mainly in the economically favored communities and schools. This is a youth of average or superior intelligence, who has done well in school until he reaches high school age, and then seems to lose his drive and direction. Some observers would identify this kind of youth as a "beatnik," but this is not a thoroughly satisfactory name for the youth of high school age whom we shall call the *privatist non-conformer.*

This kind of boy or girl has such doubts about the quality of his society that he refuses to commit himself to supporting the political and business and educational institutions around him, but prefers to lead a life of private or asocial activity.

At the coming of adolescence a person must commence to achieve his own self-esteem and his social fidelity. This is a part of his achievement of his *identity* as a person in his own right. It comes about normally as a part of his adolescent experience in school, work, play with his agemates, and association with adult citizens and workers. The youth as he achieves identity narrows and focuses his personal, occupational, sexual, and ideological commitments by getting started in one occupation, getting married and starting a family, and beginning to take part in community civic life.

Apparently this process of growth toward identity is more difficult today than it was a generation or more ago. The evidence for this statement comes from the testimony of high school counselors and teachers, from parents of intelligent and sensitive children, and from psychologists and sociologists who have studied youth culture. . . . Privatism has always been present, but has not been so noticeable formerly as in the most recent years. The tendency in former years has been to attribute youth problems to poverty. Therefore it is a shock to discover a problem group who are not poverty-stricken. . . .

[Kenneth Keniston] sees the "youth culture" as a culture which is *non-adult*, if not *anti-adult*. He says it has roles, values, and ways of behaving all its own; it emphasizes disengagement from adult values; [it plays up] sexual attractiveness, daring, immediate pleasure, and comradeship in a way that is neither of childhood nor of adulthood. Eventually a young person must leave this youth culture and enter adult life, but Keniston believes that in this process few young people are becoming deeply involved as citizens and workers. Instead, they tend to be alienated, refusing to accept the adult world with positive feeling, and retreating to a world of private and personal satisfactions. He calls this attitude *privatism*. Such a person declines to become involved with political and social problems, and prefers to spend his time with music and art. He feels powerless to affect the great society, and turns to the things closer home that he feels able to control. He may value family closeness above meaningful work because he can control things within his family, but not in his occupation. Leisure activities may be more important to him than work because he can control what he does in his free time.

> Many young people expect to find in leisure a measure of stability, enjoyment, and control which they would otherwise lack. Hence their emphasis on assuring leisure time, or spending their leisure to good advantage, or getting jobs with long vacations, and on living in areas where leisure can be well enjoyed. Indeed, some anticipate working at their leisure with a dedication that will be totally lacking in their work itself.

But Keniston does not believe this will be satisfactory. He thinks this will cause a fatal split in a person's life.

> The man who spends his working day at a job whose primary meaning is merely to earn enough money to enable him to enjoy the rest of his time can seldom really enjoy his leisure, his family, or his avocations. Life is of a piece, and if work is empty or routine, the rest will inevitably become contaminated as well, becoming a compulsive escape or a driven

effort to compensate for the absent satisfactions that should inhere in work. Similarly, to try to avoid social and political problems by cultivating one's garden can at best be only partly successful. . . . Putting work, society, and politics into one pigeon-hole, and family, leisure and enjoyment into another creates a compartmentalization which is in continual danger of collapsing.

The mood of our society includes frankness in formerly taboo areas, self-criticism, and skepticism. Youth are exposed to this mood very directly through the mass media (television, cinema, paper-back literature, etc.). They read such books as Salinger's *Catcher in the Rye* and Golding's *Lord of the Flies,* and they are encouraged to read such literature by high school teachers of literature who represent the mood of society. . . .

Under the circumstances it is not surprising that contemporary middle-class youth show a considerable degree of self-doubt and lack of confidence in the political and economic structure of modern society. It is not surprising that a *privatistic* life is preferred to one of greater social commitment. Boys find it difficult to make up their minds what occupation they will prepare for. Some of them engage in a kind of sit-down strike against the academic demands made on them by school or college. Their fathers wonder why sons are so in-grown and uncertain, as compared with the greater assurance and task-orientation they remember as normal for their generation. There is not so much concern about girls, since they are not expected to show the degree of *instrumental activism* expected of boys. With them there is more concern about their sex-role, and about the place of sexual activity in the life of a teen-age girl.

The number of privatistic non-conformers is hard to estimate because we know no measure of this quality and because a great many youth show this quality only to a limited extent. But the number who show it in such an acute form that they are recognized by their teachers and age-mates to be in a special category is probably no more than two or three per cent of an age-group. . . .

EDUCATIONAL PROGRAMS FOR THE PRIVATIST NON-CONFORMIST

What can the schools do about the difficult student who is a privatist non-conformist? If . . . [our analysis] is reasonably correct, boys and girls of average or superior intelligence need an educational program during the high school period that is designed to build self-esteem and social fidelity. The characteristics of the youth who tend toward the privatist position are the following: lack of self-esteem based on their own achievement in school and society, uncertainty about vocational choice, cognitive development more advanced than personal autonomy, lack of naive faith in society, and discontent with school.

The educational program should be designed to build social fidelity as well as self-confidence. It might contain the following elements:

1. Opportunity for service to society. A variety of projects during the school year and during the summer for improvement of the school, the local community, and the wider community. This will lead to a commitment to social welfare and a faith in the improvability of society.

2. Positively oriented study of society. Stress in courses in social studies on the achievement of modern society in solving problems of public health, poverty, educational and economic opportunity, and the building of an interdependent world.

3. Use of adult models who demonstrate both self-esteem and social fidelity. Choice of teachers who are socially optimistic, active, and oriented toward the improvement of society. There is a greater chance in the future for the selection of teachers with appropriate personalities for certain age groups, as the teacher shortage decreases and opportunity increases to select the better ones. The use of biography in literature and the social studies could stress heroes with these positive qualities. A new set of biographical films produced by Elizabeth Drews of Michigan State University centers on the lives of contemporary people who are making positive contributions to the life of society, who have faith in the improvability of this society, and who lead personal lives that can serve as models of youth.

Good education strikes a balance between analysis and affirmation. Perhaps the education of middle-class children in recent years has been too strong on analysis and too weak on affirmation. . . .

The art of teaching this kind of boy or girl is to combine experiences of basic affirmation of democratic social values with experiences of analysis and criticism of social reality, so that the youth discovers and works out for himself his identity both as a conformer to some social values and a non-conformer to some social practices.[30]

---

[30] Editor's Note: The "Student Revolters" on college campuses are very likely best understood as part of the same social movement that gives rise to the "hippies," the "juvenatrics," and to what Havighurst calls "the privatist non-conformer." The following references, therefore, are relevant not only to the article by Havighurst but also to the problem of "student revolt" discussed in extract "B" of "Democracy and Civil Disobedience: Pros and Cons" at the end of Chapter 1.

The following are a few references: "Youth: Change and Challenge," *Daedalus*, 91: 158–166, Winter 1962. See also Andrew M. Greeley, "The Temptation of the New Breed," *America*, 112: 750–752, May 22, 1965; Grace and Fred M. Hechinger, *Teen Age Tyranny*, New York: William Morrow & Company Inc., 1963; Arthur Goldberg, "Juvenatrics: Study of Prolonged Adolescence," *Clearing House* 38: 488–492, April 1964; News report, "The Hippies: Philosophy of a Subculture," *Time* 90: 18–22, July 7, 1967; G. Kerry Smith, ed., *Stress and Student Response*, Washington, D.C.: American Association of Higher Education (NEA), 1968; Nevitt Stanford, "The College Student of 1980," in *Campus 1980*, Alvin C. Eurich, ed., New York: Delacorte Press, 1968, pp. 176–199.

TOPICS FOR FURTHER STUDY

HEREDITY, ENVIRONMENT, AND "RACISM": PROS AND CONS*

Below are three brief statements dealing with the question: Are Negroes intellectually inferior to whites? Statement A summarizes a point of view widely held among contemporary psychologists. Statements B and C are pro and con statements on "Racism."

Defend or criticize one of the three following statements.

A. [This brief statement concerns the long-standing] controversy regarding the relative importance of heredity and environment in structuring the individual. A clear answer to this controversy has been given by Byron Hughes:

> No evidence indicates heredity to be more important than nurture and environment; emphatically, no evidence indicates it to be less important. . . . Heredity and nurture always operate together; one without the other is devoid of meaning. When we talk about heredity we imply nurture to be present to maintain it. When one or the other is absent there is no life. Each has implications for the other, and these implications are as varied and as numerous as are the variations in nurture and in heredity. Education is a form of nurture and is provided by the environment in which a person lives. Heredity comes from parentage. . . .

Hunt has asserted, with extensive supporting evidence, that the concepts of fixed intelligence and predetermined intelligence are no longer tenable. . . . [An] I.Q. score may vary as much as 20 to 40 points as a result of environmental stimulation or lack of environmental stimulation. . . . [In the mental development of a child] there exists a continuous reorganization of the structures of the mind contingent upon continuous creative interaction between the child and his environment. Early stimulating experiences are crucial.[31]

B. The I.Q.'s of American Negroes are from 15 to 20 points, on the average, below those of American whites. . . . Negro-white difference in mean test score occur in all types of mental tests, but the Negro lag is greatest in tests of an abstract nature—for example, problems involving reasoning, deduction, comprehension. These are the functions called for in education above the lowest levels.[32]

---

* Also relevant to this topic are pages 117–118 above, from Selection 2.9 by Allison Davis.

[31] Joe L. Frost and Glenn E. Hawkes, eds., *The Disadvantaged Child: Issues and Innovations*, Boston: Houghton Mifflin Company, 1966, pp. 5–7. See also Peter I. Rose, *The Subject is Race*, New York: Oxford University Press, 1968. This paperback contains an excellent bibliography, and would be useful as a supplement to this chapter.

[32] Carleton Putnam, *Race and Reality*, Washington, D.C.: Public Affairs Press, 1967, pp. 58–59 (bibliography).

C. [There] is no scientifically acceptable evidence for the view that ethnic groups differ in innate abilities. This is not the same as saying that there are no ethnic differences in such abilities. . . . [Although] it is exceedingly difficult to prove the absence of something. . . . we can point to the improvement in achievement when conditions of life improve. We can emphasize the tremendous variations within each ethnic group, much greater than the differences between groups even under discrepant environmental stimulation. We can insist that since innate psychological differences between ethnic groups have never been satisfactorily demonstrated, we have no right to act as if they had been. The science of psychology can offer no support to those who see in the accident of inherited skin color or other physical characteristics any excuse for denying the individuals the right to full participation in American democracy.[33]

BLACK POWER AND BLACK PRIDE: PROS AND CONS

A. The rejection of white culture by Black Muslims is . . . a symptom of more general unrest. Its essence is the desire for an identity of one's own, a rejection of something secondhand. . . .

[Some Black Muslims use] isolated Biblical texts [Jeremiah 5:15–17, 8:21, 38:7] to show that God is black, to identify themselves with Israel, to demonstrate that their oppression is the result of a curse that will end, . . . [and to show] that a man must have a nationality before he can have a God. [To recover his lost identity, the Black Muslim convert] is born again and accepts a very high standard of personal puritanism. There must be no sexual irregularity, no smoking, no drinking, no gluttony. . . . Disallowed also are cosmetics, personal display, and conspicuous spending. . . Very substantial almsgiving is required. . . .

A Muslim can trust no white man. Christianity kept the "so-called Negro" subservient to the white man; Christianity lynched Negro men and raped Negro women. Unless the Muslim—all so-called Negroes are Muslims whether they know it or not—rids himself of the slave mentality and all remnants of Christianity, he will share in the disintegration of a corrupt and dying world. . . .

---

[33] Otto Klineberg, "Negro-White Differences in Intelligence Test Performances," *American Psychologist* 18: 198–203, April 1963 (bibliography).

Observe that the opening question becomes much more specific, and more meaningful, when it is rephrased to read:

Are Negroes from deprived areas intellectually inferior to whites *or* are Negroes from upper and middle-class areas intellectually inferior to whites?

Any human being is an extremely complex subject for study, for his development depends on both personal and social, both hereditary and environmental factors. Thus, although nearly all contemporary sociologists and psychologists would tend to agree with Klineberg's rather than with Putnam's statement, the difficulties of precise measurement are tremendous. A study of the Putnam and Klineberg articles, and of their accompanying bibliographies, will be instructive, not only for a study of this specific problem but even more so for an increased awareness of the difficulties entailed in sociological or psychological measurement.

This, of course, is crude racism, as crude as anything put out by the Ku Klux Klan or the Nazis.[34]

B. The Negro does not want out [of American culture]. He wants in, and on terms that stand somewhat higher on the scale of reasonableness than the reaction to them in some corners of the white Establishment. As catalogued by the Washington Committee on Black Power, these terms include ten essentials, among them black pride ("which neither requests nor solicits; it demands"), black control of black communities, black economic productivity ("dignity through self-support"), black responsibility ("Black people themselves are responsible for their homes, their children, their schools, their streets"), black initiative, black excellence ("Let black people be the best"), black creativity and togetherness—and black self-defense.

Only human reason, black and white together, will decide whether the Negro gets what he wants. White America is only beginning to understand the new Negro mood, which is passing from the self-abasement that slavery taught to the self-sufficiency that lies still over a distant hill. The black is learning how to be black, rather than a carbon-copy white. And the pride, the new Negro institutions, the black cooperatives and the black student groups are all testimonials to his new spirit of independence. . . .

At this difficult juncture, the omens are perhaps more favorable than otherwise. One of the more thought-provoking conclusions of a poll of the U.S. Negro community reported by Harvard Sociologist Gary Marx suggests that tolerance for the white man increases in proportion to Negro civil rights militance. The black to fear is the one who has not yet been exposed to the discipline of self-pride—the unawakened 75% Negro majority that lies outside the civil rights movement, and has felt almost none of its effects. This Negro has nothing to lose by venting his frustrations in violence. The new Negro knows how much damage violence can do to his own cause.[35]

C. This is our basic conclusion: Our nation is moving toward two societies, one black, one white—separate but unequal. . . . To continue our present course will involve . . . ultimately the destruction of basic democratic

---

[34] Philip Mason, "The Revolt against Western Values," *Daedalus* 96: 328–352, Spring 1967. (Good bibliography on "Color and Race.") See also Basis Davidson, *Africa in History*, New York: Crowell-Collier and Macmillan, Inc., 1969.

Two excellent anthologies of historical as well as contemporary statements are: Leslie H. Fishel, Jr., and Benjamin Quarles, eds., *The Negro American: A Documentary History*, New York: William Morrow & Company, 1967, and Floyd B. Barbour, ed., *The Black Power Revolt*, Boston: Porter Sargent, 1968 (bibliography).

For the revolutionary communist view that Negroes must join with international communism to destroy present-day America, read Julius Lester, *Look Out, Whitey! Black Power's Gon' Get Your Mama!*, New York: International Press, 1968; and Claude M. Lightfoot, *Ghetto Rebellion and Black Liberation*, International Press, 1968.

[35] Editorial Report, *Time* 90: 20–21, December 1, 1967. Courtesy TIME, the Weekly Newsmagazine, Copyright Time Inc. 1967.

See also Harold Cruse, *The Crisis of the Negro Intellectual*, New York: William Morrow & Company Inc., 1967, pp. 535–548.

values. Large-scale and continuing violence could result, followed by white retaliation, and, ultimately, the separation of the two communities in a garrison state.[36]

THE NEIGHBORHOOD SCHOOL VERSUS BUSING: PROS AND CONS

A. Large-scale transfers of Negro children to schools in white neighborhoods . . . raise questions whose answers are by no means obvious. Should the Negro children be put in heterogeneous classes in the new school, in which case they tend to perform at the bottom of the class if the school draws from middle-class and upper-class families? Or should they be put in homogeneous classes, i.e., classes grouped according to academic ability —in which case they are again segregated in the new school? The latter seems pointless: nothing is gained by transporting youngsters several miles in order to keep them segregated. Yet dumping youngsters who are reading several years below grade level, as the New Rochelle experience suggests,

---

[36] National Advisory Commission on Civil Disorders, *National Report on Civil Disorders*, Washington, D.C.: U.S. Government Printing Office, March 1, 1968, Chapters 16–17; also New York: E. P. Dutton & Co., Inc.

On July 27, 1968, five months after the above report, the same commission (David Ginsberg, executive director) issued three

> Supplementary Studies . . . showing that the urban riots of the 1960s are a form of social protest by noncriminal elements and are justified as such by a majority of Negroes . . . [and suggesting] that short of massive suppression of millions, future riots can be prevented only by transforming the Negro slums and the institutions and attitudes that have made them.

An extensive poll of Negro and white attitudes showed that the majority of Negroes still desire integration and conciliation with whites, but that a substantial minority seem to have lost faith in the American system and are looking increasingly to militant leaders who advocate violence and separatism. Approximately 200,000 Negroes (6 percent—almost 15 percent in the Negro ghettos) favor a "separate black nation here" and feel so little a part of American society that they favor withdrawing allegiance from the United States and establishing a separate national entity. While 39 percent of the Negroes favor "laws and persuasion" to gain their rights and 38 percent favor "nonviolent protests," a substantial 15 percent believe they should "be ready to use violence."

On a more optimistic note, the survey also showed that 75 percent of the Negroes approved of the NAACP, 75 percent approved of Martin Luther King, 50 percent approved of Roy Wilkins, and 14 percent approved of Stokely Carmichael and H. Rap Brown. Although whites have a strong tendency to blame conditions of Negroes on Negroes themselves, 62 percent of the whites questioned said that Negroes have a right to live anywhere. (See *The New York Times*, July 28, 1968, p. 1 (col. 8), p. 48.)

Another 1968 survey points to the conclusion that Negro riots are the result of

> blocked opportunity . . . Negroes who riot do so because their conception of their lives and their potential has changed without commensurate improvement in their chances for a better life. . . . Negroes are still excluded from economic opportunity and occupational advancement, but they no longer have the psychological defenses or social supports that once encouraged passive adaptation to this situation. The result has been the most serious domestic violence in this country.
>
> —Nathan S. Caplan and Jeffery M. Paige, "A Study of Ghetto Rioters," *Scientific American* 219: 15–21, August 1968.

is not likely to enhance the former group's ego nor lead to meaningful encounters between the two races.[37]

B. Under segregated conditions, the minority group child identifies his social potential with his racial status. Under integrated conditions, however, the child is able to develop a sense of self based upon other dimensions. His perception of his potential is not tied to the potential attributed to his group. The realization that one can compete and make one's way in the larger society marks a giant step in the reduction of his feelings of alienation from that society. A positive identification with society and the feeling that socially approved goals are obtainable are crucial to the development and sustenance of the motivation necessary to achievement in school.[38]

C. Altogether, the sources of inequality of educational opportunity appear to lie first in the home itself and the cultural influences immediately surrounding the home; then they lie in the schools' ineffectiveness to free achievement from the impact of the home, and in the schools' cultural homogeneity which perpetuates the social influence of the home and its environs.

Given these results. . . . [s]everal elements seem clear:

(a) For those children whose family and neighborhood are educationally disadvantaged, it is important to replace this family environment as much as possible with an educational environment—by starting school at an earlier age, and by having a school which begins very early in the day and ends very late.

(b) It is important to reduce the social and racial homogeneity of the school environment, so that those agents of education that do show some effectiveness—are not mere replicas of the student himself. In the present organization of schools, it is the neighborhood school that most insures such homogeneity.

(c) The educational program of the school should be made more effective than it is at present. . . . [As things now stand] (1) these minority children have a serious educational deficiency at the start, which is obviously not a result of school, and (2) they have an even more serious deficiency at the end of school, which is obviously in part a result of school. . . . It is hard to believe that we are so inept in educating our young that we can do no more than leave young adults in the same relative competitive positions we found them in as children.[39]

---

[37] Charles E. Silberman, *Crisis in Black and White*, New York: Random House, Inc., 1964, p. 300.

[38] Dorothy K. Jessup, in *The Urban R's: Race Relations as the Problem in Urban Education*, eds. Robert A. Dentler, Bernard Mackler, and Mary Ellen Warshauer, published for the Center for Urban Education, New York: Frederick A. Praeger, Inc., 1968, p. 96.

[39] James S. Coleman, "Equal Schools or Equal Students?" *Public Interest* 4: 70–75, Summer 1966. This is a partial summary of the so-called "Coleman Report," *Equality of Educational Opportunity*, sponsored by the U.S. Office of Education and published in 1966 by the U.S. Superintendent of Documents (Catalog No. FS 5.238: 38001).

WELFARE—CUSTODIAL OR DEVELOPMENTAL? PROS AND CONS

A. The anti-poverty movement spearheaded by the new type of participating employee, the nonprofessional, and the participation of the recipient of services, the poor, can make a major contribution to the reduction of

unemployment
welfarism
alienation
the manpower shortages in the human services
the fragmentation of services.

It can be the key to the transformation of the affluent society into the Great Society.[40]

The key point in arguing for the use of these people is the fact that they can bring to the school experience and knowledge of the slum community which professionals too often lack and have little time to acquire, and which can improve the school's program. . . .[41]

B. How many persons capable of working are on welfare?

Some would say millions. But analysis disclosed that, over the next few years, out of the 7.3 million Americans on welfare, only 50,000 males may be capable of getting off—even if every program, public and private, were adequately staffed and efficiently run.

Of the 7.3 million citizens on welfare: 2.1 million, mostly women, are 65 or over, with a median age of 72; 700,000 are either blind or so severely handicapped that their work potential, if any, is extremely limited; 3.5 million are children whose parents cannot support them; the remaining 1 million are the parents of those children: about 900,000 mothers and 150,000 fathers. Two-thirds of the 150,000 fathers on welfare are incapacitated. Only some 50,000 are capable of being given job skills and training that will make them self-sufficient.[42]

C. The shortage of qualified professional personnel in the schools is the frequently heard and utterly illogical argument for utilizing the uneducated poor in instruction of the disadvantaged. But the shortage of teachers, particularly acute in the urban ghetto areas, and the need for jobs for the appallingly unprepared are two distinct and unrelated societal problems. These problems require solutions that are mutually exclusive. To use individuals for instruction, who themselves may border on illiteracy, for the dual purpose of employing them and easing the teacher shortage is

[40] Frank Riessman, "The New Anti-Poverty Ideology," *Teachers College Record* 68: 107–119, November 1966.

[41] Arthur Pearl and Frank Riessman, *New Careers for the Poor*, New York: The Free Press (Crowell-Collier and Macmillan, Inc.), 1965, p. 53. See also Frank Reissman, *Helping the Disadvantaged Pupil to Learn More Easily*, Englewood Cliffs, N.J.: Prentice-Hall, Inc., 1966, pp. 43–45.

[42] Joseph A. Califano, Jr., "Are Those on Welfare Employable?": Remarks before the Washington, D.C., Chapter of Sigma Delta Chi, April 19, 1967; reprinted in *Current*, June 1967, p. 54.

both delusory and dangerous. The rationale offered by proponents of this policy pathetically skirts the real problems: (1) the critical shortage of qualified teachers in the core areas of our cities, (2) the inferior education which racial and cultural isolation breed in our ghetto schools, and (3) the need for realistic programs of vocational education for our unemployed, undereducated, and disadvantaged adults. . . . Bootstrap operations will not serve to bring our disadvantaged children, youth, and adults into the mainstream of American life.[43]

Open Book Exam

1. In outline form, list some of the highlights in the desegregation issue since the 1954 Supreme Court decision for (a), (b), or (c).
   (a) in the Deep South
   (b) in the Border States
   (c) in Northern and Western urban areas.
2. Give a brief general statement concerning compulsory education laws (a) of 100 years ago, (b) 50 years ago, and (c) today. Explain why such laws are more necessary in an urban, industrial society than they were in a rural, agrarian culture.
3. To what degree is desegregation a racial issue and to what degree is it a social-economic issue? Explain why the social and technological changes (for example, the electronic industry) of the past few years have had an especially adverse effect on disadvantaged groups. What specific educational readjustments do these changes require?
4. Report on the particular problems of some non-Negro racial or national minority group, for example, the American Indian, the Puerto Rican, the Mexican, the Chinese, the Nisei.
5. Should educational programs in ghetto districts be radically different from those in middle-class areas? Stimulating materials on this topic may be found in Robert A. Dentler, Bernard Mackler, and Mary Ellen Warshauer, eds., *The Urban R's: Race Relations and the Problem in Urban Education*, New York: Frederick A. Praeger, Inc., 1968, pp. 198 ff.
6. Visit a poverty-stricken family with children and report on the particular handicaps experienced by these children.
7. Report on some "poor little *rich* child," who, though supplied with ample physical accommodations, is lacking in parental concern or companionship.
8. Suppose you belong to a permanent minority (that is, the Negro, the Mexican, the Indian) who can never hope to muster 51 percent of the votes needed to secure political and social reforms—reforms in perfect accord with democratic ideals. As a member of such a group, what tactics would you employ in order to achieve a fuller measure of justice?
9. Discuss the relative merits of the two ideals (a) Negro independence via black autonomy and (b) Negro achievement via integration with whites.

[43] Daniel Tanner and Lauren N. Tanner, "Teacher Aide—A Job for Anyone in Our Ghetto Schools," *Teachers College Record* 69: 743–751, May 1968.

10. Discuss the following statement (a thesis of Eli Ginsberg, Kenneth Clark, and others): "The Negro potential is tremendous, and Americans must learn to look upon the Negro community as if it were an undeveloped country waiting to be pioneered and developed."
11. Discuss the following examples of "circular reasoning":

    Negroes are too ignorant to learn, therefore they should not go to school; they do not go to school, therefore they are too ignorant to learn. Negroes are shiftless, therefore they are unable to find jobs; they are unable to find jobs, therefore they are shiftless. Negroes are poor and destitute, therefore they do not respect middle-class moral standards; they do not respect middle-class moral standards, therefore they are poor and destitute.

    How can we escape these vicious circles? The answer is that "Negroes" and "they" are vague and indefinite terms—terms that refer to "some" but not to "all" members of the group. The solution to the problem will come as we concentrate on the "some," and give special help to those among the destitute and downtrodden who show reasonable promise of rising to higher social, economic, and cultural levels. Although the number of persons in the lowest socioeconomic group who have such potential may not appear to be large at present, with persistent effort we may be confident that this number will gradually increase, until the same proportion of Negroes as of whites may realize their full potential.

Chapter 3
RELIGIOUS EDUCATION IN AN OPEN SOCIETY

Separation of Church and State

3.1 INTRODUCTION: THE AMERICAN TRADITION OF CHURCH AND STATE

In a pluralistic society no church has a privileged position, and the state refrains from any positive or negative intervention into the religious beliefs of its citizens. The only exceptions are cases in which religious beliefs upset the peace and order of society. Thus in *Davis v. Beason,* 133 U.S. 333 (1890), the Court classified bigamy and polygamy as crimes, not as religious rights. In *Zucht v. King,* 260 U.S. 174 (1922), the Court declared that school officials have a constitutional right and responsibility to require vaccination as a means of protecting public health.

However, the Court has consistently refused to act as an arbiter as to whether a religious belief is true or false. In *Watson v. Jones,* 13 Wallace, 679 (1872), which dealt with a dispute between two Louisville Presbyterian church factions, the Court held that the freedom and independence of churches would be in grave danger if *the Court* undertook to define religious heresy or orthodoxy or to decide which of two factions was the "true faith." A somewhat similar opinion is found in *Kedroff v. Saint Nicholas Cathedral,* 344 U.S. 94 (1952). Again, although laws against the fraudulent use of the mail are constitutional, the Court in *United States v. Ballard,* 322 U.S. 78 (1944), ruled that secular authorities may not use such laws to determine the truth of religious claims and beliefs—in this case, the "I am" movement; for, no matter how "preposterous" or "incredible" these claims may be, religious beliefs are not subject to findings of "truth" by fact-finding bodies.

Wherever possible, the Court has sought to accommodate secular laws to religious traditions. In *McGowan v. Maryland* and three other similar cases, 366 U.S. 420 (1961), the Court upheld the constitutionality of "Sunday Closing Laws" on the grounds that such laws were "preeminently secular" and could thus be upheld as general welfare regulations. "To say that the States cannot prescribe Sunday as a day of rest for these purposes [that is, as a day of relaxation for all citizens] solely because centuries ago such laws had their genesis in religion would give a constitutional interpretation of hostility to the public welfare rather than one of mere separation of church and state."

In a study of the American tradition of church and state, it is well to recall that 1789 is a halfway mark between 1620 and 1958. During the colonial period, when European nationality groups were becoming firmly entrenched into various forms of nationalist church-states, the American colonies were pioneering in new directions. Briefly, the American movement toward a pluralistic society progressed through three stages:

RELIGIOUS ESTABLISHMENT

This meant that a state (or colony) gave financial support to one and only one church, and that the state enforced by law the public worship and doctrines of the established church, with punishment for nonadherents.

MULTIPLE ESTABLISHMENT

This took two forms. The earlier form granted freedom of worship to dissenting groups, but maintained tax support for the established church. As time went on, the relatively isolated colonial communities came to be populated, not only by Calvinists but by Lutherans, Mennonites, Quakers, Anglicans, and other diverse groups. Under multiple establishment, each local township was required to support a minister and a school, but the religious affiliation was to be determined by the majority within each local community. Under multiple establishment (or local option), everyone still paid a general tax for religion (and for education—which was considered an integral part of religion) but the way had been opened for all religious groups to participate equally in the privilege of the establishment.

DISESTABLISHMENT

As America continued to welcome immigrants from all racial, nationality, and religious groups, its common schools could no longer be built around narrow denominational lines. Emphasis shifted to the three R's, with the fourth R, religion, steadily reduced in emphasis.

The movement from (1) establishment, to (2) multiple establishment, to (3) disestablishment (separation of church and state) has been well stated by Butts and Cremin:

> In a society where religious freedom is allowed but where education must be religious, a common public school system for all children is well

> nigh impossible. In the eighteenth century prior to the Revolution the people cherished religious freedom and a diversity of religious education more than they cherished a common school system. To maintain religious freedom and at the same time achieve a common school system the people would have to decide to exclude religion from the common school and to nourish religion in their homes and churches. The American people finally decided to take this route in the nineteenth century, but they were not yet ready to do it in the colonial period. The only other alternative is to allow each religious group to control its own schools and to share in public funds. This alternative was also tried in the colonial period and in the nineteenth century, but it was soon realized that the common values of a democratic society could not be achieved by such divisive practices. And so this alternative was likewise abandoned. But in the colonial period diversity of religion and of nationality, which often went together, seemed more important than political or social community. Thus the state patterns of education established in the colonial period began to decline until community values were elevated again in the nineteenth century in the effort to establish a new nation devoted to freedom, equality, and democracy. . . .
>
> The principle of separation of church and state was one of the achievements necessary for the creation of the new society that was in process of formation with the opening of the Revolutionary period. . . . More and more people came to believe that freedom of religion requires the assumption that there are different religious roads to the good life and that genuine religious freedom requires that the state guarantee equal rights of conscience to all religious claimants with no distinctions. . . . The test of good citizenship is morality, not religious belief. Thus, when the colonists decided to renounce their connection with Britain and become Americans, they also decided that their differing religious beliefs could not be allowed to stand in the way of the common ties of good citizenship. They therefore moved to separate the state from all churches as well as from any one church so that all Americans could become equally good citizens in the eyes of the civil law and of the state.[1]

The movement in America from religious establishment to multiple establishment to disestablishment is part of a more general trend. In predemocratic societies, religious belief was generally held to be the foundation of morality and the keystone of social unity. But in modern times, religion is often a cause of disunity. Jew and Gentile, Catholic and Protestant, Hindu and Moslem, theist and atheist—such divisions are so pronounced that no one religion seems capable of forming a center for modern society. Most religions have taught that true progress is progress in charity, all other advances being secondary thereto. But because the religions of

[1] R. Freeman Butts and Lawrence A. Cremin, *A History of Education in American Culture,* New York: Holt, Rinehart and Winston, Inc., 1953, pp. 98–99, 152, 153. By permission.

mankind remain irreconcilably plural, science, art, and the secular state have at present taken charge of those interests that alone seem capable of knitting together the many divided groups.

But the state is not almighty, and we should not look to it for everything. In a free society the worth of the individual is supreme, and the great bulk of individual affairs lies outside the province of government. The modern state is indeed a center of unity; but in a free society the state enforces unity only in terms of the practical needs of communal living: Its only obligation is to keep its citizens together in peace and harmony. Citizens may be influenced by their churches, and indirectly churches may thus have an effect on state policies. But the state deals with its citizens as citizens, not as members of any special church or creed. History affords ample proof that, united with government, religion becomes legalistic or superstitious; united with religion, government becomes despotic or totalitarian.

In the United States, all attempts to set up any one religion as an exclusive faith have met with failure. Since Washington's day, Americans have recognized that ". . . the Government of the United States of America is not in any sense founded on the Christian religion."[2] The United States government is not a Christian, a Jewish, nor a Mohammedan nation; neither is it agnostic nor atheistic. Our democratic society is a cooperative, interactive society; and where we cannot agree on a set of beliefs, such beliefs cannot be a part of our democracy—except insofar as we are free to disagree. Which is to say: America is religiously pluralistic.

Does lack of reliance on a single viewpoint mean the absence of any viewpoint? Does loss of "faith" in an *exclusive* set of beliefs mean the complete lack of religious faith? Some think so. Others, like Elliot E. Cohen, believe it implies a new type of shared conviction:

> It seems to me that the free citizen, religious or nonreligious, does have at least one shared conviction. Whether he professes to believe in God, or professes not to believe in God, he has a conviction that there is no God but God. To put it another way: I think both the religious believer and the man of secular faith in the United States come very close to holding in their hearts the Hebraic commandment "Thou shalt have no other gods before Me." I take this to mean that whether one believes in some transcendent power or not, one does not believe that there is any

[2] U.S. Treaty with Tripoli, November 4, 1796, Article XI (Barlow translation). Concerning the authenticity of Article XI, read *Treaties and Other International Acts of the United States of America*, edited by Hunter Miller, Washington, D.C.: U.S. Government Printing Office, 1931, Vol. 2, pp. 349–385, especially pp. 365, 371–372, 384. Read also Leo Pfeffer, *The Liberties of an American: The Supreme Court Speaks*, Boston: The Beacon Press, 1956, pp. 31–46.

> idea, institution, or individual—a man, a nation, an "ism"—that man can accept as a God.[3]

The democratic citizen should be humble enough not to think of himself as God or as godlike, and he is on politically safe ground so long as he permits no group or institution to arrogate to itself the attributes of the divine.

We include the state among such institutions. The order of a democracy is not a single order of the state: It is a system of orders, some in conflict with others, some even in conflict with the state itself, as presently conceived. Like the lobby of a hotel, the state is a kind of hallway whose function is to connect the more private rooms and thus to serve as a common center of communication. But free men cannot allow the state to claim overriding allegiance in all things. For the religious man, God alone may have the final claim, and such a man may freely assert: "There is a higher law than the Constitution." For the scientist, Euclid's adage still stands: "There is no royal road to geometry." As for poetry and art, "Art for art's sake" may not represent the entire truth, but it points up the fact that creative endeavors cannot be genuine unless free. As Charles Morgan has said: "If art has anything to teach it is . . . that to mistake one supposed aspect of truth for Truth itself and so to imprison man's curiosity and aspiration in the dungeon of an ideology, is the unforgivable sin against the spirit of man."[4] If society is to enjoy the maximum benefits of the aspiring saint, the reflective scientist, or the creative artist, the state dare not dictate precisely how or what such men shall think or say. The sanctions of religion, the theories of science, and the creations of art cannot be coerced.

But they can be embraced in a free manner. Woven into the three-hundred-year-old fabric that clothes American society is a dominant pattern of self-reliance and independent thought. America is a strong nation because its citizens are courageous. They are courageous because they are free to disagree, to quarrel with authority, to challenge orthodoxy. Democratic society does not provide a cloistered world where the opinions or prejudices of any group are shielded from the criticism of others. Democracy is not for weaklings, nor for indoctrinated automatons. It is for citizens

[3] Elliot E. Cohen, "The Free American Citizen, 1952," *Commentary*, 14: 219–230, at 225, September 1952. By permission. Compare Paul Tillich, *My Search for an Absolute*, New York: Simon and Schuster, Inc., 1967. But see also Robert N. Bellah, and others, "Civil Religion in America," in Donald R. Cutler, ed., *The Religious Situation: 1968*, Boston: The Beacon Press, 1968, pp. 330–398.

[4] Charles Morgan, *Liberties of the Mind*, New York: Crowell-Collier and Macmillan, Inc., 1951, p. 91. Compare Archibald MacLeish, "The Muses' Sterner Laws," *New Republic*, 128: 16–18, July 13, 1953; Ben Shahn, "Non-conformity," *Atlantic*, 200: 36–41, September 1957.

of independent convictions, but citizens who have genuine respect and affection toward others—even toward those whose views they detest.

In a democracy every citizen wears a crown. Each citizen is a trustee of freedom. Hence, because education is equally significant to democracy and to religion, contemporary Americans face such questions as the following. Can religious instruction be made a part of education without substituting indoctrination for learning, or without doing violence to our traditional separation of church and state? Can religion be taught in public schools without partiality toward some religious beliefs as against others? Can public funds be allocated to parochial schools without breaking down our traditional separation of church and state? Let us hope we can discuss these questions openly, fairly, fearlessly, and intelligently.

3.2 SUPREME COURT AND SUPREME LAW: AN AMERICAN CONTRIBUTION*

Edmond N. Cahn

[The development of the American constitution gave a new turn to the age-old philosophical] antithesis between *permanence* and *change*. . . . In the experience of the Anglo-Americans from the middle of the seventeenth century down to the time of *Marbury v. Madison,* written constitutions proved very short-lived. Of course, many adopted since 1803 have likewise fallen into history's wastebasket. But the naked fact that the United States Constitution has survived for more than a century and a half implies that something special was accomplished between 1787 and 1803 to make it an exception. Somehow or other, a sufficient balance was attained in the tension between the principle of permanence and the principle of change. If such was the case, the American solution, although it may or may not be suitable to the government of other countries, certainly merits careful study. It may constitute a major contribution to the technique of successful government. Let me therefore suggest the outlines of the historic turn which I see initiated in 1787 at the Constitutional Convention and consumated in 1803 by *Marbury v. Madison.* It was a turn in the theory of the written constitution, which may be summarized:

 (The late Edmond N. Cahn, author of many books and articles, was on the faculty of the New York Law School from 1945 to 1965.)

	As to Objective	*As to Content*	*As to Sanction*
From	perpetuity	immutability	appeal to heaven
To	efficacy	adaptation	appeal to the courts. . . .

[For many centuries the doctrine that social and moral beliefs are immutable was defended on the basis of natural law.] We owe gratitude to the long line of libertarians and egalitarians who expressed their ideals in the language of natural law. But gratitude, becoming though it is, is no substitute for honest and realistic thinking. History shows us that natural law is a flag that anyone can nail to his mast. It has been used to justify slavery as well as freedom, persecution as well as fairness, exploitation as well as equality. In ancient Athens the Sophists contended that nothing conformed so much to natural law as homosexuality, else why would so many men and women practice it? As for the apartheid program in South Africa, cannot the Nationalists contend, as Plato did, that only those whom nature has endowed with superior ethnic stock and qualified to rule should exercise political power? How often have tyrants boasted that the strong are designed by nature to dominate the weak? . . . .

Since natural law systems are so numerous and diverse, one wonders how they dare lay claim, as they do, to being fixed, eternal and immutable. On certain psychological types the effect of the mere claim is curiously soothing. The sequence of verbal sedatives—words like "fixed, eternal and immutable"—seems to bring an almost hypnotic repose to minds that are troubled in a world of flux. If you are desperately unsure about your convictions, it may relax and comfort you to call them laws of nature and thereby summon the whole physical universe to their support. Oddly enough, at the other extreme, if you feel quite dogmatic about your convictions, you are likely to do much the same thing, that is, insist that whatever you believe the entire cosmos is required to practice. Thus, at least in our time, many statements of natural law theory amount to a sort of cosmic imperialism, taking in more territory than the Russian claims to the moon. It makes no difference whether what they cloak is an extreme incertitude or an extreme certitude, for both of these may be symptoms of one and the same pathological condition. . . . Judge Jerome Frank was right when he remarked, "Man does not find his 'oughts' spelled out for him in nature, but puts them there." . . . .[5]

[Relying on the abandoned medieval theory of natural law,] aggressive

[5] Editor's Note: From Locke to Dewey, liberals have often been branded as "nominalists" or "relativists" whose ideas are "contrary to natural law." Perhaps a new climate of opinion will occur when such critics discover their own confusion—a confusion clearly stated by the great contemporary Neo-Scholastic, Father Dondeyne:

> . . . there are two fundamental ways of conceiving the natural law.
>
> 1. Natural law may be conceived as a whole of abstract, ever-present rules that

clerics present their case in terms of a choice between "God and Caesar," implying that a decision against their claims would be tantamount to a decision against God. This is completely fallacious. Our American principle of separation gives the true picture. It designates the separated entities not as "God and Caesar" but as "church and state." A free government is never so bad as Caesar and a church administered by mortal men is never so good as God.

The Founding Fathers, particularly Thomas Jefferson and James Madison, defined two distinct aspects of the American doctrine of separation: one negative and legal, the other positive and religious. They formalized the legal aspect through the First Amendment, which not only guaranteed the "free exercise" of religion but also prescribed that government "shall make no law respecting an establishment of religion." . . . . [On the negative side, the First Amendment means that our government must] attend to its own affairs and avoid intruding into the realm of religion.

Outside the margin of the law, however, one finds a wholly different aspect of the matter, that is, the positive or religious side. According to the American tradition, churches separated from the state are a religious necessity. We hold it self-evident that as long as a church speaks God's message and exemplifies God's way, it can require no assistance from the political power. If, then, the church seeks political help, it demonstrates to that extent that it deserves none.

---

are found among all peoples. This "greatest common denominator" theory constantly decreases in content as ethnology progresses.

2. Natural law may be conceived as the standard, the ideal which positive legislation must pursue in relation to a particular development of civilization, in order that its laws may be worthy of man and just. In the first sense, right to work, right to education can hardly be considered as a part of the natural law; but they are such in the second sense of natural law.

—Albert Dondeyne, *Faith and the World*, Pittsburgh: Duquesne University Press, 1963, p. 232. See also John Cogley, ed., *Natural Law and Modern Society*, Cleveland: The World Publishing Company, 1963, especially pp. 199–276.

See also F. C. Carney, "Outline of a Natural Law Procedure for Christian Ethics," *The Journal of Religion* 47: 26–38, January 1967; Margaret MacDonald, "Natural Rights," *Proceedings of the Aristotelian Society* 67: 225–250, 1946–1947; reprinted in May Brodbeck, ed., *Readings in the Philosophy of the Social Sciences*, New York: Crowell-Collier and Macmillan, Inc., 1968; Carl J. Friedrich, "Man the Measure: Personal Knowledge and the Quest for Natural Law," in *Intellect and Hope*, T. A. Langford and W. H. Poteat, eds., Durham, N.C.: Duke University Press, 1968, pp. 91–110.

As does the common law, *Crucial Issues in Education* consists of case studies. The overarching principles, or the "natural laws," which help to decide the outcome of such cases, are not clearly known. But we are more likely to discover such principles, or laws, if we begin with concrete issues and later generalize, than if we begin with what (in a prescientific, predemocratic age) were presumed to be eternal or natural laws, and then make artificial and often misleading deductions from these. On this point read Carl J. Friedrich, *Rational Decision*, New York: Atherton Press, 1964, pp. 69f., 122f.

To the believing church member, the separation of church and state is more than a barrier erected to restrain arrogant clergymen. It is also a solemn affirmation of confidence and pride in the independence of his church. The firm trust which our ancestors declared in the self-sustaining efficacy of the church was the proudest philosophy religion had ever evoked in a political society. It was a radically new idea not borrowed from England, which maintained an established church.

The new American nation embraced this new concept not only because its founders desired freedom of worship, not only because they detested the meannesses and dreaded the hostilities of sectarian conflict but—above all else—because they believed with complete fervor that religion, as Madison said, "flourishes in greater purity without than with the aid of government." . . .

[Like Jefferson and Madison] we consider the wall of separation indispensable to both church and state, and to our country's freedom.

Indispensable we know it is to the welfare of the churches; but why is it equally indispensable to the political state? Because today, more than ever before, the government of the most powerful democracy on earth needs the critical scrutiny of independent churches, their visions, exhortations, and unsparing rebukes. Organized religion knows no higher duty than to maintain the enduring ideals and universal values that exceed the jurisdiction of any earthly power, transcend the widest political boundaries, and defy the currents of popular opinion. The louder the voice of the people in a society, the more it requires the inner monitions of religious conscience. . . . In a democratic society like ours, law is tethered to the opinions and moral standards of the general public, and if religion fails to lead and edify these, the advancement of law will inevitably suffer. . . .

Here then is how a genuine effulgence of faith might illumine the road of the law. From ancient times, religion has exalted the value of individual personality and has summoned men to understand their neighbors as nearly as possible after the manner of God's understanding, for—we are told—in his eyes all men, created in his image, are equal and alike, yet every man is distinct, unique, and filled with the splendor of human dignity. This is religion's own insight. Applied wholeheartedly in the law, it could help us shape decisions of individualized and creative justice. Applied throughout our national life, it could hallow the pursuit of a free, righteous, and compassionate society. . . .

Of course, the minorities need and will always need the legal shield of the First Amendment. It safeguards their elementary rights not to suffer for believing or disbelieving, their right not to be persecuted. But the religious majority also have a certain right which the Founding Fathers were concerned to protect. Neither Madison nor Jefferson belonged to any disadvantaged or persecuted sect, neither was impelled by any personal suffering or deprivation to demand the separation of church and state. While they sympathized with the oppressed Virginia Baptists, they never thought of joining them. The legacy they intended for us is much more than the indispensable [minority] right not to be persecuted. It consists as well in the precious [majority] right not to participate in inflicting persecution. As representative government would implicate all citizens if it compelled uniformity of prayer—or, in Roger Williams' words, committed "spiritual rape," the majority as well as the minority draw protection from the prohibitions of the First Amendment. The Amendment makes it ethically safe to belong to the majority. By separating church and state, it assures the rarest, and perhaps the most excellent, of all civil rights: the constitutional right not to persecute.

3.3 THE MEANING OF RELIGIOUS PLURALISM*

Franklin H. Littell

It is a mistake to suppose that the American experiment in religious liberty and secular government derived from practical necessity or from pragmatic response to the problems of religious diversity. As the debates in the state conventions that ratified the Federal Constitution make clear, the new and radical approach to the relations of church and state derived from a view of church and a view of government quite different from that which had obtained for centuries in Christendom. The Rhode Island resolution, adopted at the point when both that state and North Carolina refused to ratify until basic liberties were guaranteed, bears quotation.

> That religion, or the duty which we owe to the Creator, and the manner of discharging it, can be directed only by reason and conviction, and not by force and violence; and therefore all men have a natural, equal and unalienable right to the exercise of religion according to the dictates of conscience; and that no particular religious sect or society ought to be favored or established, by law, in preference to others.

---

* Franklin H. Littell, "The Churches and the Body Politic," *Daedalus* 96: 22–42, Winter 1967. Reprinted by permission of *Daedalus*, Journal of the American Academy of Arts and Sciences, Boston, Mass.

Franklin H. Littell is President of Iowa Wesleyan College and author of *From State Church to Pluralism* (1962).

As believing men, which most of them were, and as champions of the full, free, and informed discussion that is the lifeblood of liberty, they left open the possibility that diverse creeds might be able to prove their case and win their way to general voluntary support. . . . This freed the church to be what the radical Reformation called "a True Church," a community of faithful people in no sense beholden to or intimidated by outside force in matters of faith. And, of barely secondary importance, it freed the state to be what government is intended to be: a human invention, limited in ultimate claims, modest in use of power, established to achieve specific ends—in a word, theologically speaking, a "creature."

Against the background of this historical development, the twin perils of dogmatic secularism and "Christian America" stand clearly defined. The ideology of secularism, always to be distinguished carefully from the historical process of secularization, is chiefly important for its influence among the intellectuals. Only occasionally has it distorted the American experiment in religious liberty, although a few published opinions in the U.S. Supreme Court report give concrete reality to the threat. Far more general is the casual acceptance of the premises of social establishment of religion, of the claims of culture-religion. Here even some outstanding church leaders have preferred to defend the mythology of "Christian America" rather than to accept the perils of religious liberty, voluntaryism, and pluralism. The public statements of such men of distinction as Henry P. Van Dusen and Reinhold Niebuhr criticizing the Supreme Court's decisions in the prayer cases attest to this. Most pertinent, however, is the way in which spokesmen for the radical right, such as Robert Welch, Carl McIntire, and George Wallace, have attempted to make defense of "Christian America" [the earlier tradition of white, Anglo-Saxon, Protestant America] a major bulwark of reactionary politics.

Quite plainly there are many who have not yet accepted the unique character of the American experiment in religious liberty and voluntaryism. . . . [where the] kinds of political cooperation open to Jews, Catholics, Protestants, and all men of good will are many and various. . . . [and where the] style of a universal spirit of dialogue is replacing the old order of coercion and arbitrament by the knife. The mind locked in a fortress, defending an ethnic complex called "Christendom," would resist such encounter by writ and by law. The mind that is fearless in faith and open to the dialogue will welcome it; it will accept the truth that a religion that cannot win its case and grow on its merits is unworthy of the future.[6]

---

[6] Editor's Note: Compare the following statement by Peter Berger:

While most spokesmen of the churches habitually deplore the secularization of Western civilization and, in one way or another, look back nostalgically on the time when (supposedly) Christendom was a reality, Bonhoeffer bids Christians to welcome secularization as an expression of the maturity and liberty of modern man. He also perceives (correctly, it seems to this writer) that secularization has its historical roots in the Biblical tradition itself. By denuding the cosmos of its divinity and placing God totally beyond its confines, the Biblical tradition prepared the way for the process we now call secularization. As Max Weber has shown convincingly, Protestantism played a key role in this modern development. It was Protestantism even more than Renaissance humanism which inaugurated the great process which Weber called "disenchantment." As Weber put it:

> That great historic process in the development of religions, the elimination of magic from the world which had begun with the old Hebrew prophets and, in conjunction with Hellenistic scientific thought, had repudiated all magical means to salvation as superstition and sin, came here to its logical conclusion. . . .

As both Dietrich Bonhoeffer and Simone Weil saw very clearly, the consciousness of abiding safely in the bosom of the church (which Simone Weil called the "patriotism of the church"—and Bonhoeffer scathingly called "cheap grace") is one of the most serious obstacles to an honest confrontation with the Christian faith. . . . The church proclaims, possesses a certain faith. This faith is addressed to each individual, in his unique existence before God. He cannot hold this faith except as the unique individual he is. As a substitute to this painful acquisition of faith, the individual can instead identify with the church, the social collectivity which. . . holds the faith as an ideology. His real act of decision, then, is not toward the faith but toward the church that claims to possess it. By identifying with the church he deludes himself into thinking that he has made a decision of faith. Actually he has only joined a club and accepted its bylaws. . . .

[But democracy encourages each citizen to think for himself, to make up his own mind about important matters. This means that he] must be totally open toward the world in all its possibilities. . . . [It] means a deliberate surrender of those religious pretensions which Dostoyevsky's Grand Inquisitor summed up in his phrase "miracle, mystery and authority." The Christian is not one possessed by irresistible forces from the beyond. He is a human being and remains one. It is as a human being that he enters into conversation with others. . . .

—Peter L. Berger, *The Precarious Vision,* New York: Doubleday & Company, Inc., 1961, pp. 177f.

Too often the First Amendment has been praised because it has allowed room for harmless rituals, meaningless myths and outmoded beliefs. Today's younger theologians are praising it because it permits the reformation of old beliefs, and the formulation of radically different outlooks to fit the needs of our technological age. On this point Michael Novak has written:

> [Today] religion appears to be struggling not so much with doubt or unbelief as with irrelevance. . . . The Christianity of the present has, of necessity shed the securities promised by the Judaeo-Christian world view of the past. The Christian today knows how profound is the darkness in which he has been left. A greater modesty, a greater sense of contingency and darkness, a greater sense of comradeship with non-Christians do not ill become Christians. What is being abandoned is not Christianity but the cultural world view that was its first matrix, its cocoon, for the first two millennia of its existence. . . . To step outside Christian institutions is not *ipso facto* to step outside Christian values.

—Michael Novak, "Christianity: Renewed or Slowly Abandoned?" *Daedalus* 96: 237–266, Winter 1967.

Sectarian Religious Instruction

3.4 INTRODUCTION: COMMITMENT VERSUS OBJECTIVITY*

Does "teaching" religion mean "teaching about" religion in an objective, impartial manner? Or does it require the "teaching of" a particular religious belief, so as to help establish commitment to that belief? Stated otherwise, if we are not teaching commitment, are we really teaching religion?

Let us briefly contrast the two opposing views, as they pertain to Christianity. Kierkegaard and others argue that objectivity is unchristian. A Christian must commit all his heart, soul, mind, and strength to the love of God (*Mark* 12:30) and can never be uncommitted or "objective" concerning the existence, commands, and promises of God. The conclusion of a religious belief is not so much a conclusion as a resolution. Hence, anyone who posits inspiration of the Scriptures, or of his Church, as a believer does, must consistently consider every critical deliberation, whether for or against, as a misdirection, as a temptation of the spirit. To allow reason to determine the content of religious doctrine is a form of idolatry, because it puts man himself in the place of God. To avoid this form of idolatry, the religious man forsakes pride in his reason, recognizing that God transcends the world and is wholly other than man, to be obeyed and worshipped, but not to be understood. St. Paul wrote: "Where is the wise man? . . . Has not God made foolish the wisdom of the world? . . . For Jews demand signs and Greeks seek wisdom, but we preach Christ crucified, a stumbling-block to Jews and folly to Gentiles" (I *Cor.* 1:20–

* These introductory paragraphs borrow heavily from Albert Guerard, *Bottle in the Sea*, Cambridge: Harvard University Press, 1954, Chap. I; from L. Harold DeWold, *The Religious Revolt Against Reason*, New York: Harper & Row, Publishers, 1949; and from Pascal: *Meditations*.

See also Robert Hanvey, "In Pursuit of Reasons," *School Review*, 69: 127–135, Summer 1961.

23). Paul delighted in paradox, and spoke of the Christian ". . . as sorrowful, yet always rejoicing; as poor, yet making many rich; as having nothing and yet possessing everything." (II *Cor.* 6:8–10). A paradox is more than a wonderful way of speaking: It is a way of speaking about the wonderful. In short, faith is not a form of knowledge. It is a direction of the will—a feeling of passionate concern, unswerving dedication, whole-hearted commitment. There are depths of feeling and heights of aspiration that reach beyond the powers of reason.

The rationalist admits that there are moments when we must let ourselves go, in love, in poetic rapture, in mystic communion. But we must be sure that the light that leads us is not darkness, and we can be reasonably sure of this only if we follow St. Paul's injunction to prove (probe) all things. The chief troubles in the world today are not caused by lack of faith, but by too much unreasoning faith in areas where reason should be free to bring order out of chaos. The truly religious person is as a little child (*Mark* 10:15; *Luke* 18:17) who finds delight in wonder, curiosity, expectancy, and who is continually surprised and reverent before the Mystery around him. A child does not look upon his beliefs as ultimate or final, but is ever eager to search for new possibilities. Thus we should approach religion in the spirit of Isaiah's "Come now, let us reason together, sayeth Jehovah" (*Isa.* 1:18). When Paul exhorts us to commit our lives to God, he adds "which is your *reasonable* service." Then he continues "Do not be conformed to this world but be transformed by the renewal of your *mind*, that you may *prove* what *is* the will of God, what is good and acceptable and perfect" (*Romans* 12:1–2). Man's mind should be regarded as God-given, and the use of reason may gratefully be regarded as the employment of a divine instrument. The injunction "Thou shalt love thy God . . . with all thy *mind* . . ." (*Matt.* 12:30) means to devote the mind at its best to the object of love. Certainly a mind that has forgotten its own essential loyalty to truth is not a mind at its best.

As for paradoxes, they should be understood as rhetorical devices for gaining attention, and for making men think about neglected aspects of experience. Thus "whoever would save his life will lose it" (*Mark* 8:35) implies no logical contradiction, since the saving and the losing have obviously to do with different levels of being.

And what are the alternatives to reason, reasonableness, tolerance, and open discussion? The alternatives are brute force, fanatical sects warring against one another, each "proud" of its own half-truth, each "perverse" in its blindness to other viewpoints. But the reasonable man is always willing to weigh and measure his own commitments against alternative commitments; for in this manner his own commitments gain in breadth and depth of meaning; and in this way the spirit of truth is both counsellor and comforter (*John* 14:16).

A few sentences from Pascal's *Thoughts* nicely summarize the two opposing points of view:

> Man is visibly made to think; that is his whole dignity and his whole merit.
>
> Reason commands us much more imperiously than a master; for if we disobey the one we are unfortunate, but if we disobey the other we are fools. [But]
>
> It is the heart which feels God, and not the reason. For that is what faith is, God touching the heart, not the reason.
>
> There is nothing so conformable to reason as the disavowal of reason in those things which belong to faith. And nothing so contrary to reason as the disavowal of reason in the things that do not belong to faith. There are two excesses equally dangerous: to exclude reason, and to admit reason alone.

Among the citizens of our pluralistic society are those who believe that our public schools overemphasize reason to the detriment of religious commitment and faith. Such persons firmly defend open discussion and freedom of dissent in *politics,* and maintain the need for critical thinking in *science;* but they nevertheless feel that such freedom and openmindedness have little or no place in *religion.* For such persons, the characteristic subject matter of religious education consists of divine revelation. These, by their very nature, should be taught as authoritative truths, not as questionable hypotheses subject to rational inquiry nor to empirical verification.

Selections 3.5 through 3.11 deal with ways in which our government has accommodated itself to such beliefs.

3.5 PUBLIC TRANSPORTATION FOR PAROCHIAL SCHOOL STUDENTS? YES.*

Hugo L. Black and Others

The "establishment of religion" clause of the First Amendment means at least this: Neither a state nor the Federal Government can set up a church. Neither can pass laws which aid one religion, aid all religions, or

* Hugo L. Black, Majority (5:4) opinion, *Everson v. Board of Education,* 330 U.S. 1 (1946). Footnotes not included in this short excerpt.

The New Jersey statute in question authorized reimbursement to parents for the transportation of children to and from schools—including payment to parents whose children attended parochial schools.

The "Yes" in the title does not mean that the Supreme Court *recommends* public

prefer one religion over another. Neither can force nor influence a person to go to or to remain away from church against his will or force him to profess a belief or disbelief in any religion. No person can be punished for entertaining or professing religious beliefs or disbeliefs, for church attendance or non-attendance. No tax in any amount, large or small, can be levied to support any religious activities or institutions, whatever they may be called, or whatever form they may adopt to teach or practice religion. Neither a state nor the Federal Government can, openly or secretly, participate in the affairs of any religious organizations or groups and *vice versa*. . . .

New Jersey cannot consistently with the "establishment of religion" clause of the First Amendment contribute tax-raised funds to the support of any institution which teaches the tenets and faith of any church. On the other hand, other language of the amendment commands that New Jersey cannot hamper its citizens in the free exercise of their own religion. Consequently, it cannot exclude individual Catholics, Lutherans, Mohammedans, Baptists, Jews, Methodists, Non-believers, Presbyterians, or the members of any other faith, *because of their faith, or lack of it,* from receiving the benefits of public-welfare legislation. While we do not mean to intimate that a state could not provide transportation only to children attending public schools, we must be careful, in protecting the citizens of New Jersey against state-established churches, to be sure that we do not inadvertently prohibit New Jersey from extending its general state law benefits to all its citizens without regard to their religious belief.

Measured by these standards [we view the provision of bus fares to parochial as well as to public school students as analogous to] . . . such general government services as ordinary police and fire protection, connections for sewage disposal, public highways and sidewalks. Of course, cutting off church schools from these services, so separate and so indisputably marked off from the religious function, would make it far more difficult for the schools to operate. But such is obviously not the purpose of the First Amendment. That Amendment requires the state to be a neutral in its relations with groups of religious believers and non-believers; it does not

---

transportation for parochial school students; it means only that the Court declares that the U.S. Constitution *permits* such transportation. The dissenting opinions indicate that this is a qualified "Yes." Furthermore, some state constitutions are very stringent with respect to using public funds to aid religion; and, following the 1946 ruling, several state courts (e.g., Missouri, Oregon, Washington) have interpreted their own state constitutions as *prohibiting* the use of state funds to transport parochial school students; whereas other states (e.g., Pennsylvania, Wisconsin) have passed laws (or amended their state constitutions) to *permit* such use.

See also Virgil C. Blum, S.J., *Freedom in Education: Federal Aid for All Children*, New York: Doubleday & Company, Inc., 1965, *versus* Edd Doerr, *The Conspiracy that Failed*, Washington, D.C.: Americans United for Separation of Church and State, 1968.

require the state to be their adversary. State power is no more to be used so as to handicap religions than it is to favor them.

Mr. Justice Jackson, Dissenting:

[The First Amendment] was intended not only to keep the states' hands out of religion, but to keep religion's hands off the state, and, above all, to keep bitter religious controversy out of public life by denying to every denomination any advantage from getting control of public policy or the public purse. Those great ends I cannot but think are immeasurably compromised by today's decision.

This policy of our Federal Constitution has never been wholly pleasing to most religious groups. They all are quick to invoke its protections; they all are irked when they feel its restraints. . . .

But we cannot have it both ways. Religious teaching cannot be a private affair when the state seeks to impose regulations which infringe on it indirectly, and a public affair when it comes to taxing citizens of one faith to aid another, or those of no faith to aid all. If these principles seem harsh in prohibiting aid to Catholic education, it must not be forgotten that it is the same Constitution that alone assures Catholics the right to maintain these schools at all when predominant local sentiment would forbid them. *Pierce v. Society of Sisters*, 268 U.S. 510. Nor should I think that those who have done so well without this aid would want to see this separation between Church and State broken down. If the state may aid these religious schools, it may therefore regulate them. Many groups have sought aid from tax funds only to find that it carried political controls with it. Indeed this Court has declared that "It is hardly lack of due process for the Government to regulate that which it subsidizes." *Wickard v. Filburn*, 317 U.S. 111, 131.[7]

---

[7] Editor's Note: Compare the following statement by Andrew Jacobs, Roman Catholic layman, and (1949) U.S. Congressman from Indiana:

> Religious freedom is a two-way street. We are free to establish and utilize our parochial schools or utilize public schools, as we choose. But the right to establish private schools does not imply the right to public financial support thereof. We have the right to build and maintain our churches, but not to build or maintain them with public funds. Our parochial schools are an adjunct of our religion, established for educational use instead of using public schools, solely for sake of the child's religious training.
>
> As long as we have the same right to send our children to public schools as anyone else, we are not discriminated against, and as Catholics we do not have a right to a separate publicly supported school system, nor does any other group of people have such right. . . .
>
> [The] legal right to maintain parochial schools does not establish the right to public maintenance. To so argue is to say with one breath, our parochial schools are in the public school category, for the purpose of public aid; while in the next breath we stoutly maintain our right to parochial schools for the purpose of religiously training our children. However, when we put our parochial schools in the public school category for one purpose, we do so for all purposes, and we must

3.6 SECTARIAN RELIGIOUS INSTRUCTION WITH PUBLIC TAX MONEY? NO.*

Hugo L. Black and Others

In 1940 interested members of the Jewish, Roman Catholic, and a few of the Protestant faiths formed a voluntary association called the Champaign Council on Religious Education. They obtained permission from the Board of Education to offer classes in religious instruction to public school pupils in grades four to nine inclusive. Classes were made up of pupils whose parents signed printed cards, requesting that their children be permitted to attend; they were held weekly, thirty minutes for the lower grades, forty-five minutes for the higher. The council employed the religious teachers at no expense to the school authorities, but the instructors were subject to approval and supervision of the superintendent of schools. The classes were taught in three separate religious groups by Protestant teachers, Catholic priests, and a Jewish rabbi, although for the past several years there have apparently been no classes instructed in the Jewish religion. Classes were conducted in the regular classrooms of the school building. Students who did not choose to take the religious instruction were not released from public school duties; they were required to leave their classrooms and go to some other place in the school building for pursuit of their secular studies. On the other hand, students who were released from secular study for the religious instructions were required to be present at the religious classes. Reports of their presence or absence were to be made to their secular teachers.

The foregoing facts, without reference to others that appear in the record, show the use of tax-supported property for religious instruction and the close cooperation between the school authorities and the religious council in promoting religious education. The operation of the state's compulsory education system thus assists and is integrated with the program of religious instruction carried on by separate religious sects. Pupils compelled by law to go to school for secular education are released in part

---

then comply with public school regulations which forbid sectarian religious teachings therein.

The issue is clear. Either you keep parochial schools and maintain them or take public funds and convert them into public schools, and they will then no longer serve the religious purpose for which they were established.

—"On Public Financial Aid to Parochial Schools," Extension of Remarks by Hon. Hugo S. Sims, July 7, 1949, *Congressional Record*, 81st Congress, 1st Session, Appendix, Vol. 95, pp. A4358–A4359.

* Hugo L. Black, Majority opinion (8–1 decision), *Illinois, ex rel McCollum v. Board of Education*, 333 U.S. 203 (1948). Footnotes omitted from these excerpts.

from their legal duty upon the condition that they attend the religious classes. This is beyond all question a utilization of the tax-established and tax-supported public school system to aid religious groups to spread their faith. And it falls squarely under the ban of the First Amendment. . . .

Mr. Justice Frankfurter, Concurring:

Separation means separation, not something less. Jefferson's metaphor in describing the relation between Church and State speaks of a "wall of separation," not of a fine line easily overstepped. The public school is at once the symbol of our democracy and the most pervasive means for promoting our common destiny. In no activity of the State is it more vital to keep out divisive forces than in its schools, to avoid confusing, not to say fusing, what the Constitution sought to keep strictly apart. "The great American principle of eternal separation"—Elihu Root's phrase bears repetition—is one of the vital reliances of our Constitutional system for assuring unities among our people stronger than our diversities. . . .

Mr. Justice Reed, Dissenting:

The phrase "an establishment of religion" may have been intended by Congress to be aimed only at a state church. . . .

Mr. Jefferson, as one of the founders of the University of Virginia, a school which from its establishment in 1819 has been wholly governed, managed and controlled by the State of Virginia, was faced with the same problem that is before this Court today: the question of the constitutional limitation upon religious education in public schools. In his annual report as Rector, to the President and Directors of the Literary Fund, dated October 7, 1822, approved by the Visitors of the University of whom Mr. Madison was one, Mr. Jefferson set forth his views at some length. These suggestions of Mr. Jefferson were adopted and Ch. II, § 1, of the Regulations of the University of October 4, 1824, provided that:

> Should the religious sects of this State, or any of them, according to the invitation held out to them, establish within, or adjacent to, the precincts of the University, schools for instruction in the religion of their sect, the students of the University will be free, and expected to attend religious worship at the establishment of their respective sects, in the morning, and in time to meet their school in the University at its stated hour.

Thus, the "wall of separation between Church and State" that Mr. Jefferson built at the University which he founded did not exclude religious education from that school. The difference between the generality of his statements on the separation of Church and State and the specificity of his conclusions on education are considerable. A rule of law should not be drawn from a figure of speech. . . .[8]

[8] Editor's Note: Extensive excerpts from Jefferson on this topic may be found in *Crusade Against Ignorance: Thomas Jefferson on Education*, Gordon C. Lee, ed., New York: Bureau of Publications, Teachers College, Columbia University, 1961.

3.7 RELEASED TIME FOR RELIGIOUS INSTRUCTION? YES.*

William O. Douglas and Others

New York City has a program which permits its public schools to release students during the school day so that they may leave the school buildings and school grounds and go to religious centers for religious instruction or devotional exercises. A student is released on written request of his parents.

The basic problem is neatly summarized by Zechariah Chaffee, Jr.:

> We have made our choice and chosen the dream of Roger Williams. It was not a choice between a good dream and a bad dream, but between a good dream which on the whole works and a good dream which occasionally turned into a nightmare of the . . . hanging of Mary Dyer on Boston Common. Sometimes nostalgia for what we have given up creeps over us. Men sometimes lament, for instance, that our public schools are godless. Suppose we admit frankly that this is a loss to the public schools, that one very important part of our nature has to be wholly neglected in the place where we receive much of the shaping of our characters and minds. It is a price to pay, but we must look at all which we have bought thereby. We cannot reject a portion of the bargain and insist on keeping the rest. If the noble ideal of the Puritan had persisted, there would be no godless schools in Massachusetts and there would be nobody in her churches except Congregationalists. Through the choice which all of the United States has made, it becomes possible for men of many different faiths to live and work together for many noble ends without allowing their divisions in spiritual matters to become, as in the old days, unbridgeable chasms running through every aspect of human lives.
>
> —Zechariah Chaffee, Jr., *The Blessings of Liberty*, Philadelphia: J. B. Lippincott Company, 1956, pp. 265–266.

* William O. Douglas, Majority opinion (6–3 decision), *Zorach v. Clauson*, 343 U.S. 306 (1951). Footnotes and bibliography not included in these excerpts.

In *Religion and the Constitution* (Baton Rouge: Louisiana State University Press, 1964), Paul G. Kauper argues that the Supreme Court has taken three positions in interpreting the "no establishment of religion" clause of our Constitution:

1. the no-aid or strict separation theory: there can be no governmental support of religion and no legislation favorable to the cultivation of religious interests.
2. the strict neutrality theory: government cannot do anything which either *aids or hinders* religion.
3. the accommodation theory: in some situations government *must*, and in other situation *may*, accommodate its policies and laws in the furtherance of religious freedom. (Sunday Closing Laws are an example of "accommodation.")

Professor Kauper cites Mr. Justice Douglas' *Zorach* opinion in support of the accommodation theory—though, as we shall see in the *Engel* case below, Mr. Douglas himself later repudiated this "accommodation" theory in favor of a strict "neutrality" theory. Professor Kauper notes that Mr. Douglas "seems to think that the idea of accommodation cannot be pushed to the point where it justifies *spending* in aid of religion," and on a state as well as a national level, notes the "constitutional tradition against use of public funds to support religious purposes and particularly to support sectarian education." (p. 105).

Those not released stay in the classrooms. The churches make weekly reports to the schools, sending a list of children who have been released from public school but who have not reported for religious instruction.

This "released-time" program involves neither religious instruction in the public school classrooms nor the expenditure of public funds. All costs, including the application blanks, are paid by the religious organizations. The case is therefore unlike *McCollum v. Board of Education,* 333 U.S. 203, which involved a "released-time" program from Illinois. In that case the classrooms were turned over to religious instructors. We accordingly held that the program violated the First Amendment which (by reason of the Fourteenth Amendment) prohibits the states from establishing religion or prohibiting its free exercise.

Appellants . . . challenge the present law . . . [and argue that] the weight and influence of the school is put behind a program for religious instruction; public school teachers police it, keeping tab on students who are released; the classroom activities come to a halt while the students who are released for religious instruction are on leave; the school is a crutch on which the churches are leaning for support in their religious training; without the cooperation of the schools this "released-time" program, like the one in the *McCollum* case, would be futile and ineffective. . . .

There is a suggestion that the system involves the use of coercion to get public school students into religious classrooms. There is no evidence in the record before us that supports that conclusion. (Nor is there any indication that the public schools enforce attendance at religious schools by punishing absentees from the released-time programs for truancy.) The present record indeed tells us that the school authorities are neutral in this regard and do no more than release students whose parents so request. If in fact coercion were used, if it were established that any one or more teachers were using their office to persuade or force students to take the religious instruction, a wholly different case would be presented. (Appellants contend that they should have been allowed to prove that the system is in fact administered in a coercive manner. The New York Court of Appeals declined to grant a trial on this issue, noting, *inter alia,* that appellants had not properly raised their claim in the manner required by state practice.) . . . Hence we put aside that claim of coercion. . . .

There cannot be the slightest doubt that the First Amendment reflects the philosophy that Church and State should be separated. And so far as interference with the "free exercise" of religion and an "establishment" of religion are concerned, the separation must be complete and unequivocal. The First Amendment within the scope of its coverage permits no exception; the prohibition is absolute. The First Amendment, however, does not say that in every and all respects there shall be a separation of Church and State. Rather, it studiously defines the manner, the specific ways, in which there shall be no concert or union or dependency one on the other. That is the common sense of the matter. Otherwise the state and religion would be aliens to each other—hostile, suspicious, and even unfriendly. Churches could not be required to pay even property taxes. Municipalities would not be permitted to render police or fire protection to religious groups. Policemen who helped parishioners into their places of worship would violate the Constitution. Prayers in our legislative halls; the appeals to the Almighty in the messages of the Chief Executive; the proclamations making Thanksgiving Day a holiday; "so help me God" in our courtroom oaths—these and all other references to the Almighty that run through our laws, our public rituals, our ceremonies would be flouting the First Amendment. A fastidious atheist or agnostic could even object to the supplication with which the Court opens each session: "God save the United States and this Honorable Court."

We would have to press the concept of separation of Church and State to these extremes to condemn the present law on constitutional grounds. The nullification of this law would have wide and profound effects. A Catholic student applies to his teacher for permission to leave the school during hours on a Holy Day of Obligation to attend a mass. A Jewish student asks his teacher for permission to be excused for Yom Kippur. A Protestant wants the afternoon off for a family baptismal ceremony. In each case the teacher requires parental consent in writing. In each case the teacher, in order to make sure the student is not a truant, goes further and requires a report from the priest, the rabbi, or the minister. The teacher in other words cooperates in a religious program to the extent of making it possible for her students to participate in it. Whether she does it occasionally for a few students, regularly for one, or pursuant to a systematized program designed to further the religious needs of all the students does not alter the character of the act.

We are a religious people whose institutions presuppose a Supreme Being. We guarantee the freedom to worship as one chooses. We make room for as wide a variety of beliefs and creeds as the spiritual needs of man deem necessary. We sponsor an attitude on the part of government that shows no partiality to any one group and that lets each flourish according to the zeal of its adherents and the appeal of its dogma. When the state encourages religious instruction or cooperates with religious authorities by adjusting the schedule of public events to sectarian needs, it follows the best of our traditions. For it then respects the religious nature of our people and accommodates the public service to their spiritual needs. To hold that it may not would be to find in the Constitution a requirement that the government show a callous indifference to religious groups. That would be preferring those who believe in no religion over those who do believe. Government may not finance religious groups nor undertake religious instruction nor blend secular and sectarian education nor use secular institutions to force one or some religion on any person. But we find no constitutional requirement which makes it necessary for government to be hostile to religion and to throw its weight against efforts to widen the effective scope of religious influence. The government must be neutral when it comes to competition between sects. It may not thrust any sect on any person. It may not make a religious observance compulsory. It may not coerce anyone to attend church, to observe a religious holiday, or to take religious instruction. But it can close its doors or suspend its operations as to those who want to repair to their religious sanctuary for worship or instruction. No more than that is undertaken here. . . .

In the *McCollum* case the classrooms were used for religious instruction and the force of the public school was used to promote that instruction. Here, as we have said, the public schools do no more than accommodate their schedules to a program of outside religious instruction. We follow the *McCollum* case. But we cannot expand it to cover the present released-time program unless separation of Church and State means that public institutions can make no adjustments of their schedules to accommodate the religious needs of the people. We cannot read into the Bill of Rights such a philosophy of hostility to religion.

Mr. Justice Black, Dissenting:

[The] sole question is whether New York can use its compulsory education laws to help religious sects get attendants presumably too unenthusiastic to go unless moved to do so by the pressure of this state machinery. That this is the plan, purpose, design and consequence of the New York program cannot be denied. The state thus makes religious sects beneficiaries of its power to compel children to attend secular schools. Any use of such coercive power by the state to help or hinder some religious sects or to prefer all religious sects over non-believers or vice versa is just what I think the First Amendment forbids. In considering whether a state has entered this forbidden field the question is not whether it has entered too far but whether it has entered at all. New York is manipulating its compulsory education laws to help religious sects get pupils. This is not separation but combination of Church and State. . . .

Under our system of religious freedom, people have gone to their religious sanctuaries not because they feared the law but because they loved their God. The choice of all has been as free as the choice of those who answered the call to worship moved only by the music of the old Sunday morning church bells. The spiritual mind of man has thus been free to believe, disbelieve, or doubt, without repression, great or small, by the heavy hand of government. Statutes authorizing such repression have been stricken. Before today, our judicial opinions have refrained from drawing invidious distinctions between those who believe in no religion and those who do believe. The First Amendment has lost much if the religious follower and the atheist are no longer to be judicially regarded as entitled to equal justice under law.

State help to religion injects political and party prejudices into a holy field. It too often substitutes force for prayer, hate for love, and persecution for persuasion. Government should not be allowed, under cover of the soft euphemism of "cooperation," to steal into the sacred area of religious choice.

Mr. Justice Frankfurter, Dissenting:

The deeply divisive controversy aroused by the attempts to secure public school pupils for sectarian instruction would promptly end if the advocates of such instruction were content to have the school "close its doors or suspend its operations"—that is, dismiss classes in their entirety, without discrimination—instead of seeking to use the public schools as the instrument for securing attendance at denominational classes. The unwillingness of the promoters of this movement to dispense with such use of the public schools betrays a surprising want of confidence in the inherent power of the various faiths to draw children to outside sectarian classes—an attitude that hardly reflects the faith of the greatest religious spirits.

Mr. Justice Jackson, Dissenting:

As one whose children, as a matter of free choice, have been sent to privately supported Church schools, I may challenge the Court's suggestion that opposition to this plan can only be antireligious, atheistic, or agnostic. My evangelistic brethren confuse an objection to compulsion with an objection to religion. It is possible to hold a faith with enough confidence to believe that what should be rendered to God does not need to be decided and collected by Caesar.

The day that this country ceases to be free for irreligion it will cease to be free for religion—except for the sect that can win political power. The same epithetical jurisprudence used by the Court today to beat down those who oppose pressuring children into some religion can devise as good epithets tomorrow against those who object to pressuring them into a favored religion. And, after all, if we concede to the State power and wisdom to single out "duly constituted religious" bodies as exclusive alternatives for compulsory secular instruction, it would be logical to also uphold the power and wisdom to choose the true faith among those "duly constituted." We start down a rough road when we begin to mix compulsory public education with compulsory godliness.

3.8 DECLARATION ON CHRISTIAN EDUCATION*

Vatican II

1. Since every man of whatever race, condition, and age is endowed with the dignity of a person, he has an inalienable right to an education corresponding to his proper destiny and suited to his native talents, his sex, his cultural background, and his ancestral heritage. At the same time, this education should pave the way to brotherly association with other peoples, so that genuine unity and peace on earth may be promoted. . . .

2. Since every Christian has become a new creature by rebirth from water and the Holy Spirit, so that he may be called what he truly is, a child of God, he is entitled to a Christian education. Such an education does not merely strive to foster in the human person the maturity already described. Rather, its principal aims are these: that as the baptized person

---

* Excerpts from *The Documents of Vatican II* edited by Walter M. Abbott, S.J. Copyright © 1966 by The America Press, used by permission of Western Publishing Company, Inc., Racine, Wisconsin.

Compare this with the 1930 Encyclical letter "On the Christian Education of Youth" of His Holiness Pope Pius XI, reprinted in English translation in *Five Great Encyclicals*, New York: Paulist Press, 1960, pp. 39–60. After describing the three societies (family, state, Church), the 1930 encyclical declares:

> Consequently, education, which is concerned with the whole man, individually and socially, in the order of nature and in the order of grace, necessarily belongs to all these three societies, in accordance with the end assigned to each in the present order of divine providence.
>
> And first of all, education belongs pre-eminently to the Church, by reason of a double title in the supernatural order, conferred exclusively upon her by God Himself; absolutely superior, therefore, to any other title in the natural order. . . . By necessary consequence the Church is independent of any sort of earthly power as well in the origin as in the exercise of her mission as educator, not merely in regard to her proper end and object, but in regard to the means suitable to attain that end. . . .
>
> Hence, every form of pedagogic naturalism, which in any way excludes or overlooks supernatural Christian formation in the teaching of youth, is false. Every method of education founded, wholly or in part, on the denial or forgetfulness of original sin and of grace, and relying on the sole powers of human nature, is unsound. . . . The school . . . if not a temple, is a den. . . .
>
> From this it follows that the so-called "neutral" or "lay" school, from which religion is excluded, is contrary to the fundamental principles of education. . . . [Hence] the frequenting of non-Catholic schools, whether neutral or mixed, those namely which are open to Catholics and non-Catholics alike, is forbidden for Catholic children and can be at most tolerated, on the approval of the Ordinary alone, under determined circumstances of place and time and with special precautions. (*Cod. Jr. Can., c.* 1374).
>
> —Reprinted with permission from *America*, the National Catholic Weekly Review.

is gradually introduced into a knowledge of the mystery of salvation, he may daily grow more conscious of the gift of faith which he has received; that he may learn to adore God the Father in spirit and in truth (cf. Jn. 4:23), especially through liturgical worship; that he may be trained to conduct his personal life in righteousness and in the sanctity of truth, according to his new standard of manhood (Eph. 4:22–24).

Thus, indeed, he may grow into manhood according to the mature measure of Christ (cf. Eph. 4:13), and devote himself to the upbuilding of the Mystical Body. Moreover, aware of his calling, he should grow accustomed to giving witness to the hope that is in him (1 Pet. 3:15), and to promoting that Christian transformation of the world by which natural values, viewed in the full perspective of humanity as redeemed by Christ, may contribute to the good of society as a whole. Therefore this holy Synod reminds pastors of souls of their acutely serious duty to make every effort to see that all the faithful enjoy a Christian education of this sort, especially young people, who are the hope of the Church.

3. Since parents have conferred life on their children, they have a most solemn obligation to educate their offspring. Hence, parents must be acknowledged as the first and foremost educators of their children. Their role as educators is so decisive that scarcely anything can compensate for their failure in it. For it devolves on parents to create a family atmosphere so animated with love and reverence for God and men that a well-rounded personal and social development will be fostered among the children. . . . Let parents, then, clearly recognize how vital a truly Christian family is for the life and development of God's own people.

While belonging primarily to the family, the task of imparting education requires the help of society as a whole. In addition, therefore, to the rights of parents and of others to whom parents entrust a share in the work of education, certain rights and duties belong to civil society. For this society exists to arrange for the temporal necessities of the common good. Part of its duty is to promote the education of the young in several ways: namely, by overseeing the duties and rights of parents and of others who have a role in education, and by providing them with assistance; by implementing the principle of subsidiarity and completing the task of education, with attention to parental wishes, whenever the efforts of parents and of other groups are insufficient; and, moreover, by building its own schools and institutes, as the common good may demand.

Finally, the office of educating belongs by a unique title to the Church, not merely because she deserves recognition as a human society capable of educating, but most of all because she has the responsibility of announcing the way of salvation to all men, of communicating the life of Christ to those who believe, and of assisting them with ceaseless concern so that they may grow into the fullness of that same life. As a mother, the Church is bound to give these children of hers the kind of education through which their entire lives can be penetrated with the spirit of Christ, while at the same time she offers her services to all peoples by way of promoting the full development of the human person, for the welfare of earthly society and the building of a world fashioned more humanly. . . .

. . . .

6. Parents, who have the first and the inalienable duty and right to educate their children, should enjoy true freedom in their choice of schools. Consequently, public authority, which has the obligation to oversee and defend the liberties of citizens, ought to see to it, out of a concern for distributive justice, that public subsidies are allocated in such a way that, when selecting schools for their children parents are genuinely free to follow their consciences.

For the rest, it is incumbent upon the state to provide all citizens with the opportunity to acquire an appropriate degree of cultural enrichment, and with the proper preparation for exercising their civic duties and rights. Therefore, the state itself ought to protect the right of children to receive an adequate schooling. It should be vigilant about the ability of teachers and the excellence of their training. It should look after the health of students and, in general, promote the whole school enterprise. But it must keep in mind the principle of subsidiarity, so that no kind of school monopoly arises. For such a monopoly would militate against the native rights of the human person, the development and spread of culture itself, the peaceful association of citizens, and the pluralism which exists today in very many societies. . . .

The Church reminds parents of the serious duty which is theirs of taking every opportunity—or of making the opportunity—for their children to be able to enjoy these helps and to pace their development as Christians with their growth as citizens of the world. For this reason, the Church gives high praise to those civil authorities and civil societies that show regard for the pluralistic character of modern society, and take into account the right of religious liberty, by helping families in such a way that in all schools the education of their children can be carried out according to the moral and religious convictions of each family. . . .

As for Catholic parents, the Council calls to mind their duty to entrust their children to Catholic schools, when and where this is possible, to support such schools to the extent of their ability, and to work along with them for the welfare of their children. . . .

3.9 AMERICAN CATHOLIC EDUCATION SINCE VATICAN II*

John W. Donohue, S.J.

Once it was thought that because American Catholic education was very sure of its purposes, it had a certain immunity from radical change. But since the close of the Second Vatican Council in December 1965 self-criticism and innovation have flourished so remarkably in this section of American education that a sympathetic Protestant observer wondered if it were almost an overcompensation.[9] In any case, the Catholic community has clearly reached a critical point after more than a century and a half of building its educational system. When the first national census was taken in 1790 there were about 35,000 Catholics, amounting to less than 1 percent of the general population of nearly 4 million. A year later John Carroll, the first native bishop, opened an academy that became Georgetown University, today the oldest Catholic institution of higher learning in the country.

By January 1965 the population of the United States was about 193 million, and some 23 percent of these Americans, or 45 million, considered themselves Catholics. The one diocese of 1790 had multiplied to 148. In them, according to the *Official Catholic Directory* for 1965, were 10,931 elementary schools (almost all of them parochial) enrolling 4,566,809 children and 2465 secondary schools (diocesan, parochial, and independent) with 1,095,519 students. This meant that approximately 14 percent of all American elementary and secondary school pupils were in Catholic schools, a proportion about twice that of 25 years earlier. In addition there were, exclusive of seminaries, 304 Catholic colleges and universities with 384,526 students. These latter institutions are not supported by the Church but by the usual fees and benefactions, and most of them are independent rather than diocesan enterprises. The whole system running from nursery school to graduate seminar was staffed by 198,756 faculty members including 104,314 Sisters. In the elementary schools Sisters outnumbered lay teachers by more than two to one, but in the colleges and universities the

---

* This article was written especially for this anthology. Father Donohue teaches educational philosophy at Fordham University, New York.

9 Martin E. Marty, under the heading "Catholic Colleges in a Time of Change," in his column for *The National Catholic Reporter*, February 1, 1967, p. 8. Dr. Marty here advises Catholic institutions to learn from the experience of Protestant colleges what dangers may be encountered in the process of secularizing themselves—for instance, the tendency toward an overreaction, leading to the neglect altogether of Religion as a field of serious study.

lay faculty was very much in the majority and included a good many men and women who are not Catholics.

These gross figures suggest the magnitude of the Catholic investment in education. One should also notice the variety of Catholic schools and the ultimate motivation that brought them into existence. Catholic education ranges from country schools in the Dakotas with two or three Sisters to complex urban universities with multimillion dollar plants (and enormous budgetary headaches), professional programs and cosmopolitan faculties; from riding classes in exclusive boarding schools to child-care centers in Harlem. This meshwork of institutions was created and sustained for a distinctive twofold purpose: to help Catholic young people achieve in their lives a development and an authentic synthesis of both the religious and the secular dimensions of their experience.[10]

Beside this basic inspiration one may distinguish some secondary motivations. In the Protestant culture of the nineteenth century Catholics had reason to think their religious faith might be compromised in the public schools or the private colleges.[11] Sometimes, too, schools were founded to

---

[10] For summaries of the history of American Catholic education within the framework of the over-all history of American Catholicism see Francis X. Curran, "Roman Catholic Church: North America," *Encyclopaedia Brittanica*, Vol. XIX, 1966 edition; and John Tracy Ellis, "United States of America," *New Catholic Encyclopaedia*, Vol. XIV. For Catholic higher education in particular, see Philip Gleason, "American Catholic Higher Education: A Historical Perspective," in *The Shape of Catholic Higher Education*, Robert Hassenger, ed., Chicago: The University of Chicago Press, 1967, pp. 15–53. For a testimony to the diversity in Catholic higher education, see Robert Hassenger and Robert Weiss, S.J., "The Catholic College Climate," *The School Review*, 74:440, Winter 1966.

[11] Editor's Note: It was not until 1925 that the First Amendment, through the Fourteenth Amendment, was interpreted to apply to state as well as federal laws. In the nineteenth century, some of the state laws were quite harsh and intolerant. For example, a child could legally be expelled from school if he followed the instructions of his priest to cut public school classes in order to attend Mass on a Holy Day, *Ferriter v. Tyler*, 48 Vt. 444 (1876). For other cases of this kind read P. A. Freund, A. E. Sutherland, M. D. Howe and E. J. Brown, *Constitutional Law*, Boston: Little, Brown & Company, 1961, Vol. II, p. 1694.

Leo Pfeffer views the extreme hostility of the Protestant majority toward the tiny Catholic minority in early nineteenth century America as a contributing factor toward the establishment of separate parochial schools:

> Catholic hostility to the public schools arose out of the bitter experiences that Catholic children suffered in them. . . . For refusing to participate in Protestant religious exercises or the reading of the Protestant Bible, Catholic public school children frequently suffered cruel persecution. They were often subjected to physical punishment, expulsion, and other indignities merely because they took seriously the guaranty of religious freedom of which the Protestants so proudly boasted. The transition from Protestant to secular public education, moreover, took place during a period when anti-Catholic bigotry was strong and extensive, when Nativism and Know-Nothingism flourished over a large part of the country. The child of the Jewish immigrant from Russia and Poland came from a background of persecution,

preserve an attachment to an ethnic group. The Germans in the Midwest or the Polish in Buffalo wanted to maintain their language and culture, and schools seemed a way of doing this to both Catholics and Protestants. For it will be remembered that the case of *Meyer vs. Nebraska* in 1923 dealt with German-language teaching in a parochial school of the Zion Evangelical Lutherans.

But the protectionist and ethnic purposes were themselves rooted in that fundamental religious aim. Building schools and conserving old country customs were designed to expedite transmission of the faith to the children. So the educational system continued to grow after the ethnocentric and protective concerns had disappeared. For there remained the goal of an education in which both religious and secular maturity would be promoted and the two zones would be harmonized. As they developed, Catholic institutions became quite thoroughly Americanized with regard to the externals of structure, administration, curricula, and methods, since they never wanted to stand apart from the cultural mainstream. According to some critics, indeed, these schools resemble their secular counterparts only too closely, except that their clientele is largely Catholic; theology is part of the curriculum (if a diminishing part at the college level), and the Catholic liturgy is celebrated in the school chapel.

By the time the Second Vatican Council convened, certain ideological conflicts between the defenders of Catholic schools and their opponents had considerably cooled, although in the 1940s they were still heated. Economic, cultural, and political factors contributed to this change and so, perhaps, did the poignantly brief but memorable ascendancies of John XXIII and John F. Kennedy. American Catholics are involved with public education because they should be and because more than half the Catholic youth between five and seventeen are in public schools. Several empirical sociological studies have dissolved the myth that Catholic schools incline Catholics to stinginess where public education is concerned or give an inferior education or promote an indefensible divisiveness—some divisions, of course, are both inevitable and healthy, which is why we have more than one political party and more than one baseball club.[12] On the other hand,

---

discrimination, and bigotry to a [twentieth century] public school of acceptance and equality. The child of the Catholic immigrant from Ireland came from a climate of equality to a public school of persecution, discrimination, and bigotry. The difference in attitudes toward the public school on the part of the Catholic and Jewish communities hardly needs any other explanation. . . .

—Excerpt from p. 61 *Creeds in Competition* by Leo Pfeffer. (Harper & Row, 1958.)

[12] Stephen K. Bailey and his associates reported in *Schoolmen and Politics: A Study of State Aid to Education in the Northeast*, Syracuse: Syracuse University Press, 1962, that "there is no evidence whatsoever to suggest that the Roman Catholic church has

the Elementary and Secondary Education Act of 1965 found some ways that are legally acceptable of extending special aids to Catholic school children. While the Act did not substantially relieve the Catholic community of the financial burden of maintaining a system costing several billions annually, it did acknowledge the place of this system in the over-all American school picture.

In the second half of the 1960s that Catholic school system was larger and more self-questioning than ever. The elementary and secondary schools confronted two major problems that were generically the same as those of public education: how to achieve equality of opportunity and how to insure quality of substance. The first aim seems impossible to realize. At present somewhat more than half the children of elementary school age and about a third of those of high school age are actually in Catholic schools. It will take all the Catholic community's financial muscle simply to maintain these proportions in face of population increase. It's not just a matter of enlarging physical facilities. Expenditures for salaries have skyrocketed because the number of teaching Sisters, Brothers, and priests available has not kept pace with mounting enrollments, and it has been necessary to employ more lay people.[13] One gets some notion of costs from an estimate offered by New York State Comptroller Arthur Levitt in a speech April 17, 1967. To absorb the state's private school children into

---

been a depressant upon state aid to education," (p. 46). But conversely there are "scores of examples" of Catholic laymen, school board members, and politicians taking the lead in promoting public education in heavily Catholic districts. A doctoral study by Ray Lindbloom at Teachers College, Columbia University, arrived at a similar conclusion. Attention is called to this latter research in an article by William S. Vincent, "Federal Aid for Parochial and Private Schools," *School and Society*, 92:357, November 28, 1964: ". . . local budget resistance is not related positively to the size of the non-public school enrollment. In fact, it is the other way round. The larger the non-public school enrollment, the less the budget resistance. . ." From a number of field studies, Peter H. Rossi and Alice S. Rossi concluded that there was no proof that parochial schooling diminished attachment to the civic community or that parents of parochial school children were any less interested in the public schools than other people who did not actually have children in these schools: "Background and Consequences of Parochial School Education," *Harvard Educational Review*, 27:191, Summer 1957. Andrew M. Greeley and Peter H. Rossi reported in *The Education of Catholic Americans*, Chicago: Aldine, 1966, that they found no evidence either that religious education was divisive or that its products were handicapped in achieving economic and social success. The report of the Carnegie-sponsored Notre Dame study, edited by Reginald A. Neuwien, *Catholic Schools in Action: The Notre Dame Study of Catholic Elementary and Secondary Schools in the United States*, Notre Dame, Indiana: University of Notre Dame Press, 1966, has copious data illustrating the above average performance of Catholic school pupils measured by national norms. See also an excellent article by Michael O'Neill, "Four Myths About Parochial Schools," *America*, 116:82–86, January 21, 1967.

[13] In the second half of the sixties the number of young men and women entering upon the life of a Sister, Brother, or priest had declined, and, at the same time, a number of communities of Sisters or Brothers were reducing their commitment to

the public system would require, he said, an additional $636 million a year—assuming there are 644,000 nonpublic pupils, whereas in 1967 the State's Catholic schools alone actually enrolled 793,834.

One can see why the Catholic community is perplexed by the problem of helping all of its children to reach religious maturity when it cannot accommodate even a majority of them in its common schools. It is true that the evidence gathered by Greeley and Rossi suggests that the quality of family life is the most significant factor in nourishing religious values. This led them to the conclusion that there is no data proving that the schools have been necessary for the survival of American Catholicism. Mary Perkins Ryan had already conjectured as much in her provocative book, *Are Parochial Schools the Answer?*[14] Her notion of Christian education was rather heavily charismatic, and she was concerned with the specifically religious formation of all members of the Church, young and old. Thus, she deplored the spending of so much manpower and money on schools reaching only a fraction. Recently some parishes have actually elected to support a catechetical center rather than a parochial school so that all the children of the parish may have one or two Released Time classes per week. There are also isolated instances of other innovations. In a largely Catholic area of northern Vermont a new educational park is being planned, and the planning has been supported by an USOE grant. The campus in the town of Swanton will replace outworn public and Catholic high schools, and will include a privately financed wing with classrooms for religious instruction and an interfaith chapel. But these cases do not amount to a trend. The Greeley–Rossi researches found that most American Catholics still strongly support parochial schools, although they are critical of such limitations as excessively large classes or inferior physical facilities. At this time there is no question of collapsing this enormous system, but the problem of equality of opportunity for all Catholic children remains.

The problem of academic quality is somewhat curious. Here again there are not many large-scale studies available, but the ones that have been made suggest that Catholic schools achieve their secular aims quite well but achieve their religious aims less effectively. Of course, it is easier to measure mathematical ability than religious commitment, but the Carnegie-financed Notre Dame investigation showed that Catholic elementary pupils tested significantly above national norms on achievement

schools in order to take on new works. In November 1967 changes of this sort were announced by the Sisters of the Immaculate Heart of Mary in Los Angeles and by the Marist Brothers in New York.

[14] Mary Perkins Ryan, *Are Parochial Schools the Answer? Catholic Education in Light of the Council*, New York: Holt, Rinehart and Winston, Inc., 1964. For the Greeley–Rossi conclusion see *The Education of Catholic Americans*, pp. 221–222.

scales and that there were analogous results at the secondary level. But neither this study nor Greeley's and Rossi's found the schools strikingly successful in developing religious maturity. The Danforth report on "Church-Sponsored Higher Education," arrived at a similar conclusion: the institutions it studied, including the Catholic ones, are stronger academically than religiously.[15]

These Catholic institutions of higher education are strung out along a spectrum ranging from tiny women's colleges to university centers, but at least two problems are common to all. One is financial. These institutions share with all nonpublic schools the formidable job of getting enough funds. The second issue is distinctive and ideological. It has been generally observed that as Catholic colleges become academically more sophisticated they also become more secularized, just as Protestant colleges did some generations ago. Concretely, this means increasing the proportion of lay men and women among both faculty and administrators, while in more advanced places all personnel, lay or not, Catholic or not, should operate according to the same professional standards as their colleagues elsewhere.[16] It also means that whereas before World War II the Catholic undergraduate in the Catholic college included in his distribution program many required courses in theology and philosophy, and was expected to attend certain religious functions, he found, as did his non-Catholic fellow students, that the faculty took rather seriously the notion of its role *in loco parentis*. Today these characteristics are everywhere gone or going.

But one of the side effects of this secularization has been the so-called crisis of identity for Catholic colleges and universities. These institutions are confronted with an especially difficult problem that is peculiar to Christian education: the harmonious interrelating of the religious and the secular, without impoverishment of either. Since they are schools, they are fully committed to secular values and share all the specifically educational problems of American higher education. In addition, they encounter special issues of their own, which may be summed up in three questions asked with varying degrees of seriousness. Is there a definable sense in which an institution can be truly Catholic and truly a university? If so, what pre-

---

[15] Manning M. Patillo, Jr., and Donald M. Mackenzie, *Church-Sponsored Higher Education in the United States: Report of the Danforth Commission*, Washington, D.C.: American Council on Education, 1966, p. 100. One study of a representative sample of 1961 college graduates found that "On most indicators of 'intellectualism' the graduates of Catholic colleges scored no lower than the national average. There seemed to be no disinclination on the part of these graduates to enter scholarly careers." Andrew M. Greeley, "Anti-Intellectualism in Catholic Colleges," *The American Catholic Sociological Review*, 23:350, Winter 1962.

[16] Andrew M. Greeley, in fact, thinks that the "desperate eagerness" with which Catholic institutions seek lay administrators is considerably overdone. "Myths and Fads in Catholic Higher Education," *America*, 117:542–543, November 11, 1967.

cisely makes such a university *Catholic*? Even if it is possible to have a Catholic university, is it desirable? Might not Catholics simply conduct good secular institutions that are no more Catholic than Harvard is Congregational?[17]

Questions of this sort are posed more insistently after the Second Vatican Council, although the Council did not simply create either the questions or the conditions stimulating them. It is rather that the Council crystallized much that the Catholic community has learned about itself and its faith from the experiences of the past several centuries. It did this by restudying the sources of Christian life and then proposing reforms or adaptations in the light of that renewal. Thereby, the Council released a number of powerful ideas, which are fermenting within Catholic education, although their effects cannot yet be fully appraised. These concepts are not found in the more obvious places. The Declaration on Christian Education, for instance, is rather conventional, and the one on Religious Freedom, though a milestone, deals with a theme that is hardly news to Americans, although it is situated here within a rich theological-philosophical context.

In the Decree on Ecumenism and in the two documents on the Church, however, there are at least four nuclear ideas that are already shaping Catholic school theory and practice. These are the themes of (1) the endorsement of the process of secularization; (2) the importance of the role and responsibility of the laity both in the Church and in the whole of human society; (3) freedom as the root of personal worth and dignity and (4) community as a focal value flowing from the human family's oneness and common destiny—demanding expression in friendship and cooperation across all lines and at all levels, including not least the international.

The first two of these concepts have had immediate resonance in American Catholic education, which has long since deepened its appreciation of secular values and has also become too large and complex for

[17] Christopher Jencks and David Riesman note the increased secularization of the better Catholic institutions in their "The Catholics and their Colleges (I)," *The Public Interest*, 7:101, Spring 1967, and "The Catholics and their Colleges (II)," 8:67–70, Summer 1967. Andrew M. Greeley also points to the process but doubts that introduction of lay trustees necessarily means eventual thorough secularization: " 'Laicization' of Catholic Colleges," *The Christian Century*, 84:372–375, March 22, 1967. Various contributors to *The Shape of Catholic Higher Education* note the same developments and issues. John Courtney Murray, S.J., recommended that Catholic seminaries form a consortium with those of other faiths and that the whole complex be linked in some way to a secular university. "Our Response to the Ecumenical Revolution," *Religious Education*, 62:91–92, March–April 1967. John Cogley hopes for total secularization, since he believes that "the Catholic University as such" has no future: "The Future of an Illusion," *Commonweal*, 86:310–316, June 2, 1967. Leonard Swidler had made a similar suggestion earlier in "Catholic Colleges: A Modest Proposal," *Commonweal*, 81:559–562, January 29, 1965.

management by ecclesiastical personnel alone. One result has been an expanding movement to create diocesan and parish school boards, composed mostly of parents and admitting laymen, including those of other faiths, to the boards of trustees of colleges and universities. But what the "Theology of the Secular" may yet mean for Catholic education is not clear. Desacralization has steadily increased since the days of medieval Christendom or the Biblical commonwealth of Massachusetts Bay, when the religious and the secular were so fused that the Church dominated the areas of art, science, technology, education, politics, and welfare work. Before secular agencies were developed for handling these concerns, the Church filled the gap by taking on earthly functions. The Second Vatican Council, while not adopting that radical secularization that declares Christianity irrelevant and the secular order absolutely independent of the Gospel, clearly did ratify the relative autonomy of the secular with its "own laws and values which must be gradually deciphered, put to use and regulated by men. . ."[18]

Some Catholics think this requires the abolition of Catholic schools as presently constituted—perhaps in favor of some good but quite secular institutions run by Catholics and open to all comers.[19] At the moment this does not seem likely so far as American Catholic elementary and secondary schools are concerned. In higher education the mounting financial pressures are making such a prospect seem less remote than it did a decade ago, and it would be rash to prophesy about tomorrow. But it would not be risky to predict that the renewed esteem for freedom will continue to affect the climate of Catholic education. Catholic college students talk a good deal about freedom and have far more of it than earlier generations did. This development, with its values as well as risks, stems in part from the contemporary culture but finds theological support in the central importance attached by Christianity to the responsible use of freedom.

On the whole, American Catholic universities have not experienced a disproportionate number of tensions over academic freedom. There have been some notorious wrangles but so have there been in respectable secular institutions. The ideal of academic freedom was itself affirmed by the Council in the document on "The Church in the Modern World": "Let it be recognized that all the faithful, clerical and lay, possess a lawful

[18] Pastoral Constitution on the Church in the Modern World," *The Documents of Vatican II*, Walter M. Abbott, S.J., ed., New York: Guild-America-Association Presses, 1966, no. 36, p. 233.

[19] Terry Eagleton, "Catholic Education and Commitment," *Catholic Education Today*, 1:8–10, January–February 1967. This is an English periodical, and the author is a member of what is called the "Catholic New Left." A somewhat similar position was argued by a French priest-educator, Michael Ducleroq, "The Church and the Question of Catholic Schools," *Cross Currents*, 15:199–212, Spring 1965. See also the articles of Cogley and Swidler cited in footnote 17 above.

freedom of inquiry and of thought, and the freedom to express their minds humbly and courageously about those matters in which they enjoy competence."[20] In the discipline of theology, however, the conceptual framework for the practical application of this ideal has not yet been fully worked out. Although theology is nowadays taught by laymen as well as clerics, speculation is quite uninhibited and it is not uncommon to find courses in Protestant theology or Jewish thought taught by scholars of these faiths.

Freedom itself is ultimately instrumental to the central Christian value of love. Christianity sees the love of God as expressing and validating itself in the love and service of others. This in turn both needs and nourishes human community. Catholic education has, therefore, to concern itself with the distinctive ways in which the school can build community. Years ago the parochial schools helped the children of immigrants to move up the social ladder. But now Catholic educators have to plan seriously and imaginatively, if they are not to be imprisoned by the world of American affluence.[21] No doubt it is getting harder for schools without tax support to reach the poor, but the Christian school must do so. Moreover, the educational experience provided by that school must effectively oppose prejudice, nationalism, and racism. For education, as the Council observed,

[20] "Pastoral Constitution on the Church in the Modern World," *The Documents of Vatican II*, 62:270. "Humbly" in this context means, we venture to suggest, not servility towards authority but respect for the prescriptive rights of evidence. In Catholic universities the faculty member rarely thinks of himself as being hampered in his teaching and research. The issues that have risen usually involved academic freedom in an extended sense. For instance, student groups have run into trouble when they wished to entertain controversial guest speakers. For a general discussion see Edward Manier and John W. Houck, eds., *Academic Freedom and the Catholic University*, Notre Dame, Ind.: Fides Publishers, 1967. Earlier essays by lay faculty members writing out of the context of a Catholic university include three by Charles Donahue, "Catholicism and Academic Freedom," *Thought*, 29:555–573, Winter 1954–1955; a review of Russell Kirk's "Academic Freedom," *Thought*, 30:274–283, Summer 1955; and "Freedom on the Campus," *America*, 97:104–108, April 27, 1957; and one by Seymour L. Gross, not himself a Catholic, "Amid the Alien Corn," *America*, 100:456–458, January 17, 1959. Two controversies centering about academic freedom in Catholic universities are discussed in Hassenger, *The Shape of Catholic Higher Education*, a treatment of the St. John's University dispute by John Leo, "Some Problem Areas in Catholic Higher Education: A. The Faculty," pp. 193–201, and Francis E. Kearns' account of his own experiences at Georgetown, "Social Consciousness and Academic Freedom in Catholic Higher Education," pp. 223–249. For a firm declaration on academic freedom and other issues, see the statement of a group of Catholic university administrators meeting at Land O'Lakes, Wisconsin, July 21–22: "The Catholic University of Today," *America*, 117:154–156, August 12, 1967.

[21] From November 5 to 10, 1967, the National Catholic Educational Association sponsored a conference to which some 120 specialists, not all of them Catholics, were invited. It was called "Blueprint for the Future: The Washington Symposium on Catholic Education," and one of its central themes was the obligation on the part of Catholic schools to invest more heavily in education for Negroes and other disadvantaged peoples.

"should pave the way to brotherly association with other peoples, so that genuine unity and peace on earth may be promoted."[22] That goal may strike us as more formidable than ever when we reflect on the difficulties symbolized by the Mekong Delta and Twelfth Street in Detroit. But these only make it more imperative.

3.10 PUBLIC FUNDS SHOULD SUPPORT PAROCHIAL SCHOOLS*

Milton Himmelfarb

As integrationist Catholics are convinced (notwithstanding Vatican II) that the marriage of Throne and Altar is God's will, so radical secularists are convinced that root-and-branch separationism is Reason's dictate. . . . As the separationists see it, the child-benefit theory is a mere device for benefiting parochial schools by the back door while evading the (presumed) constitutional prohibition of benefits by the front door, and churches and church-related institutions have no business in anti-poverty programs or anything else that gets public money. . . . [People having this point of view believe that a] country with separation is democratic, tolerant, open, free; a country without separation is despotic, persecuting, closed, unfree. The greater the separation, as in America and France, the more democracy and tolerance; the less the separation, as in Spain, Tsarist Russia, and the Papal States before the unification of Italy, the less democracy and tolerance. . . .

A good, strong case—or it would be if not for the vice of faulty enumeration. Where do you put England, Denmark, Norway, and Sweden, with their state churches? No one can deny that Great Britain and Scandinavia are free and democratic and that religious freedom is closer to being most secure there than least secure. Nor can any Jew deny that those countries

---

[22] "Declaration on Christian Education," *The Documents of Vatican II*, 1:639.

* Milton Himmelfarb, "Church and State: How High a Wall?" *Commentary*, 42: 23–29, July 1966. By permission. Milton Himmelfarb is Editor of *The American Jewish Yearbook*.

See also Rev. Neil A. McCluskey, S.J., "Public Funds for Parochial Schools? Yes!" *Teachers College Record* 72:49–56, October 1960; Daniel P. Moynihan, "How Catholics Feel About Federal School Aid," *The Reporter* 24: 34–37, May 25, 1961; Francis Canavan, "Implications of the School Prayer and Bible Reading Decisions: The Welfare State," 13 *Journal of Public Law* 439–446, Emory Law School, 1965. See also William F. O'Connor, "Aid to Education," *Commonweal*, 74: 328–329, June 23, 1961.

are, as we used to say, good for the Jews. (Proportionately, more than seven times as many Jews are in the House of Commons as in the population of the United Kingdom.) On the other hand, in the Soviet Union church and state are constitutionally separate, but the Soviet Union is neither free nor democratic nor good for the Jews, and so far from making religious freedom secure—let alone most secure—it persecutes religion. . . .[23]

To repeat: It is not true that freedom is most secure where church and state are separated; separation and separationism are not the same; even in America, separationism is potentially tyrannical; separationism needlessly repels some from the democratic consensus; it is harsh to those who prefer non-public schools for conscience' sake; and it stands in the way of a more important good. . . . the best possible education for all. . . .

[The purpose of federal aid] is not to help the Catholic schools, but to help American education; or better, to help bring about the conditions in which all Americans can have the best possible education. Since the quality of the nation's life will depend so greatly on education. . . . education has a more urgent claim on the nation than separationism. . . .

In the political and social thought that has least to apologize for, despotism is understood to prevail when state and society are all but identical, when the map of the state can almost be superimposed on the map of society. In contrast, freedom depends on society's having loci of interest, affection, and influence besides the state. It depends on more or less autonomous institutions mediating between the naked, atomized individual and the state—or rather, keeping the individual from nakedness and atomization in the first place. In short, pluralism is necessary.

---

[23] Editor's Note: To make this enumeration still more complete, we note the case of Holland:

> It is fair to ask how the public schools would be damaged if private and sectarian schools should share tax funds with them. The dividing of tax funds would mean the splintering of elementary and secondary education into denominational and other private schools and school systems. Four decades after Holland adopted a similar program, enrollment in its public schools declined from 75 percent to 30 percent of the total student population, with only the Protestant and Roman Catholic systems growing rapidly. . . .
>
> In Holland almost the total of society is organized along the lines established in the three school systems. It is divided into Catholic, Protestant and neutral clubs, civic associations, political parties, merchants' grants, labor unions and trade associations. In our country the splintering of society would probably be even more serious because of the great size and diversity of our country and its people. The minority public school with its underprivileged clientele could no longer be an effective force for unity. It could easily become as divisive in many ways as the denominational and other private schools at a time when its great unifying function would be needed as much as ever before in our national history.
>
> —Edgar Fuller, in *Current Legal Concepts in Education*, Leo O. Garber, ed., Philadelphia: University of Pennsylvania Press, 1966, pp. 43–62.

Given that a shriveling of the non-public must fatally enfeeble pluralism, . . . [let] the government see that money finds its way to the non-public schools, so that they may continue to exist side by side with the public schools. That will strengthen pluralism, and so, freedom.

3.11 PUBLIC FUNDS SHOULD NOT SUPPORT PAROCHIAL SCHOOLS*

R. Freeman Butts

. . . As we face the problem of public and private schools, we all know that the really controversial element in it for over a century has had to do with religion. As Americans sought to create a republican form of society to replace their colonial status, and as they built a public school system to be the main support for a free society, they had to face the religious problem.

During the century of political and religious conflict from 1830 to 1930, the public school idea was hammered out. As we know it and cherish it, that idea involves five basic principles: (1) Universal free education must be available for all in common public schools supported by taxation upon everyone. (2) Public schools should be maintained under the authority of the state and administered by local public authorities. (3) In order to protect freedom of conscience, the public schools should not engage in religious instruction. (4) In order to keep church separated from state, public funds cannot be given to religious schools. Finally, (5) the state can compel all children to attend some school, but children cannot be compelled to attend a public school. This idea of public education gave enormous strength, vitality, and unity to American society. It made possible, within a relatively short time, the creation of a democratic American nation out of diverse peoples. . . . The results in economic and technological progress, in political stability, and in strength of loyalty to the processes of a free society have been incalculable.

Now, the question is, "Shall we modify or possibly reverse this general

---

* R. Freeman Butts, "Public Funds for Parochial Schools? No!" *Teachers College Record*, 42: 57–61, October 1960. By permission.

Professor Butts, of Columbia University, is author of *The American Tradition in Religion and Education*, Boston: The Beacon Press, 1950.

For another useful historical supplement to this chapter, read E. S. Gausted, ed., *Religious Issues in American History*, New York: Harper & Row Publishers, Inc., 1968 (paperback).

pattern of public education?" An increasing number of voices in recent decades has begun to argue, to plead, to cajole, and to demand that we do so. One of the most dynamic forces in this process has been the Roman Catholic Church. . . . Catholic schools enrolled about 5 percent of the elementary and secondary school total in 1900, and still only 6 or 7 percent in 1940. But during the past twenty years, the rise has been spectacular. While public school enrollments increased 36 percent, nonpublic enrollments increased 118 percent. Today, about 14 percent of all schoolchildren are in Catholic schools, perhaps as much as 16 percent in all nonpublic schools. . . .

For one hundred years, the public school idea was on the march throughout America, but since 1930 or so it has been on the defensive. Piecemeal exceptions to the basic idea began to be made, such as the provision of free textbooks, bus rides, and lunches to parochial school children. "All we want," said the Catholic bishops in 1948, "is cooperation between church and state in education." "All we want," said Cardinal Spellman in 1949, "is public aid for auxiliary services, including health and welfare services." These services will benefit the child, they said, not aid the school; therefore, they are quite within the constitutional and legal limitations of the public school idea.

But since 1950 the character of the campaign has changed radically. The argument for benefits to the child and for the right of the parents to choose the school they desire had been extended to a full-blown theory of private rights in education. In 1955 the Catholic bishops spoke of the *partnership* of private and public schools, each having equal rights to public aid because they both perform a public service. Since that time we have heard more and more of the argument that the rights of parents in the education of their children are prior to the rights of the state. Similarly, the rights of the Church in education are presented as superior to those of the state. . . .[24]

---

[24] Editor's Note: In 1962 New York's Francis Cardinal Spellman said: "If the Federal Government should favor the public schools and put an additional tax on us, from which we would receive no benefit, then, my dear friends, it is the eventual end of our parochial schools."—*Time* 78: 46, February 16, 1962. Such rash statements are heard in every heated debate. In 1877 the *American Catholic Quarterly* prophesied: "Let the public school system of the free religionists do its unwholesome work ten or twelve years longer and we venture to predict that the United States of America will become a huge mass of corruption." This quotation is found in Mark Mohler, "Converting the Churches to State Education," *Current History*, 28: 47–50, April 1928.

Compare the following statement by Cardinal Cushing, Roman Catholic Archbishop of Boston (Boston *Globe*, January 26, 1964, p. A–7):

> I don't know of anywhere in the history of Christianity where the Catholic Church, the Protestant Church, or any other church has made greater progress than in the United States of America; and in my opinion the chief reason is that there is no union of church and state. . . . Once a state or government starts financing church-related schools or a church-related system of education the next step is a controlled system.

We hear the argument that the only real purpose of taxation for education is merely to subsidize parents and thus aid them to get the kind of education they wish for their children. . . . What this means is that the earlier demand for indirect aid for peripheral welfare services in justice to children has become a demand for direct financial subsidy by government or for at least tax credit as a constitutional right of parents. The *principle* of liberty and of civil rights *requires* the state to subsidize parents by full government support for the education of their children, and if the state refuses such aid, it will be infringing their rights of freedom of conscience under the First Amendment. . . .

We see this same principle being applied in the South. Just as parents who want their children to go to religious schools should have their fair share of state aid, so parents who want their children to go to all-white schools should have *their* share of state aid. . . .

If you accept the principle that the state should subsidize parents rather than maintain a common public school system, why not call on the principle to justify parents' choices on economic, political, social status, or intellectual grounds as well as on religious or racial grounds?

A proper course between voluntarism, or privatism, on the one hand, and totalitarianism, or state monopoly of education on the other, must be based on the right *and the obligation* of a free people, through its free government, to establish and maintain public schools devoted to the promotion of freedom. The people of a free state cannot rightfully create a monopoly for public education by interfering with or destroying private schools, nor can they rightfully create a monopoly for private schools by undermining or destroying their public schools.

A system of free public education is the chief means by which a free society continually regenerates itself. Public education is therefore an integral responsibility of a free and republican form of government. It is a kind of fourth branch of government, as essential to freedom as are responsible executives, elected legislatures, and independent courts. In this sense, the rights of the free people in public education are prior to the rights of individual churches or of individual parents in private education. This is the individual's guarantee that he will have any educational rights to exercise at all.

Religious Understanding—without Indoctrination

3.12 INTRODUCTION: THE RELIGIOUS EDUCATION OF FREE MEN

In moral and spiritual choices, no less than in political and scientific ones, men are continually confronted with living options—options that can be resolved only by the living thoughts of living men. This is the essential meaning of the medieval adage *semper eadem sed aliter*—"ever the same, yet ever changing"—and it is in this sense only that the past may serve as a guide to the future. Man's creative spirit is "ever the same"; but man's patterns of thought and his forms of social organization are "ever changing."

For example, in our age of high productivity per manhour, we no longer consider man to be a feeble creature whose chief virtue is humble resignation before the inevitable; and we no longer accept slavery as justified by "natural law"—even though it was so justified by Aristotle, St. Paul, St. Augustine, and other great moralists of the past. Submission and impotence seemed both natural and inevitable in an age when life was hard, hope scanty, and possibilities of improvement slight. But should not modern man assert his faith in a more positive manner? "The worship of God is not a rule of safety," said Alfred North Whitehead, "it is an adventure of the spirit, a flight after the unattainable. The death of religion comes with the repression of the high hope of adventure.[25] "Faith," wrote John Dewey, "is the power of intelligence to imagine a future which is the projection of the desirable in the present, and to invent the instrumentalities of its realization is our salvation."[26] "Not fear and submission but love and the assertion of one's own powers are the basis of the mystical experience," says Erich Fromm. "God is not a symbol of power over man

---

[25] Alfred North Whitehead, *Science and the Modern World*, New York: Crowell-Collier and Macmillan, Inc., 1936, conclusion of Chap. 12. Read also Whitehead's *Adventures in Ideas*, New York: Crowell-Collier and Macmillan, Inc., 1944, pp. 125–126.

[26] John Dewey, *Creative Intelligence*, New York: Holt, Rinehart and Winston, Inc., 1917, p. 17. Compare Harry L. Hollingworth, *Psychology and Ethics*, New York: The Ronald Press Company, 1949, p. 162.

but of man's own powers."[27] Such ideas are not new, nor are they heretical. For the European tradition has never been a static one, and it was an ancient Hebrew prophet who wrote, "Say not thou, 'What is the cause that former days were better than these?' "[28] The future, says Raymond B. Fosdick, belongs to the irresistible power of things that can grow:

> That is why democracy, rightly interpreted, is the last best hope of earth. It is rooted in the principle of growth; it is adaptable to new concepts of social justice. It is built, not on a fixed creed or on a system of regimented ideas, but on the sure knowledge that frontiers are never stationary, that the thrust of events is steadily forward, that there are no privileged ideas around which magic circles can be drawn to protect them from competition. It is only free men who dare to think, and it is only through free thought, freely expressed, that the soul of a people can be kept alive.[29]

Obstacles exist to be overcome, it is now believed, and therefore they are overcome. New frontiers await discovery, it is believed, and therefore new frontiers are discovered. When Daniel Boone's frontier is gone, Thomas Edison's frontier appears. The wider the sphere of man's knowledge, the greater its contact with the unknown; and if man will hold firm his faith in his own divine nature, the process knows no limit.

The question arises: Is it necessary for an ideal to be eternal or for an idea to be infallible, in order that the will may be firmly attached to it? Few Americans think so. A 1925 car owner may have been as attached to his "Model T" as in 1950 he becomes attached to his "V-8"; and he is not in the least dismayed because new and better models appear. Our medieval ancestors attained an integrated view of the world and of man's place in it, when they supposed that the earth was flat and stationary, and that intellectual and moral absolutes were indispensable. But twentieth-century thinkers attain an equally integrated and satisfactory viewpoint, knowing that the taboos of one culture may be accepted practices in another one without harmful consequences, and believing that ours is a spinning planet whose human inhabitants must learn to apply tentative, reconstructive thinking to ethical beliefs as well as to scientific theories. In short, intellectual theories and cultural climates of opinion are subject to change and revision, but our emotional attachment to them may be very genuine.

---

[27] Erich Fromm, *Psychoanalysis and Religion*, New Haven: Yale University Press, 1949, p. 49. Compare Rabbi Joshua Loth Liebman, *Peace of Mind*, New York: Simon and Schuster, Inc., 1946, pp. 172f.

[28] *Ecclesiastes* 7:10. Compare *Hebrews*, Chapters 11 and 12; I *Samuel* 4:9. See also Kyle Haselden, *Flux and Fidelity*, Richmond, Va.: John Knox Press, 1968.

[29] Raymond B. Fosdick, "We Must Not Be Afraid of Change," *New York Times Magazine*, April 3, 1949; slightly revised to become Chap. 8 of *Within Our Power*, by R. B. Fosdick, New York: David McKay Company, Inc., 1962.

The essence of democracy—and the ideal of democratic education—is the encouragement of freedom, responsibility and creativity on the part of all citizens. On no other basis may democracy be so clearly distinguished from totalitarianism. Dictators sometimes suppose that they do not need the opinions of dissenting groups. They try to dispense with opposition. They imprison, exile, or shoot their opponents. Democracies, on the other hand, have learned on the basis of long experience dating back to the Magna Carta and before that opposition is indispensable. Consider the British phrase "Her Majesty's *loyal opposition.*" To totalitarians, the terms "loyal" and "opposition" are contradictory: "How can anyone who opposes the government be loyal to it?" they ask. But democracies encourage criticism and dissent, and even pay public salaries to elected representatives of minority groups. For in a democracy, majorities may become minorities without any loss of rights, and minorities may become majorities without any added privileges. To still the voices of any of its citizens is to undermine the basic foundation of democratic unity—freedom of the individual citizen. The state may indeed compel obedience to laws which have won the consent of the majority of its citizens. But these laws are always open to challenge and revision. The majority is not a fixed group but a fluctuating one, and the possibility always remains open for the minority to become the majority by argument and persuasion.

In civilized societies, men learn to discuss issues, to meet their opponents face to face, to examine competing hypotheses, to restudy their traditions, to picture a type of life more ideal than that to which they are accustomed. Out of such discussion gradually emerges a body of common opinion. Roman philosophers referred to it as "natural law." Anglo-Saxon jurists called it "common law." Contemporary educators speak of it in terms such as "consensus," "pragmatic agreement," or "judicial precedent." In thus clarifying their agreements and differences, men cease to be children: They learn to modify customs and traditions, and thus develop reason and humanity, the basic virtues of civilization. Paraphrasing Edwin Markham's poem "Outwitted," Horace Kallen has expressed the social side of democracy and science thus:

> . . . other ways of thought and life draw circles which shut the differences out, as heretics, rebels, and things to flout, but democracy and science are the methods that win, for the circle they draw brings the differences in.[30]

A free society, like any other society, is held together by its traditions. But if the citizens of a free society are to cooperate with other citizens in striving for a widening social and moral outlook, then students in a free

[30] Horace M. Kallen, *Democracy's True Religion,* Boston: The Beacon Press, 1951, p. 10.

society should be encouraged to be free from a blind and unyielding acceptance of traditions. The earth does not become fruitful until torn up by the plow, nor can the mind of a student develop until challenged by new and unfamiliar points of view. A student should learn not only to answer questions, but also to question answers. Hence, writes William K. Frankena:

> In the interests of freedom of conscience, thought, and worship, the public schools, being organs of the state, cannot teach religion. Like the state itself, they must be neutral with respect to the various churches and religions; they must be neutral even as between religion and antireligious philosophies of life. They can and should teach informative courses *about* religion—its history, beliefs, institutions, influences, etc.—but they may not seek to inculcate or propagate any particular kind of ultimate creed, religious or naturalistic. What J. S. Mill says about universities applies to public education as a whole:
>
> > . . . it is not the teacher's business to impose his own judgment, but to inform and discipline that of his students. . . . The proper business of a University is . . . not to tell us from authority what we ought to believe, and make us accept the belief as a duty, but to give us information and training, and help us to form our own belief in a manner worthy of intelligent beings. . . .[31]

---

[31] William K. Frankena, "Public Education and the Good Life," *Harvard Educational Review* 31: 413–426, Fall 1966. See also Cheong Lum, George Kagehiro, and Edwin Larm, "Some Thoughts on Moral and Spiritual Values in the Secular Public School," *Progressive Education* 30: 166–171, 192, April 1953.

With respect to open-mindedness and freedom of inquiry, democracy and science have much in common. Morris R. Cohen explains why the continual reevaluation of traditional beliefs is characteristic of modern science:

> Man's ability to question that which he has from childhood been taught or accustomed to accept is very limited indeed unless it is socially cultivated and trained. It is a very rare individual who can perceive things for himself and trust his own experience or reason so as to question the currently prevailing views. For the typical Mohammedan child growing up in Central Arabia, there is no effective doubt possible as to whether Allah is the true God, and Mohammed his prophet. It is only when his community ceases to be homogeneous, when he comes into contact with those who do not believe in Mohammed, that doubt can take root and begin to flourish. Thus travellers, merchant adventurers, cosmopolitan cities, and the mixing of peoples having diverse traditions, play a predominant role as leaven in the intellectual life of mankind.
>
> As the state of doubt is intensely disagreeable, communities try to get rid of it in diverse ways, through ridicule, forcible suppression, and the like. The method of science seeks to conquer doubt by cultivating it and encouraging it to grow until it finds its natural limits and can go no further. Sober reflection soon shows that though very few propositions are in themselves absolutely unquestionable, the possibility of systematic truth cannot be impugned. . . . Any contention that the whole body of scientific or demonstrative knowledge is false will be found to be in the long run humanly untenable, i.e., incapable of being held consistently with other propositions that claim to be true. Science can be challenged only by some other system which is factually more inclusive and, through the demand for proof, logically more coherent. But such a system would simply be science improved. Sci-

3.13 OFFICIAL PUBLIC SCHOOL PRAYERS?*

Hugo L. Black and Others

[The New Hyde Park, New York] Board of Education . . . directed the School District's principal to cause the following prayer to be said aloud by each class in the presence of a teacher at the beginning of each school day:

> Almighty God, we acknowledge our dependence upon Thee, and we beg Thy blessings upon us, our parents, our teachers and our country.

This daily procedure was adopted on the recommendation of the State Board of Regents, a governmental agency. . . .

We think that by using its public school system to encourage recitation of the Regents' prayer, the State of New York has adopted a practice wholly inconsistent with the Establishment Clause. There can, of course, be no doubt that New York's program of daily classroom invocation of God's blessings as prescribed in the Regents' prayer is a religious activity. It is a solemn avowal of divine faith and supplication for the blessings of the Almighty. The nature of such a prayer has always been religious, none of the respondents has denied this and the court expressly so found. . . .

We agree . . . that the constitutional prohibition against laws respecting an establishment of religion must at least mean that in this country it is no part of the business of government to compose official prayers for any group of the American people to recite as a part of a religious program carried on by government. When the power, prestige and financial support of government is placed behind a particular religious belief, the indirect coercive pressure upon religious minorities to conform is plain.

---

ence must always be ready to abandon any one of its conclusions, but when such overthrow is based on evidence, the logical consistency of the whole system is only strengthened.

Progress in science is thus possible because no single proposition in it is so certain that it can block the search for one better founded. . . .

—Morris R. Cohen, *Reason and Nature: An Essay on the Meaning of Scientific Method*, New York: Harcourt, Brace & World, Inc., 1930, pp. 83–86. By permission. See also M. R. Cohen, *The Faith of a Liberal*, New York: Holt, Rinehart and Winston, Inc., 1946, pp. 337–361; and Alan Wood, *Bertrand Russell, the Passionate Sceptic*, London: George Allen & Unwin, Ltd., 1957.

For expressions of the same viewpoint by two Catholic writers, read Gustav Weigel, S.J., "American Catholic Intellectualism," *Review of Politics* 19: 275–307, July 1957; and Julian Pleasants, "Catholics and Science," *Commonweal* 58: 509–514, August 28, 1953.

* Majority (7–1) decision, *Engel v. Vitale*, 368 U.S. 1261 (1962). Many footnotes and references in the original decision are here omitted.

Neither the fact that the prayer may be denominationally neutral, nor the fact that its observance on the part of the students is voluntary can serve to free it from the limitation of the Establishment Clause . . . of the First Amendment [which] . . . . rested on the belief that a union of government and religion tends to destroy government and to degrade religion. . . . It is neither sacrilegious nor antireligious to say that each separate government in this country should stay out of the business of writing or sanctioning official prayers and leave that purely religious function to the people themselves and to those the people choose to look to for religious guidance.[32]

Mr. Justice [William O.] Douglas, Concurring:[33]

The point for decision is whether the Government can constitutionally finance a religious exercise. Our system at the federal and state levels is presently honeycombed with such financing.[34] Nevertheless, I think it is an unconstitutional undertaking whatever form it takes. . . .

---

[32] There is of course nothing in the decision reached here that is inconsistent with the fact that school children and others are officially encouraged to express love for our country by reciting historical documents such as the Declaration of Independence which contain references to the Deity or by singing officially espoused anthems which include the composer's professions of faith in a Supreme Being, or with the fact that there are many manifestations in our public life of belief in God. Such patriotic or ceremonial occasions bear no true resemblance to the unquestioned religious exercise that the State of New York has sponsored in this instance.

[33] Editor's Note: In *Abingdon v. Schempp* (1963), cited in the following selection, Mr. Justice Douglas' concurring opinion contained the following statement:

> The most effective way to establish any institution is to finance it; and this truth is reflected in the appeals by church groups for public funds to finance their religious schools. Financing a church either in its strictly religious activities or in its other activities is equally unconstitutional, as I understand the Establishment Clause. . . . What may not be done directly may not be done indirectly lest the Establishment Clause become a mockery.

[34] There are many "aids" to religion in this country at all levels of government. To mention but a few at the federal level, one might begin by observing that the very First Congress which wrote the First Amendment provided for chaplains in both Houses and in the armed services. There is compulsory chapel at the service academies, and religious services are held in federal hospitals and prisons. The President issues religious proclamations. The Bible is used for the administration of oaths. N.Y.A. and W.P.A. funds were available to parochial schools during the depression. Veterans receiving money under the "G.I." Bill of 1944 could attend denominational schools, to which payments were made directly by the government. During World War II, federal money was contributed to denominational schools for the training of nurses. The benefits of the National School Lunch Act are available to students in private as well as public schools. The Hospital Survey and Construction Act of 1946 specifically made money available to non-public hospitals. The slogan "In God We Trust" is used by the Treasury Department, and Congress recently added God to the pledge of allegiance. There is Bible-reading in the schools of the District of Columbia, and religious instruction is given in the District's National Training School for Boys. Religious organizations are exempt from the federal income tax and are granted postal privileges. Up to defined limits—

I cannot say that to authorize this prayer is to establish a religion in the strictly historic meaning of those words. Yet once government finances a religious exercise it inserts a divisive influence into our communities. . . .

The First Amendment leaves the Government in a position not of hostility to religion, but of neutrality. . . . The First Amendment teaches that a government neutral in the field of religion better serves all religious interests.

My problem today would be uncomplicated but for *Everson v. Board of Education* 330 U.S. 1 (1946) which allowed taxpayers' money to be used to pay "the bus fares of parochial school pupils as a part of a general program under which" the fares of pupils attending public and other schools were also paid. The *Everson* case seems in retrospect to be out of line with the First Amendment. Its result is appealing, as it allows aid to be given to needy children. Yet by the same token, public funds could be used to satisfy other needs of children in parochial schools—lunches, books, and tuition being obvious examples. Mr. Justice Rutledge stated in dissent what I think is durable First Amendment philosophy:

> The reasons underlying the Amendment's policy have not vanished with time or diminished in force. Now as when it was adopted the price of religious freedom is double. It is that the church and religion shall live both within and upon that freedom. There cannot be freedom of religion, safeguarded by the state, and intervention by the church or its agencies in the state's domain or dependency on its largesse. The great condition of religious liberty is that it be maintained free from sustenance, as also from other interferences, by the state. For when it comes to rest upon that secular foundation it vanishes with the resting. Public money devoted to payment of religious costs, educational or other, brings the quest for more. It brings too the struggle of sect against sect for the larger share or for any. Here one by numbers alone will benefit most, there another. That is precisely the history of societies which have had an established religion and dissident groups. It is the very thing Jefferson and Madison experienced and sought to guard against, whether in its blunt or in its more screened forms. The end of such strife cannot be other than to destroy the cherished liberty. The dominating group will achieve the dominant benefit; or all will embroil the state in their dissensions.

---

15 per cent of the adjusted gross income of individuals and 5 per cent of the net income of corporations—contributions to religious organizations are deductible for federal income tax purposes. There are limits to the deductibility of gifts and bequests to religious institutions made under the federal gift and estate tax laws. This list of federal "aids" could easily be expanded, and of course there is a long list in each state.

—Fellman, *The Limits of Freedom*, New Brunswick, N.J.: Rutgers University Press, 1959, pp. 40–41.

What New York does with this prayer is a break with that tradition. I therefore join the Court in reversing the judgment below.

Mr. Justice [Potter] Stewart, Dissenting:

With all respect, I think the Court has misapplied a great constitutional principle. I cannot see how an "official religion" is established by letting those who want to say a prayer say it. On the contrary, I think that to deny the wish of these school children to join in reciting this prayer is to deny them the opportunity of sharing in the spiritual heritage of our Nation. . . .

The Court today says that the state and federal governments are without constitutional power to prescribe any particular form of words to be recited by any group of the American people on any subject touching religion. The third stanza of the "Star-Spangled Banner," made our National Anthem by Act of Congress in 1931, contains these verses:

> Blest with victory and peace, may the heav'n rescued land
> Praise the Pow'r that hath made and preserved us a nation!
> Then conquer we must, when our cause it is just,
> And this be our motto "In God is our Trust."

In 1954 Congress added a phrase to the Pledge of Allegiance to the Flag so that it now contains the words "one Nation *under God*, indivisible, with liberty and justice for all." In 1952 Congress enacted legislation calling upon the President each year to proclaim a National Day of Prayer. Since 1865 the words "In God We Trust" have been impressed on our coins.

Countless similar examples could be listed, but there is no need to belabor the obvious. I do not believe that this Court, or the Congress, or the President has by the actions and practices I have mentioned established an "official religion" in violation of the Constitution. And I do not believe the State of New York has done so in this case. What each has done has been to recognize and to follow the deeply entrenched and highly cherished spiritual traditions of our Nation—traditions which come down to us from those who almost two hundred years ago avowed their "firm reliance on the Protection of Divine Providence" when they proclaimed the freedom and independence of this brave new world.

I dissent.[35]

---

[35] Editor's Note: Compare the following statement by R. Freeman Butts:

> I believe that it is an unwarranted leap of logic and of history to say that *because* we are a religious people or a religious nation, *therefore* our *government* rests on religion. This leap is sometimes made deliberately and sometimes unintentionally. So now we as educators should look again at the foundations of our governmental system. Is our Constitution a secular or a religious document? Is our government a secular institution which leaves religion to citizens as individuals or should it become an ally of religious institutions by promoting religion among the people

3.14 THE LORD'S PRAYER AND BIBLE READING AS PUBLIC SCHOOL REQUIREMENTS? NO*

Tom C. Clark and Others

[The] ideal of our people as to religious freedom [is] one of "absolute equality before the law of all religious opinions and sects. . . . The Government is neutral, and while protecting all, it prefers none, and it disparages none."

Before examining this "neutral" position in which the establishment

---

through the schools? Do the Regents and Board of Superintendents who want school children to highlight God in the Declaration of Independence also want the children to read all else its author said about God and Christianity? Does the Congress that made "One Nation, *Under God,*" the national motto want children to study the various theological meanings of God under public school teachers in public school classes? . . . Does anyone want a religious test established for public school teachers to make sure that they will promote a "proper" belief in God in the classroom? . . . Can we possibly use the schools to *encourage* belief in God or *promote* religion among the people without *persuading* students to take religious instruction? . . . I think not.

To be sure, many Americans have always been religious, more now than at any time in our history. I believe this a good thing. What it means is that religion flourishes under separation of church and state more than it did under the established religions which the founding fathers sought to abolish. But does this flourishing of religion give us license to reinterpret our history, or blur the lines between morality and religion, or identify religious individuals as the only good citizens? I think not. Freedom of religion and separation of church and state were indispensable as ingredients in forming our nation. They are even more indispensable today as ingredients in maintaining and preserving our nation.

—R. Freeman Butts, "The Relation Between Religion and Education," *Progressive Education,* 33: 140–142, September 1956.

* Tom C. Clark, Majority opinion, *School District of Abington Township, Pennsylvania v. Schempp; Murray v. Curlett* [Maryland], 83 S. Ct., 1560 (1963); or 371 U.S. 807, 907, 944 (1963).

The Court's decision dealt with two cases, from Maryland and Pennsylvania. These cases involved challenges to state law and to school district policy requiring the reading of Bible verses to the students each morning, and/or the recitation of the Lord's Prayer by the classes in unison. The 1963 decision makes it quite explicit that such enforced public school religious practices are unconstitutional; but, on the other hand, that other religious elements in public life would not be affected.

It may be noted that the majority opinion is by Justice Clark, a Presbyterian active in the affairs of his church, and that the concurring opinions include statements by Justice Goldberg, the Court's only Jew, and Justice Brennan, the Court's only Roman Catholic. The lengthy opinion by Justice Brennan canvassed the history of the church-state conflict to show long concern in this country about any breakdown of church-state separation. Brennan's opinion concluded: "The principles which we reaffirm and apply today can hardly be thought novel or radical. They are, in truth, as old as the republic itself."

The full decision constitutes an excellent summary of the recent history of the adjudication of constitutional questions regarding church-state-school relationships.

and free exercise clauses of the First Amendment place our Government it is well that we discuss the reach of the amendment under the cases of this Court.

First, this Court has decisively settled that the First Amendment's mandate that "Congress shall make no law respecting an establishment of religion, or prohibiting the free exercise thereof" has been made wholly applicable to the states by the Fourteenth Amendment. . . .

Second, this Court has rejected unequivocally the contention that the establishment clause forbids only governmental preference of one religion over another. Almost 20 years ago in *Everson* . . . the Court said that ". . . neither a state nor the Federal government can set up a church. Neither can pass laws which aid one religion, aid all religions, or prefer one religion over another," and Mr. Justice Jackson, dissenting, agreed: "There is no answer to the proposition . . . that the effect of the religious freedom Amendment to our Constitution was to take every form of propagation of religion out of the realm of things which could directly or indirectly be made public business and thereby be supported in whole or in part at taxpayers' expense. . . . This freedom was first in the Bill of Rights because it was first in the forefathers' minds; it was set forth in absolute terms, and its strength is its rigidity." . . .

Further, Mr. Justice Rutledge, joined by Justices Frankfurter, Jackson and Burton, declared:

> The [First] Amendment's purpose was not to strike merely at the official establishment of a single sect, creed or religion, outlawing only a formal relation such as had prevailed in England and some of the colonies. Necessarily it was to uproot all such relationships. But the object was broader than separating church and state in this narrow sense. It was to create a complete and permanent separation of the spheres of religious activity and civil authority by comprehensively forbidding every form of public aid or support for religion.

. . . The same conclusion has been firmly maintained ever since that time . . . and we reaffirm it now.

It is insisted that unless these religious exercises are permitted a "religion of secularism" is established in the schools. We agree of course, that the state may not establish a "religion of secularism" in the sense of affirmatively opposing or showing hostility to religion, thus "preferring those who believe in no religion over those who do believe." *Zorach v. Clauson*. . . . We do not agree, however, that this decision in any sense has that effect. In addition, it might well be said that one's education is not complete without a study of comparative religion or the history of religion and its relationship to the advancement of civilization. It certainly may be said that the Bible is worthy of study for its literary and historic qualities.

Nothing we have said here indicates that such study of the Bible or of religion, when presented objectively as part of a secular program of education, may not be effected consistent with the First Amendment. But the exercises here do not fall into those categories. They are religious exercises, required by the states in violation of the command of the First Amendment that the government maintain strict neutrality, neither aiding nor opposing religion.[36]

Finally . . . [although] the free exercise clause clearly prohibits the use of state action to deny the right of free exercise to anyone, it has never meant that a majority could use the machinery of the state to practice its beliefs. . . . In the relationship between man and religion, the state is firmly committed to a position of neutrality. . . .[37]

The place of religion in our society is an exalted one, achieved through a long tradition of reliance on the home, the church and the inviolable citadel of the individual heart and mind. We have come to recognize through bitter experience that it is not within the power of government

---

[36] Editor's Note: In religion, as in anything else, the proper function of the public schools is not indoctrination, but understanding. On this point, Theodore Powell has suggested that the Supreme Court decisions of 1962 and 1963 may in the long run prove of benefit to religion, for they may lead to a clearer understanding of the specific elements of religion which may, or which may not, be emphasized in public schools:

> Instead of bitter battles to maintain a feeble recognition of religion by means of opening exercises with little meaning or educational effectiveness, school boards should be encouraged to adopt a program based on the proper function of the public schools, not worship or indoctrination, but education. . . . The purpose of the public school is to impart knowledge, not to instill faith. This, in itself, is no small task. Real understanding by pupils of the place of religion in the development of our civilization should be a goal for every public school.
>
> —Theodore Powell, "The School Prayer Battle," *Saturday Review*, 46: 62–64, 77–78, April 20, 1963. By permission.

Compare the following statement by Albert Schweitzer:

> Christianity has need of thought that it may come to the consciousness of its real self. For centuries it treasured the great commandment of love and mercy as traditional truth without recognizing it as a reason for opposing slavery, witch burning, torture, and all the other ancient and medieval forms of inhumanity. It was only when it experienced the influence of the thinking of the Age of Enlightenment that it was stirred into entering the struggle for humanity. The remembrance of this ought to preserve it forever from assuming any air of superiority in comparison with thought.
>
> —Albert Schweitzer, *Out of My Life and Thought*, New York: Holt, Rinehart and Winston, Inc., 1933, p. 236.

[37] We are not of course presented with and therefore do not pass upon a situation such as military service, where the Government regulates the temporal and geographic environment of individuals to a point that, unless it permits voluntary religious services to be conducted with the use of government facilities, military personnel would be unable to engage in the practice of their faiths.

to invade that citadel, whether its purpose or effect be to aid or oppose, to advance or retard. In the relationship between man and religion, the state is firmly committed to a position of neutrality. Though the application of that rule requires interpretation of a delicate sort, the rule itself is clearly and concisely stated in the words of the First Amendment. . . . [Therefore] we hold that the practices at issue and the laws upholding them are unconstitutional. . . .

Mr. Justice Brennan, Concurring:

. . . What the Framers meant to foreclose, and what our decisions under the Establishment Clause have forbidden, are those involvements of religion with secular institutions which (a) serve the essentially religious activities of religious institutions; (b) employ the organs of government for essentially religious purposes; or (c) use essentially religious means to serve governmental ends, where secular means would suffice. . . .

The holding of the Court today plainly does not foreclose teaching *about* the Holy Scriptures or about the differences between religious sects in classes in literature or history. . . .

Mr. Justice Stewart, Dissenting:

I cannot agree that on these records we can say that the establishment clause has necessarily been violated. . . .

That the central value embodied in the First Amendment—and, more particularly, in the guarantee of "liberty" contained in the 14th—is the safeguarding of an individual's right to free exercise of his religion has been consistently recognized. . . . It is this concept of constitutional protection embodied in our decision which makes the cases before us such difficult ones for me. For there is involved in these cases a substantial free exercise claim on the part of those who affirmatively desire to have their children's school day open with the reading of passages from the Bible. . . .

[A] compulsory state educational system so structures a child's life that if religious exercises are held to be an impermissible activity in schools, religion is placed at an artificial and state-created disadvantage. Viewed in this light, permission of such exercises for those who want them is necessary if the schools are truly to be neutral in the matter of religion. And a refusal to permit religious exercises thus is seen, not as the realization of state neutrality, but rather as the establishment of a religion of secularism, or at the least as Government support of the beliefs of those who think that religious exercises should be conducted only in private. . . .

3.15 THE JOURNEY OF OUR HISTORY HAS NOT CEASED*

Archibald MacLeish

A world ends when its metaphor has died.
An age becomes an age, all else beside,
When sensuous poets in their pride invent
Emblems for the soul's consent
That speak the meanings men will never know
But man-imagined images can show:
It perishes when those images, though seen,
No longer mean. . . .
But are we sure
The age that died upon its metaphor
Among these Roman heads, these mediaeval towers,
Is ours?—
Or ours the ending of that story?. . . .
The journey of our history has not ceased:
Earth turns us still toward the rising east,
The metaphor still struggles in the stone. . . .
Still knocks at silence to be understood.
Poets, deserted by the world before,
Invent the age! Invent the metaphor!

---

* Archibald MacLeish, excerpt from "Hypocrit Auteur," in *Collected Poems 1917–1952*, Boston: Houghton Mifflin Company, 1952. By permission.

See also Edwin Arlington Robinson's sonnet, "Children of the Night,"—or the well-known lines of Gerard Manley Hopkins:

Eternal Silence, sing to me
And beat upon my whorlèd ear,
Pipe me to pastures still and be
The music that I care to hear.

3.16 RELIGION IN THE PUBLIC SCHOOLS*

American Association of School Administrators

ACCOMMODATIONS TO RELIGIOUS PLURALISM

Implicit in our system of government is the principle that no one religion or group of religions may dominate, but all must honor the religious convictions and practices of others. To tolerate is not enough. Honoring our differences means making room for them. It means understanding and valuing people for their differences, not merely focusing on surface similarities. It gives support to a genuinely inter-cultural education—one which strengthens mutual understanding and respect. In the long run, informed respect will strengthen the individual cultures themselves.

The public schools, as agencies of civil government, must be neutral with respect to the claims of the many religions and philosophies to the devotion and faith of their followers. At the same time they are charged, along with the civil government itself, with the responsibility to provide an environment in which practices and values that are rooted in the homes and churches can flourish. It is in response to this double duty that school policies that are truly constructive must be formulated.

The Commission proposes that constructive policy must be developed in every school district that will not only guarantee freedom from the establishment of religion but equally will foster freedom for religion. . . .

In a public school which has regularly found occasions for children to tell about their own and hear about others' religious celebrations, rites, and beliefs, few problems arise. The teacher sets the atmosphere. He or she need only be warmly interested and supportive for children to see that their differing customs and beliefs are neither strange nor the cause for estrangement but are rather wonderful and essential elements of a pluralistic society. The trap for the teacher who has not deliberately thought through his own role lies in his unconscious identification with one of the religions or groupings of religions. How easy it is for a committed Christian to speak of "we" and "our" ways, unconsciously thereby leading children to identify the "we" with the school and government or world, and perhaps themselves with the outcast or minority "they"! It then becomes hard for them to see that the schools and the government do not belong to Congregationalists or Catholics or Baptists or Adventists or Jews or Ethical Culturists or Humanists or Atheists—but to the people as citizens with their citizenship in common, whatever their religious diversities. . . .

---

* *Religion in the Public Schools*: A Report by the Commission on Religion in the Public Schools, New York: Harper & Row, Publishers, 1965 (paperback).

[For example, a] public school, whatever the feelings of its constituents, may not observe Christmas as though it were a church or combination of churches. On the other hand an educational institution for children may not, consistent with proven educational principles of readiness and interest, ignore Christmas. . . . At school the child will sing more songs from Christian heritage—not as a worshiper, of course—[but only] because there *are* more and he joins the others in wanting to share them. . . .[38] [Again, with regard to baccalaureate services, the] Commission recommends [the following] practice as being compatible with sound Constitutional and educational policy: . . . [All] religious groups represented by students in the graduating class [are free to, and may be encouraged to] conduct baccalaureate services in their own churches and synagogues. In communities where some of the churches are accustomed to unite for special services a number of them may join in a union service for their own graduates. In others, every church will hold its own. In any case, the school does not require attendance nor does it do more than inform its seniors about this opportunity as it might about any other church-sponsored youth activity. . . . The school administrator, by taking personal initiative in the matter, in one step recognizes the important role of the churches in the lives of their own young people, avoids imposing any single religious point of view on a captive audience, and yet actively suggests the importance of high school graduation as a still momentous step in the young person's development. . . .

THE CURRICULUM AND OUR RELIGIOUS HERITAGE

The public schools have as one of their principal roles the transmission of culture, the passing on of the rich heritage of the American people. Justice Jackson, in . . . the *McCollum* case, reminds us of the significant part religions have played in that cultural heritage:

> Nearly everything in our culture worth transmitting, everything which gives meaning to life, is saturated with the religious influences derived from paganism, Judaism, Christianity—both Catholic and Protestant—and other faiths accepted by a large part of the world's peoples. . . .

The Commission believes that the public school curriculum must give suitable attention to the religious influences in man's development. . . . [and] recognizes three distinct policy areas . . . where explicit educational policy, adequate materials, and effective methods need to be developed. In one large area, recognition must be given to the role of religion and the religious in literature, in history and the humanities, and in the arts.

---

[38] Editor's Note: See also "Christmas in the Schools," NEA *Journal* 56: 54–57, December 1967.

In a second area ways must be found to portray the part played by religion in establishing and maintaining the moral and ethical values that the school seeks to develop and transmit. Finally, the public schools are called on to build an understanding of the relationships between civil government and religious freedom, and to prepare youth for citizenship in a multifaithed society. . . .

RELIGION IN THE CULTURAL HERITAGE

. . . Teachers of music and art and, to some degree, of literature, often seem to have been better equipped with an appreciation of the contributions of religion in their fields. The history of these arts, usually a required study for teachers, is a history of values and of man's view of himself, his world, and his God or gods. Much of the classical work in all the arts is deeply indebted to and affected by the religion and the religious institutions of the time. True literacy in the arts almost inescapably involves a degree of religious literacy. Art history, survey and criticism, or what are commonly called "appreciation" courses, would be empty without some understanding and appreciation of the religious element.

The desirable policy in the schools, as the Commission sees it, is to deal directly and objectively with religion whenever and wherever it is intrinsic to learning experience in the various fields of study, and to seek out appropriate ways to teach what has been aptly called "the reciprocal relation" between religion and the other elements in human culture. The implementation of that policy calls for much more than an added course, either for teachers or for the high school curriculum itself. It requires topic-by-topic analysis of the separate courses, and cooperative efforts by the teachers to give appropriate attention to these relationships. . . .

VALUES [39]

The Commission . . . would have the school teach the part which organized religion has played in establishing the moral and ethical values that schools must develop and transmit. Giving due respect to the prin-

[39] Editor's Note: In a democracy, teachers should encourage students to clarify *for themselves* what they value; and this is not the same as persuading children to accept some predetermined set of values. On this point, Peck and Havighurst have written:

> It is temptingly easy and insidiously gratifying to "mold" children, or to "whip them into line" by exercising one's superior status and authority as an adult. It is often personally inconvenient to allow children time to debate alternatives, and it may be personally frustrating if their choice contradicts one's own preferences. If there is any selfish, sensitive "pride" at stake, it is very hard for most adults to refrain from controlling children in an autocratic manner. Then, too, like any dictatorship, it looks "more efficient"—to the dictator, at least. However, the effect

ciple of valuing differences in a free society, it would not seek to equate religion and morality by suggesting that religious convictions or sanctions alone undergird moral principles or ethical imperatives. It would, however, acknowledge the resources found by most people in religion as a basis for durable convictions and moral and ethical imperatives. . . . [However, it must be recognized that the] study of comparative religion and the history of religion [on the elementary and secondary levels cannot be well done until there is more] material available that is truly objective, balanced, and educationally sound. . . .

Educators have long been concerned with defining and implementing the public schools' own ethical imperatives. Their commitment to the processes and goals of education has led them to a sound distaste for "indoctrination." At the same time there is a nearly universal consensus that the schools have an important part to play in the building of character and in the development and reinforcement of value systems that are consonant with the values commonly expressed (though perhaps less commonly embodied) in the larger society. Few dispute the wisdom, even the sheer necessity for personal fulfillment, of every individual's commitment to something higher than self and more than the passing moment.

The public schools themselves represent a commitment by the American people, part of a larger commitment to "establish justice, insure domestic tranquility, provide for the common defense, promote the general welfare, and secure the blessings of liberty to ourselves and our posterity," in the words of our Constitution's Preamble. Every publc officer, in the states as in the nation, has taken an oath to support the Constitution. There seems to be no educational or ethical reason why every citizen, young or old, should not be led toward the same commitment. . . .

PREPARING FOR CITIZENSHIP IN A MULTIFAITHED SOCIETY

The early reactions to the latest Supreme Court decisions call attention to another pressing need. Far too few appeared to understand that primarily the Bill of Rights is a great bulwark designed to protect the indi-

---

on character is to arrest the development of rational judgment and to create such resentments as prevent the growth of genuine altruistic impulses. For thousands of years, the long-term effects have been ignored and sacrificed to short-term adult advantages, most of the time. Probably it is no accident that there are relatively few people who are, or ever will become, psychologically and ethically mature.

—Robert F. Peck and Robert J. Havighurst, *The Psychology of Character Development*, New York: John Wiley & Sons, Inc., 1960, p. 191. See also Louis E. Raths, Merrill Harmin, and Sidney B. Simon, *Values and Teaching*, Columbus, Ohio: Charles E. Merrill Books, Inc., 1966.

vidual from the state. Too many seemed to have overlooked or failed to attend to Justice Jackson, speaking for the Court in *West Virginia Board of Education v. Barnette* (1943):

> The very purpose of a Bill of Rights was to withdraw certain subjects from the vicissitudes of political controversy, to place them beyond the reach of majorities and officials. . . . One's right to freedom of worship . . . and other fundamental rights may not be submitted to vote; they depend on the outcome of no elections.

Few apparently heard or heeded Justice Clark's words in the last paragraph of the Court's opinion in the *Schempp* case (1963):

> The place of religion in our society is an exalted one, achieved through a long tradition of reliance on the home, the church and the inviolable citadel of the individual heart and mind. We have come to recognize through bitter experience that it is not within the power of government to invade that citadel, whether its purpose or effect be to aid or oppose, to advance or retard. In the relationship between man and religion, the State is firmly committed to a position of neutrality.

The widespread first reaction points to a real need. Surely every public school child must learn what is expressed and implied in the great compact, the Constitution of the United States of America, which undergirds our national society. He must know the history of the Bill of Rights and what it means. . . .[40]

CONCLUSION

. . . America's public schools have a long, rich, and unique history. They are founded on a singular view of the good society. They cherish differences. They respect individuality. They reflect and build an order in which differences—religious and ideological as well as natural—are regarded as

---

[40] Editor's Note:

Most persons in this country live by some philosophy of the cosmos, whether it be Catholicism, Trinitarian Protestantism, Unitarianism, Judaism, Humanism, Buddhism, agnosticism or atheism. In the eyes of the Constitution, all of these philosophies are entitled to equal respect from the civil authority. This does not mean that an equal value has been placed upon each one of them, but simply that the individual is to be completely free to make his own choice and to express his views in public places as well as private. To say that this evidences an attitude of Godlessness on the part of our constitutional system or establishes a religion of secularism is to completely misunderstand the theory of our constitution.

—Paul W. Burton, "Education, Religion and the Bill of Rights Today," in Leo O. Garber, ed., *Current Legal Concepts in Education*, Philadelphia: University of Pennsylvania Press, 1966, pp. 91–92.

contributing strength not weakness. The common faith they nourish is a faith in freedom, the matching of right with responsibility.

The power of the public school is in the opportunity it provides for the creative engagement of differences—differences in physical and mental capacities and characteristics, differences in background and culture, differences in the creeds men live by. This is a power not always understood, not uniformly supported, nor invariably exercised effectively. Concern over the role of religion in the public school that leads to a lessening of that power weakens the very institution that serves a diverse society so faithfully. Concern that leads to improvement in the methods, materials, and competence with which the school deals with the role of religion is constructive. The Commission . . . is confident that America's public schools can and will find ways to meet that challenge, to preserve the guarantees of religious freedom while reinforcing for each the free exercise of his religion, in a society which gives full respect to those of every faith and creed. . . . If and when the public schools have achieved their assigned role in the education of America's citizens, they will justify Samuel Johnson's dictum that "about things on which the public thinks *long* it commonly attains to think right." . . . .[41]

---

[41] Editor's Note: Compare the following two statements:

> Religion can, and in our judgement should, be studied in the same way as the economic and political institutions and principles of our country should be studied —not as something on which the American public school must settle all arguments and say the last word, but as something which is so much a part of the American heritage and so relevant to contemporary values that it cannot be ignored. . . .
>
> —American Council on Education, *The Function of the Public Schools in Dealing with Religion,* Washington, D.C.: National Education Association, 1953, p. 7. By permission.

> By "secular" is not meant a school unfriendly to religion, but one under community law control, not ecclesiastical control. By "secular" is also meant that the common school is an institution of the whole community, and hence recognizes the members of all its component groups as first-class citizens, irrespective of religious belief or church and synagogue connection. The emergence of the common school therefore is an expression of that tendency which progressively broadened the basis of citizenship in our country from Puritan to Protestant, to Christian, to Christian and Jew, to adherents of all religions, and, finally, to all men.
>
> —John L. Childs, "The Future of the Common School," *Educational Forum* 21: 133–141, January 1957. By permission of Kappa Delta Pi; copyright by Kappa Delta Pi.

TOPICS FOR FURTHER STUDY

CHURCH AND STATE: PROS AND CONS

A. *Religious Intoleration and the Law.* . . . The protection accorded by the laws and customs to religion as such extends automatically to religious intolerance. The belief in the exclusiveness and infallibility of the truth revealed in that religion, being part and parcel of and inseparable from the religion itself, cannot protect religion without at the same time protecting the negation of other faiths. . . . [Such a situation prevails] in the case of a State Religion, that is, where the state recognizes the monopoly of one religion as the established religion of the state, particularly where at the same time all other religions are being prohibited or outlawed.

In states in which both the religion of the majority and religions of minorities are protected by the law, which protection implicitly covers the claims of each religion to a monopoly of the truth as aforesaid, some compromise has to be found between the mutually exclusive monopolies and intolerances. It is submitted that such a compromise can be found only if the intolerance is being assigned, and restricted to, the sphere of meditation and theology, and not allowed to enter the sphere of activity and practice. In other words, the protection of the laws may extend to religious intolerance only insofar as it is passive and theoretical, never insofar as it is active and violent. . . .

As a matter of historical and sociological fact, religious intolerance has always striven to be activated; and where external conditions prevented such activation, it was often raised to the level of a holy goal to be prayed for. The understanding and insight that religious intolerance might remain passive and be restricted to the sphere of inner convictions and theological theory, is but a concomitant of the modern concept of freedom of religion.[42]

B. *Freedom of Worship.* The inalienable right of all men to worship God according to the teaching of the Catholic Church. No state can justifiably prevent the exercise of this right; and indeed it has a duty to foster this true worship, since God's supremacy calls for man's acknowledgement in worship, and Christ established one form and content of public worship in establishing one only Church, to which all are commanded to submit. But to avoid greater evil or to achieve a higher good, public authority can tolerate false religions, so long as they do not teach open immorality. The practice that should distinguish Catholics in this matter today was tersely summarized by Cardinal Gibbons in the words, "Full liberty must be

---

[42] Haim H. Cohn, "Religious Intoleration and the Law," 12 *New York Law Review* 257–274, Summer 1967. By permission.

granted to all men to worship God according to the dictates of their conscience."[43]

C. *Expanding Concepts of Religious Freedom.* . . . The genius of the Supreme Court in adapting the Constitution to changes in American society has enabled the Constitution to serve a nation which has undergone a radical transformation in a century and three quarters. In 1844, Mr. Justice Story, for a unanimous Court, could assume that this is "a Christian country" and refer to "Judaism, or Deism, or any other form of infidelity." *Vidal v. Girard's Ex'rs.*, 43 U.S. (2 How.) 127, 198 (1844). A century later the Court declared only that "we are a religious people," *Zorach v. Clauson*, 343 U.S. 306, 313 (1952), and just a few years ago it unanimously struck down a requirement "of belief in the existence of God," *Torcaso v. Watkins*, 367 U.S. 488, 495 (1961), as a condition to eligibility for public office. . . . More and more, the law has come to respect the human spirit and the dignity and worth of man.[44]

"ERROR HAS NO RIGHTS": SOME PRO-CON CATHOLIC VIEWS

A. It is true that, according to theology, there is only one true, Apostolic and Catholic Church, and this Church, as a divinely instituted perfect society, deserves a privileged position since truth has always privileges over anything that is not truth. Yet . . . [in a modern pluralistic society] the

---

[43] A *Catholic Dictionary*, Donald Attwater, ed., New York: Crowell-Collier and Macmillan, Inc., 2nd rev. ed., 1949, pp. 201–202.

[44] Arner Brodie and Harold P. Southerland, concluding remarks in their lengthy article on religious freedom, 1966 *Wisconsin Law Review*, 214–330 at 306. By permission.

In *Torcaso v. Watkins*, 367 U.S. 499 (1961), the U.S. Supreme Court held that a state could not make declaration of belief in God a condition for appointment as a notary public. Such a condition on any public benefit would put state power "on the side of one particular sort of believers. . . ." This is a forbidden establishment, since

> . . . neither a State nor the Federal Government can constitutionally force a person "to profess a belief or disbelief in any religion." Neither can constitutionally pose laws nor impose requirements which aid all religions as against non-believers, and neither can aid those religions based on a belief in the existence of God as against those religions founded on different beliefs. (Among religions in this country which do not teach what would generally be considered a belief in the existence of God are Buddhism, Taoism, Ethical Culture, Secular Humanism, and others.)

In *United States v. Seegar*, 360 U.S. 163 (1965), the Court dealt with exemption clauses for conscientious objectors to military service, and interpreted the congressional requirement of "belief in relation to a Supreme Being" to mean a

> belief that is sincere and meaningful [and that] occupies a place in the life of its possessor parallel to that filled by the orthodox belief in God of one who clearly qualifies for the exemption. Where such beliefs have parallel positions in the lives of their respective holders we cannot say that one is "in a relation to a Supreme Being" and the other is not.

See, however, Dale E. Noyd, "Credo of a Humanist," *Humanist* 27: 130–131, July–August 1967; and Jeremy Larner, "The Court-Martial of Captain Noyd," *Harper's* 236: 78–85, June 1968.

state does better to become religiously neutral; i.e., the state gives full religious freedom, retires from any positive or negative intervention into the religious life of its citizens. And it does so simply as a matter of political prudence and as the protector of the common good. It abstains from any judgment about religious truth; it abstains from intervention, not because it adheres to the theory that all religions are equally true or false. Its practice of religious freedom and separation is a mere policy, exercised in the interest of the common good without any philosophical pretense of indifferentism. . . .[45]

---

[45] Heinrich A. Rommen, *The State in Catholic Thought*, St. Louis, Mo., and London: B. Herder Book Company, 1950, pp. 602–605.

Until quite recently very few Roman Catholics defended the separation of church and state, except as a matter of practical expediency:

> It may be that under certain circumstances, such as the exceptional good will of the political powers, the Church deems it preferable to acquiesce to a factual separation of Church and State, but in no case will she ever admit that Church and State should be kept separate. Their separation remains an evil even while, for reasons of expediency, it is being tolerated. The same remark applies to the school problem.
>
> —Etienne Gilson, ed., *The Church Speaks to the Modern World: The Social Teachings of Leo XIII*, New York: Doubleday & Company, Inc. (Image D7), 1954, p. 17.

In 1948 this view was reiterated as follows:

> Is religious tolerance simply a matter of fair play? U. S. Protestants who think so often boil with indignation at the Roman Catholic Church, which accepts the advantages of tolerance in non-Catholic countries but sternly discourages other faiths in areas where Catholics are in the majority.
>
> One of the newest and clearest statements of the Catholic position appeared recently in Rome in the Jesuits' fortnightly *La Civilità Cattolica.* Excerpts are quoted in this week's *Christian Century*: "The Roman Catholic Church, convinced, through its divine prerogatives, of being the only true church, must demand the right to freedom for herself alone, because such a right can only be possessed by truth, never by error. As to other religions, the church will certainly never draw the sword, but she will require that by legitimate means they shall not be allowed to propagate false doctrine. Consequently, in a state where the majority of the people are Catholic, the church will require that legal existence be denied to error, and that if religious minorities actually exist, they shall have only a *de facto* existence without opportunity to spread their beliefs. If, however, actual circumstances. . . . make the complete application of this principle impossible, then the church will require for herself all possible concessions. . . .
>
> "In some countries, Catholics will be obliged to ask full religious freedom for all, resigned at being forced to cohabitate where they alone should rightfully be allowed to live. But in doing this the church does not renounce her thesis. . . . but merely adapts herself. . . . Hence arises the great scandal among Protestants. . . . We ask Protestants to understand that the Catholic church would betray her trust if she were to proclaim . . . that error can have the same rights as truth. . . . The church cannot blush for her own want of tolerance, as she asserts it in principle and applies it in practice."
>
> —*Time* 51: 70, June 28, 1948.

B. Religious convictions are regarded as fanatical when they prevent a man from being open to others, block his ears, and always make him misunderstand what others are saying. . . .

Man comes to be a person through dialogue with others. Man is a listener summoned to respond, and his responses constitute him in his personal being. . . .

Man is an open-ended being. He is involved in an unending dialogue which makes him to be who he is. Man is forever led into new situations, he listens to a summons that does not come from himself, and by responding to it he determines his existence as a person. . . .

Man is not an individual who grows by focussing on himself. Man does not achieve well-being by straining narcissistically after self-fulfillment. Man is a person, and hence he becomes more truly himself through communion with others. The center of man is outside of himself. . . .

Since institutions are made to promote man's life in society, they inevitably reflect the understanding of man that is current at the time they are created. The institutions in the Church—seminaries, monasteries, convents, ecclesiastical government and law courts—embody and promote the ideal of man as it was conceived at the time when they received their definitive shape. What is happening today is that with a new self-understanding many Christians find that these institutions no longer adequately promote human life. This is the deep cause for the restlessness in the Catholic Church. The present institutions of the Church operate on an anthropology that is no longer ours. . . .

Vatican Council II attempted to modify ecclesiastical institutions by making them correspond to the new anthropology. The liturgy (in the vernacular) was to make men into listeners and brothers. Participation was the key concept that inspired all the changes in institutions, whether these had to do with worship, ministry, religious life, or ecclesiastical government. Institutions in the Church must allow Christians to participate; and it is through the very process of participation that men are renewed, made sensitive to the Spirit, and open to one another. This ideal of participation in ecclesiastical institutions exists, so far, mainly on paper.

. . . .

Protestant leaders and spokesmen of other religions have repeatedly expressed their hope that the Second Vatican Council define the Church's position on religious liberty. They realize that two distinct views on this matter are taught by Catholic theologians in our century. Some theologians, the representatives of the older school, assert that error has no rights, and that therefore in "Catholic" countries governments should not tolerate Churches teaching erroneous doctrines. In such countries, they teach, the government should protect and advance the true religion. Only when Catholics are in a minority is religious liberty a good to be striven for, since in that situation it will favor the true Church. Other theologians, belonging to the newer school, the majority position today, teach that religious liberty is a good promised by the gospel, to be announced and defended by the Church in whatever situation she finds herself. These theologians reject the idea that "error has no rights," since error is an abstraction and since people who err do have rights. These theologians derive their understanding of religious liberty from the notion of man and the notion of faith revealed in the Scriptures and taught by the Church. Man is created by God to seek him with his mind and heart and this requires freedom; and the very notion of faith, through which man is reconciled and united to his God, implies a free search and a free surrender. Man can be faithful to his destiny only if he follows his good conscience. From this understanding of the gospel, these authors would say that interference and pressure by governments in the area of religion is never legitimate, except temporarily in unusual circumstances, when the exercise of a religion should interfere with the public welfare of society.[46]

PUBLIC FUNDS FOR PAROCHIAL SCHOOLS: PROS AND CONS

A. Parents have the primary obligation to educate their children and hence the primary right to choose the means of doing so. The state, like the Church is in the field of school education primarily to help the family and is the educational agent of the family. Parents who wish instruction in sacred doctrine for their children should have the help of the state in this as in other forms of education. To provide this is not to confuse church and state, since the state acts for the family, not for the Church, and does not itself espouse any religious doctrine. To refuse this help is to deny to the parents who wish it the public assistance in education to which they have a right as citizens.[47]

B. The exercise of liberty does not carry with it an option on the public treasury. I am free to go to town; this does not mean that the Government must buy me a bus ticket. I have freedom of speech; this does not mean that the Government must hire a hall for me or put me on a network. If I think the police are inadequate, I am free to hire private detectives; this does not mean the Government must pay their salaries. . . .

The argument [that grants be made to parochial school pupils for their education] comes to this: "It is constitutional for the Government to subsidize church schools if the money pauses for at least the moment in the pocket of the parents. It is the *channel*, not the *destination* that

[46] The first portion of these excerpts was from Gregory Baum, "Restlessness in the Church," *The Ecumenist: A Journal for Promoting Christian Unity* 5: 33–36, March–April 1967; the second portion is from Gregory Baum, "*Pacem in Terris* and Unity," *The Ecumenist* 1: 73–75, June–July 1963. By permission.

Father Baum is editor, *The Ecumenist*, published by the Paulist Press, New York.

[47] Herbert Johnson, A *Philosophy of Education*, New York: McGraw-Hill, Inc., 1963, p. 99. Copyright © 1963, McGraw-Hill, Inc. By permission. Herbert Johnson is Professor of Education, University of Notre Dame.

counts." This is specious reasoning. The fact that the grant pauses enroute to the clerics cannot obviate the fact that they are its true recipients.[48]

C. I would define the freedom of speech as the exclusion of governmental force from the process by which public opinion is formed on public issues. Any governmental action which makes it more difficult or hazardous to take one side of a public issue than to take the other is an abridgment, whether or not this was its avowed purpose. "Public issues" for this purpose, are not limited to those on which governmental action may be taken, but include philosophy, religion, ethics, esthetics, social sciences, etc.—all these, in other words, on which an enlightened public opinion may be deemed desirable. . . .

Governmental action which tends to regulate the content of public debate, either directly, or by singling out ideological groups or tendencies for special treatment, is permissible only if it . . . has no unnecessary deterrent effect on unprotected speech.[49]

SHARED TIME: ADVANTAGES AND DISADVANTAGES*

Shared time or dual enrollment is a plan whereby pupils of nonpublic schools enroll for part or even most of their school day in public school classes. . . . [In actual practice] shared time means that parochial school pupils attend classes in so-called "neutral" subjects in the public school and

[48] C. Stanley Lowell, "Shall the State Subsidize Church Schools," *Liberty*: 55: 11–15, October 1960. Reprinted from *Liberty*, a Magazine of Religious Freedom, Review and Herald Publishing Association, Takoma Park, Washington, D.C.: A 1961 survey of Catholic schools challenges the view that the federal aid through NDEA (National Defense Education Act) is used by parochial schools mainly for scientific purposes. George R. La Noue found that in church-related schools which had received NDEA support, textbooks in science were larded with specific religious content. Thus a mathematics textbook contained the following problems: "Jim made the Way of the Cross. He liked the sixth station very much. What Roman numeral was written above it?" "There are 37 boys in our room. Each boy says the Rosary every day. How many do we say in 20 days?" In foreign languages such lessons as "Une visite à Jesus" abound. A widely used biology text includes the study of angels as a "science" parallel to the study of the natural sciences. See G. R. La Noue, "Religious Schools and 'Secular' Subjects," *Harvard Educational Review*, 32: 255–291, Summer 1962; 33: 105–115, Winter 1963; 33: 336–359, Summer 1963 (discussion, bibliography). This study is summarized in *Phi Delta Kappan*, 43: 380–387, June 1962, and in a forty-seven page brochure by G. R. La Noue, *Public Funds for Parochial Schools*, published by the National Council of Churches, 475 Riverside Drive, New York. For a pamphlet advocating federal aid to parochial schools read "On Education" by Robert Maynard Hutchins, published in 1963 by the Center for the Study of Democratic Institutions, Box 4068, Santa Barbara, California.

[49] Laurant B. Frantz, "The First Amendment in the Balance," 71 *Yale Law Journal*, 1424–1450 at 1449, July 1962. Frantz' quotation raises this question: Does aid to parochial schools "make it more difficult or hazardous to take one side of a public issue than to take the other" with respect to such controversial problems as "naturalism," "scepticism," "birth control," "divorce?"

* Sam Dukar, *The Public Schools and Religion*, New York: Harper & Row, Publishers, 1966, pp. 221–223.

are instructed in religion and in subjects having ethical aspects in the parochial school. . . .

A. The benefits of the plan as advanced by its proponents may be summarized as follows:
   1. The integration of diverse religious groups in public school classes aids the democratization which is one of the major purposes of the public school.
   2. More pupils gain better educational training as some of the facilities used such as laboratories, etc. cannot be supplied in the private schools and would otherwise stand idle for a portion of the day.
   3. Catholic parents who share in the tax burden supporting the public school gain some direct benefits from their contributions, while the public school maintains its tradition that it is open to all comers.
   4. The public school gains support from parents of the private school pupils participating in this plan.
   5. The contact between faculties and administrations of the two types of schools tend to improve educational practice in both.
   6. The financial burden of the parochial school is eased, as are the demands on its physical facilities. It is thus able to accommodate more pupils and thereby able to satisfy the felt need of those parents wishing to obtain a religious education for their children.

B. Those who oppose shared-time plans point to a number of disadvantages. They may be summarized as follows:
   1. There are insuperable administrative difficulties inherent in shared-time plans. Among them are scheduling, discipline, observation of holidays, accreditation, grading, and the maintenance of the proper relationship between two school systems having diverse purposes.
   2. Divisiveness is strengthened rather than diminished by this plan.
   3. Public school facilities are already overtaxed and this additional burden can only result in lowering the quality of education.
   4. The large-scale adoption of this plan would lead to a proliferation of private schools, religious and secular, which would sound the death knell of the public school system as we now know it.
   5. There would be a tendency to force a modification of the public school curriculum to meet the demands of the parochial school authorities.
   6. The plan is unconstitutional under the Everson doctrine and clearly violates the provisions of the Establishment Clause of the First Amendment.

The crux of the debate lies in the question of the constitutionality of the shared-time plan under the First Amendment. There will be no final answer until the Supreme Court rules on this matter. Thus far there has been no effort to obtain such a test.

MORAL EDUCATION—PAROCHIAL OR COMMUNAL?: PROS AND CONS

A. The problem of choice between secular and other kinds of education is not a matter of choosing between the moral and the immoral. Rather, it involves a choice between two competing standards of the good life. In precise terms, the choice is between intelligence and dogma, between experience and speculation, between the demonstrable and the mystical, between diversity and uniformity; it is a choice between standards that are flexible and standards that are rigid, between methods that are critical and methods that are premised. A basic issue confronting the free, public, secular school of our time has to do with the moral struggle between freedom and the hostile remnants of a prescientific and predemocratic past. It is the issue of democracy versus absolutism.[50]

B. [We should strive for] the formulation and adoption of a faith more comprehensive and profound than the warring dogmas of most existing faiths, including scientific naturalism. This faith would rest upon the following premises: (1) that there are ultimate concerns which human beings have about such matters as the origin of existence, the meaning and purpose of human life, and the source of moral guidance; (2) that these questions arise out of the common and universal situation or predicament; (3) that to the questions there are many different answers and expressions of these answers, and that no single set of answers to the common questions has been found which will command universal assent; (4) that there is an obligation in the school program to recognize and to acknowledge the ultimate questions and in appropriate ways to help students to confront them; and (5) that the school can and ought to utilize the beliefs and practices of the historical religions (and "anti-religions") to illustrate ways in which men have sought to answer these problems. Indeed, the working out and advancement of such a common faith—one which properly balances the need for unity with commitment and diversity—is the essence of the American common school tradition.[51]

C. Rationality or reasonableness in conduct is the ability—which men possess—to envisage alternatives of action, to apply the test of observable consequences to conflicting proposals, and to accept or reconstruct these proposals in the light of consequences. The institutional expression of this rationality is the communal process of deliberation and critical assessment of evidence which alone makes possible a *freely* given consent. The willingness to sit down in the face of differences and reason together is the only categorical imperative a naturalistic humanist recognizes. . . .

Insofar as our age requires a unifying faith, it is clear that it cannot be found in any official doctrine or creed but rather in the commitment to the processes and methods of critical intelligence. Just as science made

---

[50] Frederick C. Neff, "How Moral is Secular Education?" *Christian Century*, 73: 1323–1325, November 14, 1956. By permission.

[51] Philip H. Phenix, "Religion in American Public Education," *Teachers College Record*, 57: 26–31, October 1955. By permission. For a pessimistic viewpoint concerning such a program, showing that different religious groups hold vastly different conceptions of "God," "human nature," etc., read Solomon B. Freehof, "To Find a Philosophy," *Religious Education*, 49: 112–115, March–April 1954. Read also Ronald E. Santoni, ed., *Religious Language and the Problem of Religious Knowledge*, Bloomington: Indiana University Press, 1968.

its way without an official metaphysics or theology, so it *may* be possible to build up a body of social science as a guide to action independently of the plural *over-beliefs* which its practitioners entertain provided only that those beliefs do not encourage the erection of nontrespass signs to inquiry about man and all his works.[52]

D. [The prophet Ezekiel learned that] only when God has put him on his feet can he confront God with manly self-respect and hear God's word.

> And God said unto me, Son of man, stand upon thy feet, and I will speak unto thee. And the spirit entered into me when he spoke unto me. (*Ezekiel* 2: 1–2)

This is the basic paradox of what Jacques Maritain has called "true humanism" and, therefore, the paradox both of enlightened religion and enlightened education. Only as man has faith in his own powers and respects himself is he capable of enlightened reverence; yet only in the spirit of reverence can man truly respect himself and use his powers without suicidal idolatry. Prometheus was right in resisting the god who tormented him because this god was neither righteous nor loving. But the God of Ezekiel and Job, of St. Paul and Augustine, is a God of righteousness and truth whose service is not grovelling slavery but man's highest freedom, the very source and guarantee of human dignity and human value. How can the humble service of such a God possibly do

---

[52] Sidney Hook, *The Quest for Being*, New York: Dell Publishing Co., Inc., 1961, p. 207. By permission.

Teilhard de Chardin puts the matter thus:

> Progress. . . . is the Consciousness of all that is and all that can be. Though it may encounter every kind of prejudice and resentment, this must be asserted because it is the truth: to *be* more is to *know* more.
>
> Hence the mysterious attraction . . . [of] science . . . which tells us that, to be faithful to Life, we must *know*; we must know more and still more; we must tirelessly and unceasingly search for Something, we know not what, which will appear in the end to those who have penetrated to the very heart of reality.
>
> —Pierre Teilhard de Chardin, *The Future of Man*, translated from the French by Norman Denny, New York: Harper & Row, Publishers, Inc., 1964, p. 19.

Compare the following statement from a eulogy of Judge Learned Hand:

> Judge Hand's belief in reason as a source of law, and his distrust in his own reason's results seem paradoxical at first. Yet they are logically conjoined. He who is least certain is most likely to be receptive to reason. He who is most receptive to reason is least likely to embrace those brethren of certainty—the absolute, the general principle, the formula and the controlling concept. The inquiring mind will continue to inquire.
>
> —John J. Cound, "Learned Hand," 44 *Minnesota Law Review*, 217–221, 1961.

See also Wallace Mendelson, "Learned Hand: Patient Democrat," 76 *Harvard Law Review*, 322–335, December 1962; R. W. Jepson, *Clear Thinking*, London: Longmans, Green & Co., Ltd., 1940, Chap. 4 on "Prejudice"; R. V. Sampson, *Progress in the Age of Reason*, London: William Heinemann, Ltd., 1956, p. 345f.; Abraham Kaplan, "Great Journey," *Saturday Review* 24: 26, December 23, 1961.

violence to man's proper integrity? How, indeed, can education dedicated to human worth ignore man's search for, and response to, such a God?[53]

Open Book Exam

1. Examine a specific belief of some religious minority, (for example, the Amish, Seventh Day Adventists, Mormons, Christian Scientists, Buddhists) and discuss some of the special problems that they encounter with respect to compulsory educational requirements. Then show how that belief is hindered or helped in our society.
2. Explain and illustrate each of the following meanings of the term *religion*:
   a. moral living;
   b. a feeling of humility before the unknown and a sense of reverence and awe;
   c. propitiation to the gods (or to God) for help—usually through ritual prayer;
   d. an inner sense of mystic oneness with the Ultimately Real.

   What other meanings would you add to the above four?
3. Discuss the relative merits and demerits of
   a. an education that regards a knowledge of and a reverence for God as basic to all studies and evident in all studies, as compared with
   b. an education that assumes that secular subjects can be adequately handled without reference to God.
4. Does a teacher's views concerning human nature (for example, "In Adam's fall, we sinned all"), or concerning man's ultimate destiny (for example, "salvation," "rewards in Heaven") affect the manner in which he might teach (a) mathematics, (b) music, (c) history, or (d) language? Given the same teacher, holding the same views, how would his teaching be different in a public than in a parochial school? Be specific.
5. In American society does the state exercise a monopoly in providing and maintaining schools? In *Pierce v. Society of Sisters* precisely what authority was given (and denied) to the state, to the church? Is this sound policy for the United States? Why or why not?
6. Distinguish and illustrate the following types of "friendly relationships" between church and state: (a) exemption from taxation; (b) right to establish nonpublic (private or parochial) schools; (c) participation in school lunch programs; (d) free textbooks and transportation; (e) complete financial support by the state of schools whose curriculum is determined by private or church authorities. In your view, what should be the limits (if any) to public support of sectarian education?
7. What are meant by the following: establishment of religion, multiple establishment, disestablishment? Briefly trace the history of these three church-state relationships from colonial times to the present. Are those

---

[53] Theodore M. Greene, "Religion and the Philosophies of Education," *Religious Education*, New York: Religious Education Association, March–April 1954, pp. 82–88.

who now advocate state funds for parochial schools implicitly recommending either establishment or multiple establishment?

8. Is it possible for the state to give aid to children attending a private or a denominational school (on the "child benefit theory") without at the same time providing special benefits to the denomination or private interest that controls that school?
9. In Samuel Butler's *Erehwon*, sick persons were put in jail and immoral persons were placed in hospitals. Is immorality a "sin" or a "disease"? Discuss.
10. Under what circumstances, if any, can religion be taught with the same freedom and objectivity as science and history? To appreciate the dimensions of this question, read Thomas Switzer and Everett K. Wilson's "Nobody Knows the Trouble We've Seen: Launching a High School Sociology Course," *Phi Delta Kappan* 50: 346–349, February 1969.
11. Should a child be taught to believe in, and be committed to, his own religion before he learns about other religions? What is the best age level to introduce students to the diversity of religious and nonreligious viewpoints?
12. Is education, when carried on in a public school, wholly a state activity? Or, is it an activity that has dimensions that go beyond the competence of the state and that the state may allow pupils to reach by cooperating with other agencies (for example, with religious, racial, and nationalistic minority groups), whose competence and whose interest is not identical with that of the state?
13. What are "moral and spiritual values"? Discuss the following definition: "Moral and spiritual values are values which, when shared, are enhanced rather than diminished." For example, a piece of cake is not a spiritual value because, when it is shared, it must be cut in two, and thus diminishes in "value"; whereas truth or beauty or goodness (including the attitude of a person sharing a piece of cake) is generally enhanced when shared.

Chapter 4

EXCELLENCE: HUMANISTIC AND VOCATIONAL

The Cleavage in Our Culture

4.1 INTRODUCTION

What type of liberal education best fits the needs of an industrial age? Is there a cleavage in our culture between the scientific and the technical on the one hand, and the liberal and the humanistic on the other? If so, what measures may be taken to reunite these two major strands of our civilization? Can we find a core of common learnings to cement our people into one fraternal group?

There are some who view the issue as one between "science and humanism":

> Science is organized knowledge of the law for things. Efficiency is the result of the use of this knowledge. Humanism is insight into the law for man; enrichment of life, enlargement of spirit is the fruit of this insight. Science advances by experiment; humanism builds on experience. We experiment with what happens outside ourselves; we experience what happens within. Science through controlled experiment builds the knowledge that is power; humanism through controlled experience creates the power that is character. Science as opposed to empiricism is controlled experiment; humanism as opposed to temperamentalism is controlled experience. Humanism builds up personality by enriching it with the experience of the past. This enrichment of personality by vicarious experience is culture.
>
> The conflict between the so-called cultural and the scientific type of higher education cuts to the very core of human nature, because man belongs to two worlds—the world of things and the world of experience, the world of fact and the world of faith, the world of matter and the world of mind, the world of sense and the world of spirit. The primary business of education is the unification of the two worlds in each individual.[1]

[1] John Duncan Spaeth, "Science and Humanism in University Education," an address delivered at the 69th Commencement of Washington University, June 10, 1930, St. Louis, Mo.: Washington University Studies, m.s., 1930. By permission. Mr. Spaeth was Murray Professor of English Literature at Princeton University and, from 1936 to 1938, served as president of the University of Kansas City.

The industrial revolution has drawn men away from traditional patterns of thought and action, but the changes have not all been for the better. Speed seems to have become an end in itself. Like a child with a new toy, say the critics, we are so busy making time-saving gadgets that we have time for little else. We know the price but not the value of things. We develop every kind of control except self-control. Pursued by the telephone, phonograph, radio, T.V., caught in the clamor of the factory and the uproar of the streets, we are projected through time and space like human Sputniks. Meanwhile our inner life is reduced to the level of the dime store, the comic strip, the latest music fad. The three B's of music—Bach, Beethoven, and Brahms—give way to Blues, Bebop, and Boogie-woogie. The three R's of traditional education discipline give way to the three P's of progressive education—Painting, Pasting, and Puttering. Shakespeare and the Bible stand on our shelves while we watch Westerns or read pulp magazines. In short, our outer life is killing the inner. Vulcan is killing Apollo.

The late Peter Marshall, Chaplain of the United States Senate, expressed the sentiment that progress in material things has been emphasized to the neglect of spiritual understanding:

> . . . For we have improved means, but not improved ends. . . . We need . . . to do something about the world's true problems—the problem of lying, which is called propaganda; the problem of selfishness, which is called self-interest; the problem of greed, which is often called profit; the problem of license, disguising itself as liberty; the problem of lust, masquerading as love; the problem of materialism, the hook which is baited with security.[2]

Perhaps some insight into the proper relationship between science and humanism may be gained if we begin with the premise that human freedom is never total, and that science helps man understand what sequences of natural events are invariant and what sequences may be altered to suit human purposes. Thus, pure water freezes at about 32° F., but salt may be added to this water to *make* it freeze at a lower temperature. It is man's ability to exploit the potentialities found *in* nature that makes him free, and his freedom consists in finding natural means to achieve humane ends.

Freedom, then, is not freedom *from* the world (as some Gnostics and some transcendentalists have affirmed); it is freedom *within* the world, where every option represents a mixture of features, some good and some bad. A humanistic faith holds that man may choose among alternatives within this imperfect world to attain the good life. As Carl Rogers has said,

[2] The Reverend Peter Marshall, cited in *Time*, 52: 59, July 12, 1948.

"The good life is a process, not a state of being. It is a direction, not a destination."[3]

As we move from an agrarian to an industrial economy, from a local to a worldwide community, new patterns of education are bound to occur. Before the invention of the printing press, few persons other than priests, lawyers, and doctors learned to read and write. There arose a sharp dichotomy between the ruling class whose *vocation* was that of priest, doctor, or ruler (lawgiver)—and those whose *vocations* had few, if any, academic requirements. This aristocratic class structure of the Middle Ages and the Renaissance antedates the printing press and the rise of modern science and democracy, and it should be obvious that we speak here of a bygone age. Certainly, any well-educated person should know his own traditions; but in the twentieth century the old classic education is neither realistic nor adequate. In the words of George Sarton:

> The New Humanism . . . is different from the old one in two ways. In the first place, it elucidates and defends the ideals for Eastern peoples as well as those of the West. The old humanists had been so completely hypnotized by the writings of classical antiquity and of the Old Testament that they were unable to conceive the existence of any other culture. It was necessary to show them that the Greek, Latin, and Hebrew writings, however important, were not the only ones which deserve to be considered; and their tradition would have been lost or delayed without the Arabic intervention. Moreover, other forms of beauty and wisdom were revealed in Sanskrit, Chinese, and Japanese books. It was necessary to study these books, if one wanted to be a man of the world, a full humanist.
>
> The second way is the history of science. As long as the teaching of science is concerned only with the latest results and deals with them impersonally, that teaching is practical enough but almost inhuman. Yet science is a creation of the human spirit, just as much as religion, art, or literature; it is thus an essential part of the humanities. The new humanists fully realize the spiritual importance of scientific achievements and try to emphasize them.
>
> The New Humanism is thus a fight on many fronts: . . . against the pseudohumanists who would kick science out of the humanities; . . . against the bigoted Westerners who reject Oriental ideas and Oriental religions; . . . against the narrow-minded technicians who do not appreciate spiritual values.[4]

---

[3] Carl R. Rogers, *On Becoming a Person*, Boston: Houghton Mifflin Company, 1961, p. 186.

The thesis that human freedom is not *from* the world, but only *within* the natural world is elaborated by Sterling P. Lamprecht in *The Metaphysics of Naturalism*, New York: Appleton-Century-Crofts, 1967, especially pp. 185–200.

[4] George Sarton, "The Old World and the New Humanism," in *Man's Right to Knowledge, First Series: Tradition and Change*, New York: Columbia University Press, 1954, p. 66. See also Christopher Dawson, "Schism in Education," *Commonweal*, 74: 35–37, April 7, 1961.

4.2 THE TWO CULTURES*

Martin Green

C. P. Snow's theory of the two cultures seems to me to become most irrefutable if one puts it that there is an antagonism between literary people and science; and that along with this, deriving from the same source, goes a provincialism, a contented specialization, on the part of nearly all acute intelligence today. It is from these two together that proceeds the waste of manpower and brainpower which Snow describes.

It is not, as is too commonly lamented, that everybody is blindly enthusiastic about science nowadays, and nobody cares about culture. On the contrary, it seems to me that an overrating of literature (and the arts) is just as prevalent, and even more dangerous, than any general love of science. . . . It is not the arts that are at a discount, but humanism. People no longer believe in the possibility of putting together the knowledge they find in literature with the knowledge of science and with the events of modern history, and making any important sense of them. They actively and effectively disbelieve in attempts to do that. . . .

---

* Martin Green, *Science and the Shabby Curate of Poetry,* New York: W. W. Norton Company, Inc., 1966, pp. 55, 72–74, 101. By permission.

This essay is one of many which followed C. P. Snow's *The Two Cultures and the Scientific Revolution,* London: Cambridge, 1960; rev. ed.; New York: New American Library of World Literature, Inc., 1963. Snow wrote:

> I believe the intellectual life of the whole Western society is increasingly being split into two polar groups. . . . at the one pole we have the literary intellectuals—at the other, the scientists. Between the two, a gulf of mutual incomprehension [exists]. They have a curious distorted image of each other. Their attitude is so different that, even on the level of emotion, they can't find much common ground.

Concerning the two cultures Charles R. Bowen has written:

> Since few, if any of us, can absorb *all* the new advances in knowledge, we have resorted to a narrow and potentially dangerous specialization to try to keep pace with our own sector of the "information explosion." To amplify C. P. Snow's theme, there are not only two, but dozens of different subcultures within the vast edifice known as Western knowledge. We must keep in mind that the various compartments or disciplines into which we arbitrarily have divided knowledge exist neither in the heart of matter nor of man. It is the special responsibility of education in the period ahead to see that we become neither over-specialized mandarins nor generalized ignoramuses.
>
> To paraphrase Robert Oppenheimer, it is true in regard to culture that there are two numbers, but they are one and zero, for unless tomorrow's man is as literate in science as in the humanities—and I believe this is C. P. Snow's essential point—then he can be literate in neither.
>
> —Charles R. Bowen, in *Automation, Education and Human Values,* William W. Brickman and Stanley Lehrer, eds., New York: School and Society Press, 1966, pp. 71–85. By permission.

[Nevertheless] ours is a scientific civilization, and we must be able to respond to so large a fact with something better than a wish it weren't so. . . . We need to break the tabu of incommunicability that has been laid on [scientific] knowledge; to learn to transmit it to those with equal though different intellectual experience. The belief that a nonscientist cannot achieve any significant understanding of science must be dismissed as a delusion. . . . The difficulties are of course great. But they cannot be insoluble. For the problem is not to acquire a certain amount of information, or even understanding, but to employ a certain amount of serious attention. . . . A good teacher of science can do that in a year starting literally from scratch, just as a good teacher of literature can. . . .

What distinguishes our age from earlier ones . . . is our achievement in science. . . . That is above all why, at a crude level, we must learn some science; why, at a deeper level, we must each work out the relationship of his own work to scientific work; why, deeper still, we must work out what a culture is, of which "science" can be such a huge branch. . . . Hostility to science, or to "an age dominated by science," cannot in any way serve the cause of the humanities, or the intelligence of the students to whom it is expounded. It is a form of stupidity, which teachers of literature everywhere should be actively stamping out.[5]

---

[5] Editor's Note: Perhaps it would be better to minimize "hostility to science" and speak instead of what Daniel Bell calls "the knowledge explosion." Bell points out that in 1750 there were about ten scientific journals in the entire world; by 1830 about 300; and by 1950 about 3000.

> The output in sheer words today is staggering. In 1964, nearly 320,000 separate book titles—nearly 1,000 works every day—were published throughout the world. Columbia University's new acquisitions, for example, take up two miles of bookshelves a year. In a single field, medicine, it is estimated that some 200,000 journal articles and 10,000 monographs are published annually, while in the physical and life sciences the number of books add up to about 60,000 annually, the number of research reports to about 100,000, and the number of articles in scientific and technical journals to about 1.2 million each year. Consider what will happen when writers, scholars, scientists, and professionals in the new states begin to produce in great number in these fields!
>
> But it is not the prodigious accumulation alone that is creating a distinctive change in the structure of intellectual life. It is the fact that new discoveries bring their own differentiation, or "branching," so that as a field expands subdivisions and subspecialties multiply within each field. Contrary to the nineteenth-century notion of science as a bounded or exhaustible field of knowledge whose full dimensions can ultimately be explored each advance opens up, in its own way, new fields that in turn sprout their own branches.
>
> —Daniel Bell, *The Reforming of General Education,* New York: Columbia University Press, 1966, pp. 74–75.

4.3 SOME CONTRASTS BETWEEN CLASSICAL AND MODERN CULTURE*

Bernard Lonergan

Classical culture has given way to a modern culture, and, I would submit, the crisis of our age is in no small measure the fact that modern culture has not yet reached its maturity. The classical mediation of meaning has broken down; the breakdown has been effected by a whole array of new and more effective techniques; but their very multiplicity and complexity leave us bewildered, disorientated, confused, preyed upon by anxiety, dreading lest we fall victims to the up-to-date myth of ideology and the hypnotic, highly effective magic of thought-control.

The clearest and neatest illustration of the breakdown of classical culture lies in the field of science. It is manifest, of course, that modern science understands far more things far more fully than did Greek or medieval science. But the point I would make is not quantitative but qualitative. The significant difference is not more knowledge or more adequate knowledge but the emergence of a quite different conception of science itself. The Greek conception was formulated by Aristotle in his *Posterior Analytics*; it envisaged science as true, certain knowledge of causal necessity. But modern science is not true; it is only on the way towards truth. It is not certain; for its positive affirmations it claims no more than probability. It is not knowledge but hypothesis, theory, system, the best available scientific opinion of the day. Its object is not necessity but verified possibility: bodies fall with a constant acceleration, but they could fall at a different rate; and similarly other natural laws aim at stating, not what cannot possibly be otherwise, but what in fact is so. Finally, while modern science speaks of causes, still it is not concerned with Aristotle's four causes of end, agent, matter, and form; its ultimate objective is to reach a complete explanation of all phenomena, and by such explanation is meant the determination of the terms and intelligible relationships that account for all data. So, for each of the five elements constitutive of the Greek ideal of science, for truth, certainty, knowledge, necessity, and causality, the modern ideal substitutes something less arduous, something more accesssible, something dynamic, something effective. Modern science works.

---

* F. E. Crowe, S.J., *Collection: Papers by Bernard Lonergan, S.J.*, New York: Herder and Herder, 1967, pp. 259–267. By permission.

The last sentence is taken from Bernard Lonergan, S.J., *Verbum: Word and Idea in Aquinas*, Notre Dame, Indiana: University of Notre Dame Press, 1967, p. vii.

After teaching several years at the Gregorian University in Rome, Father Lonergan is now Professor of Dogmatic Theology, Regis College, Toronto.

Now this shift in the very meaning of the word, science, affects the basic fabric of classical culture. If the object of Greek science was necessary, it also was obvious to the Greeks that in this world of ours there is very much that is not necessary but contingent. The Greek universe, accordingly, was a split universe: partly it was necessary and partly it was contingent. Moreover, this split in the object involved a corresponding split in the development of the human mind. As the universe was partly necessary and partly contingent, so man's mind was divided between science and opinion, theory and practice, wisdom and prudence. Insofar as the universe was necessary, it could be known scientifically; but insofar as it was contingent, it could be known only by opinion. Again, insofar as the universe was necessary, human operation could not change it, it could only contemplate it by theory; but insofar as the universe was contingent, there was a realm in which human operation could be effective, and that was the sphere of practise. Finally, insofar as the universe was necessary, it was possible for man to find ultimate and changeless foundations, and so philosophy was the pursuit of wisdom; but insofar as the universe was contingent, it was a realm of endless differences and variations that could not be subsumed under hard and fast rules; and to navigate on that chartless sea there was needed all the astuteness of prudence.

The modern ideal of science has no such implications. We do not contrast science and opinion; we speak of scientific opinion. We do not put theory and practise in separate compartments; on the contrary, our practise is the fruit of our theory, and our theory is orientated to practical achievement. We distinguish pure science and applied science, applied science and technology, technology and industry; but the distinctions are not separations and, however great the differences between basic research and industrial activity, the two are linked by intermediate zones of investigation, discovery, invention. Finally, if contemporary philosophic issues are far too complex to be dealt with in the present context, at least we may say that philosophy has invaded the field of the concrete, the particular, and the contingent, of the existential subject's decisions and of the history of peoples, societies, and cultures; and this entry of philosophy into the realm of the existential and the historical not merely extends the role of philosophic wisdom into concrete living but also, by that very extension, curtails the functions formerly attributed to prudence. Nor is it only from above that prudence is curtailed: its province is also invaded from below.

We do not trust the prudent man's memory but keep files and records and develop systems of information retrieval. We do not trust the prudent man's ingenuity, but call in efficiency experts or set problems for operations research. We do not trust the prudent man's judgment, but employ computers to keep track of inventories and to forecast demand. We do not rely on the prudent man's broad experience, but conduct fact-finding surveys and compile statistics. There is as great a need as ever for memory and ingenuity, judgment and experience; but they have been supplemented by a host of devices and techniques, and so they operate on a different level and in a different mode; while the old-style prudent man, whom some cultural lag sends drifting through the twentieth century, commonly is known as a stuffed shirt.

I have been indicating, very summarily, how a new notion of science has undermined and antiquated certain fundamental elements of classical culture. But besides the new notion itself, there is also its implementation. A new notion of science leads to a new science of man. Classically orientated science, from its very nature, concentrated on the essential to ignore the accidental, on the universal to ignore the particular, on the necessary to ignore the contingent. Man is a rational animal, composed of body and immortal soul, endowed with vital, sensitive, and intellectual powers, in need of habits and able to acquire them, free and responsible in his deliberations and decisions, subject to a natural law which, in accord with changing circumstances, is to be supplemented by positive laws enacted by duly constituted authority. I am very far from having exhausted the content of the classically orientated science of man, but enough has been said to indicate its style. It is limited to the essential, necessary, universal; it is so phrased as to hold for all men whether they are awake or asleep, infants or adults, morons or geniuses; it makes it abundantly plain that you can't change human nature; the multiplicity and variety, the developments and achievements, the breakdowns and catastrophes of human living, all have to be accidental, contingent, particular, and so have to lie outside the field of scientific interest as classically conceived. But modern science aims at the complete explanation of all phenomena, and so modern studies of man are interested in every human phenomenon. Not abstract man but, at least in principle, all the men of every time and place, all their thoughts and words and deeds, the accidental as well as the essential, the contingent as well as the necessary, the particular as well as the universal, are to be summoned before the bar of human understanding. If you object that such knowledge is unattainable, that the last day of general judgment cannot be anticipated, you will be answered that modern science is not a ready-made achievement stored for all time in a great book, but an ongoing process that no library, let alone any single mind, is expected to encompass. And even though this ongoing process never can master all human phenomena, still by its complete openness, by its exclusion of every obscurantism, modern study of man can achieve ever so much more than the conventional limitations of classically orientated human studies permitted. . . .

The crisis, then, that I have been attempting to depict is a crisis not of faith but of culture. . . . Classical culture cannot be jettisoned without being replaced; and what replaces it, cannot but run counter to classical expectations. There is bound to be formed a solid right that is determined to live in a world that no longer exists. There is bound to be formed a scattered left, captivated by now this, now that new development, exploring now this and now that new possibility. But what will count is a perhaps not numerous center, big enough to be at home in both the old and the new, painstaking enough to work out one by one the transitions to be made, strong enough to refuse half-measures and insist on complete solutions even though it has to wait. . . . As Professor Butterfield has observed, to correct Aristotle effectively, one must go beyond him; and to go beyond him is to set up a system equal in comprehensiveness and more successful in inner coherence and in conformity with fact.

4.4 SCIENCE AND HUMAN VALUES*

René Dubos

Since the various scientific fields include all the subjects on which reasonable men can converge objectively and exchange verifiable information, it is difficult if not impossible to state in words where science ends and where the humanities begin. The paradox, however, is that this semantic difficulty hardly ever causes any confusion in human behavior. The immense majority of the lay public shows by its reading habits that it sharply differentiates between science and non-science; this differentiation also appears in the fact that concert halls and art museums have more popular appeal than science exhibits. The "two cultures" may be an illusion, but in practice science is still regarded in our communities as a kind of foreign god, powerful and useful, yes, but so mysterious that it is feared rather than known and loved. . . . [Even among scientists themselves] Winston Churchill, Pablo Picasso and Ernest Hemingway are much more frequently discussed at the luncheon tables of scientific research institutes than are the Nobel prize winners in physics, chemistry, or biology of the same generation. And if Linus Pauling or Robert Oppenheimer is mentioned, it

* René Dubos, "Science and Man's Nature," *Daedalus* 94: 223–244, Winter 1965. This extract is used with the permission of *Daedalus*, Journal of the American Academy of Arts and Sciences, Boston, Mass.: Winter 1965 issue, "Science and Culture."

is less likely with regard to either's achievements as chemist or physicist than because their behavior makes them interesting and vital human beings. In brief, while scientists are deeply committed to their own specialized fields, they generally turn to non-scientific topics when they move outside their professional spheres.

The priority of general "human" concerns over purely scientific interests acquires particular importance in education. Whatever historians and philosophers of science may say concerning the fundamental similarities between science and the humanities as intellectual and creative pursuits, the high school or college student soon discovers from his personal experience that the two kinds of learning and activities are different as far as he is concerned. He will probably like one and despise the other; and science commonly loses in the comparison. A recent study of high school students selected for extremely high scholastic aptitude (only one per cent of the total student population!) revealed that the percentage of those selecting science decreased from 37.77 percent in 1958 to 28.87 percent in 1963. Even more serious was the finding that among those who had originally selected science 55.2 percent of the males and 58.9 percent of the females changed to other fields during their college years. The significance of these figures becomes the greater when it is realized that the trend away from science occurred during a period when great social pressure was being exerted on young people to induce them to go into scientific careers. . . .

The dissatisfaction is pungently expressed in Dewey's warning that "a culture which permits science to destroy traditional values, but which distrusts its power to create new ones, is destroying itself." . . .

Because science and technology are now advancing without the guidance of a well thought out philosophy of natural and social values, they achieve results and produce effects which in many cases no longer correspond to real human needs. Man, through science, has released disruptive forces [e.g., atomic bombs, polluted air and water, disease control—without attendant birth control] which he has not yet learned to control. . . .

Needless to say, there is nothing fundamentally new in the fact that technology alters the relationship between man and nature. For many thousand years, man has modified his environment by using fire, farming the land, building houses, opening roads, and even controlling his reproduction. The all important difference, however, is that many modern applications of science have nothing to do with human biological needs and aim only at creating new demands, even though these be inimical to health, to happiness, or to the aspirations of mankind. . . .

In reality, of course, there cannot be any retreat from science. Rather, public apprehension and hostility point to the need for an enlargement of science. Scientists must take more to heart the questions which deeply concern human beings; they must learn to give greater prominence to large human values when formulating their problems and their results. Fortunately, this is probably easier than is commonly believed because. . . . history shows that the broad implications of science can become integrated in the intellectual fabric of modern societies. Human cultures, like organisms and societies, depend for survival on their internal integration, an integration which can be achieved only to the extent that science remains meaningful to the living experience of man.

Liberal Education for a Scientific Age

4.5 INTRODUCTION

In an era of universal education, what can be done so that *all* students may find their formal schooling psychologically interesting, morally uplifting, and vocationally worthwhile? With the growing emphasis on science and technology in school curricula, can the newer courses be taught in a manner that will make them less narrow and technical, more liberal and humane? Is philosophy inherently more liberal than chemistry, Latin than journalism, history than contemporary events? Or are these traditional subjects more liberal only because the newer subjects are not yet taught in a liberal manner?

Before reading the following selections dealing with these topics, it may be well for the reader to learn the editor's viewpoint. Briefly, it is this: Since leisure is a necessary prerequisite of civilized living, democratic education should insure sufficient productivity per man-hour so that leisure is available to all or nearly all citizens of our society. High productivity per man-hour means skill in some special area; it means efficiency. Thus, in a democratic society, vocational education is a necessary prerequisite of any liberal education.

But it is not a sufficient condition. For, even if we have the necessary leisure to live in moderate affluence, we still must learn to live in as excellent a manner as the human condition allows. In short, we must both "learn to live" (by gaining vocational efficiency so that we have more leisure), and we must "live to learn" (by gaining the understanding, the wisdom, and the humanity that makes for civilized living).

Our society is based on the ideal that every citizen is both subject and ruler; producer and consumer; an end-in-himself and a contributor to the needs of others. In such a society excellence will appear in many and varied forms, but in all of them the vocational and humanistic ideals must complement one another.

4.6 THE IDEA OF EXCELLENCE*

John W. Gardner

Taking the whole span of history and literature, the images of excellence are amply varied: Confucius teaching the feudal lords to govern wisely . . . Leonidas defending the pass at Thermopylae . . . Saint Francis preaching to the birds at Alviano . . . Lincoln writing the second inaugural "with malice toward none" . . . Mozart composing his first oratorio at the age of eleven . . . Galileo dropping weights from the Tower of Pisa . . . Emily Dickinson jotting her "letters to the world" on scraps of paper . . . Jesus saying, "Father, forgive them; for they know not what they do." . . . Florence Nightingale nursing the wounded at Balaclava . . . Eli Whitney pioneering the manufacture of interchangeable parts . . . Ruth saying to Naomi, "Thy people shall be my people."

The list is long and the variety is great. Taken collectively, human societies have gone a long way toward exploring the full range of human excellences. But a particular society at a given moment in history is apt to honor only a portion of the full range. And wise indeed is the society that is not afraid to face hard questions about its own practices on this point. Is it honoring the excellences which are most fruitful for its own continued vitality? To what excellences is it relatively insensitive; and what does this imply for the tone and texture of its life? Is it squandering approbation on kinds of high performance which have nothing to contribute to its creativity as a society?

If any one among us can contemplate those questions without uneasiness, he has not thought very long nor very hard about excellence in the United States.

A conception which embraces many kinds of excellence at many levels is the only one which fully accords with the richly varied potentialities of mankind; it is the only one which will permit high morale throughout the society.

Our society cannot achieve greatness unless individuals at many levels

---

* John W. Gardner, *Excellence: Can We Be Equal and Excellent Too?*, New York: Harper & Row, Publishers, 1961, pp. 130–134, 85–86. Copyright © 1961 by John W. Gardner. Reprinted with the permission of Harper & Row, Publishers, Incorporated.

Author of several books, and for many years president of the Carnegie Corporation and of the Carnegie Foundation for the Advancement of Teaching, John W. Gardner was Secretary of Health, Education, and Welfare under President Johnson. In 1967 he resigned from the Cabinet to take charge of the Urban Coalition, a new attempt to engage private business organizations to work toward the reduction of poverty. His book *Self-Renewal*, New York: Harper & Row Publishers, Inc., 1964, might well be used to supplement this chapter.

of ability accept the need for high standards of performance and strive to achieve those standards within the limits possible for them. We want the highest conceivable excellence, of course, in the activities crucial to our effectiveness and creativity as a society; but that isn't enough. If the man in the street says, "Those fellows at the top have to be good, but I'm just a slob and can act like one"—then our days of greatness are behind us. We must foster a conception of excellence which may be applied to every degree of ability and to every socially acceptable activity. A missile may blow up on its launching pad because the designer was incompetent or because the mechanic who adjusted the last valve was incompetent. The same is true of everything else in our society. We need excellent physicists and excellent mechanics. We need excellent cabinet members and excellent first-grade teachers. The tone and fiber of our society depend upon a pervasive and almost universal striving for good performance.

And we are not going to get that kind of striving, that kind of alert and proud attention to performance, unless we can instruct the whole society in a conception of excellence that leaves room for everybody who is willing to strive—a conception of excellence which means that whoever I am or whatever I am doing, provided that I am engaged in a socially acceptable activity, some kind of excellence is within my reach. . . . As I said in another connection:

> An excellent plumber is infinitely more admirable than an incompetent philosopher. The society which scorns excellence in plumbing because plumbing is a humble activity and tolerates shoddiness in philosophy because it is an exalted activity will have neither good plumbing nor good philosophy. Neither its pipes nor its theories will hold water. . . .

We cannot meet the challenge facing our free society unless we can achieve and maintain a high level of morale and drive throughout the society. One might argue that in any society which has spread prosperity as widely as ours has, morale will be universally high. But prosperity and morale are not inseparable. It is possible to be prosperous and apathetic. It is possible to be fat and demoralized. Men must have goals which, in their eyes, merit effort and commitment; and they must believe that their efforts will win them self-respect and the respect of others.

This is the condition of society we must work toward. Then, unhampered by popular attitudes disparaging excellence, we can dedicate ourselves to the cultivation of distinction and a sense of quality. We can demand the best of our most gifted, most talented, most spirited youngsters. And we can render appropriate honor to that striving for excellence which has produced so many of mankind's greatest achievements.

It is important to bear in mind that we are now talking about an approach to excellence and a conception of excellence that will bring a whole society to the peak of performance. The gifted individual absorbed in his own problems of creativity and workmanship may wish to set himself much narrower and very much more severe standards of excellence. The critic concerned with a particular development in art, let us say, may wish to impose a far narrower and more specialized criterion of excellence. This is understandable. But we are concerned with the broader objective of toning up a whole society.

This broader objective is critically important, even for those who have set themselves far loftier (and narrower) personal standards of excellence. We cannot have islands of excellence in a sea of slovenly indifference to standards. In an era when the masses of people were mute and powerless it may have been possible for a tiny minority to maintain high standards regardless of their surroundings. But today the masses of people are neither mute nor powerless. As consumers, as voters, as the source of Public Opinion, they heavily influence levels of taste and performance. They can create a climate supremely inimical to standards of any sort.

I am not saying that we can expect every man to be excellent. It would please me if this were possible: I am not one of those who believe that a goal is somehow unworthy if everyone can achieve it. But those who achieve excellence will be few at best. All too many lack the qualities of mind or spirit which would allow them to conceive excellence as a goal, or to achieve it if they conceived it.

But many more can achieve it than now do. Many, many more can *try* to achieve it than now do. *And the society is bettered not only by those who achieve it but by those who are trying.*

The broad conception of excellence we have outlined must be built on two foundation stones—and both of them exist in our society.

1. A *pluralistic approach to values.* American society has always leaned toward such pluralism. We need only be true to our deepest inclinations to honor the many facets and depths and dimensions of human experience and to seek the many kinds of excellence of which the human spirit is capable.

2. A *universally honored philosophy of individual fulfillment.* We have such a philosophy, deeply embedded in our tradition. Whether we have given it the prominence it deserves is the question which we must now explore. . . .

4.7 VOCATIONAL EDUCATION FOR TODAY*

Grant Venn

A facade of affluence hides the spreading blight of social crisis in America—a crisis compounded by insufficient economic growth, a rising number of unemployed, increasing racial tensions, juvenile delinquency, swelling public welfare rolls, chronically depressed areas, an expanding ratio of youth to total population, and a growing disparity of educational opportunity. At the center of the crisis is a system of education that is failing to prepare individuals for a new world of work in an advanced technological society.

Regardless of his race, intelligence, or place of birth, the human being is the greatest resource any nation can possess. . . . Each time this precious resource is wasted, to whatever degree, it represents a grave loss to the nation and the world. . . .

[Directly or indirectly, all of these problems are related to the technological revolution, and it seems reasonable] to accept Donald Michael's thesis that the new technology is something "so different in degree as to be a profound difference in kind."

The landmark of technological developments has been the introduction of automation and computers into industry and commerce. *Automation*

---

* Excerpts from Grant Venn, *Man, Education and Work,* Washington, D.C.: American Council on Education, 1964, pp. 4, 5, 13, 16–17, 23, 24, 28, 32, 130, 131, 139, 140, 157.

Compare the following statement from Garth L. Mangum, and others, *The Manpower Revolution,* New York: Doubleday & Company, Inc., 1965, p. 210:

> The essential feature of the industrial revolution was the amplification of man's muscle through the use of engines. In the information revolution the emphasis has shifted to the amplification of his brain through the use of computers and information processing systems. Already, there are as many different kinds of computers as there are kinds of engines. The applications of digital processing are limited only by the ingenuity of our scientists and technologists.
>
> There is a basic and fundamental difference between brawn and brain—a difference that is exaggerated when these faculties are extended and amplified by either mechanical engines or electronic processors. The key ingredient in a muscle or engine is the energy that powers it. This energy, or fuel, is consumed; it can never be recovered and reused. In contrast, the key ingredient in a brain, or information handling system, is information. And this information is not consumed by the process of using and applying it. In fact, it can be used over and over again, and by using it we often augment it, actually increase the original supply. . . .
>
> The point is—information processing, unlike the engine, is a self-feeding growth process. Perhaps this difference explains why the information revolution has been faster and more widespread in its implications than the industrial revolution.

See also Donald H. Michael, *The Next Generation,* New York: Random House, Inc., 1965.

encompasses a class of devices that automatically perform both the sensing and the motor tasks formerly performed by human labor. Thus, automated machines can mine coal, pick cotton, cast and finish engine blocks, sort bank checks, roll aluminum, grade oranges, and weave cloth. *Computers* are devices which rapidly perform traditional human tasks involving experience, memory, analysis, logic, and decision-making. Such devices now can diagnose symptoms for the physician, research a case for the lawyer, read envelopes for the postman, analyze market portfolios for the broker, design a plant for the architect, prepare war and defense plans for the military, fly missiles for the scientist, screen volunteers for the Peace Corps, and keep inventory for the merchant. These machines are being "taught" to translate languages, compose music, play chess, transcribe speech, and "see" objects; already they correct their mistakes and identify trouble spots in their mechanism.

The impact of these devices on the labor market has been profound. Automatic elevators have recently displaced 40,000 elevator operators in New York City alone. New equipment in the Census Bureau enabled 50 statisticians to do the work in 1960 that required 4,000 such people in 1950. The check-writing staff in the Treasury Department has been reduced from 400 people to four. . . . Thirty thousand packinghouse workers have been "automated out" of their jobs in the past few years. Enormous machines have helped reduce employment in the coal fields from 415,000 in 1950 to 136,000 in 1962. While construction work has leaped 32 percent since 1956, construction jobs have shown a 24 percent decline. Comparable statistics exist for the chemical, aircraft, communications, metals, transportation, and other industries. In many additional cases where automation and computers have been introduced, the effect has not yet been to fire or lay off, but rather to put a moratorium, or freeze, on new hiring.

[In this transition] into what Daniel Bell labels a "postindustrial society". . . . [the] population as a whole and the labor force in particular are increasingly mobile in where they live and work, in a manner recalling the movements of the great western migrations and the depression. In a recent year more than 8 million different workers changed jobs. In that same year there were 11.5 million job changes, two-thirds of which were to a completely different industry, one-half to a completely different occupational category. Nearly half of the people in the United States have changed their residence during the last five years, a fifth of them to a different state. The most frequent cause of residence change is employment opportunity. . . . [but with the speed of change in occupations, this requires better ways] to facilitate [the] rapid occupational changes [which] the new technology is bringing to employment. . . . Norman C. Harris [has summarized these changes quite clearly]:

Professional jobs, making up six percent of the labor force in 1930, will probably constitute 12 percent by 1970. At the other extreme, unskilled, semi-skilled, and service jobs, which together accounted for 56 percent of the labor force in the 1930's, will by 1970 decrease to only 26 percent of the labor force. But the really significant changes in our labor force, and in society in general, have occurred at the level of the semi-professional and technical; the managerial, business, and sales; and the highly skilled jobs. These jobs taken together, will account for over 50 percent of the labor force by 1970. . . .

It is an open question whether present forms of vocational and technical education are equal to the demands of a changing world of work. . . . [Some] schools pride themselves on how close their shop facilities duplicate real job conditions, and many of them do have excellent first-job placement records for their graduates. But this does *not necessarily* mean that the school has given the graduate the education he may really need. What is called for is more and better occupational education, to be sure, but occupational education on a more general basis—teaching certain basic skills, of course, but also devoting more time to the development of broader technical understanding, of communication and computational abilities, and of an appreciation of civic, cultural, and leisure activities. . . . Obviously, many of the assumptions underlying the existing structure of vocational education need re-examination in the light of the new relationship between man, his work and his education. . . .[6]

---

[6] Editor's Note:

Between 1929 and 1962, our population grew 53 percent, while our gross national product, in constant (1954) dollars, grew 159 percent. The result is the high standard of living of our affluent society and the economic power that is a major deterrent to foreign aggression.

Technology has brought great gains and also has given rise to serious problems. A major problem is the imbalance between the type of labor force our new technology increasingly requires and the skills and qualifications of large numbers of workers in our present labor force. Far too many receive inadequate education and meager training, while the demand grows for broader education and more specialized skills. . . .

The paradox . . . is that all over the nation jobs go unfilled. . . . There seems to be no lack of people on the one hand or unfilled jobs on the other; what appears to be lacking is people with sufficient training and the right skills. The jobless worker in the wrong place with the wrong skills and aptitudes, has become the fall guy. . . .

—John K. Norton, *Changing Demands on Education and Their Fiscal Implications*: A report prepared by the National Committee for the Support of Public Schools, Washington, D.C.: 1963, pp. 6–9.

Aston R. Williams points to another aspect of this problem:

Very frequently the view is expressed in the United States that the purpose of general education is not to prepare a man for the job he takes the day after he graduates, but for the job he takes ten years after graduation. The story is often

[Perhaps our present problem will be better understood if it is seen in historical perspective. For the past 100 years, the] key to equality of opportunity was the development of a unique educational system, free and open to all, regardless of station in life. This belief gave rise to an educational program which has, historically, offered essentially the same curriculum to all regardless of ability, background, or aspiration. . . . [But the] best education for some is not the best education for all. Each individual is different, and should have the benefit of an educational program to fit his capacities and develop his full potential. For many young people this will mean occupationally oriented curricula, both within secondary and higher education. . . . [Today] the academic course tends to be crowded with students who do not belong in it. . . . [It] is a strange state of affairs in an industrial democracy when those very subjects are held in disrepute which are at the heart of the national economy and those students by implication condemned who will become its operators. . . .

[The school dropout illustrates the problem.] The image of the dropout is of a dull, rebellious young person. Yet study after study has shown no substantial difference in intelligence between the dropout and his age group as a whole; a recently completed study showed, for example, that *two-thirds* of them were in the I.Q. range of 90 to 109. These are *average* young men and women, with considerable potential for occupational development within the schools. And they are rebellious only in the sense that for most of them the subjects they studied in school were of little interest. Professor Harris declares that "without a doubt the biggest task facing the American high school today is to make its curriculum meaningful to students. For hundreds of thousands of boys and girls this meaning must be found in subject and curriculums related to the world of work." . . .

[It should be obvious that this problem is closely connected with that of the Negro, and other underprivileged groups.] Since 1955, the jobless rate among Negro youth has risen twice as fast as among white. . . . Comparing only nonfarm workers, one of three white workers is classified as unskilled or semiskilled; but three out of four Negro workers are in this category.

---

told of the dean of the engineering school who keeps three envelopes in a desk drawer for visiting alumni, who are always only too ready to explain how their own curricula in engineering might have been improved. The dean interrupts the visitor to ask how many years back he had left, and produces an envelope from the desk drawer either with 0–5, or 5–10, or 10+ written on the front, wherein, before the alumnus can speak, is found what he was about to say. Those who had left up to five years before would have liked more engineering subjects. After five years the alumni decide that they would have preferred more basic mathematics and physics and chemistry; after ten years?—more humanities and social sciences. By this time the engineer has discovered that his problems are as likely to be human as technical.

—*General Education in Higher Education*, New York: Columbia University, Teachers College Press, 1968, p. 11.

With jobs at this level shrinking, the employment gaps between whites and nonwhites are bound to become even more pronounced.[7]

[The problem of unemployment is more than an economic problem, because a] man's occupation in American society is now his single most significant status-conferring role. Whether it be high or low, a job status allows the individual to form some stable conception of himself and his position in the community.

The social and psychological effects of joblessness are painfully apparent in America today. They can be seen in the faces of those citizens standing in line for relief checks; none of them may be starving, and there may be work around the home that could keep them busy, but without a job they are lost. Tens of thousands of jobless youth cast about at loose ends, with 80 to 90 percent of the juvenile cases in the courts coming from their ranks. Job discrimination creates a hard knot of frustration in the Negro, frustration that explodes in bitter racial conflict. In this picture should also be noted the woman in her forties, her children grown up, going out to get a job: there still may be plenty of work around the home and the family may not need the money, but she feels a need for new identifications found only in holding a job. This crucial importance of the job to the individual in American society must be borne in mind in a discussion of man, his work, and his education. Statistical compilations of the effect of technology on the labor market can be compelling, but for millions of Americans the problem of joblessness is real and personal. . . .

A job is vital to the young person, and it is also vital that the job provide an outlet for his abilities, that it be compatible with his considered aspirations. . . . The high school dropout may find a job washing dishes or parking cars; if he has graduated from high school or attended college awhile, he may clerk in a store or become a route salesman. These are dead-end jobs, and he knows it. He becomes frustrated; initiation for him has become a personal defeat. . . .

The evidence is that in the decades ahead the rate of economic growth will be increasingly dependent upon the rate of technological development. And since the rate of technological advance depends on the availability of technical personnel, the education of people in the professional, technical, and skilled occupations becomes a prime factor in increasing the growth rate of the national enterprise. . . .

---

[7] Editor's Note:

[The] Labor Department . . . reported that in June [1968] the U.S. work force . . . reached 80 million for the first time in history . . . [but with] 3.6 million [3.8 per cent] still jobless . . . The jobless rate for all nonwhite workers rose . . . to 7.2 per cent . . . largely reflecting the rise in Negro teen-age joblessness, which, at 30 per cent, is double the rate for white youths.

—News item: "Employment: Superlatives & Paradoxes," *Time* 92: 64–65, July 19, 1968.

The technical, skilled, and semiprofessional occupations all demand substantial amounts of postsecondary education for entrance. In the accelerating job-upgrading process of technology there is a steady increase of higher education and skills needed for entry and retention. Education has become the crucial ladder to the reward positions in society. Of the undereducated and untrained, Secretary Wirtz says:

> The reason for the increasing concentration of unemployment among unskilled workers is that machines are taking over the unskilled jobs. These are the jobs which have, up to this time, absorbed the casualties of the educational system: Those who for one reason or another have left school without having added to the strength which is in their arms and backs the skill it takes to do something more than "common labor." This wasn't too bad when there were enough common labor jobs around. Now there aren't.
>
> Today, unskilled workers make up 5 percent of the work force, but almost 15 percent of all the unemployed are in this group. Unemployment is over twice as high among the young worker groups and among nonwhite workers—the two groups in which there are the largest percentages of unskilled workers—than it is in the work force as a whole. . . .

The relationship between education and work, in terms of occupational entry and upgrading, is fixed and firm. . . .[8]

---

[8] Editor's Note: As a case study in modern industrialization, consider agriculture:

> In 1790 agriculture occupied 90 percent of the U.S. population. Half a century later the proportion had dropped to 70 percent, and by 1890 only 43 percent of the people were farmers. The principal events responsible for this trend were John Deere's production of the steel plow, Cyrus McCormick's invention of the reaper (which he began to manufacture in 1847) and John Appleby's development (in 1879) of the grain binder. After 1890 the substitution of machines for manpower on U.S. farms proceeded at a much more rapid rate. The farm population declined to 30 percent in 1915 and to 18 percent by 1940. The gasoline engine was, of course, the prime factor, and it became the motive power of a variety of mass-production harvesting machines: the self-propelled wheat combine, the hay baler, the cotton and corn pickers. Since World War II a proliferation of other harvesting devices, handling perishable as well as nonperishable crops, has been partly responsible for the further reduction of the farm labor force to the present 5 percent. . . . [Thus,] whereas the average bean picker picked 1.06 bushels per hour by hand, a single operator could pick 95.8 bushels per hour by machine. Moreover, there are a number of side benefits from harvesting by machine, including delivery of cleaner fruits and vegetables to the consumer.
>
> —Clarence F. Kelly, "Mechanical Harvesting," *Scientific American* 217: 50–59, August 1967. By permission.

In the developing countries of the world, 90 percent of whose population is still occupied in farming, the changes likely to occur within the next few decades are appalling. Within the United States, since World War II over 5,000,000 (about 25 percent) of all U.S. Negroes have moved from the "cotton picking" South to the "industrial" North. Their present plight is described by Roger Beardwood, "The Southern Roots of Urban Crisis," *Fortune* 78: 80–87, 151–156, August 1968.

4.8 GREAT BOOKS CONSTITUTE THE CORE OF LIBERAL EDUCATION*

St. John's College Faculty

No one would dispute that a technological civilization like ours requires many trained specialists and technicians; but the need for these, urgent as it may be, should not blind us to the even more urgent need for reasonable and well-educated men. Specialized work should be sustained and criticized by minds able to view specific problems in a context of general principles and related theory. If these conditions are not met, specialized work becomes routine and uninspired technique, pedantry, or pretentious nonsense. . . .

The useful arts, in the final analysis always the application of general truths and theories to concrete problems and situations, require a foundation of theory before they become very useful, or at least before they become other than hit-or-miss empirical procedures. . . .

The intellectual arts have a utilitarian dimension, but this does not make the end of the liberal college a utilitarian one. A liberal education concentrating upon instruction in the proper use and understanding of linguistic and mathematical symbols possesses a truly universal significance. . . . An earlier faculty report says:

> It is an integral part of the American dream that each man in our society may and must perform the highest functions. These functions consist in the intelligent free choice of the ends and means of both our common and individual life. This is a most glorious and most difficult proposition to which we are dedicated. Among other things it means that each man must have his measure of liberal education, since choices can be neither free nor intelligent without relevant training and understanding. These trainings and understandings are parts of the liberal arts and sciences. Professional and vocational schools study, or should study, their respective minimal amounts of theoretical science. But there are basic trainings and understandings common to all vocations and therefore common necessities of all free men. . . .

---

* Excerpted from *The St. John's Program: A Report*, Annapolis, Md.: St. John's College Press, 1955. By permission. Read also David Boroff, "St. John's College: Four Years with the Great Books," *Saturday Review*, 46: 58–61, March 23, 1963.

Compare also the following statement by Plato:

> In heaven, methinks, there is laid up a pattern of the good city which he who desires may behold, and beholding, may set his own house in order. But whether it exists or ever will exist on earth is no matter, for the wise man will live after the manner of it, having nothing to do with any other.

—Plato, *Republic* IX, 592 (Jowett translation).

THE GREAT BOOKS IN THE CURRICULUM

. . . It has been said that the authors of these books are the real St. John's faculty. If so, they are subjected to more severe standards of selection than most faculties. Furthermore, they are never granted tenure. To be selected for the curriculum, a book must meet the following requirements:

First, it must be a masterpiece in the liberal arts. The author must possess and his work must exemplify those intellectual arts and habits the student is supposed to acquire—rigorous and honest thinking, imagination, an effort to transcend the merely factual and historical, and, above all, the direction of these to the end of learning and communicating the truth.

Second, it must be a work of fine art. It must possess a clarity and grace that tempt the mind of a reader to yield willingly to the discipline of its logic and to explore the intricacies of its thought.

Third, it must have many possible interpretations. From the first two criteria it follows that a great book can be understood on a certain level without the support of commentary and is thus immediately intelligible. On other levels different interpretations may be equally valid, and the texture of possible meanings develops as the book finds its place in the context of an intellectual tradition. It is endlessly provocative.

Fourth, it must raise significant questions, even though it may not answer them. These questions and the answers we make to them are the essential aspects of our individual and social lives. In facing them the author must be conscious of the limits of human analysis and exposition; and he must be willing, where necessary, to follow reason to these limits.

Fifth, each book, in addition to its independent contribution, must be related to the other books in the curriculum. Whether the relations are those of agreement or opposition does not matter. In this way the understanding of any one book is cumulative and corrected by the reading of the others.

It would seem legitimate to describe books conforming to the above criteria as "great books." . . . St. John's believes that such books provide the best possible material for students to work with. . . .[9]

---

[9] Editor's Note: Here is a brief criticism of "Great Books" as the core of a curriculum:

> That we should read "great books" rather than poor ones is a venerable truism; that we should make them the core of a liberal education is not quite so obvious. . . . Books do not grow in a vacuum, and books do not grow purely out of other books. At all times, the essential relation is not between book and book, but between book and life. A revolution in literature is part of a general revolution in thought, itself inseparable from a change in social conditions. . . . Certain immense changes, of

4.9 THE INSPIRATION OF GREAT BOOKS*

Gilbert Highet

THREE ERRORS

There are three errors which help to account for the weaknesses of contemporary education.

The first is the mistaken idea that schools exist principally to train boys and girls to be sociable, "integrated with their group," "equipped with the skills of social living," "adjusted to family and community co-operation," and so forth. Obviously that is *one* of the aims of schooling, sometimes neglected in the past though usually emerging as a by-product. It was a necessary and valuable function of school and college at the most recent stage in American history to create a more or less uniform pattern of culture for the new middle class, and a stable social order in which the children of the unparalleled flood of immigrants who reached the country between 1880 and 1920 could find their place as Americans. But another

---

the utmost importance to mankind, never were recorded in commensurate books. The Industrial Revolution had incalculable consequences; but even if James Watt had happened to write a book, it might well not have deserved to be considered a world classic. And in the mounting tide of socialism for the last century and a half, no single book, however mighty, can be treated even as an adequate symbol. . . .

But the chief ambiguity in selecting the Hundred Best Books results from the effort to combine two criteria, the intrinsic (artistic or scientific) and the social: books that live because of their beauty and truth, books which once were events in the history of mankind. When the two criteria happen to be in agreement, it is little short of a miracle. The most miraculous case of all is that of Plato. St. Paul, in rare passages, reaches supreme heights of spiritual and literary power; Jean Jacques Rousseau was not merely a portent, but, once in a while, a poet. But as a rule, the scales are not the same. . . . If *Hamlet* had never been written, mankind would have been deprived of a jewel; but, because Luther nailed his ninety-five theses on the church door at Wittenberg, the lives of millions were transformed. There is an abyss between a classic and a document. . . .

—Albert Guerard, *The Education of a Humanist*, Cambridge, Mass.: Harvard University Press, 1949, pp. 128–132. By permission. Professor Guerard is an authority on "great books" having authored *Preface to World Literature*, New York: Holt, Rinehart and Winston, Inc., 1949, and numerous books on literature and humanism.

For further criticisms of "great books" read Dwight McDonald, "Book-of-the-Millennium Club," *The New Yorker*, 28: 171f., November 29, 1952; F. R. Leavis, "Great Books and a Liberal Education," *Commentary*, 16: 224–232, September 1953.

* Gilbert Highet, *Man's Unconquerable Mind*, New York: Columbia University Press, 1954, paperback 1960, pp. 40–45, 75–78. By permission.

The editor recommends this inexpensive paperback as a supplement to this chapter. Gilbert Highet is Professor of the Classic Languages at Columbia University.

aim of education, equally important or more important, is to train the individual mind as intensely and to encourage it as variously as possible—since much of our better and our more essential life is lived by us as individuals, and since (in the advancing age of mass-culture) it is vital for us to maintain personal independence.

The second of these three errors is the belief that education is a closed-end process, which stops completely as soon as adult life begins. . . . It is like learning music for nearly a decade, and then never going to a concert or playing a single note. Here the schools, colleges, and teachers are surely to blame. Too many teachers (especially in college) seem to limit the interest of their students by implying that their own true and central aim is to train professional scholars, and that amateur interest in their subject is to be deprecated.

The third error which limits the use of knowledge in the Western world is the notion that learning and teaching always ought to have immediate results, show a profit, lead to success. . . . The result is that important and long-fruitful subjects tend to be squeezed out of education, neglected, even ignored and deformed. For instance, English literature is one of the finest literatures in the entire world: a thing to be proud of and to enjoy. To be brought up speaking and reading English is to be presented with the key to a massive and incorruptible treasure. Our literature from Chaucer to Eliot contains enough to make a man happy, thoughtful, and eloquent through an entire lifetime. And yet many unfortunate boys and girls in the English-speaking countries are being denied that opportunity. Their teachers tell their parents that language is a "tool"; and instead of showing them how to read and appreciate the best fifty of those miraculous books, they instruct them in a dreary pastiche sometimes called "language arts," which is to literature as finger painting is to the National Gallery. Year by year, more youngsters go to high school and to college. Year by year, standards go down and down—and not because there is an inevitable degradation in admitting large crowds into our educational system, but simply because we are recklessly ready to waste both the minds of the young and the rich inheritance of the past. . . .

TRAINING THE THINKER

. . . We can never tell how great minds arise, and it is very hard to tell how to detect and encourage them when they do appear. But we do know two methods of feeding them as they grow.

One is to give them constant challenge and stimulus. Put problems before them. Make things difficult for them. They need to think. Produce things for them to think about and question their thinking at every stage.

They are inventive and original. Propose experiments to them. Tell them to discover what is hidden.

The second method is to bring them into contact with other eminent minds. It is not enough, not nearly enough, for a clever boy or girl to meet his fellows and his teachers and his parents. He (or she) must meet men and women of real and undeniable distinction. That is, he must meet the immortals. That brilliant and pessimistic scoundrel Plato died just over 2,300 years ago, but through his books he is still talking and thinking and leading others to think; and there is no better way, none, for a young man to start thinking about any kind of philosophical problem—human conduct, political action, logical analysis, metaphysics, aesthetics—than by reading Plato and trying to answer his arguments, detect his sophisms, resist his skillful persuasions, and become both his pupil and his critic. No one can learn to write music better than by studying *The Well-tempered Clavier* of Bach and the symphonies of Beethoven. A young composer who does so will not, if he is any good, write music like Bach and Beethoven. He will write music more like the music that he wanted to write. A man may become a routine diplomat by following the rule book and solving every problem as it comes up, but if he is to grow into a statesman he must read his Machiavelli and consider the lives of Bismarck and Lincoln and Disraeli. The best way toward greatness is to mix with the great.

Challenge and experiment; association with immortal minds: these are the two sure ways of rearing intelligent men and women. And these two opportunities for greatness are, or ought to be, provided by schools and colleges and universities. "But," you will ask, "do schools exist only to train geniuses?" No, but they do not exist only to train the average and to neglect or benumb the talented. They exist to make the best of both. One of the heaviest responsibilities in education is to do justice to exceptional minds, remembering that they may emerge in any place, at any time, and in any body—even a clumsy and misshapen frame may hold a brilliant mind. It must be a strange experience to teach in a little country school, the same subjects year after year to the same families, and then to find a gifted young engineer or a born dramatist among one's pupils. Disconcerting. Difficult. Difficult to know how to encourage without patronizing; difficult not to be a little jealous. Yet the history of knowledge is filled with true stories of teachers who recognized outstanding gifts in a pupil and gave him all he needed to set him on his way to eminence: touching and encouraging, these tales. Such is the story of the Spanish peasant boy who was drawing with charcoal on a plank when a teacher saw him, started training him, and helped to make the artist Goya. Such is the tale of the thin sensitive undersized London schoolboy whose schoolmaster's son gave him the run of his private library: it was among those shelves and as a result of that kindness that the youngster wrote a poem called *On First*

Looking into Chapman's Homer. Behind every great man there stands either a good parent or a good teacher.

Education in America and in the other countries of the West is an inspiriting achievement: all those light, healthy schools, those myriad colleges, so many youngsters having a fine time and not working too hard. . . . Schools do exist for the average. They also exist to serve the distinguished. America was built both by a multitude of common men and women and also by a few eccentrics, heroes, and giants. . . .

The life of every teacher is partly dedicated to discovering and encouraging those few powerful minds who will influence our future, and the secret of education is never to forget the possibility of greatness.

We owe them reverence, the great minds of the past and present and future. It is inspiring and delightful even to scan their names. One shines on another, receiving light in return. It is like looking at the stars, when the eye travels from the Bear to Orion, from Aldebaran to Sirius and Vega, from glory to glory. . . . To read the life of even one such thinker is to renew one's faith in humanity, one's sense of duty to the world. To move freely among the captain minds of any one great age—say the seventeenth century, or the century that produced Cicero, Lucretius, Vergil, Horace, and Livy, or the nineteenth century—is to be perpetually astounded at the depth unplumbable, the infinite variety of the human mind, and to repeat the words of the Greek tragedian:

Wonders are many, but none,
none is more wondrous than man.[10]

---

[10] Editor's Note:

Great books are for the able, not for dull or mediocre students. . . . Forgetting the simple truth that a small and clumsy mind cannot engage a great idea or a subtly rendered complex emotion and that one without some significant dimension of emerging greatness cannot hold conversation with the great, we act, in deference to our "democratic faith" as if this were not so; and we become involved in a myriad of teaching devices unwittingly designed to subvert the educative process. . . .

There is nothing one can do with Stephen Vincent Benét, Carl Sandburg, Tolstoy, or Shakespeare to make them suitable for below average students. Shakespeare, for one, has been rewritten in simplified language for the young and the less able; but *Shakespeare* is gone. They are nice little stories, but they are no longer value exemplars. . . . No work of art, whether painting, music or literature, can be tampered with in an over-all way, taking out the higher order abstractions or intricate details of design or subtle nuances and remain an exemplar. Exemplars are great because they are demanding. We must rise to them, they cannot be brought down to us. . . .

The blind spot of the classical realist lies in his failure to realize that this heritage [of great books and other classics] can . . . do inestimable harm when forced upon those not equipped to receive it. . . . Such students live in a dim and confusing world. They are hounded by failure and fear which slowly turns into rebellion. The student comes to detest the school, the teacher, and finally himself. The number of juvenile delinquents that teachers following this outworn faith have driven into lives of crime must be tremendous. . . .

4.10 SCIENTIFIC STUDY SHOULD BE LIBERAL*

H. M. Dowling

[During] the second half of the nineteenth century . . . a dichotomy was set up between the humanities which dealt with human nature and the sciences and technology which dealt with nature. It is a dichotomy which has persisted ever since so that, no less than the great Victorians, we have failed to grasp and exploit the cultural possibilities of what for a majority is now not merely the "new learning," but the only learning.

Writing forty years ago in his *The Aims of Education*, Alfred North Whitehead disposed of the fallacious antithesis [between a liberal and a technical education]: "There can be no adequate technical education which is not liberal," he said, "and no liberal education which is not technical; that is, there is no education which does not impart both technique and intellectual vision." He distinguished three different roads to culture—the literary . . . the technical . . . the scientific. . . . Whichever of these three courses a student selected, it should give him [said Whitehead] "a technique, a science, an assortment of general ideas, and esthetic appreciation, and each of these sides of his training should be illuminated by the others."

Obviously such views as these have great relevance to the debate now going on concerning the proper way to teach science and technology. Are we in our teaching exploring and exploiting to the full the cultural resources of scientific and technical subjects? Accepting specialization as necessary and inevitable, as I think we must, have we really grasped the idea that this specialization could become the avenue to a deep and wide culture? Have we considered, moreover, that for many students in this modern age science or technology may, in fact, be the best and most acceptable road to culture, since it accords with their aptitudes, inclinations and ambitions? . . .

The blind spot of those attacking it [the attempt to bring great classics into the school curriculum] lies in their failure to realize that withholding it from those with the intellectual and imaginative power to benefit from it would result in cultural disaster. A hallowed place must be made for the humanistic disciplines in the junior-senior secondary schools of tomorrow. . . .

—Everett J. Kircher, "Broudy's Educational Aspirations: Reality or Utopia?" *Studies in Philosophy and Education* 2: 241–258, Summer 1962. By permission of the Executive Editor, Southern Illinois University, Edwardsville, Illinois. Broudy's position, which was discussed at length in the article from which this excerpt was taken, is quite similar to the one stated above by Gilbert Highet.

* H. M. Dowling, "Science and Culture: A False Antithesis," London: *New Scientist*, 11: 727–729, September 21, 1961. Mr. Dowling is Headmaster of the Crewe County Grammar School, England. By permission.

The fact is that a science like chemistry or physics, or a technical subject like metallurgy, or a craft like woodwork or metalwork, can be taught in one of three different ways. It can be taught simply as a technique, a way of doing something practical; or it can be taught as both a technique and a science; or it can be taught as a technique, a science *and a culture*. If it is taught as a culture as well as a technique and a science it will certainly include a way of doing things (technique) and a systemized body of facts and principles (science), but it will also allow scope for such intellectual, esthetic and even social ideas as would if not impeded, arise naturally from a serious study of the subject. . . .

Now it is certain that much of our science and technology is not being taught in this way. Recently I asked a man who had gained a doctorate in chemistry whether he thought his subject could be made a cultural medium. He was obviously startled by the question, and immediately afterwards confessed that he had never thought of his subject in that way. Obviously his university courses in chemistry had given him no insight into its wider and deeper cultural potentialities. He had learned chemistry purely as a science (a systemized body of fact and principle) and as a technique.

It is essential, of course, that our science and technology should continue to be taught at this high and exacting scientific and technical level.[11] But it is a pity, nevertheless, that other intellectual and esthetic areas which properly belong to a liberal study of the subject, should remain altogether unexplored and undeveloped. Similarly, crafts like woodwork and metalwork are often taught on a purely technical level, with little, if any, reference to their scientific basis and their intellectual and esthetic implications. This is a tragedy, because for many people the learning of a craft may be the very best introduction to the realms of science and esthetics.

It would be foolish and unfair, of course, to blame individual teachers for this situation. The fault lies in the whole tradition in which scientific and technical training has been conceived and practiced.

May I crystallize the present argument in two statements which may seem dogmatic, but which I am convinced express important truths?

1. No technical process ought to be taught at any educational level without some reference to the science (that is, the organized body of facts

[11] Editor's Note: A study of 6000 executives by the Harvard Graduate School of Public Administration reveals that "The percentage of top corporation officials having a degree in science or engineering rose steadily from 7 percent in 1900 to 20 percent in 1950 . . . to 26 percent in 1963." If this trend continues, "the proportion of top industrial management with a background in science and engineering will have risen to more than 50 percent by 1980."—Milton H. Spencer and Harvey Nussbaum, "Meeting the Needs of Negroes for Careers in Management," *The Negro Educational Review* 18: 53–64, July–October 1967.

and principles) involved in it. *Technical training not based on science is illiberal.*

2. No science or technical subject ought to be taught without reference to the general ideas—for example, in the fields of history, esthetics, economics—which a generous treatment of the subject would naturally evoke. *Science or technology without general ideas is illiberal.* . . .

Frankly it terrifies me to think that the vast expansion of technical and scientific education to which we are now being committed may be implemented in largely noncultural terms, and without any serious effort to explore its liberal potentialities. Thousands of men and women may learn their science and technology simply on the plane of technique or narrowly specialized knowledge, without that lifting and liberalization of the mind which a wider exploration of the subject is bound to encourage. Some idealists will hope that a bit of poetry or philosophy twined round the edges will make these students cultured men and women. It will do nothing of the sort.

We cannot afford to go on outlawing science and technology to the noncultural wilderness. In our school, college and university courses we must ensure, by reform and coordination of syllabuses, that whether the student is learning elementary metalwork or degree physics he is acquiring a technique, a science, a collection of general ideas and esthetic appreciation.[12]

---

[12] Editor's Note: More recently, two other British writers have expressed these ideas as follows:

> From early times the belief has existed that effects of certain studies were general and refining whilst others were limited and specific, or, in social terms, that some studies were worthy of the gentleman, the freeman and the scholar whilst others were deemed servile, base, fit only for a "mechanical man." An education thought to be narrow and limited was concerned with the vocational aspects of learning, in the past with science and the "mechanical arts," and today, to a great extent, with the technical subjects. On the other hand, a liberal or general education was, and still tends to be, associated with the arts subjects, the humanities. We consider a liberal education to be one concerned with the development of the whole personality of each individual, one in which the approach to studies is wide in sympathy and free from narrow prejudice, in a word, enlightened, and the products of such an education should be men and women who are both able to satisfy the technical and professional demands of work and who are candid, mature people.
>
> A subject can be taught in such a way that it consists mainly in acquiring knowledge or skill. The pupil can only apply this knowledge or skill in a situation very similar to the one in which he first learned it, and its use is thus strictly limited. The pupil becomes a reproducer of facts and his success depends largely upon his ability to memorize. The same knowledge or skill can, however, be taught in such a way that the pupil recognizes and understands the relevant general principles. He is helped to realize that these principles can be applied in other circumstances and he both looks for and is provided with opportunities to apply them. Here we have the application of the knowledge or skill in a wide variety of circumstances, the emphasis being placed on the pupil's power of adaptation and intellectual

4.11 THE EDUCATION OF TECHNOLOGISTS*

H. N. Sheldon

The White Paper on *Technical Education* (1956) defined a technologist as one who ". . . has studied the fundamental principles of his chosen technology and should be able to use his knowledge and experience to initiate practical developments. He is expected to accept a high degree of responsibility and in many cases to push forward the boundaries of knowledge in his own particular field." Since the technologist may alternatively be described as an applied scientist, breadth of outlook is an essential quality for him, since his function is to apply scientific and technological principles ultimately for the benefit of society. Certainly he cannot function without affecting profoundly the society of which he is a member.

It is against this background of the concept of the technologist and the institutions specially conceived for his higher education that we must examine the claim that such education is, indeed, liberal education. The concern that the training of the technologist should contain more than specialized know-how (more appropriate to the technician) arose very largely from the technologists themselves—staffs of colleges, professional institutions and industrialists. Indeed, the main pressure for a more liberal influence came from industry which demanded recruits at this level "with the ability to think independently and constructively," "with initiative and ability to make judgements," "with a good scientific and cultural background," etc. There was no shortage of advice from outside the technological professions—educational reformers and philosophers and leading thinkers in science and the humanities all attempted to grapple with this specific aspect of the general problem of "overspecialization" (an expression incapable of objective definition or measurement), and to offer suggestions as to solution of the problem.

---

ability although the achievement of this application depends to a large extent on our approach and method of presentation, . . . [i.e.,] the various subjects studied should be integrated and the relationships between them made clear, the pupil being given an idea of all or most of the bodies of knowledge which are his cultural heritage and which an educated citizen should possess.

—P. R. May and S. Turner (Lecturers in Education, The University of Durham), in *The Aims and Organization of Liberal Studies,* D. F. Bratchell and Morrell Heald, eds., London: Pergamon Press, 1966, pp. 88–89. By permission.

* H. N. Sheldon, "Liberal Studies in Colleges of Advanced Technology," in *The Aims and Organization of Liberal Studies,* D. F. Bratchell and Morrell Heald, eds., London and New York: Pergamon Press, 1966, pp. 69–74. By permission.

H. N. Sheldon is Acting Head of the Department of Liberal Studies, Royal College of Advanced Technology (Proposed University of Salford), Salford, England.

There are two barren arguments which need debunking in order to clear the air. Stated bluntly, they are: (1) that specialized study in applied science or technology is illiberal *per se* whilst specialized study in other fields such as the humanities is not, or to express it another way—some subjects are "liberal" whilst others, by implication, are not; (2) vocational studies are less liberal than studies with less vocational relevance.

Neither postulate would be admitted by the colleges of advanced technology. Specialized study of anything is only meaningful within the whole cultural context and the culture of a society includes every element—science, technology, philosophy, religion, economic activity, aesthetics, literature, social studies—and the theologian who is *completely ignorant* of economics, sociology and science, and whose mind is closed to the influences of these disciplines merits the description, narrow, illiberal or over-specialized, just as much as any specialist in pure or applied science, who is ignorant of or uninfluenced by the humanities. In any case, the former is more likely to exist than the latter.

As far as the vocational/non-vocational argument is concerned, not only is the distinction devoid of reality but in the case of the technologist one might argue that balance and all-roundness are a vocational necessity and that non-technical studies are at least as vocationally relevant as technical.

The colleges of advanced technology, therefore, regard themselves as institutions of higher learning providing a liberal education for their students. The nucleus of this liberal education is the specialized and disciplined study of a branch of applied science, whilst around this nucleus are grouped other less-specialized studies which are regarded as complementary and, indeed, highly relevant. . . .

The particular function of liberal studies is to counter the danger of excessive specialization and to assist in the all-round development of the student as an individual and as a member of society so that he may bring qualities of balance and perception to bear in every field of his activity.

More specifically, liberal studies in colleges of advanced technology have four main aims based upon the needs of the student, namely to help him:

1. to think clearly and independently in fields of knowledge and experience outside his own technology;
2. to express his ideas effectively in speech and in writing;
3. to gain an understanding of people and of the society in which he lives;
4. to develop his aesthetic interests and sensibility.

These objectives are interrelated and in large measure interdependent.

Clear and independent thought enables the individual to form his own philosophy and to make his own judgements on matters of value. It assists him in resisting prejudice and acquiring objectivity. It enables him to resist the dangerous pressures in society tending to narrowness, conformity, selfish materialism and political apathy or confusion, all of which threaten the continuance of healthy democracy.

Effective expression, valuable for anyone, is vital to the technologist. He is accustomed to dealing with problems where the answer is clear-cut, but he will be increasingly called on to deal with non-technical problems involving human beings. Here the answers are in terms that are not measurable, but which nevertheless require the maximum precision of thought and expression. Language is the basic tool of civilized communication and is thus the measure of intellectual discipline; further, its proper use involves both scientific and aesthetic qualities.

The technologist is the agent by which contemporary society is being profoundly affected. He must have an understanding of this society, the traditions by which it has been built up, the nature of the changes which he is helping to bring about, and the effects they will have on human beings. He must appreciate the importance, both to society and to the individual, of the process of mental and emotional adjustment to new conditions. The arts play an essential part in effecting this adjustment. Their role must be fully recognized, and not confused with mere decoration. An understanding of art illumines the nature of society and of man. Aesthetic experience aids in the fuller development of human personality, and in the education of feeling. In dealing with human problems, insight gained from such sources as literature may be more valuable than abstract analysis.

To sum up, liberal studies aim less to impart factual information than to bring out the unity of the many branches of human knowledge and activity; to foster the ability to think intelligently, with sympathetic understanding and alert interest; to evolve a full personality capable of dealing with problems of human relations; to assist the individual in the difficult process of adapting himself to the society in which he lives.[13]

---

[13] Editor's Note: Francis H. Horn, President of Rhode Island University, has expressed very similar ideas in the context of American higher education:

> I believe . . . that each person, within the period of his formal schooling, should have as much liberal education as possible, consistent with the requirements of his particular vocation and the time he can devote to his schooling. But I also believe—and here I part company with all the liberal arts people—that the vocational preparation must take precedence over the liberal education. . . . If an individual can give seven years to his higher education, the liberal part of this education will exceed the professional part. But if he has only four years to give to college—and he wants to be an engineer or a cattle breeder for example—the larger proportion of his program will be vocational. . . .
>
> Regardless of how much liberal education a person gets in his formal schooling, it is a great mistake to have it concentrated as preprofessional or prevocational education. This, however, is the normal pattern of higher education in this country . . . [and it contributes] to the idea that the liberal arts part of one's education is something to be completed and forgotten; a hurdle which, once surmounted, leaves

4.12 THE GREAT AMERICAN FRUSTRATION*

Archibald MacLeish

From the beginning of what we used to call the industrial revolution—what we see today more clearly as a sort of technological coup d'état—men and women, particularly men and women of imaginative sensibility, have seen that something was happening to the human role in the shaping of civilization. . . . Who were *we* in this strange new world? What part did *we* play in it? Someone had written a new equation somewhere, pushed the doors of ignorance back a little, entered the darkened room of knowledge by one more step. Someone else had found a way to make use of that new knowledge, put it to work. Our lives had changed but without *our* changing them, without our intending them to change. Improvements had appeared and we had accepted them. We had bought Mr. Ford's machines by the hundreds of thousands. We had ordered radios by the

---

the individual to devote himself to the really important part of his education, the vocational part. I contend that liberal and vocational education should be intermingled at every stage of a student's career, unless he happens to be someone who is still uncertain in his choice of occupation. Then a broad exploratory program exclusively in the liberal arts is desirable. . . . [In such an exploratory program] some subjects will inculcate better than other subjects those values we recognize as characteristic of a liberal education . . . engineering drawing, well taught, will open "windows of the mind," but literature or philosophy, equally well taught, will open many more. The more windows opened for the individual the better, for man does not live by bread alone.

But he does live by bread. My major quarrel with the liberal arts people, I suppose, is their failure to recognize this fact. They skip over, as if it didn't exist, the major dilemma of higher education in our day. That dilemma is this: how can the colleges and universities provide graduates prepared for the thousands of specialized tasks which must be carried on in our technological civilization, and at the same time prepared for the demanding responsibilities of intelligent and informed citizenship—including satisfying personal living—in our democratic society?

I suggest that it is time to end this current battle of the books of liberal and vocational education, general and specialized knowledge, culture and training. We must . . . recognize first that the individual and society need both types of education; second, that the problem, both for the student and for the college, is the right relationship between the two; third, that the relationship will not be the same for all individuals . . . or for all institutions . . . ; and fourth, that the diversity of curricula and schools within American higher education resulting from these different approaches to the relationship of liberal to vocational education is a matter of strength, and efforts to force a common pattern, especially the pattern of the traditional four-year curriculum in the liberal arts, must be resisted.

—Francis H. Horn, "Liberal Education Reexamined," *Harvard Educational Review* 26: 303–314, Fall 1956. By permission.

* Archibald MacLeish, "The Great American Frustration," *Saturday Review* 51: 13–16, July 13, 1968. By permission.
Compare Selection 1.6, also by Archibald MacLeish.

millions and then installed TVs. And now we took to the air, flew from city to city, from continent to continent, from climate to climate, following summer up and down the earth like birds. We were new men in a new life in a new world . . . but a world *we* had not made—had not, at least, intended to make.

And a new world, moreover, that we were increasingly unsure, as time went by, we would have wanted to make. We wanted its conveniences, yes. Its comforts, certainly. But the world as a world to live in? As a human world? . . .

Prior to Hiroshima it had still been possible—increasingly difficult but still possible—to believe that science was by nature a human tool obedient to human wishes and that the world science and its technology could create would therefore be a human world reflecting our human needs, our human purposes. After Hiroshima it was obvious that the loyalty of science was not to humanity but to truth—its own truth—and that the law of science was not the law of the good—what humanity thinks of as good, meaning moral, decent, humane—but the law of the possible. What it is *possible* for science to know science must know. What it is possible for technology to do technology will have done. If it is possible to split the atom, then the atom must be split. Regardless. Regardless of . . . anything. . . .

In the brief time [after Hiroshima] when we alone possessed what was called "the secret," the American Government offered to share it with the world (the Baruch Plan) for peaceful exploitation. What we proposed, though we did not put it in these words, was that humanity as a whole should assert its control of science, or at least of this particular branch of science, nuclear physics, limiting its pursuit of possibility to possibilities which served mankind. But the Russians, with their faith in the dialectics of matter, demurred. They preferred to put their trust in *things*, and within a few short months their trust was justified: they had the bomb themselves.

The immediate effect in the United States was, of course, the soaring fear of Russia which fed the Cold War abroad and made the black plague of McCarthyism possible at home. But there was also a deeper and more enduring consequence. Our original American belief in our human capability, our human capacity to manage our affairs ourselves, "govern ourselves," faltered with our failure to control the greatest and most immediate of human dangers. We began to see science as a kind of absolute beyond our reach, beyond our understanding even, known, if it was known at all, through proxies who, like priests in other centuries, could not tell us what they knew.

In short, our belief in ourselves declined at the very moment when the Russian belief in the mechanics of the universe confirmed itself. No one talked any longer of a Baruch Plan, or even remembered that there had been one. The freedom of science to follow the laws of absolute possibility to whatever conclusions they might lead had been established, or so we thought, as the unchallengeable fixed assumption of our age, and the freedom of technology to invent whatever world it happened to invent was taken as the underlying law of modern life. It was enough for a manufacturer of automobiles to announce on TV that he had a better idea—any better idea: pop-open gas-tank covers or headlights that hide by day. No one thought any longer of asking whether his new idea matched a human purpose.

What was happening in those years, as the bitterly satirical fictions of the period never tired of pointing out, was that we were ceasing to think of ourselves as men, as self-governing men, as proudly self-governing makers of a new nation, and were becoming instead a society of consumers: recipients—grateful recipients—of the blessings of a technological civilization. We no longer talked in the old way of the American Proposition, either at home or abroad—particularly abroad. We talked instead of the American Way of Life. It never crossed our minds apparently—or if it did we turned our minds away—that a population of consumers, though it may constitute an affluent society, can never compose a nation in the great, the human, sense.

But the satirical novels, revealing as they were, missed the essential fact that we were becoming a population of consumers, an affluent society, not because we preferred to think of ourselves in this somewhat less than noble role but because we were no longer able to think of ourselves in that other role—the role our grandfathers had conceived for us two hundred years ago. We were not, and knew we were not, Whitman's Pioneers O Pioneers.

It is here, rather than in the floundering failures and futile disappointments of Vietnam, that this famous frustration of ours is rooted. Vietnam alone, disastrous as that whole experience has been, could never have produced, in a confident and self-reliant people such as the Americans once were, a mood like the American mood of these past months. Not even the riots of last summer and this spring could have afflicted us as we are now afflicted if we had still believed that our principal business was the making of a nation, the government of ourselves. Indeed the riots are, if anything, the consequence, not the cause, of our self-doubt—or, more precisely, the consequence of the actual causes of that doubt. It is not without significance that the targets of the mobs in the burning streets are supermarkets and television outlets rather than the courthouses and city halls which would have drawn the mobs of earlier times. Courthouses and city halls stand—or stood once—for the American Proposition. Supermarkets and television outlets are the symbols of the American Way of Life. Mobs strike for the Bastille in any rising and the Bastille in the United States today is whatever stands for the American Way of Life: the goods and services, the material wealth, which the majority claim as the mark of their Americanism and which the minority are denied.

It is because we are unwilling to recognize this fact and unable to face the crisis as a crisis in the long struggle for the creation of a true Republic —because, indeed, we are no longer primarily concerned with the creation of a true Republic—that the majority respond to these riots with nothing but a demand for more police and more repression, while the Congress sits impotent and paralyzed in Washington.

Which means, of course, however we put it, that we no longer believe in man. And it is that fact which raises, in its turn, the most disturbing of all the swarming questions which surround us: how did we come to this defeated helplessness? How were we persuaded of our impotence as men? What convinced us that the fundamental law of a scientific age must be the scientific law of possibility and that our human part must be a passive part, a subservient part, the part of the recipient, the beneficiary . . . the victim? Have the scientists taught us this? A few months ago one of the greatest of living scientists told an international gathering composed of other scientists: "We must not ask where science and technology are taking us, but rather how we can manage science and technology so that they can help us get where we want to go." It is not reported that Dr. René Dubos was shouted down by his audience, and yet what he was asserting was precisely what we as a people seem to have dismissed as unthinkable: that "we," which apparently means mankind, must abandon our modern practice of asking where science and technology are "taking *us*," and must ask instead how *we* can "manage" science and technology so that they will help us to achieve *our* purposes—our purposes, that is to say, as men.

Dr. Dubos, it appears, scientist though he is and [a] great scientist, believes rather more in man than we do. Why, then, do we believe so little? Perhaps we can answer that question best by asking another: how was our original, American belief in man achieved? Where did it come from? Thomas Jefferson, who had as much to do with the definition of our American belief as anyone, reflected on that subject toward his life's end. It was that famous trio at William and Mary, he decided, who "fixed" his "destinies." It was his education in his college, the teaching of Small and Wythe and the rest, which shaped his mind, gave it its direction. John Adams would have said the same and doubtless did: it was in Harvard College that he found those Greeks and Romans who taught him what a man could be and therefore *should.*

Is it *our* education, then, which has shaped the very different estimate of man we live by? In part, I think; in considerable part. Education, particularly higher education, has altered its relation to the idea of man in fundamental ways since Adams' day and Jefferson's. From the time when Harvard President Charles Eliot introduced the elective system there—from the time, that is to say, of the renunciation by the university of an intention to produce a certain *kind* of man, a man shaped by certain models, certain texts—the university's concern with "man" as such has grown less and less and its concern with what it calls "subjects" has become greater and greater. The important thing has become the academic "offering" (revealing word): the range of subjects from which the student, with his eye on his career, may choose. And the ultimate consequence, only too evident in the time we live in, has been the vocationalization of the higher schools. The college no longer exists to produce men *qua* men, men prepared for life in a society of men, but men as specialized experts, men prepared for employment in an industry or a profession.

"Getting ahead in the world," says Professor Allen Tate of the University of Minnesota, "is now the purpose of education and the University must therefore provide education for our time, not for all time: it must discover and then give to society what society thinks it wants. . . ." Some of us, looking at the present state of American society—the decay of its cities, the bewilderment of its citizens—may wonder whether the university has really provided "education for our time," but no one, I think, will deny that Professor Tate's emphatic irony has its bite. The vocationalism which a technological society demands of the graduate schools has produced a secondary vocationalism which the graduate schools impose on the colleges, and the result is that undergraduate education—far more important to the preparation for citizenship than graduate education—is increasingly affected by the vocational taint.

What is happening, and in the greatest universities as well as in the less great, is that the entire educational process is becoming fixed—hung-up as the phrase goes now—on its vocational end result. The job out there in the profession or the industry dictates the "training" (their word, not mine) in the graduate schools, and the graduate schools dictate the preparation in the colleges, and the whole system congeals from the top down like a pond freezing. The danger is that the society may congeal with it, for nothing is more certain in the history of our kind than the fact that frozen societies perish.

As specialized, professional training, higher education in the United States today is often magnificent. Young doctors are better and better as their specialties become more specialized: so much better that it is now a recommendation in almost any field to say of a young doctor that he is young. Student physicists in the great graduate schools are so notoriously productive at twenty-two that a professional physicist of thirty regards himself, or is regarded by his juniors, as middle-aged. But the educated *man*, the man capable not of providing specialized answers, but of asking the great and liberating questions by which humanity makes its way through time, is not more frequently encountered than he was two hundred years ago. On the contrary, he is rarely discovered in public life at all.

I am not arguing—though I deeply believe—that the future of the Republic and the hope for a recovery of its old vitality and confidence depend on the university. I am confining myself to Dr. Dubos's admonition that we must give up the childishness of our present attitude toward science and technology, our constant question where *they* are taking *us*, and begin instead to ask how *we* can manage *them* "so that they can help us get where we want to go." "Where we want to go" depends, of course, on ourselves and, more particularly, on our conception of ourselves. If our conception of ourselves as the university teaches it or fails to teach it is the conception of the applicant preparing for his job, the professional preparing for his profession, then the question will not be answered because it will not be asked. But if our conception of ourselves as the university teaches it is that of men preparing to be men, to achieve themselves as men, then the question will be asked *and* answered because it cannot be avoided. Where do we want to go? Where men can be most themselves. How should science and technology be managed? To help us to become what we can be.

There is no quarrel between the humanities and the sciences. There is only a need, common to them both, to put the idea of man back where it once stood, at the focus of our lives; to make the end of education the preparation of men to be men, and so to restore to mankind—and above all to this nation of mankind—a conception of humanity with which humanity can live.

The frustration—and it is a real and debasing frustration—in which we are mired today will not leave us until we believe in ourselves again, assume again the mastery of our lives, the management of our means.

Education for a New Era

4.13 INTRODUCTION: THE SPIRIT OF INQUIRY

This is a book about liberal education—about education that stimulates in each person a compelling urge to explore the unknown and to exercise to a fuller degree the vast possibilities of his mind. The man on the street may say "I think" when he means "I feel" (that is, "I am attached to these prejudices"). But for a scholar, "I think" is intellectually meaningless unless that thinking has included a fair and impartial study of competing points of view. No pattern of ideas is so sacred that the thinker's mind should be closed to other alternatives. "You have been told to prove you are right," said Louis Pasteur, "but I say, try to prove you are *wrong*." The scientist, like the inventor, believes that if we all worked on the assumption that what is accepted as true is really true, there would be little hope for advance. Hence the heritage of knowledge is always slightly tentative and subject to reconstruction in the light of new discovery. But through the cooperative endeavors of many investigators, "the great community"[14] gradually accumulates a body of knowledge which progressively acquires the virtues characteristic of science: clarity and consistency, testability and adequacy, precision and objectivity. In the words of Nobel prizewinner P. W. Bridgman:

> . . . the most vital feature of the scientist's procedure has been merely to do his utmost with his mind, *no holds barred*. This means in particular that no special privileges are accorded to authority or to tradition, that personal prejudices and predilections are carefully guarded against, that one makes continued check to assure oneself that one is not making mistakes, and that any line of inquiry will be followed that appears at all promising.[15]

[14] Concerning "The Great Community" as an ideal in American philosophy, read Max H. Fisch, ed., *Classic American Philosophers*, New York: Appleton-Century-Crofts, 1951, pp. 34–39.

[15] P. W. Bridgman, *Reflections of a Physicist*, New York: Philosophical Library, Inc., 1950, p. 370.

In an authoritarian society, teachers are expected to transmit a fixed set of values; education is indistinguishable from indoctrination. Problems are approached from an "official" or "approved" point of view, while opposing viewpoints are presented as mere straw men easily knocked over. Such "education" develops minds undisciplined in resourcefulness and versatility, minds either soft or inflexible. The few adults who outgrow such "education in immaturity" look back on their schooling as a form of prolonged infancy, and upon their teachers as intellectual baby sitters hired to keep young minds asleep.

In a democratic society, schools also transmit truths and values; but here they are transmitted in a tentative, experimental manner—as the best that openly critical thinking has arrived at thus far. The democratic teacher has a profound respect for traditions, but he views them as subject to modification and improvement. The present is enriched by the past, and tradition is a splendid banquet that our ancestors have provided for us. But in a society that has respect for the new as well as the old, for the living as well as for the dead, each generation must study anew to determine which of tradition's foods are still edible, which no longer are nourishing. This process can occur when all viewpoints are privileged to defend themselves and thereby fairly win or lose a place in the living world. We cannot avoid this confidence in ourselves or in the generations to come. There is an element of truth in the saying that American democracy places more emphasis on its "Ten Amendments" than it does on the "Ten Commandments," and that the basic ethics of our society is "contentless." But it is not contentless in the sense that we have no cherished traditions or beliefs to sustain our personal and social behavior. It is contentless only in the sense that each and every one of our traditional beliefs is subject to critical scrutiny.

Thus, democratic education has two major functions: to impart accumulated knowledge and traditions, and to encourage the discovery of new truth. On the one hand, schools should train men to shape the society of their generation on the basis of the accumulated wisdom of the past. On the other hand, schools should stimulate creative thinking—thinking which continually renders previous knowledge suspect. This dual function of education was expressed by the founder of Christianity who came "not to destroy but to fulfill the law" and "not to send peace but a sword."[16]

If these two purposes seem contradictory, it is only because the nature of our dynamic society is not understood. In a democracy, liberty depends on liberalism—defined as faith in change by reason and persuasion rather than by force or violence. By placing its primary emphasis on the individual, democracy becomes an open society, in which individuals can

[16] *Matthew* 5:17; 10:34.

challenge any and all traditions; in which private experience is the ultimate criterion of truth and value; and in which informed public criticism is the primary means of improving our heritage. The strength of an open society rests on independent, self-reliant citizens who are free to talk, to meet, to think, to seek truth, to move about, to be different, to try something new, to make the most of their lives according to their own ideals.

"The case for democracy," wrote Carl Becker, "is that it accepts the rational and humane values as ends, and proposes as the means of realizing them the minimum of coercion and the maximum of voluntary assent."[17] In democratic schools, the rational side of human nature should be disciplined to think independently, the humane side to think cooperatively. If education is properly balanced, democratic citizens must, in the neat phrase of Alexander Meiklejohn, learn "to think independently together." When reason and humanity are properly balanced, men learn to think for themselves, but they also learn to modify their thinking (or rationalization) in terms of opposing opinions of other men—men for whom they have respect and affection, but who happen to think differently from them. In short, "It is one thing to educate people to the end that control *of* them may be developed; it is quite another thing to educate to the end that control *by* the people may be increased and perfected."[18]

In a dynamic society, debate and controversy are signs of health, not of sickness. Varied and conflicting ideas and interests are the very lifeblood of a free society, provided that citizens are willing to compromise and to pool their many diverse ideas through joint, cooperative thinking. Schools do not fulfill their major function unless scholars act as social catalysts, forcing others to reconsider their opinions, and leading them to develop viewpoints more appropriate to the times. In this manner, education helps to break the "crust of custom" that tends to form over inherited beliefs and prejudices, there is an ever-evolving synthesis of old and new, and progress is both possible and peaceable.

---

[17] Carl Becker, *New Liberties for Old*, New Haven, Conn.: Yale University Press, 1941, p. 151.

[18] A. V. Sayers, A *First Course in the Philosophy of Education*, New York: Holt, Rinehart and Winston, Inc., 1952, pp. 3–4.

4.14 EDUCATION FOR CHANGE*

Margaret Mead

Is not the break between past and present—and so the whole problem of outdating in our educational system—related to a change in the rate of change? For change has become so rapid that adjustment cannot be left to the next generation; adults must—not once, but continually—take in, adjust to, use, and make innovations in a steady stream of discovery and new conditions. . . .

[Our] education system today . . . combines these different functions: (1) The protection of the child against exploitation and the protection of society against precocity and inexperience. (2) The maintenance of learners in a state of moral and economic dependency. (3) Giving to all children the special, wider education once reserved for the children of privileged groups, in an attempt to form the citizen of a democracy as once the son of a noble house was formed. (4) The teaching of complex and specialized skills which, under our complex system of division of labor, is too difficult and time-consuming for each set of parents to master or to hand on to their own children. (5) The transmission of something which the parents' generation does *not* know (in the case of immigrants with varied cultural and linguistic backgrounds) to children whom the authorities or the parents wish to have educated.

To these multiple functions of an educational system, which, in a slowly changing society, were variously performed, we have added slowly and reluctantly a quite new function: *education for rapid and self-conscious adaptation to a changing world*. . . . [For this is] the most vivid truth of the new age: *no one will live all his life in the world into which he was born, and no one will die in the world in which he worked in his maturity*. . . .

In this world, no one can "complete an education." The students we need are not just children who are learning to walk and talk and to read and write plus older students, conceived of as minors, who are either

---

* Margaret Mead, "Why is Education Obsolescent?" *Harvard Business Review* 36: 23–36, 164–170, November–December 1958. By permission.

Compare the following:

> The world of the future—and the very near future—will call for such traits as originality, boldness and flexibility. Whereas, I wonder if many of our schools don't unconsciously encourage conformity, timidity and rigidity. Often what the school wants out of the student is the "right answers"—forgetting that often the right answer is the trite answer.
>
> —Peter G. Peterson, "The Class of 1964—Where Is It Going?" Washington, D.C.: National Committee for the Support of the Public Schools, 1966, p. 15.

"going on" with or "going back" to specialized education. Rather, we need children *and* adolescents *and* young *and* mature *and* "senior" adults, each of whom is learning at the appropriate pace and with all the special advantages of experience peculiar to his own age.

If we are to incorporate fully each new advance, we need simultaneously: (1) The wide-eyed freshness of the inquiring child; (2) The puzzlement of the near-dunce who, if the system is to work, must still be part of it; (3) The developing capacities of the adolescent for abstract thinking; (4) The interest of the young adult whose motives have been forged in the responsibilities of parenthood and first contacts with a job; (5) The special awareness of the mature man who has tempered experience, skepticism, and the power to implement whatever changes he regards as valuable; (6) The balance of the older man who has lived through cycles of change and can use this wisdom to place what is new.

Each and every one of these is a learner, not of something old and tried—the alphabet or multiplication tables or Latin declensions or French irregular verbs or the rules of rhetoric or the binomial theorem, all the paraphernalia of learning which children with different levels of aspiration must acquire—but of new, hardly tried theories and methods: pattern analysis, general system theory, space lattices, cybernetics, and so on. . . .

In this world the age of the teacher is no longer necessarily relevant. For instance, children teach grandparents how to manage TV, young expediters come into the factory along with the new equipment, and young men invent automatic programing for computers over which their seniors struggle because they, too, need it for their research.

This, then, is what we call the *lateral transmission* of knowledge. It is not an outpouring of knowledge from the "wise old teacher" into the minds of young pupils, as in vertical transmission. Rather, it is a sharing of knowledge by the informed with the uninformed, whatever their ages. The primary prerequisite is the desire to know. . . .

In thinking about an effective educational system we should recognize that the adolescent's need and right to work is as great as (perhaps greater than) his immediate need and right to study. And we must recognize that the adult's need and right to study more is as great as (perhaps greater than) his need and right to hold the same job until he is 65 years old. . . .[19]

[19] Editor's Note: Compare the following statement by Robert Oppenheimer:

In an important sense this world of ours is a new world, in which the unity of knowledge, the nature of human communities, the order of society, the order of ideas, the very notions of society and culture have changed and will not return to what they have been in the past. What is new is new not because it has never been there before, but because it has changed in quality. One thing that is new is the prevalence of newness, the changing scale and scope of change itself, so that the world alters as we walk in it, so that the years of man's life measure not some small growth or rearrangement or moderation of what he learned in childhood, but

4.15 ENCOURAGING VERSATILE AND INDEPENDENT MINDS*

Peter Schrag

"When one considers . . . the education of a nation's young," said Whitehead in *The Aims of Education,* "the broken lives, the defeated hopes, the national failures, which result from the frivolous inertia with which it is treated, it is difficult to restrain within oneself a savage rage. In the conditions of modern life the rule is absolute, the race which does not value trained intelligence is doomed. Not all your heroism, not all your social charm, not all your wit, not all your victories on land or at sea, can move back the finger of fate. Today we maintain ourselves. Tomorrow science will have moved forward yet one more step, and there will be no appeal from the judgment which will then be pronounced on the uneducated."

The statement was made to the Mathematical Association of England in the year 1916—it deserves to be repeated, even in America a half century later.

Our schools have come a long way in recent years, and a long way indeed since 1916. There are new courses and techniques, special programs for the gifted and the underprivileged, better pay for teachers and, in general, a greater understanding and concern for education. And yet many schools are still inadequate, not because their buildings are ancient and their teachers underpaid, or because they have not adopted all the new gimmicks on the market (which, in some places, have merely been added to

---

a great upheaval. . . . To assail the changes that have unmoored us from the past is futile, and in a deep sense, I think, it is wicked. We need to recognize the change and learn what resources we have.

—Robert Oppenheimer, "Prospects in the Arts and Sciences," *Perspectives* USA, No. 11, Spring 1955, pp. 5–14 at 10–11.

See also W. G. Fleming, ed., *Emerging Strategies and Structures for Change,* Ontario Institute for Studies in Education, Toronto, Canada, 1966, especially pp. 18–24; Robert Chim, "Change and Human Relations," in *A Multidisciplinary Focus on Educational Change,* Richard I. Miller, ed., Bulletin of the Bureau of School Service, College of Education, University of Kentucky 38: 26f., 1965; George Axtelle, "Democracy, Education and Progress," *Educational Method* 19: 99–104, November 1939; Morris E. Opler (Chapter IV), in T. Brameld and Stan Elam, eds., *Values in American Education,* Bloomington, Ind.: Phi Delta Kappan, 1964; Kyle Haselden and Philip Hefner, *Changing Man: The Threat and the Promise,* New York: Doubleday & Company, Inc., 1968 (bibliography).

* Peter Schrag, *Voices in the Classroom,* Boston: The Beacon Press, 1965, pp. 275–281.

the old program, like mushrooms in a dull sauce) but because so many schools are committed to the wrong enterprise at the wrong time. "Education," to quote Whitehead again, "is the acquisition of the art of the utilization of knowledge." It is not the random distribution of inert ideas, the regurgitation of prepackaged facts, or the formal exchange of clichés between teacher and student.

Many schools are still storage bins, twelve-year warehouses for the young where, ideally, very little is supposed to happen, and where all events are subject to intensive control. Organized from the outside in, they were created on the basis of buildings, budgets, administrative efficiency, pupil headcounts, accounting procedures and rigid structures. Variety, flexibility and originality are intolerable because they make administration difficult, they ruin normal accounting and scheduling systems, and they make the citizens suspicious. Thus the textbook and the syllabus become the academic analogs of fenders, or tail-lights and spray paint on the assembly line: they are added to the kids as they move through on the curricular belt. It is easy to teach "facts" not only because the culture is fact-ridden, but because it is easy to test for learning when "facts" are to be regurgitated. So far we have no machines for evaluating good prose, originality, or the elegance and effectiveness of a student's power to reason. Even the teachers of some of the prestigious suburban advanced placement courses are sometimes afraid to experiment; their object is to prepare students for the College Board advanced placement examination. They are not there to teach them how to think.

Too many schools, too many teachers, too many communities are fearful of the one thing that education is supposed to achieve: the capacity to think. Thinking students ask nasty questions. Thinkers get too big for their britches. They want to change things. If you challenge students too much they may turn around and challenge you. Ask them real questions and they start discussing things that the teacher or the community doesn't like to discuss: why Negroes are treated badly, why adults aren't a little more honest about sex and morals, why the local politicians are corrupt. In the Bible belt the idea that God created the universe in six days is not a discussable issue, and all the ideas and prejudices rooted in rural South fundamentalism and racial segregation remain almost as untouchable now as they have ever been. J. Evetts Haley, one of the leaders of the right-wing Texans for America, issued a manifesto a few years ago proclaiming that "the stressing of both sides of a controversy only confuses the young and encourages them to make snap judgments based on insufficient evidence. Until they are old enough to understand both sides of a question, they should be taught only the American side."

But the inadequacies are rooted not only in local or regional prejudices—in Catholic strictures against sex education in Chicago, in fundamentalist

Protestant opposition to the teaching of evolution, or in Alabama redneck resistance to honest discussions of integration, civil rights and human dignity—but also in outgrown and irrelevant notions about the nature of education and the purposes of schools. Because it was—and is—a creature of the community, the public school was traditionally oriented to the small world at hand, drew its ideas and values from that world, and prepared children for life as the community lived it, not for success in, and mastery of a larger, rapidly changing world beyond its borders. Grandpa survived without the new math—just as he survived without many other things—but when his schools failed him, he always had the farm, the shop and the frontier to fill the gaps. But the school of hard knocks is closed and the dehydrated textbook wisdom of the past is inadequate to the problems of the future. The children of Appalachia can only be successful in the accustomed existence of relief, unemployment and despair because they are not being trained for anything else. . . . The simple maxims of an agrarian society are meaningless and sometimes dangerous in a complex technological world. The universe demands challenge as much as obedience, toleration as much as rectitude. . . .

What are the possibilities? . . . . The possibilities lie in the teaching of processes—in trying to get students to *do* physics or history, not talk about them, to achieve their own conclusions, not merely memorize those of others. Good teachers have always attempted to do this, even before the new courses came along, but they now have materials that have never been available before. If they are taught correctly the new courses in mathematics, physics, biology, and other fields *demand* independent investigation, the formulation of generalizations by well-defined inductive and deductive methods, the testing of hypotheses and the evaluation of conclusions. They are aimed toward generating a sense of what a discipline is, of what one can do with it, and what its limitations are. They lie in a self-consciousness about thought. Any discipline, after all, is a human construct, not something that lies *out there* as an objective kind of reality waiting to be discovered.

The rationale for such education lies in teaching students to learn for themselves, to assimilate and organize data, to evaluate opinions and impressions and propaganda. It rests not on teaching life adjustment, but on propagating techniques of control, of stimulating curiosity, and on developing effective means of making choices. It is devoted not so much to preparation for this or that vocation or a certain kind of college or the enjoyment of the good life in a California suburb, but to the development of attitudes and skills which are necessary for all of them. To a certain extent almost all secondary education is still organized around vocational assumptions, and students are forced to choose at the age of thirteen or fourteen, and sometimes earlier, whether they are going to follow a college track or a "general" track (leading, often, to no particular goal) or a vocational track. Thus, as adolescents they already have to close doors behind them, have already been selected in or selected out. It is a harsh choice to impose on people of their age. And it is probably unnecessary. The greatest danger is not that kids will lose time, but that they will lose their humanity.

Critics of American society have often noted the dichotomy between our respect for education and our streak of anti-intellectualism. Democratic attitudes, frontier independence and the practical concerns of everyday life made us impatient with authority, and especially with what we came to regard as the presumptions of an effete intellectuality. A simple education in school taught you all you had to know.

In recent years that dichotomy has begun to disappear. There is more respect for intellectual achievement because its fruits, especially in science and technology, are now becoming apparent to most Americans. Nevertheless, we still tend to identify intellectuality with *knowing a lot* and we are, therefore, trying to achieve it—have been trying to achieve it for years—through an education oriented toward the distribution of data. In a sense we have begun to accept the worst of what we traditionally rejected and to ignore the best of what we had. The man we have always respected is not the one crammed with a lot of information but the one who could solve problems, who was able to find out what he needed to know and use it for the improvement of himself and his society. One of the challenges for education is to adapt that healthy frontier attitude and its techniques to the demands of modern understanding, to teach people how to think, and how to use the intellectual tools that our culture has produced in such abundance.

TOPICS FOR FURTHER STUDY

CULTURAL PLURALISM IN A SCIENTIFIC AGE: PROS AND CONS

In this chapter we have contrasted what C. P. Snow has called the "two cultures," that is, the culture of a prescientific *Western* man versus that of a *Western* man in the twentieth century. The following short statements are intended to dramatize the contrast between the culture of modern Western man and that of some *non*-Western traditions. For here the "cleavage" is much greater. Read these—and other statements dealing with this topic[20]—and then discuss the educational issues involved.

A. The people of the world may be regarded as gathered before one large receiver or television set. . . . A world community is being formed by communication, by shared knowledge, by intellectual exchanges, by economic ties, by travel, and by a sense of a common destiny, or at least of a common fate.

The sweep of Western science and technology is preparing the way, if we survive, for a world civilization. This civilization may not be attractive, but it will nevertheless be one in the sense that it will be based on common knowledge, common assumptions, and a common style of life.

As Harvey Wheeler puts it, "In unconsciously creating a unitary industrial world order, man has made his survival depend upon his ability to follow it by a consciously created political order." . . . *Homo sapiens* is everywhere the same. . . . The forces of science, technology, urbanization, industrial development, the mass media, and world integration carry the same imperatives wherever they reach.[21]

B. As long as the [Mexican] Indian continues to believe that natural phenomena result from supernatural agencies, that drought and rain, insect plagues, and disease are consequences of divine whim and affected only by his piety with the priest as intermediary, it will be almost impossible to rouse him from his apathy, to make him self-reliant, dependent on his own initiative, to secure his cooperation, to lessen the terrible infant mortality, to make him, in short, a civilized member of a modern Community.[22]

---

[20] For a description of a college course designed to help young Americans gain a better understanding and appreciation of non-Western values, read Francis Shoemaker, "New Dimensions for World Culture," *Teachers College Record* 69: 685–697, April 1968 (Contains annotated bibliography).

[21] Robert M. Hutchins, *The Learning Society*, New York: Frederick A. Praeger, Inc., 1968, p. 64. Read also Israel Scheffler, *Science and Subjectivity*, Indianapolis: The Bobbs-Merrill Company, Inc., 1967.

[22] José Vasconcelos, cited in N. L. Whetan, *Rural Mexico*, Chicago: University of Chicago Press, 1948, p. 476; Copyright 1948 by the University of Chicago.

C. For an African the impact of a university education is something inconceivable to a European. It separates him from his family and his village (though he will, with intense feeling and loyalty, return regularly to his home and accept what are often crushing family responsibilities). It obliges him to live in a Western way, whether he likes to or not. It stretches his nerve between two spiritual worlds, two systems of ethics, two horizons of thought. . . . You cannot import television sets and automobiles without importing the social philosophy which goes with these things. Technology is inseparable from a money economy. It assumes a competitive society. It assumes obedience to the clock. It assumes that the individual can detach himself from the matrix of his family and village, and exercise his individuality. All these assumptions are anathema to traditional African society.[23]

ABSORBING KNOWLEDGE—THINKING INDEPENDENTLY: PROS AND CONS

A. Ours are the schools of a democracy, which *all* the children attend. At least half of them never had an original idea of any general nature, and never will. But they must behave as if they had *sound* ideas. Whether those ideas are original or not matters not in the least. It is better to be right than to be original. What the duller half of the population needs, therefore, is to have their reflexes conditioned into behavior that is socially suitable. And the wholesale memorizing of catchwords . . . is the only practical means of establishing bonds in the duller intellects between the findings of social scientists and the corresponding social behavior of the masses. Instead of trying to teach dullards to think for themselves, the intellectual leaders must think for them and drill the results . . . into their synapses.[24]

B. Teachers who are concerned to encourage creativity among their pupils must resolutely oppose the concept of education as information-feeding. It is, of course, wasteful for children to have to rediscover for themselves everything that has already been discovered. And it is necessary to gain some basic knowledge to use it as a springboard for creative work. The problem is how to help children to gain this knowledge without, in the process, killing their creative drive because of the *way* in which the knowledge is assimilated. We know that spoon-feeding and mechanical, ground-covering methods are most likely to kill creativity. Teaching children thoughts rather than how to think is one example of this approach. Readymade thoughts that have to be absorbed into the memory work against the encouragement of originality. If we insist that children memorize hundreds of isolated scraps of information, we must be prepared for

---

[23] Eric Ashby, *African Universities and Western Tradition,* Cambridge, Mass.: Harvard University Press, 1964, pp. 41, 100.

[24] R. L. Finney, A *Sociological Philosophy of Education,* New York: Crowell-Collier and Macmillan, Inc., 1928, p. 395.

the fact that, with their time totally taken up with absorbing mountains of data, there will be no time or energy left for thinking. . . . A good teacher, like Socrates, should make us feel a little uncomfortable, should prod us into creative activity. . . .

[However] Creativity is not just a throwing over of accepted standards in art, literature, music, and so on. This sort of destructive iconoclasm is usually the refuge of the incompetent. Creativity is essentially constructive and reconstructive and takes place within the canons and standards of one's own cultural tradition. . . . The maturing process must take place within a tradition: the mature, creative person transcends his tradition. But only he can transcend tradition, who has first immersed himself in it.[25]

C. . . . we need to distinguish between honest appreciation of creative behavior in the school situation, and mere sentimentality toward the "cute" and the "precious" without reference to standards of intellectual merit. The one leads to respect for creative functioning and the integrity of the individual, the other leads to manipulating children's behavior for exhibitionistic purposes bearing only "Kids-Say-the-Darndest-Things" results. . . .

We need to distinguish between remembering and discovering, between information and knowledge, between the fact-filled quiz kid and the educated student. Possessing isolated facts is not the same as being broadly educated (either over a whole range of subjects or in one subject). To be well-informed we need only a good memory, to be knowledgeable we must also be able to discover. The merely informed person holds on irrevocably to a once conceived fact. The educated person deals flexibly with presently conceived facts in the full realization that today's fact was yesterday's fancy, and today's fancy may very well turn out to be tomorrow's fact.[26]

D. The greatest weakness in present evaluation of the outcomes of education relates to a trait not closely connected with the capacity to absorb knowledge—an abiding interest in things of the mind. Some of the so-called late bloomers, the students with mediocre or poor high school records, who were intellectually awakened by an interested and inspiring college teacher, dramatically highlight the need to appraise the outcomes of such teaching. . . .

Though the factors involved in genuine intellectualism cannot now be described with precision, prominent among them is a compulsive interest in ideas, in things of the mind, in all aspects of the world and of man. Perhaps the *sine qua non* in the mosaic of intellectualism is an interest in ideas and their consequences in the history, the present condition and the future welfare of mankind. Other facilities and qualities which deserve analysis and assessment include: (1) the unremitting urge to pursue new knowledge; (2) the capacity to perceive subtle relationships between seem-

---

[25] Paul Nash, *Authority and Freedom in Education*, New York: John Wiley & Sons, Inc., 1966, pp. 258–287. By permission.

[26] Jacob W. Getzels and Philip W. Jackson, *Creativity and Intelligence*, New York: John Wiley & Sons, Inc., 1962, pp. 131, 137. By permission.

ingly unrelated facts or events; (3) an impulsion to play with ideas, unrestrained by the tenebrific forces of pedantry and the intimidating pontifications of established authority; (4) the ability to suspend judgment in all situations in which one is intellectually not at home; (5) a reasonably wide acquaintance with basic theories, principles and key ideas in the major branches of learning; and (6) the ability and the desire to read steadily and widely throughout life. A review of even this incomplete catalogue of traits indicates that though no one can be an intellectual without possessing average intelligence and a body of reliable knowledge, learning and intelligence should not be confused with intellectualism.[27]

LIBERAL EDUCATION FOR ALL: PROS AND CONS

A. We begin with the hypothesis that any subject can be taught effectively in some intellectually honest form to any child at any stage of development. It is a bold hypothesis and an essential one in thinking about the nature of a curriculum. No evidence exists to contradict it; considerable evidence is being amassed that supports it.[28]

B. The politician tells us "You must educate the masses because they are going to be masters." The clergy join in the cry for education, for they affirm that the people are drifting away from church and chapel into the broadest infidelity. The manufacturers and the capitalists swell the chorus lustily. They declare that ignorance makes bad workmen; that England will soon be unable to turn out cotton goods, or steam engines, cheaper than other people; and then, Ichabod! Ichabod! the glory will be departed from us. And a few voices are lifted up in favour of the doctrine that the masses should be educated because they are men and women with unlimited capacity of being, doing, and suffering, and that it is as true now, as ever it was, that the people perish for lack of knowledge. . . . [In] my judgment, the preparatory education of the handicraftsman ought to have nothing of what is ordinarily understood by "technical" about it. The workshop is the only real school for a handicraft.[29]

C. [Education is the] organized, deliberate attempt to help people to become intelligent. . . . [The aim of liberal education] is manhood, not manpower. It prepares the young for anything that may happen; it has value under any circumstances. . . . It gets them ready for a lifetime of learning. It connects man with man. It introduces all men to the dialogue about the common good of their own country and of the world community. It frees

---

[27] Earl J. McGrath, "Observations on the Meaning of Academic Excellence," *Liberal Education* 48: 214–231, May 1962.

[28] Jerome S. Bruner, *The Process of Education*, Cambridge, Mass.: Harvard University Press, 1960, p. 33.

[29] T. H. Huxley, *Science and Education* (1877), New York: Philosophical Library, Inc., 1964, pp. 266–267, 348.

Compare John Dewey, "Individuality, Equality and Superiority," *New Republic* 33: 61–63, December 13, 1922; reprinted in Gross, Wronski, and Hanson, *School and Society*, Boston: D. C. Heath and Company, 1962, pp. 291–295.

their mind of prejudice. It lays the basis of practical wisdom. All this implies the habit of thinking and the capacity to think about the most important matters. This, in turn, implies the capacity to distinguish the most important from the unimportant. It implies the development of critical standards of thought and action. . . .

Machines can do for every modern man what slavery did for the fortunate few in Athens. The vision of the learning society, or, as Sir Julian Huxley has put it, the fulfillment society, can be realized. A world community learning to be civilized, learning to be human, is at least a possibility. Education may come into its own.[30]

D. [Hutchins has been criticized for] his oft-repeated statement "Men are everywhere the same" and hence should get the same kind of education. The fact that such a judgment seems to fly in the face of all the empirical evidence has been a major reason for the rejection of Hutchins' views by psychologists and educators. Teachers have replied that such a statement could not be made by anyone who has tried to teach slow learners in an elementary school, and psychologists have pointed to the vast differences in intellectual capacity indicated by the distribution of scores on tests of intelligence.

But the fact that Hutchins now concedes that children cannot all proceed at the same pace may help to appease his opponents, while the growing evidence that the differences in test scores may, in many cases, reflect early childhood experiences rather than genetic differences gives rise to the hope that if provision can be made for enriching these experiences for children now deprived during the preschool years, we may find that true education, as distinct from training, is appropriate for more children than has ever been considered possible.[31]

Open Book Exam

1. Choose any profession or vocation and analyze carefully various ways in which it has been affected by technological changes. What corresponding changes, if any, would this imply for the schools' preparatory work?
2. Give examples illustrating the contention that the "liberal" education of today is simply a carry-over of the "professional" or "vocational" education

[30] Robert M. Hutchins, *The Learning Society*, New York: Frederick A. Praeger, Inc., 1968, pp. vii, 91, 135. See also Arthur A. Cohen, ed., *Humanistic Education and Western Civilization: Essays for Robert M. Hutchins*, especially pp. 38–39 by Mortimer J. Adler, New York: Holt, Rinehart and Winston, Inc., 1964.

[31] Paul Woodring, "Toward a Life of Learning" (review of R. M. Hutchins, *The Learning Society*), New York: Frederick A. Praeger, Inc., 1968; *Saturday Review* 51: 52, July 20, 1968.

Hutchins' statement that "Men are everywhere the same" is usually cited as a capsule statement of the philosophy of "idealism" or of "perennialism." Numerous and varied criticisms of this viewpoint by "experimentalists," "pragmatists," "reconstructionists," and others may be found in contemporary books on the Philosophy of Education.

of bygone ages. Inasmuch as these "professions" of former ages included the Hebrew "scribe," the Greek "philosopher," and the medieval "scholar," perhaps the education suited for such "vocations" remains quite "liberal" even today. Discuss pros and cons.

3. Discuss *one* of the following:
   a. It is widely held that *all* children (save the genuinely mentally retarded) should, in the course of their elementary-secondary schooling, become acquainted with such great men as Homer, Shakespeare, and Beethoven. What position do you take on this matter, and what do you regard as the most compelling arguments for the stand you take?
   b. Many secondary schools are including (some are requiring) courses in automobile driving in their curricula. This is expensive and time-consuming, but some studies show a direct correlation between such instruction and reduced traffic accident rates. Is this a justifiable function for the high school? Why or why not?
4. Defend or criticize the following statement: There should be some general (or liberal) education, and also some specialized (or vocational) education, at every level from the kindergarten through graduate school, and every student should partake of both—at all levels.
5. Do all subjects in the curriculum have aesthetic values, practical uses, liberal outcomes? Do all subjects have these values for all students? Do they have them in equal degree for any individual student?
6. For the prospective teacher, what is the proper balance between general or liberal education, specialization in some subject-matter field, and strictly professional or pedagogical preparation?
7. For the experienced teacher seeking in-service training or an advanced degree, indicate cases, if any, where the present options between graduate courses in education and graduate courses in a specialized subject-matter area may not adequately provide for a teacher's real needs (for example, a music teacher who would like to know more about literature or philosophy; an art major, who, in his undergraduate studies, had no time to study history or chemistry).
8. Discuss "the cleavage in our culture."
   a. as a cleavage between the new science and the old humanism;
   b. as a cleavage between the new secularism and the old ecclesiasticism;
   c. as a cleavage between the "existential" and the "essential or general";
   d. as based on some other dichotomy.

   Try to give examples of teachers you have known whose approach to teaching may have been affected by one or more of these "cleavages."
9. Discuss the relative merits of the following two poems for use in English classes:

> I strove with none, for none was worth my strife;
> Nature I loved, and next to Nature, Art;
> I warmed both hands before the fire of life,—
> It sinks, and I am ready to depart.
>
> —William Savage Lander, "On His Seventy-Fifth Birthday"

I play it cool and dig all jive.
That's the reason I stay alive.
My motto, as I live and learn,
Is: Dig and Be Dug in Return.

—Langston Hughes, "Motto," from *The Panther and the Lash*, New York: Alfred A. Knopf. By permission.

Chapter 5
CHANGING INSTRUCTIONAL STRATEGIES

Encouraging Giftedness and Creativity

5.1 INTRODUCTION

The ancients declared that it took five slaves to make one free man. Today machinery has taken the place of the slaves; but, without adequate education, the new class of "displaced persons" cannot truly be called free men. Since social mobility is the essence of democracy, our society denies its most cherished traditions unless the exceptionally talented children from every race, creed, cultural, and economic group are helped to develop their talents and encouraged to elevate themselves "from log cabin to white house" or "from inner city to suburbia."

Not all children have outstanding ability, but many do; hence, in the words of Morris Meister, we must

> . . . face up to the idea that the intellectual human resources of any nation are finite; that not more than a third of the individuals in an age group can be educated for intellectual work; that from this segment of the population come nearly all of our scientists, scholars, lawyers, teachers, writers, inventors, artists, musicians, etc.; that individuals from the top third contribute to civilization out of all proportion to their number; that manpower shortages have developed in almost every professional and technical field; and that these shortages are a real danger to our way of life. Our great concern for the proper education of high-ability youth stems from the critical need for conserving human talent and resources.[1]

The dependence of society upon this top group, and the crucial importance of the quality of the education which it receives, can hardly be exaggerated.

But should a person who believes in the brotherhood of man, who is brought up in the tradition of liberty, equality, and fraternity, strive to excel, to surpass his fellow men? To be different? To become one of society's elite? Or do our traditions imply that we are all so many peas in the democratic pod, that it is the *common* in "commonwealth" which must receive priority?

[1] From Robert G. Andree and Morris Meister, "What Are Some Promising Programs for Gifted Students?" *Proceedings of the Thirty-Eighth National Convention, National Association of Secondary School Principals Bulletin,* April 1954, p. 314.

We all know Jefferson's famous words in the Declaration of Independence: "We hold these truths to be self-evident: that all men are created equal. . . ." But in a letter to John Adams, in 1813, Jefferson wrote: "There is a natural aristocracy among men. The grounds of this are virtue and talents. . . . The natural aristocracy I consider the most precious gift of nature, for the instruction, the trusts, and government of society." Jefferson agreed with Adams that there is a natural aristocracy among men; but he was careful to differentiate the natural aristocracy based on virtue and talent, from the artificial ones based on occupation, wealth, birth, race or religious creed. In working for the more "general diffusion of knowledge," a prime aim of any school or college is to discover those who are "really wise and good," to uncover, from the children of *all* classes, those who may develop into the true leaders of an open society; in short, to promote "democracy's aristocracy." It is entirely consonant with our democratic ideals that persons of quality and talent raise themselves above the commonplace. Indeed, such superior individuals are both the fruit and the seed of our free society.

Clearly, genius *is* the possession of a talented few. But in an equally genuine sense, genius exists in each of us, and manifests itself wherever there is natural growth, wherever there is a full, free play of natural faculties. Booker T. Washington was right when he said that American society will not prosper until it puts worth and dignity into the common occupations of men.

One function of democratic education, then, is to help talented youth find their way into the more demanding professions—to climb higher on the social and professional ladder. But an equally important function is to add worth and dignity to the common occupations. These two functions are realized when mind and body, science and art, labor and leisure, education and recreation, are governed by a single vision of excellence and a continuous passion for achieving it.

Thus, on the one hand, we have the American ideal that there are not merely five or ten "higher" professions, or five or seven "liberal" arts; but rather, that every occupation is worthwhile, and that there are thousands of arts. Or rather, there is one art—the art of life manifesting itself in every work of man, where all have learned to give in kind for what they receive and every man becomes a true enrichment of others.

On the other hand, it is simply untrue to say of *all* American citizens that immaturity yields to maturity, rudeness to culture, self-indulgence to self-control. In any society, the fullest human potentialities are realized by very few men and women. Earlier sections of this anthology have emphasized the fact that no criterion (ideological, religious, racial, or financial) should be permitted to make second-class citizens of any members of our democratic community. But emphasis on *equality* should not blind us to the need for *quality*. American education will not serve society well enough until all students with high potential—democracy's aristocracy—receive an education which brings out their special talents to the fullest measure. The problem, as Will French neatly put it, is to find "the means for creating social unity without crushing individuality and for developing individuality without cultivating social cleavages. . . ." And perhaps no issue is more crucial, for in the words of Eugene Sayers: "If it is possible to teach genius instead of merely hoping it will come along, the future will belong to the society which first discovers how."

5.2 THREE WAYS TO HELP TALENTED CHILDREN*

D. A. Worcester

ACCELERATION

Skipping is, administratively, the easiest method—with the exception, perhaps, of early entrance—of adjusting to children of advanced mentality. It is the method which has been used most. When it is used with care, the children who have skipped make good progress and are well adjusted. The danger of gaps in knowledge and skill must be kept in mind. If other methods of acceleration are not available, the bright child should skip a grade. . . .

[One value of] acceleration [is that it] recognizes the facts of life. Chil-

---

* D. A. Worcester, *The Education of Children of Above-Average Mentality*, Lincoln: University of Nebraska Press, 1956, pp. 30–34, 42–49 *passim*. By permission. Footnotes to research references cited in the original article are omitted here.

D. A. Worcester, now retired, was in 1956 professor of education at the University of Nebraska, and later taught at the University of Arizona.

This selection should perhaps have been given the title "Three Ways to Help Talented Children—Using Traditional Textbooks and Traditional Methods of Classroom Organization." For, as later readings in this chapter will show, our approach to these problems has changed very considerably with the use of programmed learning, teaching machines, and nongraded classrooms.

It is instructive to note the tempo of change in contemporary education. Sputnik and the cold war undoubtedly had much to do with the influence of Admiral Rickover and others who in the 1950s criticized American education for its relative neglect of talented students. But the 1960s have witnessed a better understanding of the psychology of learning, the development of many new types of teaching machines and programmed materials, as well as widespread experimentation with various forms of nongraded classrooms. Thus, within ten or twenty years, what was viewed as a special problem (Selections 5.1–5.4 educating the gifted child) has developed into a reevaluation and a restructuring of all levels and aspects of education (Selections 5.5–5.14).

dren do differ from each other markedly. Some develop much more rapidly than do others. Usually those of greater academic potentialities are also more mature socially and emotionally and fully as well-developed physically.

[Moreover] failure to accelerate involves dangers. There is evidence to show that gifted children who are held back with those of their CA (chronological age) are more likely to develop behavior and personality problems than are those who are accelerated. There is danger also of producing lazy and careless work habits among those who are educationally beyond their classmates but who are held back with them. . . .[2]

The time saved by acceleration is important. . . . Let us assume that there are 34,000,000 school children in the United States. Ten percent of these should, according to our evidence, be able to save a year of time. But assume that only three percent of them could save a year each. Then our country would have gained for its use more than 1,000,000 years of its best brains in a single generation. Don't we need these brains?

[Acceleration can mean] financial saving. . . . If a million children went to school for only eleven years instead of twelve, the saving to school budgets would be considerable. . . .

ENRICHMENT

Enrichment should be provided for all children who can profit from it whatever type of program they are in.[3] The accelerated child should have enrichment. Indeed, if it *be* enrichment, acceleration in the sense of

---

[2] Editor's Note: For talented students, acceleration usually acts as a challenge and added incentive. Dale B. Harris has written:

> There is an increasing conviction among psychologists that early and intense stimulation of a varied nature has something to do with the actual level of, or quality of, the organism. Not only does the appetite for learning of gifted children require opportunity for exercise in order to be developed, but possibly the appetite itself can be cultivated if children quite early are subjected to a fairly intense degree of academic, abstract, conceptual stimulation. . . . We must not let our very worthy concern with the expansion of education for all children any longer continue to blind us to the need to make special provisions for highly talented youngsters.
>
> —Dale B. Harris, "Acceleration," in *Talent and Education*, The Modern School Practices Series #4, E. Paul Torrance, ed., Minneapolis: University of Minnesota Press, 1960, pp. 131–132. Copyright © 1960 by the University of Minnesota.

[3] Editor's Note: Natural ability may be less significant than motivation as a factor of success:

> Within the upper 1 or 2 percent of the population, based on intellectual ability, it appears that success in life and contributions to society depend more on motivational factors than on variations in intelligence. This conclusion is borne out by Anne Roe's studies of distinguished American scientists. [See Anne Roe, *The Making of a Scientist*, New York: Dodd, Mead & Company, Inc., 1953.] She found

becoming more and more separated from the average group is inevitable, whether or not it is recognized by name, and whether or not the individual meets classes in another school building. . . .

If [the program is] truly enriching, it has to be of value. In small schools where there may be only one gifted child at a particular educational level, or in schools with limited facilities but good teachers, or in schools where there is prejudice against acceleration, enrichment is particularly needed.

At the senior high school-freshman college level, much of the present overlapping could be obviated by planned enrichment. . . .

SELECTED CLASSES

Classes designed for gifted or mentally advanced children have been variously named. The more common general titles have been *segregated,* sometimes *partially segregated* or *special.* This writer prefers the word *selected,* as proposed by Hildreth. . . . The present trend is toward more of these classes.

Where the school is so large that there is more than one class of a given grade in the same building, it is relatively easy to put the brighter ones together unobtrusively. In the secondary school, divisions can be made among those who show differences in competence in particular subjects. There is no implication of superiority-inferiority difference in the fact that one student is studying algebra and another general mathematics, or that one is doing more advanced mathematics than another. Some people just like mathematics. . . .

[Selected] classes are feasible only in those school systems whose enrollment is large enough to justify a special room and a special teacher. While such classes may combine more than one grade level—although in large systems this might not be necessary—perhaps twelve pupils of approximately the same educational level will be the minimum requirement. There are those who think this minimum too low. However, when one thinks of the willingness to provide special instruction for the physically handicapped and the mentally retarded in classes of this size, and when he thinks of the stupendous contributions which society may expect from the finest training of its finest minds, he becomes eager to see what can be done when a teacher really has time to devote to the needs of a few outstanding pupils. Possibly the maximum size of such a class may be as high as twenty, but it must be remembered that time for attention to individual pupils is of first importance.

---

several of these fifty-nine outstanding men to be only moderately above average in intelligence. Above a certain level, intelligence is a poor predictor of performance.

—R. F. DeHaan and R. J. Havighurst, *Educating Gifted Children,* Chicago: University of Chicago Press, 1957, pp. 129–130.

[Many ask:] Are selected classes democratic? A democratic society selects individuals for all kinds of special purposes. In school we select for the band, the school paper, the football team. So long as the selection is based upon ability and no one is excluded because of race, social or economic status, or other factors not related to ability, there can be no basis to the charge that selected classes are undemocratic. . . .

It is sometimes feared that these classes will result in their members' thinking too highly of themselves. Much careful observation has been given to children in selected classes with the almost 100 percent conclusion that such fears are groundless. Children are working together in groups and on individual projects. In group activities they find others who are their equals or superiors. They learn to respect the knowledge which each possesses concerning his own project. . . .

It is much more likely that an attitude of superiority will develop, if the gifted child is in a mixed class. Here he is almost always right—he knows the answers and the others know that he does. He may constantly compare himself with those who do not have the answers. He is frequently resented by the others.

An exceedingly common practice, and one far more likely to produce snobs than a selected class, is to have those in a single classroom divided into fast learners, slow learners, and, perhaps, a middle group. No situation could be devised which is better adapted to making the bright feel superior and the slower one believe he is "dumb." . . .

When upper grades are reached there may be selected classes in special subjects. For example, a group interested in mathematics, science, or literature may be formed which will not only cover the regular work in the subject but roam far afield in it. This is one of the best ways of encouraging talent. Where there are not enough children for a class, laboratory or library facilities or special correspondence courses may be made available to an individual. . . .

Some schools organize what are usually called partially segregated classes. The children of high ability are kept together . . . for their academic work but are undifferentiated from other pupils for social activities, music, and the like. . . .

This type of class is almost always employed as an enrichment procedure. It usually *assumes* that the gifted children are like, or ought to be like, others in all except "intellectual" matters. The assumption is of doubtful validity. However, when a well-organized program of work is provided, children in these classes do profit substantially, and the lack of social contact with other children . . . is lessened. . . .

It is unfortunate that we have no good studies which reliably compare the merits of various methods of caring for the needs of the gifted. Apparently *any* scheme which tries to do something for them yields value. . . .

5.3 WHY ARE GIFTED CHILDREN OVERLOOKED?*

Ralph W. Tyler

In the first place, many have little or no opportunity for demonstrating their superior abilities. Parents differ markedly in the degree to which they encourage their children to show achievements in the presence of adults. Many children have limited opportunities for demonstrating abilities in school. . . .

In the second place, we often overlook gifted children because we adults are not sensitive to some of the signs of giftedness. For example, the child who works out by himself the relationships among number combinations, rather than simply repeating the arithmetic facts we give him, may seem slow to us rather than being recognized as a child who has given a sign of awakened curiosity and superior mathematical ability.

In the third place, a gifted child or youth may have characteristics which are disliked by many adults and this fact makes it difficult for us to perceive his giftedness. The young gifted child is often one who . . . asks "Why?" again and again . . . he seeks to develop a chain of explanation in his thinking. Busy adults may find these continuing questions distracting and irritating and thus fail to recognize the child's unusual abilities. Then, too, gifted children often seek to test their developing ideas and skills at levels beyond those commonly expected for their age group. A budding "scientist" blows up his home laboratory, or a highly motivated child "artist" tries to paint a mural on his bedroom wall. Such efforts are less likely to be interpreted as indications of giftedness than as signs of "cussedness."

In the fourth place, some gifted youth are overlooked because they have exceptional abilities in certain areas only and in other areas show no superior abilities. The artistic child who has difficulties with reading and arithmetic is not likely to have his artistic gifts recognized by his teacher. . . .

Finally, many gifted children and youth are overlooked because they come from working classes, from families where many parents are not looking for genius and where teachers are likely to anticipate learning problems rather than giftedness. . . .[4]

---

* Ralph W. Tyler, "Meeting the Challenge of the Gifted," *The Elementary School Journal*, 58: 76–77, November 1957. By permission.

Professor Tyler, an eminent educational psychologist, has been on the faculty of the University of Chicago for many years. He was formerly director of the Center for Advanced Study in Behavioral Sciences at Stanford University.

[4] Editor's Note: Children, no less than prison guards, know the dreadful meaning of "solitary confinement," and may, to avoid such confinement, conceal their own talents:

> Sometimes the bright child will do what he can to be just like the rest, even to

5.4 CREATIVITY AND INTELLIGENCE*

J. P. Guilford

Creative thinking is best distinguished by the fact that there are novel aspects to it—novel for the thinker himself, that is. It is obvious that the same response cannot be both novel and previously practiced in the same immediate context. . . . [although] there is always some degree of transfer in every act of creative thinking. Items of information are recalled and used in some connection other than that with which they were learned or in some new form in which they were not experienced before. The implication of this is that the *general* aspects of information should be

---

the point of not seeming to know the answers in examinations or class discussions. In an effort to subdue an inferiority he might feel because he is different in a way which is not readily accepted by the others, he may deliberately feign either stupidity or averageness. Although he believes the games and conversations in which others participate are foolish, he will pretend enjoyment of them in order to be "one of the gang." For some children solitariness is a natural and enjoyable state, but for most the companionship of those with similar interests is more to be desired.

To the gifted child the choice may resolve itself in this way: "The kids my own age are silly, and the older ones won't let me play with them. But the worst thing is playing alone. Since I can't fake my size and age, the least I can do is to pretend I don't know and am not interested in so many things. Then maybe the ones as young as I am will let me play with them."

—Willard Abraham, *Common Sense About Gifted Children*, New York: Harper & Row, Publishers, 1958, pp. 17–20, 40, 28, 190, 68. By permission.

The old rule to "get it or get out" once made it relatively easy to rid schools of all but the talented and the obedient. But compulsory attendance laws created quite a different school atmosphere, in which social adjustment took precedence over subject-matter mastery. But "adjustment" takes various forms:

Adjustment, if the term is taken to mean getting-along, is something that most of the gifted seem to have mastered—better than their duller agemates. With them, however, adjustment may mean, as it does for many in our culture, conforming attitudes rather than creative ones. When we give our best grades to the docile child, and fail to credit originality and individuality, we are showing the gifted that it pays to conform and, perhaps, are teaching little else.

—Elizabeth Monroe Drews, "What About the Gifted Child?" Michigan State University, *College of Education Quarterly* 3: 3–6f., October 1957.

See also Lawrence A. Cremin, *The Transformation of the School: Progressivism in American Education 1876–1957*, New York: Alfred A. Knopf, 1961, especially pp. 127–128; Carleton Washburne, "An Eighty-Year Perspective on Education," *Phi Delta Kappan* 45: 145–150, December 1963; Raymond P. Harris, *American Education: Facts, Fancies, Folklore*, New York: Random House, Inc., 1961, especially pp. 226–241.

* J. P. Guilford, in *Instructional Media and Creativity*, Calvin W. Taylor and Frank E. Williams, eds., New York: John Wiley & Sons, Inc., 1966, pp. 74–76. By permission. Compare the following:

The student who ranks first in his class may be genuinely brilliant or he may be a compulsive worker or the instrument of domineering-parents' ambitions or a self-centered careerist who has shrewdly calculated his teachers' prejudices and expecta-

emphasized in the learning of information and strategies should be learned that have *general* application in connection with new information. . . .

The relation of creative abilities to intelligence, as traditionally known and measured, has been investigated quite a number of times, usually by means of correlating scores from traditional intelligence scales with scores from tests of divergent-thinking abilities. . . . [From such studies] we may say that individuals with high intelligence scores may have scores on divergent-production tests ranging from low to high, but individuals with low intelligence scores very rarely have high divergent-production scores. From these facts we may state the generalization that being high on what is measured by intelligence tests is a necessary condition for high creativity, but it is not a sufficient condition. . . .

We may also say that no one can be very low in intelligence score and also very creative. . . . [In] whatever field of information the individual aspires to be creative, it is important for him to have a good fund of information of that kind in his memory storage, as indicated by tests of cognitive abilities in those areas. This deduction focuses our attention on the possession of an abundance of information and on abilities other than those more directly and more obviously involved in creative thinking.

The same implication arises from another line of reasoning. I have elsewhere proposed the thesis that creative thinking and problem-solving are essentially the same mental phenomenon. . . . Now problem-solving is just about as broad as behavior itself. . . .: the structure of intellects offers a broad and systematic taxonomy of behavior, and novel behavior may touch upon almost any aspect of it. Thus, I cannot help urging that a plan for creativity training should be sufficiently broad to take into account all potentially useful intellectual contributions. . . .

In order that something in memory storage [may be used creatively] . . .

---

tions and discovered how to regurgitate efficiently what they want. Or he may have focused narrowly on grade-setting as compensation for his inadequacies in other areas, because he lacks other interests or talents or lacks passion and warmth or normal healthy instincts or is afraid of life. The top high school student is often, frankly, a pretty dull and bloodless or peculiar fellow. The adolescent with wide-ranging curiosity and stubborn independence, with a vivid imagination and desire to explore fascinating bypaths, to follow his own interests, to contemplate, to read the unrequired books, the boy filled with sheer love of life and exuberance, may well seem to his teachers troublesome, undisciplined, a rebel, may not conform to their stereotype, and may not get the top grades and the highest rank in class. He may not even score at the highest level in the standard multiple choice admission tests, which may well reward the glib, facile mind at the expense of the questioning, independent, or slower but more powerful, more subtle, and more interesting and original mind. . . . We need a new definition of excellence. . . . We must find ways to identify such characteristics as motivation, creativity, imagination, and emotional maturity.

—William Bender [formerly Dean of Admissions at Harvard], cited by Ronald C. Doll and Robert S. Fleming, eds., in *Children Under Pressure*, Columbus, Ohio: Charles E. Merrill Books, Inc., 1966, p. 57.

the information in storage must [be well coded and labeled] . . . Much therefore depends upon the ways in which information is committed to storage. The manner of learning the information is undoubtedly important. The practice of rote or senseless learning is often condemned, but not severely enough, and not enough action has been taken to correct learning practices in this respect.

As much as possible, the learner should take the initiative in exploring and discovering things for himself. Things the learner discovers for himself are rarely forgotten, and it can be confidently expected that their availability in recall will be relatively high, other conditions being comparable. In order to give acquired information transferable possibilities, the information should not be kept in isolation, but should be given connections with other information, in the form of implications, relations, class memberships, and system memberships. . . . Since classification is so important in providing addresses of information in memory storage, considerable emphasis should be given to habits of forming classes and relationships between classes. . . . subjects to which Piaget has given considerable attention in his studies of the logical aspects of intellectual development.[5]

---

[5] Editor's Note: Compare the following statement by Calvin W. Taylor:

For those who have the idea that I.Q. tests measure creative talent with at least some degree of validity, I would like to cite a few results. In factor analysis studies by many research workers across the country, the factors which get at the ability to sense problem areas, to be flexible, and to produce new and original ideas tend to be *unrelated* or to have only low relations with the types of tests entering into our current measures of intelligence. Getzels and Jackson, in the College of Education at the University of Chicago, as well as Torrance, in the Bureau of Educational Research at Minnesota, have reported that if an I.Q. test is used to select top level talent, about 70% of the persons who have the highest 20% of the scores on a creativity test battery will be missed. (Or stated otherwise, more cases with high creativity scores are missed than are identified by using an I.Q. test to locate creative talent.). . . .

[In a recent study,] Guilford and Allen . . . selected some 28 dimensions of the mind which they felt were relevant to success on the job in the physical sciences. Then they prepared plain English descriptions and also a sample item of a best test for each of these 28 intellectual characteristics. A sizable number of scientists on the job were interviewed by Allen, after which he asked them to arrange these 28 characteristics in terms of importance on their job. The 28 characteristics were arranged in rank order according to their judged importance by the total group of scientists. Traditional intelligence tests have included about 5 or 6 of these characteristics, such as general reasoning, vocabulary ability, number ability, memory for ideas, ability to visualize spatially, and perhaps perceptual speed. All but one of these traditional intelligence factors ranked below 20th in the list. In other words, 19 of the 20 intellectual characteristics ranking at the top on the job in science were *non-intelligence intellectual characteristics*. Some examples are intellectual flexibilities, fluencies, originality, penetration, redefinition ability, sensitivity to problems.

—Calvin W. Taylor, "A Tentative Description of the Creative Individual," *A Source Book for Creative Thinking*, S. J. Parnes and H. D. Harding, eds., New York: Charles Scribner's Sons, 1962. By permission. See also Calvin W. Taylor, "Be Talent Developers," *Today's Education* 57: 33–36, December 1968.

Programmed Learning

5.5 TOWARD A THEORY OF INSTRUCTION*

Jerome Bruner

A theory of instruction is *prescriptive* in the sense that it sets forth rules concerning the most effective way of achieving knowledge or skill. . . . It sets up criteria and states the conditions for meeting them. The criteria must have a high degree of generality [There should not be separate rules or norms for each subject or for each grade level]; for example, a theory of instruction should not specify in *ad hoc* fashion the conditions for efficient learning of third-grade arithmetic. . . .

A theory of instruction has four major features.

[*Predisposition*] First, a theory should specify the experiences which most effectively implant in the individual a predisposition toward learning—learning in general or a particular type of learning. For example, what sorts of relationships with people and things in the preschool environment will tend to make the child willing and able to learn when he enters school?. . . .

The will to learn is an intrinsic motive, one that finds both its source and its reward in its own exercise. The will to learn becomes a "problem" only under specialized circumstances like those of a school, where a curriculum is set, students confined, and a path fixed. The problem exists not so much in learning itself, but in the fact that what the school imposes often fails to enlist the natural energies that sustain spontaneous learning—curiosity, a desire for competence, aspiration to emulate a model, and a deep-sensed commitment to the web of social reciprocity. . . .

[*Structure*] Second, a theory of instruction must specify the ways in which a body of knowledge should be structured so that it can be most readily grasped by the learner. "Optimal structure" refers to a set of propositions from which a larger body of knowledge can be generated, and it is characteristic that the formulation of such structure depends upon the state

---

* J. Bruner, *Toward a Theory of Instruction*, Cambridge: Harvard University Press, 1966, pp. 40–42, 49, 71, 72, 127, 134, 171.

Jerome Bruner is Professor of Psychology at Harvard.

of advance of a particular field of knowledge. . . . Since the merit of a structure depends upon its power for *simplifying information,* for *generating new propositions,* and for *increasing the manipulability of a body of knowledge,* structure must always be related to the status and gifts of the learner. Viewed in this way, the optimal structure of a body of knowledge is not absolute but relative. . . .[6]

To instruct someone . . . is to teach him to participate in the process that makes possible the establishment of knowledge. We teach a subject not to produce little living libraries on that subject, but rather to get a student to think mathematically for himself, to consider matters as an historian does, to take part in the process of knowledge-getting. Knowing is a process, not a product. . . .

[*Sequence*] Third, a theory of instruction should specify the most effective sequences in which to present the materials to be learned. Given, for example, that one wishes to teach the structure of modern physical theory, how does one proceed? Does one present concrete materials first in such a way as to elicit questions about recurrent regularities? Or does one begin with a formalized mathematical notation that makes it simpler to represent regularities later encountered? What results are in fact produced by each method? And how describe the ideal mix?. . . .

Instruction consists of leading the learner through a sequence of statements and re-statements of a problem or body of knowledge that increases the learner's ability to grasp, transform, and transfer what he is learning. In short, the sequence in which a learner encounters materials within a domain of knowledge affects the difficulty he will have in achieving mastery.

There are usually various sequences that are equivalent in their ease and difficulty for learners. There is no unique sequence for all learners, and the optimum in any particular case will depend upon a variety of factors, including past learning, stage of development, nature of the material, and individual differences. . . .

---

[6] Editor's Note: Five years earlier, Bruner emphasized structure as follows:

> Knowledge is a model we construct to give meaning and structure to regularities in experience. The organizing ideas of any body of knowledge are inventions for rendering experience economical and connected. We invent concepts such as force in physics, the bond in chemistry, motives in psychology, style in literature as means to the end of comprehension. . . . The structure of knowledge—its connectedness and the derivations that make one idea follow another—is the proper emphasis in education. For it is structure, the great conceptual inventions that bring order to the congeries of disconnected observations, that gives meaning to what we may learn and makes possible the opening up of new realms of experience.
>
> —J. S. Bruner, *On Knowing,* Cambridge, Mass.: Harvard University Press, 1962, p. 120.

See also Stanley Elam, ed., *Education and the Structure of Knowledge,* Skokie, Ill.: Rand, McNally & Company, 1964.

No single ideal sequence exists for any group of children. . . . [Hence] if a curriculum is to be effective in the classroom it must contain different ways of activating children, different ways of presenting sequences, different opportunities for some children to "skip" parts while others work their way through, different ways of putting things. A curriculum, in short, must contain many tracks leading to the same general goal. . . .

[*Reinforcement*] Finally, a theory of instruction should specify the nature and pacing of rewards and punishments in the process of learning and teaching. Intuitively it seems quite clear that as learning progresses there is a point at which it is better to shift away from extrinsic rewards, such as a teacher's praise, toward the intrinsic rewards inherent in solving a complex problem for oneself. So, too, there is a point at which immediate reward for performance should be replaced by deferred reward. The timing of the shift from extrinsic to intrinsic and from immediate to deferred reward is poorly understood and obviously important. . . .

Effective cognitive learning . . . involves at least three things. . . . There must first develop a system of cognitive organization that detaches concepts from the modes of action that they evoke. A hole is to dig, but it is also a hole. Secondly, it requires the development of a capacity to detach concepts from their affective contexts. A hole is not just a reminder of a hidden orifice. Finally, it demands a capacity to delay gratification so that the outcomes of acts can be treated as information rather than as simply punishing or rewarding. . . .

[In contemporary education] what is needed is the daring and freshness of hypotheses that do not take for granted as true what has merely become habitual. I can only hope that in pursuing a theory of instruction we shall have the courage to recognize what we do not understand and to permit ourselves a new and innocent look.[7]

---

[7] Editor's Note:

Thorpe and Schmuller [1953]. . . . suggest that only five principles of learning may be stated . . . [and] that learning is generally facilitated and tends to be most permanent when:

1. The learner is motivated—when he has some stake in the activity.
2. The learning is geared to the learner's level—when it is compatible with the learner's physical and intellectual ability.
3. The learning is patterned—when the learner can see meaningful relationships between the activity and the goal.
4. The learning is evaluated—when the learner has some way of knowing what progress he is making.
5. The learning is integrated with personal-social development—when the learner experiences satisfactory growth and adjustment.

Of these same principles, another psychologist [B. R. Bugelski (1956)] makes the following observation: "These five principles are the harvest of the thousands of experiments performed in the field of learning as they look to educators. Whether these are really principles of learning or just prejudices and platitudes might very

5.6 TOWARD A TECHNOLOGY OF INSTRUCTION*

B. F. Skinner

No matter how well structured a subject matter may be, it must still be taught. . . . It is not true that "the two essentials of a good teacher are (a) enthusiasm and (b) thorough knowledge of and interest in his subject." A third essential is knowing how to teach. . . .

[In the early 20th century, E. L. Thorndike attempted to develop a science of pedagogy. Thorndike] turned to the measurement of mental abilities and to matched-group comparisons of teaching practices. He pioneered in a kind of research which, with the encouragement offered

---

well be questioned. As practical propositions, only the fourth (knowledge of results) has any real basis for implementation."

—H. Gordon Hullfish and Philip G. Smith, *Reflective Thinking*, New York: Dodd, Mead & Company, Inc., 1961, pp. 170–171. By permission. The student will find it instructive to compare these five principles with Bruner's four.

See also John B. Carroll, "Basic and Applied Research in Education: Definitions, Distinctions, and Implications," *Harvard Educational Review* 38: 263–276, Spring 1968 (bibliography).

* Excerpts from two articles by B. F. Skinner. The first is "Reflections on a Decade of Teaching Machines," *Teachers College Record* 65: 168–177, January 1964; by permission. The second, "Why We Need Teaching Machines" [originally in the *Harvard Educational Review* 31: 377–398, Fall 1961], is from *Cumulative Record*, enlarged ed., Copyright © 1961 by Appleton-Century-Crofts. Reprinted by permission of Appleton-Century-Crofts, Division of Meredith Corporation.

B. F. Skinner is the name most generally associated with *teaching machines, step-increment learning, reinforcement, programmed instruction,* and *contemporary behaviorism.* After having taught at the University of Minnesota and the University of Indiana, he has been at Harvard since 1948.

Skinner's teaching machines may be viewed as an attempt to fuse ends and means, and in this respect represent an application of the pragmatic philosophy, so characteristic of America:

> There is no better way to distinguish science from superstition than by asking to what degree means and ends are joined. The essence of magic is the assumption that results can be accomplished without the accommodation of human aspirations to physical conditions. We may shout "hocus-pocus" and wave a magic wand in the fond hope that words and wishes will bring results. But until we discover the operative conditions of nature we are indulging in magic or wishful thinking. In contrast to magic, a law of science states an invariant relation or connection between one state of affairs and another. In the words of John Dewey, "It signifies that *if* one is to attain a specified result, *if* one is to get the result with the maximum of efficiency, there are conditions having a necessary relationship to that intent."
>
> —H. Ehlers, "Democracy as a Fusion of Ends and Means," *Educational Theory* 7: 12–18, January 1957.

by promising new statistical techniques, was to dominate educational psychology for decades. It led to a serious neglect of the process of instruction. . . .

The contrast between statistical evaluation and the experimental analysis of teaching has an illuminating parallel in the field of medicine. Various drugs, regimens, surgical procedures, and so on, must be examined with respect to a very practical question: Does the health of the patient improve? But "health" is only a general description of specific physiological processes, and changes in these processes induced by a given treatment. Medicine has reached the point where research on specific processes is a much more fertile source of new kinds of therapy than evaluations in terms of improvement in health. Similarly, in education, no matter how important improvement in the student's performance may be, it remains a by-product of specific changes in behavior resulting from the specific changes in the environment wrought by the teacher. Educational research patterned on an experimental analysis of behavior leads to a much better understanding of these basic processes. . . . We have long since passed the point at which our basic knowledge of human behavior can be applied to education through the use of a few general principles. . . . Traditional views may not have been actually wrong, but they were vague and were not entertained with sufficient commitment to work substantial technological changes. . . .

The changes in the behavior of the individual student brought about by manipulating the environment are usually immediate and specific. The results of statistical comparisons of group performances usually are not. From his study of the behavior of the individual student, the investigator gains a special kind of confidence. He usually knows what he has done to get one effect and what he must do to get another. . . .

The student is more than a receiver of information. He must take some kind of action. The traditional view is that he must "associate." The stream of information flowing from teacher to student contains pairs of items which, being close together or otherwise related, become connected in the student's mind. This is the old doctrine of the association of ideas now strengthened by a scientific, if uncritical, appeal to conditioned reflexes; two things occurring together in experience somehow become connected so that one of them later reminds the student of the other. The teacher has little control over the process except to make sure that things occur together often and that the student pays attention to them—for example, by making the experiences vivid or, as we say, memorable. Some devices called teaching machines are simply ways of presenting things together in ways which attract attention. The student listens to recorded speech, for example, while looking at pictures. The theory is that he will associate these auditory and visual presentations.

But the action demanded of the student is not some sort of mental association of continuous experiences. It is more objective and, fortunately, more controllable than that. To acquire behavior, *the student must engage in behavior*. This has long been known. The principle is implied in any philosophy of "learning by doing." But it is not enough simply to acknowledge its validity. Teaching machines provide the conditions needed to apply the principle effectively. . . .

Traditionally, for example, something called a "knowledge of French" is said to permit the student who possesses it to do many things. One who possesses it can (1) repeat a French phrase with a good accent, (2) read a French text. . . , (3) take dictation in French, (4) find a word spoken in French on a printed list, (5) obey instructions spoken in French, (6) comment in French upon objects or events, (7) give orders in French, and so on. If he also "knows English," he can give the English equivalents of French words or phrases or the French equivalents of English words or phrases.

The concept of "a knowledge of French" offers very little help to the would-be teacher. As in the case of reading, we must turn to the behavioral repertoires themselves, for these are all that have been taught when education has been effective. The definition of a subject matter in such terms may be extraordinarily difficult. Students who are "competent in first-year college physics," for example, obviously differ from those who are not—but in what way? Even a tentative answer to that question should clarify the problem of teaching physics. . . .

In the broadest sense, teaching machines are simply devices which make it possible to apply our technical knowledge of human behavior to the practical field of education. Teaching is the expediting of learning. Students learn without teaching, but the teacher arranges conditions under which they learn more rapidly and effectively. . . . It is usually not enough simply to tell the student something or induce him to read a book; he must be told or must read and then be questioned. In this "tell-and-test" pattern, the test is not given to measure what he has learned, but to show him what he has not learned and thus induce him to listen and read more carefully in the future. . . .

An analysis of learning which concentrates on the behavior applies most directly to a technology, for the task of the teacher is to bring about changes in the student's behavior. His methods are equally conspicuous: He makes changes in the environment. His teaching method is simply a way of arranging an environment which expedites learning. . . .

An important condition is the relation between behavior and its consequences; learning occurs when behavior is "reinforced." The power of reinforcement is not easily appreciated by those who have not had first-hand experience in its use or have not at least seen some sort of experimental demonstration. Extensive changes in behavior can be brought about by arranging so-called contingencies of reinforcement. Various kinds of contingencies are concealed in the teacher's discussions with his students, in the books he gives them to read, in the charts and other materials he shows them, in the questions he asks them, and in the comments he makes on their answers. An experimental analysis clarifies these contingencies and suggests many improvements. . . .[8]

In arranging contingencies of reinforcement, machines do many of the things teachers do; in that sense, they teach. The resulting instruction is

---

[8] *From Pigeons to Pupils.* The modern teaching machine and the technique of programmed instruction owe their existence mainly to the development, by Skinner and other experimental psychologists, of a process called operant conditioning. It is often demonstrated to students something like this: A hungry pigeon is placed in a box or cage, and the demonstrator undertakes to teach it to do a simple trick—for example, to turn around in a clockwise direction. He begins by watching for the pigeon to make some move—turning its head to the right, perhaps—that might lead to the execution of a clockwise turn. When he sees such a move, he instantly "reinforces" it by giving the pigeon a grain of corn. As a rule, the pigeon will immediately repeat the move, and the demonstrator will again reinforce it. He will then withhold the corn until the pigeon chances not only to turn its head to the right but at the same time, let us say, steps forward with its left foot. This move, too, will be reinforced with corn.

Proceeding in this fashion, an experienced demonstrator can usually manage within two or three minutes to get the pigeon whirling rapidly in a clockwise turn. In a few minutes more, he can often teach the pigeon to whirl in the opposite direction and, finally, to combine the two turns so as to execute a sort of figure 8 maneuver. By this same method, pigeons have been conditioned to discriminate among playing cards of different suits, to peck out tunes on a toy piano, and to play a kind of table tennis.

About ten years ago, Skinner was struck with the idea of trying to teach people like pigeons—that is, by arranging matters so that a student, like a pigeon being taught to execute a figure 8, would be reinforced instantly each time he took a step in the right direction. In 1954, he published an article setting forth his views and arguing that the necessary reinforcement should be provided by a machine. . . .

Unlike the pigeon trainer, programmers do not simply wait until the student happens to do what they want. . . . The reinforcement does not consist in giving the students corn but in telling him that he is right. "Human behavior is remarkably influenced by small results," Skinner has written. ". . . We might say that the human organism is reinforced by any simple gain in competence. . . ."

The advantage of programming in short steps is that in the process of revising, the programmer, by noting which questions his subjects miss, can tell exactly where he has been ambiguous or confusing. Questions can, of course, be made too easy. By consistent "overprompting," as it is known in the trade, a programmer may produce a text that students will race through, answering every question correctly but learning very little. If, however, the programmer also tests his subjects carefully to make sure that they are learning what they are supposed to learn, he should be able to produce a program that is not only clear—and therefore "easy"—but one that teaches with great efficiency. . . .

[In this new type of pedagogy] "The programmer has the privilege of deciding what will be taught," [P. Kenneth] Komoski has said, "But the students show him how to teach it. . . ."

—Spencer Klaw, "What Can We Learn from the Teaching Machines?" *Reporter* 27: 19–26, July 19, 1962. By permission. Copyright 1962 by The Reporter Magazine Company.

not impersonal, however. A machine presents a program designed by someone who knew what was to be taught and could prepare an appropriate series of contingencies. It is most effective if used by a teacher who knows the student, has followed his progress, and can adapt available machines and materials to his needs. Instrumentation simply makes it possible for programmer and teacher to provide conditions which maximally expedite learning. . . . It is merely an effective formulation of those activities of teacher and student which have always been the concern of educational specialists. . . .

Machine teaching is unusually efficient because (1) the student is frequently and immediately reinforced, (2) he is free to move at his natural rate, and (3) he follows a coherent sequence. These are the more obvious advantages, and they may well explain current successes. But there are more promising possibilities: the conditions arranged by a good teaching machine make it possible to apply to education what we have learned from laboratory research and to extend our knowledge through rigorous experiments in schools and colleges. . . .[9]

Professor Skinner regrets that his success in training pigeons has led some people to the mistaken conclusion that his behavioristic methods of learning apply only on the animal level. On this point read M. G. Hall, "Interview with B. F. Skinner," *Psychology Today* 1: 20–24f., September 1967.

[9] Editor's Note: Skinner's main thesis is illustrated in the following analogy by Phil C. Lange, *Sixty-Sixth Yearbook of the National Society for the Study of Education*, Part II: *Programmed Instructions*, Chicago: University of Chicago Press, 1967, p. 161:

In the local community of this writer's childhood there were few shoe sizes but an excellent shoe clerk who was highly expert in stretching shoes, in softening and shrinking leather, and in using a tool to make comfortable bulges for corns and bunions. The total market of shoes was too limited to justify an elaborate technology and distribution system to fit individual needs; every new purchase required "breaking-in" and there was pleasure in old shoes. By contrast, now over 625 million pairs of shoes are sold annually in our nation. Some stores now advertise that in any style you have fifty-four different sizes from which to choose. Today you expect a shoe to fit perfectly even if it was mass produced by a manufacturer who never knew you existed, who built it to the specifications of a model foot. The shoe salesman is no longer an adapter of shoes; instead he is expert in getting your interest, appraising your need, judging your taste—and knowing where and when to go into his store's inventory to select the best fit. By analogy, most teachers today are still shoe stretchers.

When there are more people, more are different in the same ways. Eventually it becomes profitable to mass produce for specialities and differentiation. It is interesting that the field of special education, with its tradition for knowing the learner and for tutorial and custom-made instruction, is one of the earliest and most active exploiters of programmed instruction. . . .

In the same NSSE *Yearbook*, pp. 243, 229–230, C. H. Lindvall and John O. Colvin write:

If instruction is to be efficient and challenging . . . it must place the pupil at the point in the learning sequence which is appropriate for him, and it must accom-

5.7 THE EDUCATION INDUSTRY; 1967*

Peter Schrag

Ever since the first flurry of announcements about the new corporate entries in the education business—the mergers of electronics firms and publishing houses, and the creation of new corporate divisions for education—there has been increasing concern that academic decisions will eventually be made in company board rooms, that children will become appendages to electronic monsters, and that the teacher will find himself

---

modate his program to his needs. For this reason . . . [it has been] necessary to develop placement tests within each area of each subject. For example, in arithmetic there are placement tests in numeration, in addition, in subtraction, and so on. . . . The placement testing makes it possible to say of each pupil, "He should start at level B-Numeration, level D-Addition, level C-Subtraction (and so on).". . . That is, the process places the pupil at his proper level in the curriculum sequence in every sub-area of reading, of arithmetic, and of science. . . .

A major problem encountered by teachers who use programs in such a way as to permit each pupil to proceed as fast as he is able is what to do with a pupil when he completes a given programmed course well before the end of the term. As a rather typical example of such a situation, we note the case of a high-school student, taking a programmed course in algebra, who completes the full year's work by February. The obvious and appropriate procedure, according to his school's curriculum, would be to have him proceed to a program in geometry. If such a procedure is actually followed, however, the student finishes the school year having completed a full year of algebra and a fraction of a year's work in geometry. The problem then arises of where to place this student next year. If he enters a geometry class, he will have to repeat a great deal of material. Under a plan involving the most efficient use of programs, he would start the next year at the exact point where he left off the preceding one. But this flexibility in progress is difficult to achieve within the typical class-and-grade organization of a school, and those schools that have attempted it have eventually encountered difficulties in scheduling and in the promotion of pupils. If individualized progress is actually to be achieved, some organizational pattern must be developed which will not limit flexibility in progress to that which can be achieved within the structure of one class. Each student should be permitted to work at his own particular point of achievement in some well-defined instructional sequence, regardless of the grade level or class to which he happens to be assigned. This, of course, points to the need for the development of sequences of instructional objectives that represent a continuity that is not broken by grade levels or particular classes. . . . [Hence, unless there are to be many additional teachers,] it is essential that lesson materials be largely self-instructional. . . .

* Peter Schrag, "Kids, Computers, and Corporations," *Saturday Review* 50: 78–80, 93–96, May 20, 1967. Copyright 1967 *Saturday Review*, Inc.

Here is a brief explanation of the meaning of "programmed instruction":

The elements combined by instructional programming to produce optimal learning are as follows:

a. Active response by the student . . . [Whether by] writing, speaking, selecting [or] matching . . . a response must occur before it can be reinforced or rewarded and so become established. To learn is to be able to do, and to understand is to be able to explain. . . .

b. Small steps in which careful control of stimuli produces gradual increments in mastery of the subject . . . Each frame (the basic unit of instructional material)

technologically obsolete. Confronting this image of the pedagogical Big Brother is a sylvan vision of the "truly child-centered school" based on the individualized instruction that computers seem to make possible. The child sitting at that keyboard *must* be living modern. To start him playing with electronic machines at the age of four is really to prepare him for the world in which he'll live. No more slates, blackboards, and golden rules: The work will now be displayed by a cathode ray tube (CRT), spoken by a computer-controlled tape, and registered and evaluated through infinitely patient electronic circuits that can play chess, do calculus, and say "Good morning, Mary."

Although several firms, among them RCA, IBM, and Responsive Environments Corporation, are working intensively with instruction by computer, the interests, significance, and dangers of the industry are far more pervasive. . . . Westinghouse has just invested more than $2,000,000 in the development of a computerized system to allow schools to plan each child's work not according to some track or level, but as a genuinely individualized program; Litton has designed a complete junior college; Xerox and Westinghouse operate Job Corps centers which may ultimately provide experience and models for the design of other educational systems. Meanwhile, in a number of university centers, scholars and researchers, often working as industry consultants, are refining techniques of instruction and programming, and are compiling data on the performance of the children who sit at those keyboards. For some people in the industry, the future will lie not only in selling machines, but in providing a complete package of educational services from workbook to teacher training for a market that includes industry and the federal government, as well as schools and individual buyers. In such a vision, the smaller school district of the year 2000

---

presents material that is carefully arranged in terms of what the learner knows already: the learner, in mastering such a step, need not refer back to earlier material or look ahead to later material. . . .

c. Immediate feedback for each response . . . Knowing the correct answer rewards the behavior, gives the learner confidence, and encourages retention. . . .

d. Self-pacing, or individualization of the rate at which the learner masters the material. . . . [In most] classroom teaching . . . the rapid learner is held back, and the slow learner—who might nonetheless be a good student—is dragged forward too quickly. . . . In contrast, programmed instruction is learner-centered, and encourages each student to work at his own best rate. . . . Working at a comfortable speed, the learner is, at the same time, given incentives for steady advance through constant reinforcement. The total instructional cycle—increment question, response, feedback—can take place dozens, or even hundreds or more, times an hour, with teaching and testing blended into one seamless process. . . .

e. Low error rate for the individual learner, as a consequence of the effective operation of the first four principles. . . . Error-free learning is not only simpler, but its effects improve morale, motivation and retention. . . .

—Donald Cook and Francis Mechner, in *Applied Programed Instruction*, Stuart Margulies and Lewis D. Eigen, eds., New York: John Wiley & Sons, Inc., 1962, pp. 3–5. Reprinted with the permission of the publisher. Copyright 1962 John Wiley & Sons, Inc.

(or perhaps even 1984) will be like the local television station, producing some of its own material and techniques, but relying largely on one or several national networks. . . .

On the horizon seemed to be a vast market that spent $50 billion a year (most of it in instructional salaries), a growing national interest in education, and a mounting series of educational problems that seemed to demand (but never really got) radically new approaches.

Professor Patrick Suppes of Stanford University, now an RCA consultant, Moore at Pittsburgh, and others have demonstrated that the computer or the talking typewriter can be highly effective in teaching and upgrading skills in the three R's. . . . Moore feels that the whole American educational system applies its resources backwards: At the graduate level the ratio of students to teachers is close to one-to-one; in the second grade it is thirty-to-one. By developing student independence early, he believes, the ratios could be reversed. And John Henry Martin, former superintendent of schools in Mount Vernon, New York, and now an executive of Responsive Environments (the company that markets the talking typewriter), calculates that the machine can "produce readers cheaper" than conventional instruction can; by the beginning of second grade, he claims, children using the machines can develop a reading vocabulary of 200 to 250 words with 90 percent effectiveness, even in disadvantaged areas. . . . But Martin . . . [has] considerable doubt that machines can be programmed economically for anything but fairly well-defined skills and operations. "The computer cannot develop the capability of the student to communicate effectively with other people," said R. Louis Bright, the United States Associate Commissioner of Education. "It cannot train the pupil to originate ideas or to talk confidently before a group." It is possible to put into a machine a whole mathematical or physical system, and to let students ask the machine questions. But no computer can respond to questions or operations for which it has not been programmed; it cannot evaluate the quality of a work of prose, and cannot deal with the moral and personal ambiguities of contemporary life.

This is not to say that machines can only teach "facts"; perhaps more than anything else, they can help students understand processes—whether in chemistry or in calculus. Testifying before a congressional committee last summer, Maurice B. Mitchell, the president of Encyclopaedia Britannica, said:

> You can tell a child that a caterpillar turns into a butterfly, and identify that as metamorphosis. That is a long word. A child will not know what the word means, until you show him that process in time-lapse photography. Then a big word like metamorphosis gets to be just another ordinary word to the youngster in the third grade.

It is clear, moreover, that the "software"—the curricular materials—will be developed for computers. RCA and the City of New York recently launched a program (financed by the federal government) which will place computer terminals (essentially teletype machines wired to a central computer) in 200 elementary classrooms. Children will be working with material developed by Suppes in California in reading, mathematics, and writing for grades one to six. Concurrently, Responsive Environments Corporation is translating the Bank Street Urban Readers into material for the talking typewriter. In the meantime IBM is trying its own materials at every level from elementary to graduate school and plans to have some fifteen of its model 1500 computers (each with audio and visual components) in experimental use within a year.

And yet most of this activity involves the translation of existing material into machines: It deals with the same skills, the same ideas and concepts. Few people have begun to ask whether the whole process of mechanizing educational materials involves anything more than streamlining what was already inadequate in [the hands of ordinary classroom teachers]. "People in education," said a Xerox official, "don't seem to be interested in the why question. Something which can reproduce garbage more quickly is not necessarily a service." . . .[10]

[The] introduction of programmed learning will demand of every teacher an answer to the question: "What can you do that the machine can't?" At the same time, it may stimulate better evaluation of *all* educational techniques. The machine, moreover, will be only a small part of the process: The diversity of goods and services—and experience—offered by the industry is likely to touch every aspect of learning and training, inside the schools and out. It may well be, indeed, that the prime impact of the industry will be as important outside the formal educational structure as in the classroom. The possibilities of quick data retrieval of library resources, long distance xerography, and computer terminals make it possible for people to study at home (or anywhere else) on their own time and at their own pace. There is nothing about the new technology that limits it to schools or to use at certain hours. . . .

More important for the future is the relative unwillingness of the education establishment to make changes on its own initiative. This inertia, rather than being a barrier to the industry, may be an asset. The demonstrated inadequacies of the schools—and especially in the most visible disaster areas (in the slums, for example) provide an opening for the

---

[10] Editor's Note:

The fact is that we do not know how far we can go in teaching. . . . Experiments are finding that the young learner is capable of mastering many concepts we have traditionally refrained from teaching him. What is the capacity of a brain with an I.Q. of 50, 100, 150? No one really knows, but with teaching machines and basic research on instructional programming, we might find out.

—Lawrence M. Stolurow, "Teaching Machines," *The Nation* 195: 66–68, August 26, 1962.

entrepreneur. To date, federal funds spent by individual districts on conventional techniques have shown few results; at the same time, what the national corporations learn in one area they can—because they are national—immediately apply somewhere else. The machine, moreover, can offer options of enrichment and advancement to those for whom education is the very essence of competitive success. If the ghetto schools succeed with new techniques, is there any question that the suburbs will buy them as well?

The American romance with the machine and with efficiency has its dark side, but it is a romance nevertheless. At a time when Americans are being told that it is possible to teach children more about almost everything at an increasingly younger age, and when a child's greatest heritage appears to be education itself, there is no reason to doubt that in the long run most parents and communities will turn to those resources that offer the greatest possibilities. . . .

It used to be said that certain social problems were too large for private initiative, and justified government involvement. In recent years they have apparently become too large for local government as well. Education and welfare are becoming commercially profitable and that, finally, is why the industry is here. . . .[11]

---

[11] Editor's Note: Phil C. Lange lists the following as *forces which operate against programmed instruction:*

Lack of precise behavioral descriptions and taxonomies for learner characteristics.
Difficulties in changing teacher roles.
Apprehension over change (automation).
Absence of a continuous system of individual diagnosis and prescription for learning. . . .
Inadequate and incomplete choice of programs; inadequate system for selection and precise prescription. . . .
The high cost of innovation and retooling. . . .

[The following are *forces which operate in favor of programmed instruction*]:

Appeal of scientific and systems approach.
Promise of individualization.
Increase in school's range of individual differences: also more students with similar differences.
Curriculum reforms that develop new materials that go directly to learner; more curricular and instructional decisions outside the local school. . . .
Increased use of nongraded school organization, continuous progress, and advancement based on performance.
More recognition of the importance of preteaching planning and arrangements.
More programming in teacher education. . . .
Dissatisfaction with school's failures to retain pupils and in teaching basic skills.
New financial resources for and new investors in the production of instructional materials and media. . . .
Increased instances of success with programmed instruction in business, industry, military, and in adult education. . . .

—Phil C. Lange, in *Programmed Instruction*: Sixty-Sixth Yearbook of the NSSE, Part II, Chicago: University of Chicago Press, 1967, p. 310 (slightly adapted). By permission.

The Human Element in Teaching

5.8 WHAT CAN WE EXPECT FROM THE UNPROGRAMMED TEACHER?*

Henry Winthrop

Devotees of cybernetics and automated teaching occasionally create the impression that they see no limitation in the scientific revolution opened up by the Age of Computers. They seem to consider that there is no skill, no aptitude, no trait, no quality, and no function of man which cannot be taken over by the machine. . . . [and they fail to mention] what a great teacher can accomplish which a machine cannot. . . . It is of these distinctively *human* potentialities that we need to be reminded.

All education which has left an impact upon those exposed to it bears witness to the fact that an inspiring teacher who can convey his enthusiasm for his subject leaves an indelible impression upon the memories of a large number of his students. The history of Western culture confirms this, from the personal magnetism of Socrates to the platform charm exercised by William James. Though we pay tribute to the stimulus value of a programmed question, how does it compare with the stimulus value of the unprogrammed teacher?. . . .

We must not overlook, I think, the value which the living teacher

---

* *Teachers College Record* 67: 315–329, February 1966. Footnotes omitted.

Professor Winthrop is Chairman, Department of Interdisciplinary Social Science, University of South Florida, Tampa.

The notion that teaching machines could be substituted for teachers was cleverly satirized in the following limerick, which appeared in *Current*, January 1961, p. 46:

The latest report from the Dean
In praise of the teaching machine
  Is that Oepidus Rex
  Could have learned about sex
By himself, and not bothered the Queen.

For another satire, read "Learn with BOOK," *Phi Delta Kappan* 44: 153, December 1962. See also Bill Surface, "What Computers Cannot Do," *Saturday Review* 51: 58–59, 66, July 13, 1968.

possesses by virtue of the fact that he can point out the relevancy of his subject to the *personal* and *social concerns* of the student. . . . Since an *ideal*, automated teaching device [admittedly not yet produced] would have to be asked a clear question or, at least, be given a clear answer before it could proceed, a confused question or an unclear response would most likely gum up its works. This is precisely where the programming of the biped is of a superior type. He is programmed to furnish answers to unclear questions and vague or muddled answers by *knowing how to recast these.* These he can recast precisely because he is *sensitive to the intent* of the speaker or the questioner and precisely because he can be sympathetic to the concerns, anxieties, groping and *Weltschmerz* of the student whose reach unfortunately exceeds his grasp. Perhaps the first-rate teacher creates an existential sense of understanding for the student listener by the tone of his voice, by the expression on his face or by the touch of his hand upon the student's shoulder. It matters not. But create it he does. No teaching machine to date has been endowed with the tragic sense of life, and yet without this sense much of human learning must be as ashes in the mouth. As for the future, I am definitely *not* expecting to see the day when a rubber pad at the end of a steel arm, comes down upon the shoulder of a student and a taped voice, speaking in sepulchral tones from the remote electronics interior of some marvelously advanced teaching machine, says "Yes. I know *just* how you feel!". . . .

As a full man, the really outstanding teacher sees to it that, wherever possible, learning is related to life. . . . [and the student should be stimulated to seek] answers to such questions as "What is the good life?" or "What is the ideal society?". . . . A true education and culture must provide for the unfolding of the moral grain in every man. Few question the great importance of this task. All of us, at some time or other, have been deeply impressed by the examples of greatness of soul. . . . [for] the molding of character is still one of the major goals of education. In what respect, may I ask, can automated instruction, providing chiefly facts clothed in representative language rather than ideals of character described in expressive language, help to achieve [greatness of soul]? . . . Better still, in what sense can the impact of nobility of life and purpose, given by a great man we have been privileged to know or a great teacher at whose feet we have been privileged to sit, ever be furnished by a teaching machine? Only written descriptions of such great souls, delineated in expressive language, have the power to move us and to serve as models for our moral development. The very techniques of programming destroy the inspirational function and the moving drama which are frequently the virtues of great prose. This function is forever lost in the fractionation of information which a proper program requires and in the matter-of-fact, unadorned style which the items of automated instruction require. The moving power of great novels, distinguished plays, poetry which touches us in depth, and even the non-fictional classics are clearly alien to the objectives of automated instruction. Every form of aesthetic catharsis, producible in the theatre or by great forms of art, is eternally foreign to the mission of a teaching machine. . . . Only the human being can provide a sense of what a lived culture can be. This he does, not only by example but also by bringing to the fore the importance of the dimensions of feeling and sensitivity for the human condition. Knowledge is not enough. One must distinguish, as Archibald MacLeish once put it, between a fact and the feel of a fact. . . .

The dedicated teacher, possessing largeness of outlook and greatness of soul, a respect for truth and for painstaking detail as well as some understanding of that which is transcendent to the merely stimulus-bound . . . [provides a service] beyond calculation. Once more we are forced to emphasize for the reader that mechanical aids to teaching will never be able to fulfill these functions. Yet without these functions learning would lose its savor and teaching would fail in one of its most crucial missions. . . .

I turn finally to that quality so characteristic of man. . . . his sense of humor. The capacity to laugh at human foibles, to see the incongruity between human behavior and human ideals, to see the unexpected and surprising relationships of similarity between what at first glance seem to be disparate elements of human experience—all these are of inestimable value in moving ever closer to our definitions of the good life. . . . There is no limit to what a fine teacher can do with a good sense of humor. One barb which punctures a pattern of intellectual or social affectation, is worth a mint of dull chapters in a textbook. A single satire may do more to change the course of history than a mountain of learned monographs. . . . [To] the extent that humor can provide the common touch and sweep up both instructor and student in a bond of mutual appreciation, there are few substitutes for it.

Automated instruction, I am strongly convinced, will never provide a commodity which is competitive with an outstanding teacher's sense of humor. I will apologize for the strength of this conviction on the day when I hear the first side-splitting, belly laugh emerge from the interior of a teaching machine. . . .

5.9 THE PERSONAL FACTOR IN TEACHING*

Harry S. Broudy

Civilization and education . . . are consistently on the side of knowledge and purpose and against ignorance and chance. This is as it should be, save for the circumstance that increasing knowledge and purposeful action does not necessarily decrease the volume of life controlled by ignorance and chance. The reason is simple: every deliberately instituted act—driving to the shopping center to buy groceries, for example—sets up chains of events other than and in addition to those that result in buying the groceries. For example, one waves to the postman on the way, or one inadvertently fails to return the greeting of a diffident student. These events in turn set up their own chains of events that in turn intersect with other chains. . . .

[Many schoolroom situations] exemplify the frightening fact that in the act of teaching we create situations and stimuli whose consequences are beyond calculation, even if it occurred to us to calculate them. . . . Will a teacher who makes a child secure inspire him to a significant change in his motivational pattern? Or will a teacher who destroys a child's security inspire him to unusual achievement? That depends, one is told, on the nature of the child and presumably on the nature of the teacher also. So there seems to be no easy substitute for studying the child, the teacher, and, one might add, all other relevant circumstances in their particulars. But is it the duty or is it within the competence of the teacher to undertake such clinical study?

Those who argue that teaching is an art rather than a science probably have in mind this difficulty of predicting pupil behavior from general principles. . . .

When such small behaviors produce such great results, who is to blame a teacher for trembling with anxiety at the close of each day? What remark, what gesture, what grimace, what quip, what praise, what reproof produced what effects on which pupils? And what effects will tomorrow and the day after that engender?

The engineer responsible for the structural integrity of a huge span, the surgeon whose every movement is significant, the general with thousands of lives at his command are familiar symbols of vast responsibility. We wonder at times how these men bear up under it. Yet a teacher—not a

---

* Harry S. Broudy, *Paradox and Promise*, New York: Spectrum Books, 1961, Excerpts from "Mirabile Dictu," pp. 74–85, 153–154.

Harry Broudy is professor of education at the University of Illinois.

mighty person on any scale—daily radiates influences on many many children. The engineer has control over what is being built; the surgeon sees the effect of his movements; the general, one hopes, takes only well-calculated risks. The teacher, however, is often playing blind man's buff, not knowing whom he touches and how the touch is received. Responsibility in such a situation takes on a tinge of desperation.

Mercifully not many teachers are like Socrates, who could never forget the gravity of the teaching relation, who so carefully desisted from letting himself intrude into the learning process. He was the midwife merely helping the pupil bring his own conceptions to birth. But it was an impossible role. His pupils could not help learning Socrates as well as themselves. Perhaps it is wrong to say that we teach subjects, and it is difficult to understand what is meant by saying that we teach pupils, but the teacher never fails to teach himself to the pupil.

That is why teaching machines may well take over the bulk of instruction in the years to come.[12] Even the best of human teachers is not an efficient teaching machine. All that a human teacher can add to the mechanics of instruction is himself, his peculiar organization of experience, which, fortunately or not, is induplicable. His thoughts are not merely true or false; they are profound or shallow, significant or trivial, interesting or boring. Most important of all, he is a source of praise and reproof.

[As for the precise effects of various instructional devices, teachers' mannerisms, or pedagogical methods, very little is known for sure.] About all one can say is that the teacher, first of all, must be himself, and, second, that he be concerned about the pupil, but in a peculiar way. He is himself *for* the pupil, while his concern for the pupil is disguised behind a concern for a subject of instruction. Thus it looks as if Teacher X is teaching arithmetic, but his concern, as Rousseau pointed out, is what is happening to the pupil when he has an arithmetical insight. In exemplifying a genuine human perspective of life, the teacher must seem to be wholly unconscious of being an example. . . .

---

[12] Editor's Note:

Far from dehumanizing the learning process, in fact, computers and other electronic and mechanical aids are likely to *increase* the contact between students and teachers. By taking over much—perhaps most—of the rote and drill that now occupy teachers' time, the new technological devices will free teachers to do the kinds of things only human beings can do, playing the role of catalyst in group discussions and spending far more time working with students individually or in small groups. In short, the teacher will become a diagnostician, tutor, and Socratic leader rather than a drill-master—the role he or she is usually forced to play today.

—Charles E. Silberman, "Technology is Knocking at the Schoolhouse Door," *Fortune* 74: 120–125, August 1966. See also Charles E. Silberman and the Editors of *Fortune, The Myths of Automation,* New York: Harper & Row, Publishers, 1966.

If a teacher is a source of non-standardized insights, if the teacher is creative enough to produce a highly personal reaction to the world and to the subjects he teaches, then he is a valuable asset and not a machine at all. If he is an inciter to thought, if he can engage in enlightening dialogue, if he enacts a life style that persuades as it reveals, then it is not a teaching machine we are talking about. In this sense there is no more point in talking about any one type of "good" teacher than there is to talk about any one type of "good" artist or "good" personality. The goodness lies in their willingness, indeed, their inability to refrain from interacting with the young in an educative way, and this they do in as many ways as there are individual patterns in their respective lives.

Great and wonderful is the institution that attracts to its faculty a variety of personalities who exemplify the diverse patterns of the good life and who, by teaching, conduct their pupils on their own individual guided tour in the wisdom of the race. In such an institution each classroom is a new perspective from which the world looks new and fresh and revelatory. Great and wonderful are the years one is privileged to spend exploring the world in the company of such teachers. The pressure of life's business makes these years tragically few.

The advent of a teaching machine that can drill the learner with marvelous efficiency and has mechanical means of duplicating a lesson a millionfold through the miracles of electronics only serves to make us ask anew: Just what is teaching and what are teachers for? The answer is at once disturbingly old and suggestively new. Why, teachers teach *themselves*. They themselves are the only subject matter that they alone can teach.

5.10 EVALUATION OF SOCRATES AS A TEACHER*

A. PERSONAL QUALIFICATIONS

	Rating (high to low) 1	2	3	4	5	Comments
1. Personal appearance	☐	☐	☐	☐	☒	Dresses in an old sheet draped about his body
2. Self-confidence	☐	☐	☐	☐	☒	Not sure of himself—always asking questions
3. Use of English	☐	☐	☐	☒	☐	Speaks with a heavy Greek accent
4. Adaptability	☐	☐	☐	☐	☒	Prone to suicide by poison when under duress

B. CLASS MANAGEMENT

	1	2	3	4	5	Comments
1. Organization	☐	☐	☐	☐	☒	Does not keep a seating chart
2. Room appearance	☐	☐	☐	☒	☐	Does not have eye-catching bulletin boards
3. Utilization of supplies	☒	☐	☐	☐	☐	Does not use supplies

C. TEACHER–PUPIL RELATIONSHIPS

	1	2	3	4	5	Comments
1. Tact and consideration	☐	☐	☐	☐	☒	Places student in embarrassing situation by asking questions
2. Attitude of class	☐	☒	☐	☐	☐	Class is friendly

D. TECHNIQUES OF TEACHING

	1	2	3	4	5	Comments
1. Daily preparation	☐	☐	☐	☐	☒	Does not keep daily lesson plans
2. Attention to course of study	☐	☐	☒	☐	☐	Quite flexible—allows students to wander to different topics
3. Knowledge of subject matter	☐	☐	☐	☐	☒	Does not know material—has to question pupils to gain knowledge

E. PROFESSIONAL ATTITUDE

	Rating (high to low) 1	2	3	4	5	Comments
1. Professional ethics	☐	☐	☐	☐	☒	Does not belong to professional association or PTA
2. In-service training	☐	☐	☐	☐	☒	Complete failure here—has not even bothered to attend college
3. Parent relationships	☐	☐	☐	☐	☒	Needs to improve in this area—parents are trying to get rid of him

RECOMMENDATION: Does not have a place in Education. Should not be rehired.

* *Source*: This chart is by John Gauss (El Cajon, Calif.), *Phi Delta Kappan* 43: Outside Back Cover, January 1962. By permission.

Reorganizing the Classroom

5.11 THE IMPOSSIBILITY OF STANDARDIZATION*

Walter W. Cook

When a random group of six-year-olds enters the first grade, two percent of them will be below the average four-year-olds in general mental development, and two percent will be above the average eight-year-old. Disregarding the extreme two percent at either end, there is a four-year range in

* Walter W. Cook, "The Gifted and the Retarded in Historical Perspective," *Phi Delta Kappan,* 39: 249–256, March 1958. Footnotes omitted. By permission.

Until his death in 1963, Walter Cook was Dean of the College of Education, University of Minnesota.

general intelligence. By the time this group has reached the age of twelve (seventh grade level), the range will have increased to almost eight years. As long as all the children of all the people remain in school, the range continues to increase. When the educational achievement of a typical sixth grade class is measured, we find a range of approximately eight years in reading comprehension, vocabulary, arithmetic reasoning, arithmetic computation, mechanics of English composition, and other forms of achievement. In almost any sixth grade class will be found a pupil with first or second grade reading ability, and another with eleventh or twelfth grade reading ability. In any grade above the primary level will be found the complete range of elementary school achievement. . . .

When the *General Culture Battery*, consisting of achievement tests in general science, foreign literature, fine arts, and social studies, was administered to high school and college seniors in Pennsylvania, it was found that the upper ten percent of high school seniors were above the college senior median and could have been given B.A. degrees without lowering the intellectual standards of such degrees. It was also found that the lower ten percent of college seniors were below the high school senior median.

Although these facts should be basic data in educational thinking and call for revision of our postulates, they are largely ignored. The idea that the process of schooling *must* consist of homogeneous groups of pupils receiving uniform instruction by mass educational techniques from uniform textbooks is the axiom which prevents constructive approaches to the problem of variability in the classroom. It leads to the further assumptions that grade levels should signify rather definite states of educational achievement; that the course of study for a grade is the prescribed academic requirement, to be administered uniformly to all pupils; that a pupil should not be promoted to a grade until he is able to do the work outlined for that grade; that when individual differences are provided for by good teaching, all pupils can be brought up to standard; that maintaining a passing mark results in homogeneous instructional groups; and that when relative homogeneity does not prevail, it is a result of poor teaching or lax standards. These assumptions underlie most of the criticisms of public education. These assumptions are contrary to fact. . . . The range of ability in the classes of the elementary and high school is so great that if the slow learner in the eighth grade were demoted to the fourth, he would still be a slow learner in the fourth, and below the median of the class. If the top pupil of the fourth grade were accelerated to the eighth, he would still be a bright pupil in the eighth, and above the median of that class. . . .

Our conclusion must be that the more effective the instruction—the more adequately we meet the needs of all pupils—*the more heterogeneous groups become.*

The central problem of meeting the needs of the slow pupil and the gifted pupil, as well as the average pupil, is how best to meet the needs of individuals in groups of widely varying ability. Since all instructional groups vary widely in interests and ability, it seems wiser to attempt to develop techniques for meeting the needs in such groups instead of constantly striving for a homogeneity which cannot be achieved. This calls for changes in beliefs, attitudes, and understandings which will result in more defensible administrative and curriculum policies. Let us suggest some of them.

The administrative policy should have two purposes: (1) to make it possible for the teacher to know the pupil well enough to meet his needs and (2) to provide instructional material with a range of difficulty and interest appeal commensurate with the needs of the instructional group:

A. The size of classes must be reduced to not more than twenty-five pupils. The practice of giving each elementary teacher a class of from thirty to forty pupils and having the high-school teacher meet from 150 to 250 different pupils a day, with instruction based on a uniform textbook, precludes the possibility of meeting individual needs.

B. A systematic testing program revealing status and growth in the basic intellectual skills and abilities (not facts) required for optimum adjustment in the culture must be instituted, with the results for each pupil from kindergarten to college graphically portrayed. The purposes of these tests are not the traditional ones—those of holding teacher and pupils to standards or as a basis for promotion or marking; the purpose is rather to enable the teacher to know more about the pupil, the books he can read, the type of problems he can solve, the amount of improvement that can be expected—in short, to know the educational experiences that he needs.

C. A permanent record folder, containing in addition to the superimposed profiles of the test results, the health record, samples of handwriting, creative written work, and other evidences of achievement showing the pupil's development from kindergarten on, should be in the hands of each teacher.

D. Each teacher should have an opportunity for a personal conference with the parents of each pupil not less than twice each year in order that both the parents and teacher may understand the pupil better.

E. The primary basis for grouping children should be physical and social development (probably best indicated by chronological age), since these are the most obvious criteria of status in childhood groups. A child should live and work with the group he most obviously belongs with—one which accepts him and which he accepts.

F. There must be grouping within classes on the basis of status and needs in specific learning areas. These groups should be flexible as to size and duration and specific in purpose.

G. The practice of labeling school books by grade should be discontinued. A code number indicating to the teacher the difficulty of the material is sufficient.

H. In both the elementary and high school, the practice of having a teacher instruct the same group of pupils from three to six years should be encouraged.

I. At the high school level there should be special honors courses for students who demonstrate unusual ability in mathematics, science, language, and other subjects.

J. In the high school the practice of integrating English and the social studies in a four-to-six-year coordinated sequence with two- or three-hour daily periods in a laboratory workshop should be encouraged.

K. A wealth of instructional material should be provided in each classroom. It should have a range of difficulty, interest appeal, and content commensurate with the range of abilities and interests of the class. It must be placed in the classroom and not in the library or other special room. Perhaps the best way to meet the needs of the potential geniuses in our classes is to place them in intellectual contact with the geniuses of the ages. This can be done through books. This should be an item of first priority in any school system. The most serious indictment that can be brought against public education today is its failure to furnish the teacher with adequate books and instructional materials and to surround every pupil with a wealth of reading materials of both a literary and a factual nature. Textbooks are necessary, but they are far from sufficient as instructional material. . . .[13]

5.12 GENERALISTS AND SPECIALISTS IN THE ELEMENTARY SCHOOL*

George D. Stoddard

In American education, the idea of a school grade is only about a century old. As in other nations the earlier forms of organization were less structured. On the whole, the grade may be regarded as a good invention, but

[13] Editor's Note: Compare Henry David Thoreau: "If a man does not keep pace with his companions, perhaps it is because he hears a different drummer. Let him step to the music which he hears, however measured or far away."

* G. D. Stoddard, *The Dual Progress Plan*, New York: Harper & Row Publishers, Inc., 1961, pp. 2–4, 20–21, 35–41, 64, 151, 155, 222.

like so many other inventions it has become obsolete. To the extent that a grade embodies appropriate attention to individual differences, is based on common cultural demands, and is capable of being competently taught, it is a useful device. It is consistent with other guideposts of maturity such as age, size, weight, and mental maturity.

When the grade idea was applied only to common learning (i.e., the three R's), it was closer to its ideal than it is now. We have no common learnings in abstract mathematics, science, music, or art; in these areas not much is expected of the American adult, even by way of appreciation. On the other hand, a great deal is expected of the adult in terms of the language arts and social studies, *so much so, that they form practically the whole content of our standardized tests of intelligence.* Tests of general mental ability scarcely get beyond reading comprehension; they make only a bow to science or the arts, or to originality in any form.

Somehow there has developed throughout the grade system a distrust of the specialist. Perhaps there was felt to be little need for specialized training. Engineering and other technologies scarcely entered into the planning of the elementary school; before the Land-Grant College movement, such studies were not the general rule in higher education. The average American child, while often adept in mechanical manipulation, remains essentially indifferent to pure science. This indifference is not a necessary by-product of his nervous system; it is more often a result of his schooling. . . .

The Education of Teachers for the Dual Progress Plan. Paul Woodring has written a compact account of the course of teacher education in the United States, with emphasis on the proliferation which has taken place in the last few decades. He shows how a perversion of the teachings of John Dewey led to the false assumption that the teaching of the whole child did not require excellence in subject matter or any consistent philosophy of education. . . .

[But the new age demands much more than schooling in the three R's; for the explosion of knowledge results in] what might be called *the insurmountable task* of the all-purpose teacher:

> Being responsible for the teaching of all subjects taught in the elementary school, she [the ideal teacher?] should command a scholarly knowledge of mathematics, literature, history, science, geography, government, music, and art. An elementary knowledge of these fields is not sufficient,

---

Read also G. D. Stoddard, "Creativity in Education," Chapter 12 of *Creativity and its Cultivation,* Harold H. Anderson, ed., New York: Harper & Row, Publishers, 1959. See also "A Critical Look at Team Teaching," *The Instructor* (70th Anniversary issue), 71: 33–42, October 1961 (bibliography).

Dr. Stoddard was formerly Chancellor and Executive Vice-President, New York University, and is author of many books on educational psychology.

> for in each sixth-grade class there will be a few children with mental ages of sixteen, eighteen, or higher and some of these will have marked aptitudes in special fields. The ideal teacher must have advanced knowledge in all areas if she is to provide maximal learning opportunity for gifted children. She would be an expert in the teaching of reading and able to diagnose reading difficulties. She must teach handwriting, spelling, and many more skills. She should have a thorough grasp of language and should know how to teach children to use it effectively, both in speech and in writing. Probably she should know some language other than her own for foreign language instruction is increasingly becoming a part of the elementary curriculum.[14]

All that on the side of subject matter! As a result, we have accepted teachers who can do *something* in all these fields, propped up by a few specialists and the ever-ready textbooks and canned examinations; we have, at least, demanded a humane person who generally likes children and gets along well with people. Clearly, the problem is to combine learning in depth (by restricting the content spectrum) with the humane and proficient approach, on the ground that good intentions are not enough. I feel that the team approach, together with specialization fed by a strong program in the liberal arts, in the future, will be looked upon as so rational a combination as to make students wonder what the mid-century conflicts in teacher education were all about. . . .

[In the Dual Progress Plan] a *home teacher* is placed in charge of *two rooms*, on a half-day basis for each. She is responsible for registration and counseling; she teaches reading and the social studies. The other half-day is assigned to special teachers who teach mathematics and science, music, arts and crafts, recreation and health, and—beginning with grade five—an optional sequence in a foreign language. The special teachers in each subject or cluster of subjects offer the work on a longitudinal basis straight through the elementary grades, and in a combined school throughout the twelve grades. Thus the special teachers, as a team, are in a good position to judge the quality of special aptitudes and their course of growth throughout the child's school life. Test scores, profiles, ratings, and sample items furnish a continuous comprehensive record. All special teachers are to encourage pupils to form social clubs based on content interest that cut across the grades.

Generally a pupil's grade standing will be determined by his home teacher, but he will be free to pursue avidly a specialty according to his aptitude. A fifth-grade pupil may play in the high school band or orchestra, and a pupil gifted in mathematics or science may be brigaded with like-minded students in more advanced grades.

---

[14] Paul Woodring, *New Directions in Teacher Education*, New York: The Fund for the Advancement of Education, 1957, pp. 71–72.

The home teacher (usually a woman) is in charge of both sections of her grade. Since one of her functions is to be concerned with pupil orientation, she concentrates on knowing the pupils, the families, and the neighborhoods, linking this knowledge [to that of the subject-matter specialists who work closely with her].

[To see how the Dual Progress Plan operates, let us consider mathematics. Analogous principles and procedures would apply to art, music, and the sciences. The importance of early instruction has been well stated by] John R. Dunning, dean of the School of Engineering of Columbia University:

> . . . If we are to wipe out scientific illiteracy and mathematical illiteracy, we must start in our elementary schools. For just as the child who does not want to read is more incurably illiterate than the child who does not know how to read, so the child who misses the point of science is more ignorant than the child who lacks information about science; and it is in the first few years of school that we are now almost systematically crushing that lovely combination of wonderment and shrewd inquiry which is the real point of science.
>
> There is no such creature as a child too young for science. In fact, since toddlers are more interested in discovering the world outside themselves than in probing their own psyches or their interpersonal relations (unless they are pretty sick toddlers), the beginning of all rational intellectual activity lies in the realm of elementary science and mathematics. . . .[15]

Under the Dual Progress Plan, it will be better, after full testing, *to allow the mentally backward child to abandon mathematics beyond the commonest skills,* in order that he may concentrate on what surely will be demanded of him, namely, an optimum proficiency in the language arts and social studies. He can improve, however slowly, in reading comprehension and general information; through such means, as far as subject matter can help, he will best be able to achieve personal satisfaction and vocational fitness. After all, his need of science will be no more than a modicum, thus placing him, if we were to be cynical about it, near the average rating of adults in the mid-twentieth century. Any special talents may help to take up the mathematics-science slack; they can be emphasized, in school and out. There is more "low-level" reading, performing (in sports or art), and deciding (in family affairs) than "high-level." It is no part of scholastic virtue to force upon a pupil standards which he is truly unable to meet. It is better to have a child's resources fully mobilized toward a modest success than to have them continually serve receding, impossible goals.

In short, when necessary it is all right to "take the heat off," especially

[15] *New York Times Magazine,* November 29, 1959, p. 80.

for content outside the cultural imperatives, provided we know what we are doing. This is different from "relaxing standards"; it is, rather, a reaffirmation of the basic principle of individual differences in ability. In the Dual Progress Plan standards of achievement should rise, for each pupil is expected to perform at his highest potential level. . . . [If we can] discover the slow, the average, and the fast learners, and adjust their programs accordingly . . . [we may] put an end to the concept of average ability for a class, calling for average performance under average teaching effectiveness. This means a playing up of the spread of talent as a means of reducing, on the one hand, the nagging of the dull and, on the other, the indefensible neglect of the gifted. . . .

As we move from the self-contained classroom to the Dual Progress Plan, we should not entertain the thought that the specialists in the ungraded section are more praise-worthy than the teachers in the core section devoted to the language arts and social studies. In fact, the latter also become specialists, though the range is broad. We might with justice say that in the new plan all teachers are both specialists and generalists. . . .

If we are given teacher specialization superimposed upon a sound basis of the liberal arts and child development, and hold to clear but not fixed ideas as to what is imperative and what is elective in our society, it seems to me we are well prepared to design the school of the future. . . .[16]

---

[16] Editor's Note: Speaking of secondary education, R. Freeman Butts has written:

The college preparatory function of high schools promises again to be a major, if not the major, function of high school education. In the thirty years from 1929 to 1959 the high school enrollment has almost doubled (4,800,000 to 9,200,000), but college enrollment has more than tripled (from 1,100,000 to 3,700,000). We must recognize the growing necessity for a larger body of highly trained persons in all fields and the increasing aspiration and intention of the American people that more and more young people shall continue their education beyond high school. . . .

We must not be apologetic for the college preparatory function of the public high school. We must improve the academic courses in English, mathematics, science, and foreign language. . . .

We must find ways to deal constructively with differences of ability but without stratifying differences into rigid categories of social or intellectual inferiority or superiority. How can we deal with the wide range of abilities, motivating, challenging, and pushing toward excellent performance but without creating attitudes of inferiority or defeat among the less able and attitudes of superiority or snobbishness among the more able? This is an important challenge to the comprehensive high school. If it cannot do this, then we might as well have separate secondary schools as our European friends do. That is, if separation into ability groupings really aids learning. Do we know that it does, or is it just easier and nicer for the teacher? Most of us believe in the *social* advantages of the comprehensive high school; but are there *intellectual* advantages, even for the high ability students? Are there certain conditions or certain subjects in which able students learn better in mixed classes than they do in separate sections? And similarly for the slow learners? And by all means do not forget all those in between.

Finally, we must respond to the challenge to define the needs of students in such a way as to strike a proper balance between their need for intellectual achievement,

5.13 INDEPENDENT STUDY*

Anne Patrick and Others

The term *independent study* means a learning situation within the school day which allows a student to develop personal competencies through experiences as an individual but in interaction with others when needed. It is characterized by freedom from constant supervision. Students read, write, contemplate, listen to records and tapes, view, record, memorize, create, build, practice, exercise, experiment, examine, analyze, investigate, question, discover, and converse. Independent study emphasizes the individual's role in learning. It implies that all students possess potentialities for self-initiative, self-discipline, resourcefulness, productivity, and self-evaluation. . . .

Independent study is not study carried out by a student entirely on his own. When a student is seeking procedural authority, defining a problem, developing ideas, testing points of view, taking certain risks, he needs to feel the undergirding influence of a teacher whom he respects. A skillful teacher can provide the right amount of help at a time when it is needed most and thus prevent a student engaging needlessly in large amounts of unproductive activity. In this role, the teacher counsels, advises, and plans. . . .

The final success of independent study will depend upon the person

---

their need for social responsibility, and their need for self-development. For the half of our students who are not going on to college I should say that a proper balance in the educational program would consist of these three ingredients in about equal proportion. For the half who are going on to higher study I should say the educational and cultural priorities require that the ingredients be three parts scholarship, two parts social responsibility, and one part self-development.

Schooling without rigorous knowledge is no education at all; but if the acquisition of organized knowledge is the *only* goal, then education may become rigid and lifeless. Schooling without self-development becomes routinized and oppressive, but if self-development is the *only* goal, education may become undisciplined and soft-headed. Schooling without social responsibility makes of education the impractical plaything of dilettantes, but if social responsibility is the *only* goal, education may impose a cheerless and drab conformity, throttling the creative sparks of originality and choking the freedom for individuals which we cherish so highly. The purpose of our schooling is to speed the process by which the child learns to become a man of learning in freedom.

—R. Freeman Butts, "Scholarship and Education in a Free Society," *Teachers College Record*, 61: 279–289, March 1960. By permission.

* Excerpts from David W. Beggs, III, Edward G. Buffie, W. M. Griffin, Anne Patrick, and others, *Independent Study*, Bloomington: Indiana University Press, 1965, 2, 5, 39, 46, 80–82, 211–212. By permission.

See also Donald C. Manlove and David W. Beggs, III, *Bold New Venture: Flexible Scheduling*, Bloomington: Indiana University Press, 1965. (Contains bibliography.)

who actually puts it into effect, the classroom teacher. A teacher needs to be willing, even eager, to encourage independent study. This is the same kind of desire for personal satisfaction as the child who wants to find out why thunder booms or what makes a desert. The teacher who has a curious mind and sincerely enjoys new explorations will like to work with independent study. She will willingly forsake the single text and happily work with individuals more than with groups. The enthusiasm a teacher feels for independent study is transmitted to her students. The teacher who will be effective in nurturing independent study will not be one who wants her class neatly organized with each child rigidly attempting to cover the same material or one who looks upon any interruption of her planned activities or deviation from the curriculum guide as a minor irritation.

The teacher in a successful independent study operation must be ready to accept change, change in plans, in activities, in work habits, and in teaching procedures. She is no longer the source of all knowledge, the lecturer, the explainer, the assignment giver; rather, she is the counselor, the guide, the listener, and the friend of her students. She will help children steer away from unproductive activities, help them use resources properly, encourage them with the patience of Job. She must be the kind of person who is willing to give free rein to children to work outside her circle of influence and to respond to any accomplishment, even though she has not been at the center of the learning experience. . . .

[*Individualized Instruction* is a broader term than *Independent Study*, for students vary in their need and desire for independent study.] In spite of the long-held notion about teen-agers desiring freedom to work out their own destinies, when given the opportunity to plan their programs, to select modes of study and to take the consequences for these selections, only about half of the [college] freshman students in a high ability student population really are comfortable with such a situation and wish to have it continue. A sizable percentage of them (about fifteen percent) are so uncomfortable with this situation that they react almost violently against the idea after having been subjected to it. On the other hand, a similar percentage (again about fifteen percent) are tremendously enthusiastic about the program and feel cheated when such opportunities are terminated.

[Independent study, like other teaching, must accommodate itself to the fact that a group of students will exhibit] varying levels of mental processes. Students who learn simply by answering questions to workbook problems or through teaching machines Skinnerian-type stimuli are working at one level of mental process, while the graduate doctorial candidate who, on his own, identifies an original problem for study and carries this problem through to completion is working at an entirely different level of mental process. Somehow, classes might be developed which could involve varying proportions of lower and higher mental process dimension expectations. . . .

Pupils should work toward defined goals in their independent study program. These objectives should be understood by the student. . . . Part of the thrill for any traveler is to know how far he is from his destination. Students want to know, and profit from knowing, how they are doing. . . . They want and have a right to the teacher's critical and positive evaluation of their efforts. This may be done in a number of ways, through discussion, by placing work on display, with written comments, in reports to the class, or through a note to the parents. . . .

At the beginning of the school year, the teacher needs to work with her group in order to find out what kinds of experiences they have had in independent study. She needs to know what kind of environment will help children discover and develop areas which will be of interest to them. In summary her tasks boil down to five significant jobs:

1. To motivate the student toward whatever level of independent study appears most appropriate for him.
2. To counsel the student regarding his area of concern and guide him to the resources to enrich the area.
3. To teach him the effective use of multiple resources.
4. To continue to encourage and aid him as he works toward his goals.
5. To recognize his efforts and evaluate his products.

To those teachers who doubt the value of independent study in the elementary school, there can be only one comment: Try it for a sustained period of time and thrill to the advantages to you, and, more important, to your students!. . . .

PROCESS AND CONTENT GOALS

While there will always be a debate about what is desirable in a school program and what the outcomes should be, there is new attention being given to how the student learns rather than to what he learns.

For example, Glenn Heathers has identified three major sets of goals which are sharp, broad, and current with accumulated theory:

1. *The content goals*—included here are such things as: the learning of terminology, classification, information, explanation theory, and technical application of information and theory. You will note that the first three concern themselves primarily with the teaching of information or facts.

2. *The process goals*—instead of stressing acquisition of particular bodies of knowledge or content, emphasis is placed upon teaching students how to acquire, interpret, evaluate, and communicate knowledge. The tool skills,

critical thinking, inquiry, *self-evaluation*, development of personal interest, and study habits receive central emphasis.

3. *The personal-social goals*—these relate to such things as values (social, esthetic, theoretical), personality makeup (emotional security, positive self-concept, self-assertion, etc.). . . . Learning products as measured by achievement test scores were once given a high value in evaluating educational progress. The ability to use these products was assumed to be a direct follow-up from knowledge. Definitely the trend today is to place emphasis on teaching students how to use ideas and develop concepts. Examination of the newer programs in science, mathematics, and social studies will validate this assertion. Emphasis is upon the search, the discovery, the investigation, or the process of inquiry. Students are led to search for interrelationships, patterns, and structures of ideas.

Independent study is the vehicle for students to use in reaching the process understandings the school designates as important. The accumulation of information and storage of facts should be given less stress than basic understanding of broad ideas. This is not to say that content is not important. Content acquisition is essential as a tool to use in the development of process understandings; however, it is not an end in itself. Often educators go too far in the direction of teaching only facts or in the other direction of teaching only unsupported generalizations. A balance is required for a useful and enduring education.[17]

[17] Editor's Note: Here is a recent optimistic assessment of the independent study program for secondary schools:

1. It is now certain that more responsibility for their own learning can effectively be placed on the more able and mature high school students.
2. Much greater flexibility of scheduling and what is studied is practical. It is quite possible, for example, to schedule a whole class made up of students on independent study on a two-or-three-times-weekly basis such as the typical college class.
3. Use of teacher time and the nature of the teacher role can be greatly changed. The teacher with a class that meets three times a week instead of five will have more time for planning and for conferences with individual students. The role of the teacher as a guide to individual learning will be enhanced by such arrangements.
4. Perhaps most important, procedures for independent study give the school new ways of awakening interests and talents of students whose zest for learning might otherwise be stultified by the regime of the traditional schedule of class study.
5. Finally, independent study shows promise of helping young men and women to develop qualities of resourcefulness and self-guided learning that will improve their future education and indeed help prepare them for independent lifelong learning. This broader spirit of individual inquiry is well expressed by John Gardner: "The ultimate goal of the educational system is to shift to the individual the burden of pursuing his own education."

—Don H. Richardson, "Independent Study: What Difference Does it Make?" *National Association of Secondary School Principals Bulletin* 51: 53–62, September 1967. By permission. The quotation is from John Gardner, *Self-Renewal: The Individual and the Innovative Society*, New York: Harper & Row, Publishers, 1964.

5.14 THE NONGRADED SCHOOL*

John I. Goodlad

Nongrading . . . [embraces] a few simple but nonetheless compelling principles of child development, learning, school function, and pedagogical practice.

First, children are different, much more different than we have up to

---

* Excerpted from John I. Goodlad, "Meeting Children Where They Are," *School Curriculum and the Individual* (1966) by permission of Blaisdell Publishing Company, A Division of Ginn and Company.

John I. Goodlad is Professor and Director, University Elementary School, University of California, Los Angeles, and Assistant to the Chancellor for Education, University of California, Irvine.

The "nongraded school" in elementary education has its counterpart in high school and junior high school "flexible scheduling," which means this:

> Two short words symbolize very well some significant shortcomings of today's schools. The words are *walls* and *bells*. . . . *Walls* divide schools into look-alike classrooms. . . . [and] bar team teaching, large group instruction, economical use of technical aids, and effective independent study. . . . *Bells* divide the school day into standard segments of time for most (in some schools, all) school subjects. These look-alike periods get in the way of varying time with the purposes and activities of instruction and prevent the school from dealing effectively with individual differences among students and teachers. . . .
>
> Flexible scheduling—with other arrangements that go along with it—is designed to cope with the problems of the *walls* and the *bells*. . . . [It is based] on a number of observations:
>
> 1. Duration and frequency of class periods should reflect the importance and complexity of the subject. All classes need not meet the same number of periods per week or the same amount of time each day.
> 2. Students learn at different rates of speed.
> 3. Youngsters grow physically, emotionally, and intellectually at varying rates throughout the school year. Thus, the school program must be flexible enough to accommodate the changing development of each youngster.
> 4. The principal should give teachers the control of time.
> 5. Teachers possess different and varied abilities. Not all teaching jobs need the same skill, preparation, or time allotment.
> 6. Students are capable of personal responsibilities and can make mature decisions.
> 7. Time allotments, methods of teaching, student grouping, and teachers' and pupils' activities are the responsibility of teachers and counselors, not of the administration. Professional teachers, after all, are trained in the area of curriculum and instruction. Hence, they should be allowed to determine group abilities, units of instruction, amount of time needed to accomplish objectives of the unit, and the facility best suited to the method of instruction.
> 8. Learning is more important than teaching; learning can take place without the teacher. Students can learn from each other or independently.
> 9. Substantial improvement must take place in the instructional program; the teacher has the obligation to innovate and to create ways to improve instruction.

—Gardner Swenson, Donald Keys and J. Lloyd Trump, *Providing for Flexibility in Scheduling and Instruction*, Englewood Cliffs, N.J.: Prentice-Hall, Inc., 1966,

now recognized. We have been shamefully remiss in taking these differences into account in our educational planning and teaching.

Second, an essential in seeking to provide intelligently for these differences is educational diagnosis of and prescription for the individual. Mass techniques and common expectations for all are inimical to these highly sensitive human processes.

Third, there must be alternatives from which to fill the prescription. A monolithic school structure providing only pass or fail as the alternatives in regulating pupil progress simply does not square with the range of alternatives necessary to coping imaginatively with human variability.

Fourth, the proper question to ask in starting a child off on his school career is not, "Is this child ready for school?" but, "What is this child ready for?" This is the most pregnant idea and is, indeed, at the heart of nongrading.

Fifth, criterion standards replace norm-based standards as the measure of pupil progress. Norm-based standards are sloppy standards geared to group performance. They tend to result in unjustified rewards for high but inadequate performance on the part of the able and relentless, punishing failure for the slow and deprived. It has been estimated that 25 percent of children in school receive 75 percent of the failing grades based on group standards. These children ultimately come to regard themselves as failures —not just in school but in life itself. Most of this loss to mankind could have been prevented by asking and carefully answering the question, "What is this child ready for?"

Criterion standards seek to arrange a sequence of difficulty or a meaningful progression in work assignments. Instead of pronouncing the child to be at the fourth-grade level, which tells us very little and most of that misleading, these standards seek to provide a profile of where the child is now functioning with respect to the skills and concepts comprising the sequence of learning. These are really tougher standards, each child pitting himself against the rigor of the material rather than the uncertainties of group competence and variability. Unfortunately, we are still at a rela-

---

pp. 5–12. By permission. See also Robert M. Bush and Dwight W. Allen, *A New Design for High School Education: Assuming a Flexible Schedule*, New York: McGraw-Hill, Inc., 1964.

Flexible scheduling and the ungraded school are based on a common philosophy:

> The ungraded primary school . . . is a philosophy of education that includes the notion of continuous pupil progress, which promotes flexibility in grouping by the device of removing grade labels, which is designed to facilitate the teacher's role in providing for pupils' individual differences, and which is intended to eliminate or lessen the problems of retention and acceleration.

—Frank R. Dufay, *Ungrading the Elementary School*, West Nyack, N. Y.: Parker Publishing Company, 1966, pp. 23–24.

tively primitive stage in the development of these criterion measures but rapid progress is being made in projects designed to change the curricula of America's schools.

Sixth, sound learning is meaningfully cumulative. That is, the child's progression does not suffer from what psychologists call retroactive and proactive interference. A percentage problem for the child who has no conception of parts and wholes, let alone the number base on which percent depends, contaminates his present mathematical knowledge and interferes with what follows. Such is the unhappy, cumulative product of several "bare passes" in a graded system.[18]

The graded school was brought into being at a time when we knew little about individual differences in learning. The assumption then, in the middle of the nineteenth century, was that the content of instruction could be divided into roughly equal packages and mastered, a year at a time, by children of the same age. Soon, there came to be graded content, graded textbooks, graded children, graded teachers, and graded expectations for schooling. Graded tests and graded norms came later. The entire graded machinery was efficient in classifying the hordes of children pouring into our schools in increasing numbers throughout the balance of the nineteenth century and into the twentieth.

But the children didn't fit. Some simply could not master the work of a grade in a year; others romped through it. Good teaching raised the level throughout; poor teaching lowered it. A formidable gap between the swift and the slow remained.

* * *

The usual fourth-grade class contains children achieving at second, third, fourth, fifth, and sixth grades in some aspects of their school work—and even occasionally above and below these levels. The average spread in achievement is four years. In a fifth-grade class it is five; in a sixth, six years in tested achievement, and so on. These are not fourth or fifth or

---

[18] Editor's Note: B. Frank Brown believes that

Every nongraded plan should be tested against several propositions: (1) it must make possible an accurate classification of students of near equal achievement, (2) it must provide for frequent reclassification so that students are permitted to move forward on an individual basis as fast as they can go, (3) it must permit the establishment of individualized goals for each student, (4) it must have standards compatible with the varying rates at which students learn.

—B. Frank Brown, "The Non-Graded School," *National Association of Secondary School Principals Bulletin* 47: 64–67, May 1963. See also Frederick Shaw, "The Educational Park in New York: Archetype of the School of the Future?" *Phi Delta Kappan* 50: 329–331, February 1969; Arthur I. Berman, "Seminar/Autolecture," *Today's Education* 57: 33–36, December 1968.

sixth grades except in name. They are composites of many grades, each graded class overlapping graded classes above and below. In a field like reading, the picture is even more startling. Children in a fifth-grade class commonly range in reading from the second or third to the ninth or tenth.

The common-sense protest here is that, given ideal school conditions, these slow pupils could be pulled up substantially. True, but given equally ideal conditions for the able, they too would move up beyond these performances.

A common-sense solution to managing this vast range of attainments, frequently posed by lay critics of the schools, is to group those of like achievement in a single class. (The term used often but incorrectly for this achievement grouping is ability grouping.) But some additional evidence gives us pause. The variability in attainments within one child sometimes parallels the variability in an entire class. A child, like a class, is not a second, fourth, or sixth grader. Johnny can be in the fifth grade for arithmetic computation, the sixth for arithmetic reasoning, the seventh for spelling, the eighth for word meaning, the ninth for paragraph meaning, and the tenth for language—and yet be officially registered in the sixth grade. In the same class is Jean, whose scores range from low third to high seventh; Bill, from high second to high fifth; and Pat, from fourth to tenth. (These figures, incidentally, are taken from actual class roles.) Children are downright ornery. They refuse to grow up all of a piece.

Under a plan of grouping for likeness in achievement, Johnny, Jean, Bill and Pat would join a new group for each subject and rarely would be together in the same groups. Their class groups, to be closely homogeneous (that is, comparable in attainment), would be composed of children from throughout the building, brought together because of their assumed readiness for identical learnings. A monstrous scheduling problem is involved. This can readily be managed through modern computer techniques.[19]

* * *

. . . It is not easy to escape more than a century of gradedness. . . . [Moreover, even in the most ideal of contemporary nongraded schools] as quickly as one goal is attained, others come into view. As former Chancellor Lawrence Kimpton once said about the University of Chicago over which he presided, "This probably isn't a very good place for the pursuit of happiness, but it's a wonderful place to find happiness in pursuit." . . .

---

[19] Editor's Note:

Teaching methods which permit the learner to operate autonomously in the search for new understandings utilize creative thinking to promote concept de-

TOPICS FOR FURTHER STUDY

SEGREGATING THE GIFTED: PROS AND CONS

A. Unfortunately, our social mores always have been hostile to the concept that children of superior mentality ought to be educated apart from those of average ability. In our democratic society we are committed to the basic assumption that there is no person who can claim to be an indispensable man. We proceed from this entirely correct assumption to the incorrect conclusion that neither does a democracy have indispensable men. This is obviously erroneous. A moment's reflection will show that no society can function without its indispensable men. By this I mean the men who because of natural endowment and careful training possess the intellectual, artistic, and moral abilities to carry forward the momentum of civilization.[20]

B. There is a great danger that the current "quest for excellence" will turn into an emphasis on the education of the easily educable. . . . A decade ago, the line of least resistance was to organize a program so easy that nobody could get mad at the superintendent because his child was flunking. Today, the line of least resistance is to work only with children who don't need much work.[21]

---

velopment. . . . One way to promote the use of creative thinking as an aid to conceptual growth is to make the teacher's role less directive and more responsive, to have the learner focus on a problem, and allow him to gather data freely with the help but not the direction of the teacher. . . . [For example, O. K. Moore] allows his subjects to manipulate freely the keys of an electric typewriter. The teacher says the name of each letter as it is imprinted on the paper. No goals are set, no instructions given. Every time a child performs an operation by hitting a letter or a group of letters, he gets a response. When he hits groups of letters that are words, he is given the sound of the whole word. Through this method (which I have drastically oversimplified) three- and four-year-olds learn to read and type incredibly well and very quickly.

The key to Moore's approach is the responsive environment. He gives the learner freedom to operate in his own way, at his own pace, without any extrinsic rewards and pressures. The environment is highly responsive to each action the child performs. Moore opens the door to creative thinking by maximizing the child's autonomy and the feedback data he gets from his operations.

—J. Richard Suchman, "Creative Thinking and Conceptual Growth," *Gifted Child Quarterly*, 6: 95–99, Autumn 1962; reprinted in *Creativity: Its Educational Implications*, J. C. Gowan, G. D. Demos, and E. P. Torrance, eds., New York: John Wiley & Sons, Inc., 1967.

[20] Rear Admiral Hyman S. Rickover, USN, "Let's Stop Wasting Our Greatest Resource," *Saturday Evening Post*, 229: 19f., March 2, 1957. By permission of E. P. Dutton & Co., Inc. See also H. G. Rickover, *American Education—A National Failure*, New York: E. P. Dutton & Co., Inc., 1963.

[21] Martin Mayer, *The Schools*, New York: Harper & Row, Publishers, 1961, p. 156.

C. Crucial for the development of talent in a democracy is a democratic attitude toward it, and a democratic attitude of the talented toward themselves. Outstanding talent is greatly to be desired and its emergence causes rejoicing. But if the talented feel a vain superiority, the talent sours. The most effective of the gifted are those least touched by a sense of their otherness. Absorbed in living the life of talent, they share their knowledge, their skill, their interest, and their enthusiasm in the cooperative business of living and learning and doing.[22]

D. Separating gifted students from other students for part or all of their educational experience has evoked conflicting opinions. . . . The commission, weighing all factors, believes that some grouping of students by ability is desirable policy.

A strong practical argument in favor of special grouping is that it greatly facilitates both enrichment and acceleration. In a class consisting entirely of gifted pupils it is much easier—and therefore much more likely to happen in actual practice—for the teacher to provide enriched learning experiences than when a wide variety of assignments is required in a heterogeneous class. Also, an all-bright group can be accelerated smoothly without the disadvantage of sudden grade jumps that skip important learning experiences, as sometimes happens when acceleration is an individual matter. *Every pupil, however, should have some experience in ungrouped classes.*[23]

COMPUTERIZED INDIVIDUALIZED INSTRUCTION: PROS AND CONS

A. The best single reason for using computers for instruction is that computer technology provides the only serious hope for accommodation of individual differences in subject-matter learning.[24]

B. The key claim of the new technology is that individualized instruction only now can be truly achieved. The chores of drill, exercises, skill development will be taken over by computers and the talking typewriters. Total packages of books tied to films, filmstrips, tapes, et cetera, will replace dramatized presentations. The teacher will be freed for human interaction. He has opportunities for the kinds of open discussion that seem unlikely to become characteristics of machines. He can become a person who is related to other human beings, a guide and a problem sharer with the young. He can foster creativity and problem-solving based on facts assembled by machine sources. He can live up to the conception of the

---

[22] Catherine Cox Miles, in *Talent and Education,* The Modern School Practices Series #4, E. Paul Torrance, ed., Minneapolis: University of Minnesota Press, 1960, p. 64. Copyright © 1960 by the University of Minnesota.

[23] Educational Policies Commission, *Manpower and Education,* Washington, D.C.: National Education Association, 1956, pp. 104–105. By permission. Italics added.

[24] Patrick Suppes, "Computer-Based Instruction," *RCA Electronic Age* 26: 2–6, Summer 1967, and reprinted in *Educational Digest* 33: 8–10, October 1967. See also William Keppel, *The Necessary Revolution in Education,* New York: Harper & Row, Publishers, 1966.

teacher implied in the comment, "Any teacher who can be replaced by a machine should be!"[25]

C. J. P. Eckert (who with J. W. Mauchey was responsible for the design of ENIAC, the first digital electronic computer) [said] . . . . "After seventeen years, I've finally been forced to adopt the definition that thinking is what computers cannot do. This definition is very workable, since it changes from year to year as computer progress is made."[26]

D. [We are repeatedly told] that, thanks to modern technology, the necessary educational revolution is just around the corner. But is it?

I share with many of my fellow computer scientists and engineers a solid faith that computers will ultimately influence the evolution of human thought as profoundly as has writing. I sympathize with hopes for programmed instruction, language laboratories, television, and film in strips, loops, or reels. Ultimately, however, is not tomorrow. Education's institutional rigidity combined with infant technology's erratic behavior preclude really significant progress in the next decade, if significant progress is interpreted as widespread and *meaningful* adoption, integration, and use of technological devices (including books and blackboards) within the schools. . . .

The President and the Congress set great store on education as a weapon of social reform. The Office of Education is consequently under great pressure to produce immediate results. But when a program must be successful by definition, the need for a good show often overwhelms scientific objectivity; after the curtain falls, little remains either of practical value or of added insight. . . . When ideas that are promising as objects of research and honest experiment give birth, through artificial dissemination, to a brood of hysterical fads, there is the danger that angry reaction will dump out the egg with the shell.[27]

E. We have for the past century conceived of mastery of a subject as being possible for only a minority of students. With this assumption we have adjusted our grading system so as to certify that only a small percent of students (no matter how carefully selected) are awarded a grade of A. If a group of students learns a subject in a superior way (as contrasted with a previous group of students) we still persist in awarding the A (or mastery) to only the top 10 or 15 percent of the students. We grudgingly recognize that the majority of students have "gotten by" by awarding them grades of D or C. Mastery and recognition of mastery under the present relative grading system is unattainable for the majority of students —but this is the result of the way in which we have "rigged" the educa-

[25] William Van Til, and others, members of the executive board of the John Dewey Society, "Educational Technology and Professional Practice," *Insights* [by members of the John Dewey Society]. Volume 4, No. 2, June 1967.

[26] Donald G. Fink, *Computers and the Human Mind*, Garden City, New York: Doubleday, 1966, p. 208.

[27] Anthony G. Oettinger, "The Myths of Educational Technology," *Saturday Review* 51: 76–77, 91 f., May 18, 1968. A member of the Harvard IBM team, Professor Oettinger is author of *Run, Computer, Run,* Cambridge, Mass.: Harvard University Press, 1969.

tional system. . . . [rigged] on the assumption that there is a standard classroom situation for all students. . . . We persist in asking such questions as: What is the best teacher for the *group*? What is the best method of instruction for the *group*? What is the best instructional material for the *group*?

One may start with the very different assumption that individual students may need very different types and qualities of instruction to achieve mastery. . . . [and] define quality of instruction in terms of the degree to which the presentation, explanation, and order of elements of the task to be learned approach the *optimum for a given learner*. . . . [Some] students will need more concrete illustrations and explanations than will others; some students may need more examples to get an idea than do others; some students may need more approval and reinforcement than others; and some students may even need to have several repetitions of the explanation while others may be able to get it the first time. . . . The main point to be stressed is that the quality of instruction is to be considered in terms of its effects on *individual* learners rather than on random *groups* of learners.[28]

THE DROPOUT PROBLEM AND JUVENILE DELINQUENCY: PROS AND CONS

"More than half the inmates in our prisons for adults were once juvenile delinquents. Given proper treatment when they were still young, these men and women might have become responsible citizens, able to contribute their share to society." Are these two statements in quotation marks true? If so, is the lack of "proper treatment" due to racial prejudice or cultural maladjustment (Chapter 2)? Is it due to lack of meaningful religious experience (Chapter 3)? Is it due to outmoded courses of study (Chapter 4)? Is it due to lack of understanding and failure to give the child the needed individual attention (Chapter 5)?

With so many possible answers—and with so little certain knowledge—this topic is obviously one where prejudice and hasty generalizations may easily hold sway. And it should be obvious that the following brief "Pros and Cons" are neither complete nor adequate.

A. It is often said that the lower class child fails in school because he is apathetic or aggressive. Without denying this, some would turn it around and raise the further question whether he is not also increasingly apathetic and aggressive in school because he fails. For what can be more tormenting than to be faced day upon day with a situation you cannot handle and yet may not leave on pain of severe punishment? Insofar as the pre-

[28] Originally published in the UCLA Center for the Study of Evaluation of Instructional Programs, May 1968, Vol. 1, No. 2, the article from which this short excerpt is taken will appear in Bloom, Hastings, and Madaus, *Formative and Summative Evaluation of Student Learning*, New York: McGraw-Hill, Inc., 1970. [Italics added.]

school experiences of the lower class child have not prepared him for school, school can only be a source of frustration: he is neither ready to do what is required nor can he escape. The reaction to this type of frustration is hopelessness and rage. In school, the hopelessness is manifested in apathy, i.e., psychological withdrawal from the source of frustration, and the rage in aggression, i.e., physical attack upon the source of frustration. Ultimately, not only does this failure lead to dropping-out with consequent unemployability, but the patterns of apathy and aggression maintained over the compulsory school years often become stabilized into deep-seated maladjustment and delinquency. From this point of view, compensatory pre-school education may be seen as an effort to bring the experience of the lower class child into greater continuity with the expectations of the school—expectations that presuppose middle class value and language codes for its children—not only in order to increase learning but to avoid the frustrating consequences of the discontinuities between the home and the school.[29]

B. The fundamental problem of the highly creative individual in maintaining his creativity is in learning how to cope with the discomfort which arises from divergency—of so often being a minority of one. Of the problems which arise in this process some of the more important ones include: coping with the sanctions of society against divergency, the alienation of one's friends through the expression of a talent, pressures to be a well-rounded personality, divergence from sex-role norms, desires to learn on one's own, attempts at tasks which are too difficult, searching for a purpose, having different values and being motivated by different rewards, and searching for one's uniqueness. Running throughout all of these problems, of course, are factors which lead to psychological estrangement from others—parents, teachers, and peers.[30]

C. There is no scientific evidence regarding the effect of religion as such on crime.[31]

D. We must assume that there is a reason for all human behavior. This is something that we have learned only recently. We assume, curiously, that the behavior of animals is wise, so that a bird building a nest in an unexpected place teaches us something new. But when we see a human do something a little different that we cannot interpret immediately, we think he is very foolish. We must take the view, heuristically, that every action by a normal human being has some positive reason for existing. . . . If some action seems foolish to us, it is because *we* do not understand

[29] J. W. Getzels, "Pre-School Education," *Teachers College Record* 48: 218–228, December 1966. (Contains excellent bibliography.) See also Sarah H. Lepper and others, *Good Schools for Young Children: A Guide for Working with Three-, Four-, and Five-Year-Old Children*, New York: Crowell-Collier and Macmillan, Inc., 2nd ed., 1968.

[30] E. Paul Torrance, *Guiding Creative Talent*, Englewood Cliffs, N.J.: Prentice-Hall, Inc., © 1962, p. 124. By permission. See also Banish Hoffman, *The Tyranny of Testing*, New York: Crowell-Collier and Macmillan, Inc., 1962.

[31] Father R. W. Murray and F. T. Flynn, *Social Problems*, New York: Appleton-Century-Crofts, 1938, p. 471.

the reasons, and it is we who are foolish when we act on the opposite assumption. The first rule that I have learned as an anthropologist is to assume optimistically that there is some positive reason for the behavior of any person or any community. Thus, nothing is to be treated negatively. We do not say that groups lack something or they would not do this; rather we recognize limitations on our own understanding of why each group acts in a particular way. . . .

Therefore, when we come to think of reasons why people do not accept literacy, we have to think not that there is something wrong with them. Rather we must seek some positive reason either why they have rejected literacy (if they have had it) or why it is felt to be dysfunctional in their situation. . . . It is not enough to say, "Well, they must be a cultural difference." What we need to know are the reasons why they act as they do. In thinking of the disadvantaged Negroes living under slum conditions, we must understand that many do not see the *function* of literacy, and hence respond poorly to education. It isn't going to substantially improve any individual's position in society to give him a fourth grade education. . . . The language which Negro children speak with their families is only one of several attributes of Negro culture which seem to be under attack in many schools. Teachers need to accept the language which Negro children bring to school, to recognize that it is a perfectly appropriate vehicle for communicating ideas in the Negro home and subculture. The teacher must encourage Negro children to learn a new English dialect, the informal English dialect of the school room, without making an attack on the dialect which children associate with their homes and their identity as Negroes.[32]

Open Book Exam

1. Are schools today overemphasizing the talented few, or the exceptionally weak, and neglecting the average or mediocre student? Rosenhaupt and others warn of the possibility that an overemphasis upon academic brilliance will stultify creativity, fail to provide the college-level preparation required for a host of vital occupations, and produce a "disenfranchised and mal-content middle class" analogous to that which supported Adolf Hitler. (For the Rosenhaupt statement, see "In Defense of the Average," *Education, USA*, National Education Association, October 4, 1962, p. 19.) How valid are these concerns and what are the preeminent school reforms or modifications they seem to require?
2. Some critics argue that special public education for the gifted is inherently undemocratic and is tantamount to unequal educational opportunities. The concern is that such separate treatment tends to isolate the potential leaders from the larger society and to restrict their intimate

[32] Sol Tax, "Group Identity and Educating the Disadvantaged," in *Language Programs for the Disadvantaged*, National Council of Teachers of English, Champaign, Ill.: 1966, pp. 205–215.

association with most of those with whom, or for whom, they will ultimately have to work as adults. Is there any evidence to support these contentions, in whole or in part? Is there any evidence to indicate that the schooling of the average student (and the below-average) is enhanced by the removal of the more able students from the regular classroom?

3. Increasing numbers of able students are enrolling in "advanced placement programs," or in special college level classes while still in high school. Discuss the merits and demerits (and the practical difficulties) of such programs. Assess the benefits claimed for a longer period in high school as compared with the advantages associated with graduation from school one or two years sooner.
4. Distinguish between the gifted and the creative child. Should these children be grouped heterogeneously or homogeneously? Support your answer.
5. Discuss the relative merits and demerits of "segregation by talent or ability" versus "homogeneous ability grouping."

   A series of short two- to three-minute discussions on this topic might be organized by showing the relation of the above problem to such other types of segregation as:

   a. Segregation by sex versus coeducation.
   b. Segregation on the basis of economic or social status versus common schooling for all economic and social classes.
   c. Segregation by age levels (as in the typical graded school) versus the "one-room school."
   d. Segregation into religious denominations versus common or "secular" schools.
   e. Segregation by race versus desegregation.
   f. Segregation of child "workers" (for example, "C.C.C. programs") versus academic students.

   The same topic may also be approached as it applies:

   g. to the elementary grades;
   h. to the secondary schools;
   i. to colleges and universities.

6. Discuss "preparation," "incubation," "insight," and "verification" as sequences or stages in the history of science. (For data, read John W. Haefele, *Creativity and Innovation*, New York: Reinhold Publishing Corporation, 1962; and Arthur Koestler, *The Act of Creation*, New York: Dell Publishing Co. Inc., 1966.) Assuming this fourfold analysis of constructive thinking is a valid one, discuss specific ways in which it might be applied in education.
7. Discuss the "drill now, think later" theory of education. Would you rate as *superior* a teacher who is able to provoke genuine interest on the part of students in their work, and rate as *inferior* a teacher whose chief emphasis is drill and rote memorization? Or would you rate as the most superior teacher one whose teaching represents a happy balance between (a) drill (habit formation), (b) understanding (comprehension, insight), and (c) appreciation (emotional responsiveness)?
8. Examine specific programmed materials for the subject area (for example,

mathematics), or the grade level (for example, Junior High School) in which you are particularly interested (for example, the programmed text *English 2600* by Joseph C. Blumenthal, published by Harcourt, Brace & World, Inc., 1960). Then, in outline form, list several possible advantages and several possible disadvantages of programmed learning and of teaching machines.

9. Illustrate the meaning of the following statement: A student who has not fully mastered a first lesson is less able to master a second; and any child who is left behind too many times may give up and stop learning anything at all. Do you believe that teaching machines and the nongraded school would help reduce the number of students who are "left behind too many times"? If so, explain why. Be specific.
10. Is pedagogy a science, or is it an art that sometimes employs sciences such as psychology and sociology? Or is it both? Explain. When we speak of teaching as an art, do we mean the art of organizing subject matter? Is it the artful handling of students? Or is it the art of self-mastery and self-control whereby a teacher's personality has an impact on students?
11. Explain the meaning of "team teaching," and illustrate its application in (a) subject matter areas, and (b) in the lower or upper elementary grades. Will team teaching result in a greater differential between "master teachers," "run-of-the-mill teachers," "apprentice teachers," and "teaching assistants"? Will this differential mean that superior *teachers* (as well as counselors or administrators) will receive better financial rewards? (This last question relates more to Chapter 6 than to Chapter 5.)

Chapter 6

NEW PERSPECTIVES FOR THE TEACHING PROFESSION

Toward Greater Professionalism

6.1 INTRODUCTION: THE NEED FOR BETTER TEACHERS

When parents entrust their most precious possessions to the schools it is in the hope that their children may come in contact with the best that has been felt and thought in the world. Insofar as social progress occurs, the best of yesterday becomes the average of today, and the best of today becomes the commonplace of tomorrow. Education cannot be satisfied with the average, the commonplace, the reduction of all to a least common denominator. If our schools are to perform their maximum service, they must transmit the highest product, the ripest fruit, the nearest approximation to truth yet realized by the minds of men.

This includes contact with minds that are discontented with our present best, minds that reach forward to future improvements in unforeseen directions. The issue arises: Who is to decide what *is* best? Those who believe in academic freedom insist that the scholar who is disciplined in and dedicated to his special area of competence should be given freedom to make that decision for himself. If we heed the politician or the pressure group instead of the specialist and scholar, we may be sure that the average, the mediocre, the group with the largest numbers, will prevail. But if we heed the scholar, we have at least a reasonable chance that superiority will win out. Such superiority, of course, is contingent upon the quality of professional knowledge, skill, and expertness of the teacher.

In his field of competence, the technical expert is supposed to be "professional"—that is, capable and objective in his thinking. Hence, if teaching is to be considered a profession—one comparable to the medical profession—the teacher must be allowed great latitude of judgment. A teacher's relation to a student is analogous to that of a doctor advising a patient, or a judge trying a case of law. If such professional people are to make their proper contributions to society, they should be free from intimidation and subordination. Indeed, they should be beyond reasonable suspicion of subjection to such influences, whether from political, religious, or economic pressure groups. When such freedom prevails, the scholar enjoys "academic freedom."

For democracy to survive, each oncoming generation of children must understand the ideals on which democratic society is based. For this purpose, good teachers are of crucial importance. And the questions arise: "What are the attributes of a 'good' teacher?" and "Does the teaching profession, as it exists today, attract people who possess these attributes?"

Nearly everyone will claim to have known at least one remarkable teacher. Of what did his remarkableness consist? The list of characteristics is endless; the desirable qualities are universally respected, yet the definition always eludes us. We speak of the teachers of English and professors of history we have known, and we pay tribute to their knowledge of the subject at hand. Surely, this had much to do with their effectiveness—but not all. Teachers in the fullest sense of their calling are essentially models of the spirit; they represent far more than they present. It is here that their genius, or at least their talent, will lie—and it is this that frustrates any explicit discussion of the ultimate in the art of teaching.

Very well, you say, but why are there so few such teachers? Why are so many, the vast majority, so decidedly otherwise? What must we do to bring more of these artist-teachers into the classroom and onto the campus? Here we are on more solid ground; the answers are not so nebulous. In any age, in any field, the true artists are scarce—and perhaps scarcest of all is that artistry of which Emerson was speaking when in his essay on "Education," he wrote:

> Nature provided for the communication of thought, by planting with it in the receiving mind *a fury to impart* it. 'Tis so in every art, in every science. One burns to tell the new fact, the other burns to hear it. See how far a young doctor will ride or walk to witness a new surgical operation. I have seen a carriage-maker's shop emptied of all its workmen into the street, to scrutinize a new pattern from New York. So in literature, the young man who has taste for poetry, for fine images, for noble thoughts, is insatiable for this nourishment, and forgets all the world for the more learned friend—who finds equal *joy in dealing out his treasures.* (As quoted in Robert Ulich, *Three Thousand Years of Educational Wisdom,* Cambridge: Harvard University Press, 1947, p. 589. Italics added.)

Today the competition for the best minds, the most skillful people, is unprecedentedly intense, not only among institutions within the U.S. but for service around the world. Moreover, as emerging nations sense their needs for literacy, technical skills, and professional sophistication, the demand for education—and therefore for teachers—must mount still higher. Paul Woodring neatly epitomized the basic problem in his perceptive discussion of *New Directions in Teacher Education.* The truly "liberally educated man" (he wrote)

> is one who can make wise decisions independently. He can choose between good and bad, truth and falsehood, the beautiful and the ugly, the worthwhile and the trivial. His education will improve his ability to make ethical decisions, political decisions, decisions within the home and on the job. It will enable him to choose and to appreciate a good book, a good painting, or a good piece of music. It will free him of provincialism and prepare him to understand cultures other than his own. It will enable him to make the many decisions necessary in planning a good life and conducting it properly. This education should be common to all, and independent of vocational choice.[1]

This, of course, is the sort of person who should be teaching our children. But (says Woodring in the same work):

> Unless the quality of people drawn into the teaching profession is maintained and projected on an increasingly higher level, the education of our children is bound to deteriorate. The long-range welfare of our society requires that a reasonable proportion of our ablest young people invest their lives in the development of succeeding generations.
>
> The question facing the schools is how to attract more of the ablest men and women into the profession, how to provide them with the best possible education for the important work they are to do, how to utilize their talents most effectively in the classrooms and laboratories, and how to retain them in the face of competition from other professions.

6.2 TURMOIL IN TEACHING*

T. M. Stinnett

[The status of the teaching profession] depends largely upon the quality of the teacher. . . . Some idea of the rate at which professions have grown may be obtained from the facts that in 1850, professional workers constituted only 1.9 percent of the total labor force and in 1900 only 3.8 percent

---

[1] Paul Woodring, *New Directions in Teacher Education*, New York: Fund for the Advancement of Education, 1957, pp. 8, 14.

* The first portion of this selection is from T. M. Stinnett, *The Profession of Teaching*, Washington, D.C.: The Center for Applied Research in Education, 1962, pp. v, 2, 3, 85, 99. The second portion is reprinted with permission of the Macmillan Company from *Turmoil in Teaching* by T. M. Stinnett (pp. 34–37). Copyright © by T. M. Stinnett, 1968.

T. M. Stinnett is Visiting Professor of Education, Texas A & M University, College Station, and former Assistant Executive Secretary for Professional Development and Welfare, National Education Association of the United States.

We may recall Flexner's brief definition of a profession. "The essence of . . . profes-

[whereas in 1950 they constituted 6.4 percent]. To state the development in another way, the total working force of the United States increased 8 times between 1850 and 1950, but professional workers increased 26 times. . . . Flexner enumerates six criteria of professions:

1. They involve essentially intellectual operations.
2. They derive their raw materials from science and learning.
3. They work up this material to a practical and definite end.
4. They possess an educationally communicable technique.
5. They tend toward self-organization.
6. They are becoming increasingly altruistic in nature.

To the list above [Myron] Lieberman would add two criteria of great significance:

1. A broad range of autonomy for both the individual practitioners and for the occupational group as a whole; and
2. An acceptance by the practitioners of broad personal responsibility for judgments made and acts performed within the scope of professional autonomy. . . .

[L. D.] Haskew has identified the difference between professional education and nonprofessional education as threefold. (1) Professional education does not leave to chance the cultivation of those attributes—ethics, disciplines, methods of thought, allegiances—which make the professional fit to assume the trusteeship which society entrusts to him. (2) Professional education focuses upon the person as an individual who is to practice and seeks to broaden his human—that is, his mental, moral, and emotional—capacities. (3) Professional education simply cannot stop short of performance; it cannot accept without unmistakable proof the dictum that knowledge alone is power. . . .

Perhaps the single greatest need of teaching—to achieve recognized professional status—depends upon raising minimum preparation levels to those of the other professions. This movement is underway with goals of five years preservice preparation for classroom teachers for elementary and secondary school teachers, and of six years for special-school-service personnel. These plans are generally endorsed by the profession and have been implemented already in some states. In addition to extending the years of preparation, there are equally important goals of achieving more rigorous and selective admission requirements and of improving the quality of the preparing programs. The fact that responsibility for a good teacher education program is being assumed by the entire faculties of colleges and universities, rather than simply by the education or teacher training depart-

sions resides in the application of free, resourceful, unhampered intelligence to the comprehension of problems."—Abraham Flexner, *Universities—American, English, German*, New York: Oxford University Press, 1930, p. 29.

ments, indicates that the job of providing teachers has been accepted by the higher education institutions as an endeavor of first importance.

[The increasing awareness that teaching is a profession is only one of several] causes of new militancy among teachers. . . . *The first and obvious causal factor is the mounting anger of teachers with economic injustice specifically and with the relative economic neglect of schools generally*. . . . Teachers behold the spectacle of national groups plugging for ever growing Federal appropriations for military hardware but consistently fighting general grants for the schools. They see the most menial kind of laborers being rewarded far beyond teachers. They know that some 40 per cent of the young men in teaching, those who want to make a career of their profession—and up to 75 percent of the married men—have to moonlight in one, two, three, and even four extra jobs to support their families. The general public rationale for teachers' moonlighting often is not that salaries are inadequate but that teachers want to keep up with the Joneses.

The second causal factor in the upsurge of teacher restiveness is the changed working conditions and the changed fabric of the teaching profession.

Some of the obvious changes are as follows:

1. *The rapid decrease in the number of school districts, with a consequent enlargement of the size of the average school district.* This is a factor of considerable import. In 1931–32, for example, there were in the United States a total of 127,422 districts. By 1965–66, this total had dwindled to about 27,000 with as many as 2,500 not operating schools.

The significance of this decline is that, as districts grow larger, paternalism in staff relations declines in appeal; also, staffs are better prepared.

The enlarged size of school districts, of course, tends to impersonalize staff relationships, as well as to make more complex and difficult effective communications between the administration and staff. Often the result is staff dissatisfaction and frustration, and a rebellious attitude tends to develop among segments of the staff.

2. *A recent and steady increase in the number of young people, especially men, in the teaching force.* In 1955–56, about 26 per cent of the public-school teaching staff were men; in 1963–64 this percent had increased to 32. In 1955–56, the median age of all teachers in the public schools was 42.9; in 1963–64 this median had dropped to 39.9. In the latter year, the median age of men was 34; of women, 44.3. In 1963–64, about one third of all men were under 30 years of age.

These are factors of great significance. The new college graduates entering teaching are a new breed. They have grown up in a new social and economic milieu. Their preparation for teaching is different, more comprehensive, more realistic. They have a different concept of the roles and rights of teachers. The traditional image—an image held by society generally and too often by teachers themselves—of the teacher as a sort of indentured servant or often timid hired hand, something of a third-class citizen, inept and bumbling, who must be told by his betters what to do and when to do it, is not acceptable to teachers in general any more. This has been a subtle, almost imperceptible change in the teaching profession. Its impact is profound and cannot be ignored in the future.

3. A *fact closely allied to the infusion of new blood into the teaching ranks: the increasingly higher levels of preparation and, thus, of competence of any given total teaching staff.*

In the short span of a decade and a half, the requirements for preparation and licensure of beginning elementary-school teachers has risen drastically. From little or no requirement of college work in many states the minimum requirement of the bachelor's degree is now almost universal. Preparation for high-school teachers is rapidly climbing toward the master's degree. In 1955–56 the percent of public-school teachers with preparation below the bachelor's degree was 22.2. By 1965–66, it had dropped to 7.0.

For high-school teachers the preparation levels are, of course, still higher. In 1955–56, about 97 percent of high-school teachers held bachelor's degrees or had higher preparations; by 1965–66 the percent had increased to about 99.4. Perhaps the most significant factor of all is that elementary-school teachers are rapidly closing the gap between their preparation and that of their high-school colleagues. . . . The significance here is that, as this gap in preparation is closed, staff attitudes become more uniform and perhaps on the more aggressive side.

These figures point up clearly that the era of the typical teacher as a normal-school graduate, equipped only with meager general and liberal education and a bag of tricks, has ended. Typically, the new teacher now is well-educated, competent, and confident. The profile of the nation's public-school teaching staff has changed. So has its outlook and its posture. Yesterday's paternalistic treatment of teachers is likewise outmoded.

The third causal factor, which obviously is at the heart of the new and aggressive climate among teachers, is the hunger to be a real part of a creative enterprise, not cogs in a well-oiled machine. . . . This means participation of the staff in the decision-making regarding policies under which teachers work. There seems to be an automatic assumption that the term *professional negotiations* applies exclusively to salaries. This is erroneous. Salary policy is only one among many problems. The process has to do with conditions of work, teacher load, personnel policies, grievances, conditions of employment, promotion, tenure and dismissal, academic freedom, textbook selection, curriculum determination, and a whole cluster of related policies. . . .

To put the matter bluntly, the period of the old line-staff relationship, of the benevolent despot or the benevolent paternalist, of the hierarchial concept in administration is rapidly fading from the American scene. There are still some pockets left where there are such attitudes on the part of both school boards and school administrators, but they are on their way out.

6.3 TEACHER EDUCATION: LIBERAL AND PEDAGOGICAL*

Hugo Beck

[There is a mistaken view that] the content of teacher education . . . [is] a contest between liberal education and professional education . . . between liberal arts and pedagogical methodology . . . [with the implicit assumption that there is a] dualism of content and method, liberal and pedagogical. . . .

It is not our intention here to define a sound liberal education. We assume that every liberal arts graduate has been exposed to the four domains of knowledge; physical science, biological science, social science, and humanistic studies. Further, we hope that every liberal arts graduate is familiar with the methods of inquiry developed in each domain, methods that account for discovering, testing, revising, extending, and communicating knowledge in that area.

In our approach to the education of secondary-school teachers, the undergraduate program would be the responsibility of the liberal arts college, since the education of future teachers is similar in content to the education of students in other professions. Beyond the point of undergraduate education, however, the training of future teachers begins to develop in specialized areas.

The first area is competence in education as an academic discipline in its own right with its own identifiable subject matter. Education is but one field of knowledge in the larger context of the social sciences. It takes its place along with sociology, political science, anthropology, and economics as a field that attempts to study some aspect of society and the relationships of the individual within that particular area of concern. Specifically, education is inquiry into the way in which society transmits the culture

* Hugo Beck, "An Approach to the Teaching of Secondary-School Teachers," *School Review* 69: 437–448, Winter 1961. Footnote references and bibliography here omitted.

Hugo Beck is Administrative Coordinator of the Master of Arts in Teaching Program at the University of Chicago.

and the accumulated wisdom of that culture to each new generation. Education is the study of the transformation of the individual from a dependent, immature being into one who, by communication with his fellow men, comes to understand the natural forces in his environment and is able to exercise more and more control over that environment. Even if there were no departments of education in the conventional sense and no pedagogical methodology, education would still have a legitimate place in the curriculum of the social sciences.

The secondary-school teacher also needs competence in the specialized subject-matter fields he plans to teach. Whether his field is biology, history, English, or foreign languages, he must be thoroughly conversant with the methods of inquiry of that field. Competent scholars in these fields can assist the teacher-scholar in developing criteria for the selection of materials that are crucial for course content for secondary-school students.

Third, the secondary-school teacher must have facility in areas of education that are germane to the teaching-learning situation. He must have insights into theories of learning, into motivation, evaluation, individual differences, group influence, the structure of social organizations, the effect of the social and the natural milieu—all areas grounded in and developed through the liberal arts tradition and of special concern to the behavioral sciences. An interdisciplinary approach is needed so that each department does not perpetually rediscover the wheel. The lines of communication must be kept open so that when knowledge is discovered in one discipline that has relevance to another the knowledge may be readily shared.

Fourth, the secondary-school teacher must have competence in the technological and the technical aspects of education. This area includes the methods of teaching a specific subject, the development of learning materials, the use of audio-visual techniques to supplement and complement the teacher's role. In short, we are concerned here with the teaching process. If these areas are taught in teacher-education institutions as accumulated folklore, as tried and true practices, as recipes for action, or as "seat of the pants" judgment, the academician may validly object that education courses lack a scientific approach. But this area of pedagogy can be taught, and in a few departments of education is being taught, with as much rigor and as much dedication to a theoretical rationale as any of the social sciences.

The education of teachers has still one more dimension: the art of teaching, which is a synthesis of the four areas described here and which culminates in the actual teaching-learning situation that the teacher meets in the classroom. In the art of teaching, insights and concepts gleaned from all four of these areas are brought to bear on the child to facilitate his learning. The blending of these insights and concepts into a meaningful approach is a task that calls for personal inquiry and reflection, a task that the teacher must do for himself. No one can do it for him. Many sources of competent assistance are available, however: scholars from the great categories of human knowledge, scholars in the field of education, intelligent schoolmen who are skilled practitioners, and master teachers under whose direction the beginning teacher observes and teaches. Here again responsibility must be shared. A department of education, in isolation, cannot by itself enable the teacher to develop the art of teaching. All who are involved in the advancement of learning need to share this responsibility, which, in the past, academic scholars and practitioners have often shirked. . . .

The approach to teacher-education we have sketched would not replace a liberal education. It would be an extension of a liberal education. It would combine the talents of a variety of scholars. It would present the opportunity for members of academic departments in colleges and universities and members of the teaching profession in the field to assume a more vigorous role in the education of teachers. Whether this program can resolve the basic dilemma in teacher education remains to be seen. It may carry the seeds of a better plan for developing the inquiring teachers desperately needed in our schools today.

Education is not the sole concern of a single department. It depends on a variety of disciplines for insights and concepts. It is a fruitless task to try to determine which portion of the education of teachers belongs to the education department and which belongs to the academic tradition. Teacher education is an invitation to inquiry that embraces all disciplines.[2]

---

[2] Editor's Note: For examples of education as an art, or as a craft, read Stanley L. Clement, "Seven Principles of Learning," *Clearing House*, 36: 23–26, Sept. 1961; also W. E. McPhee, R. A. Granger, and others, in *Bulletin of the National Association of Secondary-School Principals*, 45: 80–93, December 1961.

The foregoing essay by Hugo Beck is concerned with the preparation of teachers for secondary schools and may suggest, by implication, that the preparation of elementary school teachers must be conceived in fundamentally different terms. But there is a growing body of professional and scholarly opinion, reflected in Selection 5.12 by George D. Stoddard, to the effect that the elementary school teacher too must be an expert in some field. Recent developments in the study of the teaching of mathematics and physics, for example, indicate that the primary grades may be the best places to introduce fundamental mathematical or physical principles. To be sure, this instruction will be in suitably elementary terms, but it means that at least some primary teachers should have been mathematics majors—and, of course, that all primary teachers will have carried their study of mathematics farther than is presently customary. And who more than the elementary teacher requires a broad, liberal education?

6.4 ACADEMIC FREEDOM IN THE PUBLIC SCHOOLS*

E. Edmund Reutter, Jr.

MEANING OF ACADEMIC FREEDOM

To most educators "academic freedom" is a cherished concept, although frequently it is a nebulous one when specifics are involved.

It is important to note that academic freedom is essentially a tradition—not a right of educators in the legal sense of rights. It is not found in the Bill of Rights with such rights as freedom of religion, of the press, of assembly. Nor does it frequently find its way directly into statutes. Furthermore, only scant help has been furnished by the courts which over the years have woven patterns of interpretation of other rights and freedoms.

"Freedom" connotes an absence of restraints. Legal restraints on teachers are to be found primarily in state statutes and in local board of education regulations—and of course in the interpretations of the courts when these have been litigated. . . .

The concept of academic freedom was born and raised on the college level, and the classic statement of its meaning is to be found in that of the American Association of University Professors. Excerpts from this statement follow:

> The teacher is entitled to freedom in the classroom in discussing his subject, but he should be careful not to introduce into his teaching controversial matter which has no relation to his subject. . . . The college or university teacher is a citizen, a member of a learned profession, and an officer of an educational institution. When he speaks or writes as a citizen, he should be free from institutional censorship or discipline, but his special position in the community imposes special obligations. As a man of learning and an educational officer, he should remember that the public may judge his profession and his institution by his utterances. Hence he should at all times be accurate, should exercise appropriate restraint, should show respect for the opinions of others and should make every effort to indicate that he is not an institutional spokesman.

---

* E. E. Reutter, Jr., "Legal Aspects of Academic Freedom," in Leo O. Garber, ed., *Current Legal Concepts in Education*, Philadelphia: University of Pennsylvania Press, 1966, pp. 253–268. Footnote references here omitted.

Edmund Reutter, Jr., is Professor of Education at Teachers College, Columbia University, and author of many books and articles on school law and administration.

APPLICATION TO THE PUBLIC SCHOOLS

Attempts to apply this college tradition of academic freedom to the public schools sometimes meet with difficulties of philosophy as well as of implementation. . . .

On the university level, professors are engaged essentially in extending the frontiers of knowledge. The nature of the university is to derive and test new ideas and theories. The prototype of the university professor is that of an authority in his academic field. He is a scholar, more than he is a teacher. Conversely, in schools below the college level, instructors are primarily disseminators, rather than producers, of knowledge.

A second possibly pertinent difference between colleges and lower levels of education relates to the maturity of students. Presumedly, chronological age and prior training make the typical college student better able to weigh evidence and to reach independent conclusions than his brothers and sisters in elementary and secondary schools. A third consideration is based on the fact that children are required to attend public school—or an appropriate equivalent—whereas college attendance is voluntary and not required by the state. Also, in most colleges and universities there is an opportunity for students to avoid certain courses or instructors. Choice is much more limited in the typical school below college level.

Whether these differences are germane may depend upon the situations in which "academic freedom" is called into play. . . .

RECENT JUDICIAL INTERPRETATIONS: EMPLOYMENT

Eligibility for employment in the public schools is circumscribed to a considerable extent by state-administered certification requirements. While many of these indirectly affect teacher freedoms, they are generally not of serious concern to this topic. It is clear that the state can require good moral character as well as academic qualifications. The Supreme Court of Oregon in 1963 sustained the denial of a certificate to a man who had several years before been convicted of several burglaries. The Supreme Court of California the year before found valid a statute prohibiting employment in the public schools of persons convicted of certain sex offenses where the statute was applied prospectively only.

Of considerable concern within the employment area are state statutes requiring teachers to take oaths indicating that they will not do certain kinds of things related to violent overthrow of the government, or that they will not teach certain types of doctrines. . . . It was in 1961 that the United States Supreme Court, treating again the question of loyalty oaths as a condition of employment, sustained the validity of the requirement of an oath in general but struck down a specific provision in the oath required of Florida teachers. The offensive element to which the person had to swear was that he had never knowingly lent his "aid, support, advice, counsel, or influence to the Communist Party." In a unanimous decision the United States Supreme Court found that "the provision is completely lacking in . . . terms susceptible of objective measurement . . . [and thus] violates the first essential of due process of law."

In June of 1964, the Supreme Court by a 7–2 margin invalidated a pair of Washington oaths on the grounds of "vagueness." The majority re-emphasized, however, "We do not question the power of a state to take proper measures safeguarding the public service from disloyal conduct. But measures which purport to define disloyalty must allow public servants to know what is and is not disloyal." . . . .

CLASSROOM PERFORMANCE

Recent court actions involving classroom performance include a wide variety of situations.

The Supreme Court of Wisconsin held that a teacher's discussion of sex matters in class was of a nature such as to warrant his removal. An instructor in speech, introduced certain items which, in the eyes of the court, constituted conduct transcending contemporary standards of propriety. The fact that the teacher had had some graduate work in the field of home and family living did not give him the right under "academic freedom" to introduce such matters. The decision was based primarily upon the nature of the comments made by the teacher, although two concurring judges emphasized the fact that the teacher was not certified in biology and therefore was not entitled to discuss such matters in his speech class. . . .

An appellate court in Illinois has concluded that a local board of education could require tenure teachers who did not have bachelors' degrees to earn a reasonable number of college credits within a reasonable period of time and could dismiss those teachers who failed to comply with the regulation. The case would appear to sustain the point of view that academic freedom does not involve the right to be judged solely on performance when one's qualifications fall far below those that are required in the present day to do a particular job.

SCHOOL-RELATED ACTIVITIES

Litigation is increasing in situations which are clearly school-related but do not involve the teaching function directly. For example, can a teacher be required to supervise a bowling club which meets after school hours off school premises and is not officially a school-sponsored activity, although it is sanctioned by the school board? "No," said the Supreme Court of Pennsylvania late in 1963. It found the assignment not closely enough related to the school program to justify a teacher's being required to accept the assignment.

On the other hand, according to another Pennsylvania court, a teacher can be required to attend "open house" at school during American Education Week. . . .

In Louisiana a teacher of industrial arts was directed to have his students, as part of their instructional program, construct wooden forms for a sidewalk leading to the school. He refused, claiming that the activity was construction work. The appellate court found the assignment reasonably related to the curriculum and therefore ruled against the teacher.

In New York City a teacher refused to participate in school-conducted Civil Defense drills on the grounds of conscience. He was dismissed and his license revoked. In 1963 this matter came before a court, which held that the action of the school authorities was sound legally because the teacher could "constitutionally be required to participate in the . . . [Civil Defense] drills, notwithstanding his scruples against nuclear warfare, since drills are purely a defensive measure and not coercive of preparation for nuclear war against such scruples."

PERSONAL ACTIVITIES

. . . In the area of out-of-school activities of a personal nature, which activities reflect on the teacher's role as an example to students, the courts continue to find that where the conduct is such that a board can reasonably determine it to be prejudicial to the teacher's reputation, grounds for dismissal exist. Recent examples include an Illinois teacher who became intoxicated in public on several occasions and was arrested therefor, and a New Mexico teacher who had pleaded guilty to a charge of assault on a woman following a brawl in a tavern. In New York, however, the Appellate Division ordered reinstated a teacher who had been arrested in a gambling raid, pleaded guilty and paid a fine. . . .

A very significant judicial decision by an appellate court of California concerned the freedom of a public junior college teacher to publish in the local newspaper letters criticizing the schools of the county where the teacher taught. In some of the letters the teacher was exceptionally critical of the administration, and some of his statements were highly emotional. The case is of particular significance because the teacher's conduct was examined by the Commission of Personnel Standards of the California Teachers Association (a panel having statutory status in the expert witness category). This commission recommended that the teacher's employment be terminated as it would be likely to lead to difficulties both for him and for the district. The appellate court, however, disagreed, and while recognizing that his language might have been "somewhat intemperate," held that the teacher could not be kept from joining in the public debate on the subject of education by virtue of the fact that he happened to be a teacher in the system. (The trial court had upheld the dismissal, but the court of appeal reversed.)

That a degree of restraint in expressing attitudes is expected of teachers is illustrated in a recent Massachusetts case. The highest court of that state added to our knowledge of legal limits on academic freedom by establishing the point that a teacher can be discharged for calling the superintendent an "s. o. b.!". . . . The many legal aspects in the area of collective action of teachers are only beginning to be clarified.[3]

AN ASSESSMENT

How, then, has academic freedom fared over the last few years? My conclusion is that this has been neither a dramatically good nor a dramatically poor period for academic freedom so far as legal aspects are concerned. In some respects legislatures have continued their proclivity to restrict certain teacher freedoms, but not nearly so much in the political area as they did in the immediate post-World War II period. At the same time legislatures have shown some inclination to be more generous in according freedoms to teachers in such areas as collective action, recognition of professional associations and determination of teacher qualifications. . . .

It is my belief that there is need for the profession to come to grips with just what academic freedom implies in the way of responsibilities to accompany the right and in terms of determining when the freedom has been abridged. Once there is some agreement here the next step is to communicate the concept to the public. . . .

It is important to keep in mind, however, that most of the situations that might be considered to involve academic freedom are handled without resort to the courts. Tenure laws and actions of professional associations have tended to put a brake on some flagrant abuses of academic freedom. Also there is reason to be encouraged by some evidence that the public may be beginning more to recognize that it is in the public interest to protect academic freedom. (I must hasten to add, however, that I wish I felt more secure in noting this to be a trend.). . . .

[3] Editor's Note: See Myron Lieberman, "Collective Negotiations: Status and Trends," *American School Board Journal* 155: 7–10, October 1967; summarized in *The Education Digest* 33: 24–26, December 1967. Problems of local versus regional control, as well as UFT—AFT—NEA conflicts, are discussed in the *Phi Delta Kappan* 50: 249–305, January 1969.

It also seems pertinent to emphasize another non-legal point. . . . Self-imposed restraints [by teachers on themselves] are no less detrimental to a good educational program than are the more tangible ones. Probably they are more insidious because they cannot be combated as effectively. Often a teacher does not realize that he is weakening his teaching by avoiding controversial matters or that he is undermining his profession by meekly submitting to all sorts of pressures. Not infrequently, moreover, a teacher may be unaware of the restrictions he actually is placing on himself and his teaching.

If we compare the restrictions placed on public school teachers today with those placed on them a few decades ago, the progress is remarkable. On the other hand, there may be some reason to believe that for the last few years we have been on something of a plateau in regard to freedom of the public school teacher. Such a plateau on a higher level has also existed for a longer period of time in regard to the university teacher.

Most gains for academic freedom made in the past have been interwoven with improvements in two basic factors—professionalization of the occupation of teaching and public understanding of the process of education. Any progress in connection with these factors will be progress toward more academic freedom, more secure academic freedom and more responsible academic freedom in the educational system of our country. Here lies the challenge of educators.[4]

---

[4] Editor's Note: Compare the following:

There is little doubt that given the present governmental structure teachers' organizations could, if they choose to do so, exert considerably more influence over the future of education than they are now doing. . . .

A concerted effort needs to be made to consolidate and integrate the many organizational segments within the broad institution of education. . . . The achievement of unity within a profession of education will not come easily. . . . [because] there are forces at work which tend to fractionate the profession, such as the trend toward specialization in administration and guidance services for example, and the elevated statuses of certain groups such as science and mathematics teachers as a consequence of the National Science Foundation programs. The objective of the profession must be to achieve consensus on important questions confronting the profession as a whole and at the same time to maintain an internal governing structure that can tolerate the emergence of powerful subdivisions within itself. . . .

[To improve] the professional character of their service . . . the following steps seem to be warranted: (1) Teachers themselves must take more responsibility for controlling entry into the practice of teaching—such action would involve modifying the control now exercised by certification boards, legislatures, and/or teacher training institutions. (2) Teachers must accept the sometimes distasteful, but most essential, task of policing their own membership. . . . (3) Teachers must refine and extend their stockpile of esoteric knowledge. This step will not be an easy one, judging from difficulty experienced in the past in deciding just what the content of education is. . . .

—R. L. Campbell, L. L. Cunningham, and R. F. McPhee, *The Organization and Control of American Education*, Columbus, Ohio: Charles E. Merrill Books, Inc., 1965, pp. 260, 284, 285.

6.5 FREE TEACHERS—THE PRIESTHOOD OF DEMOCRACY*

David Fellman

In many ways, democratic government asks much of people. Since it relies upon persuasion and reason, it asks them to do some thinking, and particularly, to think a great deal about difficult public questions. Every educator knows how very painful thinking really is, both for himself and his students. It can hardly be denied that many people have found a considerable measure of satisfaction in dictatorship because it releases them from the irksome obligation of thinking. Furthermore, democracy asks us to be tolerant even of those with whom we may be in sharpest disagreement. Since intolerance of dissident opinions is certainly as "natural" as tolerance, and in fact seems to require much less of an exertion of will, this too is asking a good deal of us. Democracy is incorrigibly skeptical and tends therefore to be unsatisfying for those who demand the security of a full set of the correct answers to all the questions which perplex the human race. Democracy is not so much concerned with correct answers as it is with a methodology for reaching essentially tentative decisions in a workaday world.

We have to recognize that the price we must pay for living in a free speech society is very great, though of course we are persuaded that the price is not too great. . . . Far more wonderful than our oversized automobiles, our television and air-conditioning, our jet planes and our hydrogen bombs, is the free human mind. Good government, the cultivation of the arts, the progress of the sciences and technology, all require an atmosphere of freedom of thought and of freedom to put thought into words. The price may seem to be a steep one, but what is purchased is the greatest bargain in all history. . . .

No one can deny that academic freedom, like all freedoms, must operate within the terms of the accepted and dominant culture, in all countries, but for us the difference lies in the character of the American culture, which is based upon freedom and democracy. We agree with Lord Acton

* The first two paragraphs of this essay are from David Fellman, *The Limits of Freedom*, New Brunswick, N.J.: Rutgers University Press, 1959, pp. 92, 122–123. By permission. The remaining paragraphs are from David Fellman, "Academic Freedom in American Law," 1961 *Wisconsin Law Review*, 3–46, January 1961. By permission. David Fellman is Professor of Law at the University of Wisconsin. See also W. P. Murphy, "Educational Freedom in the Courts," *AAUP Bulletin*, 49: 328–359, December 1963.

that "at the root of all liberty is the liberty to learn." Our view of higher education is reflected in the famous remarks which Thomas Jefferson made about the time of the founding of the University of Virginia in 1820: "This institution will be based upon the illimitable freedom of the human mind. For here we are not afraid to follow truth, wherever it may lead, nor to tolerate any error so long as reason is left free to combat it." We also agree with Cardinal Newman that a university is a place

> . . . in which the intellect may safely range and speculate, sure to find its equal in some antagonistic activity, and its judge in the tribunal of truth. It is a place where inquiry is pushed forward, and discoveries verified and perfected, and rashness rendered innocuous, and error exposed, by the collision of mind with mind, and knowledge with knowledge.

Thus in our American civilization the university must operate without intellectual boundaries because it must be completely free to search for the truth, and, as W. T. Couch once observed: "Academic freedom is the principle designed to protect the teacher from hazards that tend to prevent him from meeting his obligations in the pursuit of truth."

The principal device for preserving academic freedom is a tenure system. Briefly, tenure has come to mean that after a defined probationary period the teacher acquires a permanent position from which he cannot be discharged without good cause shown, upon specific notice and a fair hearing, or what has come to be known as academic due process. Tenure does not mean that a teacher cannot be discharged from his job at all, but it does mean that he cannot be dismissed arbitrarily. . . .

All sorts of subjects have caused trouble in the schools, including religion, science, history, politics, questions of war and peace, and above all, social and economic issues, such as those dealing with free trade, monetary policy, labor problems, government regulation of business, public utilities, communism and other varieties of radicalism, sex and birth control, prohibition and race questions. As long ago as 1901, President Hyde of Bowdoin College pointed out that one of the basic reasons for the rise in academic freedom cases at that time was that increasingly the colleges and universities were concerning themselves with social and economic questions which divide the public and which people care about. In a broader sense, it must be noted that in the nature of things the scholar is necessarily a disturbing person, since he is professionally committed to raising questions about accepted ideas and institutions which, as in the case of Socrates, are bound to evoke reactions ranging from uneasiness to alarm. Professors deal with new ideas, and as Walter Bagehot once observed, "one of the greatest pains to human nature is the pain of a new idea." . . .

No teacher, whether protected by legal tenure or not, has a right to his job if he does his work incompetently, and appellate courts have often upheld dismissals for reasons of incompetence or negligence. Such facts as inability to maintain discipline, lack of knowledge of subject matter and inability to cooperate with colleagues, serving as a barmaid in her husband's beer garden after school hours, publicly advocating no participation in any way in a war effort on grounds of conscientious objection, subjection to epileptic fits, or striking a child in anger, have been held by courts to justify dismissals for incompetence. Of course, the burden of proving incompetence is on the school authorities, and dismissals on this ground have been set aside by reviewing courts where they found the proof insufficient. Thus, it has been held that incompetence is not established by the mere fact that the teacher signed the nominating papers of a communist candidate for office, nor by the fact that the teacher committed in the course of a long and faithful service a single breach of strict ethics by feigning illness to go hunting, nor by the mere fact that pupils and parents express dissatisfaction.

Courts have sanctioned many other reasons for dismissing teachers from their posts . . . lack of students . . . neglect of duty . . . unprofessional conduct . . . insubordination . . . belonging, contrary to regulations, to trade unions . . . marriage. . . .

[Nevertheless] the United States Supreme Court has spoken out more and more clearly in defense of academic freedom. . . . [Thus] Mr. Justice Frankfurter said:

> That our democracy ultimately rests on public opinion is a platitude of speech but not a commonplace in action. Public opinion is the ultimate reliance of our society only if it be disciplined and responsible. It can be disciplined and responsible only if habits of open-mindedness and of critical inquiry are acquired in the formative years of our citizens. The process of education has naturally enough been the basis of hope for the perdurance of our democracy on the part of all our great leaders, from Thomas Jefferson onwards.
>
> To regard teachers—in our entire educational system, from the primary grades to the university—as the priests of our democracy is therefore not to indulge in hyperbole. It is the special task of teachers to foster those habits of open-mindedness and critical inquiry which alone make for responsible citizens, who, in turn, make possible an enlightened and effective public opinion. Teachers must fulfill their function by precept and practice, by the very atmosphere which they generate; they must be exemplars of open-mindedness and free inquiry. They cannot carry out their noble task if the conditions for the practice of a responsible and critical mind are denied to them. They must have the freedom of responsible inquiry, by thought and action, into the meaning of social and economic ideas, into the checkered history of social and economic dogma. They must be free to sift evanescent doctrine, qualified by time and circumstance, from that

restless, enduring process of extending the bounds of understanding and wisdom, to assure which the freedoms of thought, of speech, of inquiry, of worship are guaranteed by the Constitution. . . .[5]

---

[5] Felix Frankfurter, *Wieman v. Updegraff*, 344 U.S. 183 (1952) (majority opinion). See also the minority opinion of Justice William O. Douglas, *Adler v. Board of Education*, 342 U.S. 485 (1952).

The Role of the Teacher in Policy Making

6.6 INCREASING TEACHER PARTICIPATION IN POLICY MAKING*

American Association of School Administrators

Basic to the recent upsurge of teacher demands for participation in school policy making is the rapid elevation of teacher competence as reflected in increased preparation. At the close of World War II, it is estimated that not more than 35 percent of public-school teachers held degrees. In 1965–66 it is estimated that 92 percent held one or more degrees and that the average preparation of all public-school teachers was about 4.6 years of college.

The significance of this drastic upgrading is to be found in the feeling of self-confidence of teachers. Their reasoning is that if teachers are competent to teach adequately the nation's children, they are competent to have a meaningful role in the planning of educational programs for these children.

The steady diminution in the number of school districts and the steady growth in their size were twin factors of great significance in the development of teacher aggressiveness. The more individual identity tends to be submerged in numbers, the more the individual struggles for recognition and the more he is likely to join an organization for mutual benefit and strength. . . .

There was ample evidence in the postwar years and on into the early 1950's that restiveness among school staffs was climbing, and from 1955 to 1960 teacher discontent reached the boiling point. The dangerous situation was readily discernible to those who really wanted to read these signs, but few did. . . .

---

* American Association of School Administrators *Yearbook,* 1966: 19–30, 53–58; summarized in *Educational Digest* 32: 12–15, April 1967.

For a longer discussion of this topic, read Benjamin Epstein, "What Status and Voice for Principals and Administrators in 'Collective Bargaining' and 'Professional Negotiation' by Teacher Organizations?" *National Association of Secondary School Principals Bulletin* 49: 226–259, March 1965.

As early as 1946, as a result of a bitter strike, the Norwalk, Connecticut, board of education and the Norwalk Teachers Association entered into what is believed to be the first collective negotiation agreement for teachers. At this time, there were a few collective bargaining contracts between boards and AFT affiliates. The Norwalk agreement was broadened in 1957 to provide an appeals procedure, which is believed to be the first provision of its kind in the professional negotiation context.

Connecticut appears to have been the early leader in pressing for collective agreements for school staff. Several such agreements were adopted between 1946 and 1962 by a process generally designated *cooperative determination.*

A resolution entitled "Teacher-Board of Education Relationships" and approved by the NEA Representative Assembly in 1961 was the first resolution on professional negotiation to become official NEA policy. A 1962 NEA resolution used for the first time the term *professional negotiation* and denounced the use of labor procedures, declaring, "Industrial . . . conciliation machinery, which assumes a conflict of interest and diversity of purpose . . . is not appropriate to professional negotiation." Included in the 1962 resolution was a demand for legislation assuring teachers the rights to professional negotiation and for an appeals procedure. The 1964 convention repealed the negative paragraph about labor machinery and gave greater visibility to the role of the superintendent. In 1965, a significant deletion was made in the professional negotiation resolution in the paragraph, "The seeking of consensus and mutual agreement on a professional basis should preclude the arbitrary exercise of unilateral authority by boards of education, administrators, and teachers." Part of the sentence was changed from ". . . should preclude the arbitrary exercise of unilateral authority by boards of education *and the use of strikes by teachers.*"

Adoption by boards of education of formal, written negotiation or bargaining agreements is a relatively recent phenomenon, dating back no more than four years. The speed with which such procedures are spreading, however, is unparalleled in recent educational history. The passage of state legislation dealing with relationships between teachers and their employing boards is adding increased impetus to the drive. In 1965 alone, seven statutes were enacted, and a total of 11 are now in existence.

The variety in the provisions of these statutes almost defies categorization. State affiliates of the NEA favor legislation applicable solely to educational employees, while the American Federation of Teachers supports legislation in many states that would bring educational employees under the same collective bargaining laws which cover all public employees. Another basic difference lies in the determination of the negotiation unit, i.e., whether the unit is restricted to classroom teachers. . . .

The superintendent's role in professional negotiation has been much discussed. Since his basic obligation is to the welfare of the pupils and to leadership in the formulation of sound educational policy, he should be an independent third party in negotiation. He, or his representative acting under his direct supervision, must carry this role into formal negotiation where, in most cases, with legal advice, he will continue to serve as interpreter in difficult communications between the board and the staff. He should exercise free and independent judgment on all educational matters, providing resource material and information to assist all parties in arriving at reasoned decisions, clarifying issues, and making proposals based on what is best for the district and its educational program. The superintendent under no circumstances should be bypassed. Anything which weakens the effectiveness of his position in the district will ultimately weaken the schools.

New patterns of staff relationships require many changes in local school administration, and their pace will quicken rather than abate in the years ahead. New processes and new insights into the nature and means of policy formulation are needed, not only to upgrade the professional status of teachers but also to improve the conditions under which they work, thus enhancing the quality of education.

It is the firm belief of AASA that problems are better prevented than solved, and that satisfactory negotiation procedures are best developed in a climate of goodwill before the need for them becomes acute. It is believed that the superintendent, if he is to continue in his position of educational leadership, must assume responsibility for initiating and guiding changes in patterns of staff relationships. . . .[6]

---

[6] Editor's Note: Compare the following statement by Jack R. Gibb in "Expanding Role of the Administrator," *Bulletin of the National Association of Secondary School Principals* (NASSP) 51: 46–52, May 1967:

> The most effective administrator is the one who acts as a catalyst, a consultant, and a resource to the group. His job is to help the group to grow, to emerge, and to become more free. He serves the team, the group, the school best when he is a whole person, is direct, real, open, spontaneous, permissive, emotional, and highly personal. The leader at his best is an effective member . . . he's with the group *as a person* and not as a role. . . .
>
> The primary mission of the secondary school is to create conditions in which students, teachers, and administrators grow. People grow (1) when the climate is one of trust, warmth, acceptance, and personal worth; (2) when communication is open and in depth; (3) when people have an opportunity to determine their own goals and to evaluate progress toward these goals; and (4) when there are emergent freedoms and a sense of interdependence. It is the responsibility of the administrator to help create conditions in which this growth occurs.

6.7 PUBLIC-EMPLOYEE NEGOTIATING VERSUS SCHOOL-BOARD AUTHORITY*

Reynolds C. Seitz

The argument in support of the attitude that the public employer should not be required to bargain collectively with public employees can be briefly summarized as follows: (1) The fixing of conditions of work in the public service is a legislative function, (2) Neither the executive nor legislative body may delegate such functions to any outside group, (3) The legislative or executive must be free to change the conditions of employment at any time.

NATURE OF GOOD-FAITH COLLECTIVE BARGAINING

It is submitted that these arguments are based upon a misconception of what is actually meant by good-faith collective bargaining. The concept of what constitutes good-faith collective bargaining has been worked out to a large extent by the federal courts and the National Labor Relations Board in interpreting Section 8(d) of the National Labor Relations Act which by its specific language imposes a duty on employers and unions to "meet at reasonable times and confer in good faith with respect to wages, hours and other terms and conditions of employment" and goes on to state "such obligation does not compel either party to agree to a proposal or require the making of a concession." . . . .

I feel that the guidelines laid down by the National Labor Relations Board and the federal courts quite definitely establish that it is a misconception to say that good-faith bargaining requires the legislative (school board) or executive to surrender authority. . . .

The United States Supreme Court in interpreting the meaning of good-faith collective bargaining under the National Labor Relations Act has recognized three categories of proposals:

1. Those that are illegal and therefore cannot be bargained about.
2. Those that may be bargained about if the parties voluntarily wish to do so.
3. Those that are mandatory and must be bargained about.

Proposals that come within the category of wages, hours and other terms and conditions of employment fall within the mandatory area. . . .

---

* Essay in Leo O. Garber, ed., *Current Legal Concepts in Education,* Philadelphia: University of Pennsylvania Press, 1966, pp. 94–112, 97–99, 106–110. Footnote references here omitted. R. C. Seitz is Dean and Professor of Law at Marquette University.

THE RIGHT OF TEACHERS TO ENGAGE IN CONCERTED ACTIVITY

. . . Woodrow Wilson called strikes by public employees "an intolerable crime against civilization." The *Norwalk* case (1951) quotes Franklin D. Roosevelt, whom it identifies as certainly no enemy of labor, as saying "A strike of public employees manifests nothing less than an intent on their part to prevent or obstruct the operation of government and such action is unthinkable and intolerable." *Norwalk* goes on to say:

> Under our system, the government is established by and run for all of the people, not for the benefit of any person or group. The profit motive is absent. It should be the aim of every employee of the government to do his or her part to make it function as efficiently and economically as possible. The drastic remedy of the organized strike to enforce the demand of union of government employees is in direct contravention of this principle.

As far as striking against school boards is concerned, there is an additional good argument. Teachers cannot forget that they work in a delicate area where it is of the utmost importance that young people be encouraged to respect the legitimate authority of school personnel. Is there not a serious question that teachers risk such respect when they go on strike, granted that sometimes they may have a good cause? But will the immature young people in school be able to appreciate the fact or will they merely feel that authority has been flaunted? Certainly it seems very disconcerting when teachers and teachers' unions openly defy existing law and assert that, regardless of the law, they will strike.

It seems pretty much the same arguments are pertinent as respects teacher picketing of schools, granted there is such free speech in picketing. Can the young person fully understand the teacher picket line or does it do something which causes him to question the authority of the teacher?

Is there a remedy if teachers do not have the right to strike? Surely to be realistic teachers will need to exert some kind of pressure in order to accomplish certain goals. The argument that there is a need to strike and picket overlooks the fact that there is indeed a certain kind of pressure inherent in collective bargaining. Although, as has been indicated, the pressure does not require capitulation, collective bargaining does demand a give and take—responses to demands—often counter-proposals—full explanations when demands are rejected. This very process is calculated to produce some sane and logical compromises. By a succession of free choices each party determines the order of importance of his bargaining proposals. As these proposals are pressed and rejected, each party balances what is desired against known costs of unresolved disagreement. In the school field these costs on the one side are such things as loss of good teachers and fostering a general low morale with consequent effects on end goals of education and on the other side the loss of community support for the schools if unreasonable demands are made.

A fact-finding statute such as that in Wisconsin is an interesting substitute for a strike and picketing. Remember the fact finder is not empowered to render a binding decision. But the [Wisconsin] statute does provide for enlisting public opinion to help bring about a settlement.

There is another kind of concerted effort which some have proposed. I refer to sanctions—the chief exponent of which is the National Education Association. Under this suggestion the teacher organizations encourage teachers not to return a signed contract and advise teachers not to accept jobs in the area. It is true that, if effective, sanctions have the same result as a strike in the sense that teachers are not in classrooms. The great difference, however, is that teachers are not leaving their posts during a contract term.

It is hard to find any illegality in the sanction which is sparked only by an appeal to teachers not to sign contracts or take jobs in an area. This sort of appeal is surely free speech and the individual certainly has a right to determine if he will work. Illegality would appear only if the organization induced some kind of boycott pressure which resulted in teachers who did not heed the sanction call losing job opportunities.

In spite of the facts that strikes by public employees and teachers are held to be illegal, they have occurred and are likely to take place again. From a purely practical viewpoint, teachers in mass cannot be discharged. Perhaps the most effective way to attack the strike problem is to aim legislation at the union treasury if the union calls the strike. . . .

CONCLUSION

This discussion should have established that school board authority will not be undermined just because collective bargaining is decreed by law. It is submitted that the tide is running in favor of giving public employees more bargaining rights. It does not appear that the trend can be stopped for long by school boards. It seems they will have no more success in this respect than the industrialist of the 1930's—who, incidentally, tried to halt the movement to give the laborer increased bargaining rights with very much the same kind of arguments that some boards of education are using today. There was the contention of improper delegation of authority.

It appears, therefore, that boards of education might very well stop trying to label provisions for collective bargaining illegal and turn their attention toward working out procedures which will make of public-employee bargaining something which is practical and expeditious. . . .

If boards of education will work out satisfactory procedures and engage in good-faith bargaining there is every reason to believe that there will be created a climate that will produce better education for children.

6.8 AN ACADEMIC ALTERNATIVE TO COLLECTIVE NEGOTIATIONS*

Richard C. Williams

The 1960's will likely be remembered as a period unique in U.S. education. Certainly one of the characteristics that will distinguish this decade from others is the emergence of teacher militancy. Nationally, teachers are using various devices to achieve higher salaries and more effective participation in decision making. It is becoming increasingly apparent that teachers have enormous power to enforce their demands when they resort to collective action.

Smythe has suggested a conceptual framework for analyzing the economic power potential of any group of employees, public or private. According to Smythe, when estimating power potential, five components must be considered:

1. Employees must be irreplaceable for one reason or another—either their skill must be so specialized that they cannot be replaced or their employers do not dare to replace them.
2. Employees must be critical to the operation of the organization—that is, the organization must be unable to function in the absence of the employees.
3. Cost of disagreement for the employer must exceed the cost of agreement —dissension must be too damaging to management to continue the impasse.
4. Employees must be keenly aware that they possess these three strengths: They must realize that they are irreplaceable, critical to the operation, and that disagreement will be much more costly to the employer than the proposed agreement.

---

* Richard C. Williams, "An Academic Alternative to Collective Negotiations," *Phi Delta Kappan* 49: 571–574, June 1968. By permission.

Mr. Williams is Assistant Professor of Education, U.C.L.A.

His footnote references to Cyrus F. Smythe [University of Minnesota] and to others are here omitted.

5. Employees must have the militancy and cohesiveness to bring effective pressure on the employer.

Any group possessing *all* of these components maintains enormous bargaining power. Indeed, the question of whether the group has the legal right to bring their collective power to bear on a situation through the use or threatened use of a strike or sanction becomes largely academic.

Smythe contends, too, that teachers possess the first three components of this power framework and that they are rapidly acquiring the last two. . . .

The question is no longer whether teachers will participate; it is, instead: What form will their participation take? Will it be the industrial relations or academic alternative? The ultimate answer to this question rests heavily upon the kinds of decisions made by school management and legislatures as regards teacher responsibility and participation in decisions. Perhaps rather than spending their energies solely on the passage of "collective negotiations" laws, the many state legislatives should also be considering permissive laws that will pave the way for school boards to widen the decision-making scope to include the teachers, without causing teachers to force the issue through militancy.

6.9 THE SCHOLAR'S EXPANDING POLITICAL ROLE*

John Kenneth Galbraith

In the thirteen years from 1951 to 1964, although the labor force in the United States grew by about 10 million—from 60.9 millions to 70.6 millions—blue-collar employment did not increase at all. . . . Recent studies suggest, in general, that these trends will continue. There will be a rapid increase in professional and white-collar requirements, only a modest increase in blue-collar employment. . . .

In the early stages of industrialization, the educational requirement for industrial manpower was in the shape of a very squat pyramid. A few men of varying qualifications—managers, engineers, bookkeepers, timekeepers and clerks—were needed in the office. The wide base reflected the large requirement for repetitive labor power for which even literacy was some-

* J. K. Galbraith, *The New Industrial State*, Boston: Houghton Mifflin Company, 1967, pp. 236–241, 274, 281, 294, 349–352, 364–367, 370–387. By permission. Also by permission Hamish Hamilton, London.

thing of a luxury. To this pyramid the educational system conformed. . . . [Even today, it] is assumed that an old mill town will have bad schools.

By contrast the manpower requirements of the industrial system are in the shape of a tall urn. It widens out below the top to reflect the need of the technostructure for administrative, coordinating and planning talent, for scientists and engineers, for sales executives, salesmen, those learned in the other arts of persuasion and for those who program and command the computers. It widens further to reflect the need for white-collar talent. And it curves in sharply toward the base to reflect the more limited demand for those who are qualified only for muscular and repetitive tasks and who are readily replaced by machines. . . . [In today's world] the mature corporation must acknowledge dependence on the state for a factor of production [i.e., education] more critical for its success than capital. . . . [As an example of the changing point of view, in today's world a] well-educated Negro is not so necessarily the first fired or the last hired.

The industrial system, it seems clear, is unfavorable to the union. Power passes to the technostructure and this lessens the conflict of interest between employer and employee which gave the union much of its reason for existence. Capital and technology allow the firm to substitute white-collar workers and machines that cannot be organized for blue-collar workers that can. The regulation of aggregate demand, the resulting high level of employment together with the general increase in well-being all, on balance, make the union less necessary or less powerful or both. . . .

In fact the industrial system has now largely encompassed the labor movement. It has dissolved some of its most important functions; it has greatly narrowed its area of action; and it has bent its residual operations very largely to its own needs. Since World War II, the acceptance of the union by the industrial firm and the emergence thereafter of an era of comparatively peaceful industrial relations have been hailed as the final triumph of trade unionism. On closer examination it is seen to reveal many of the features of Jonah's triumph over the whale. . . .

THE EDUCATIONAL AND SCIENTIFIC ESTATE

As the trade unions retreat, more or less permanently, into the shadows, a rapidly growing body of educators and research scientists emerges. This group connects at the edges with scientists and engineers within the technostructure and with civil servants, journalists, writers and artists outside. Most directly nurtured by the industrial system are the educators and scientists in the schools, colleges, universities and research institutions. They stand in relation to the industrial system much as did the banking and financial community to the earlier stages of industrial development. Then capital was decisive, and a vast network of banks, savings banks, insurance companies, brokerage houses and investment bankers came into existence to mobilize savings and thus to meet the need. In the mature corporation the decisive factor of production [is an adequate] supply of qualified talent. . . .

The nature of this educational and scientific estate, the sources of its influence and its relation to the technostructure and the state [deserves careful study]. . . .

Until well along in the present century the educational community in the United States was very small and concerned largely with elementary education. This has changed explosively in recent times. College and university teachers, who numbered 24,000 in 1900 and 49,000 in 1920 will total 480,000 by the end of this decade. This is a twenty-fold increase in seventy years. Only 238,000 students were enrolled in all colleges and universities in 1900 as compared with 3,377,000 in 1959 and a prospective 6,700,000 in 1969. Only 669,000 were in high school grades in 1900 as compared with 9,271,000 in 1959 and a prospective 14,600,000 in 1969. In the early industrial system only a modest number were needed with advanced technical or other skills. Colleges and universities were principally required to train men for the learned professions—medicine, law, the church, veterinary medicine and the like—or to supply the very exiguous cultural adornment thought appropriate to the offspring of the well-to-do.

Apart from their numerical insignificance, educators in the earlier stages of industrial development—in the United States until well into this century—were also, economically, an inferior caste. Funds for financing higher education in private colleges and universities came from the well-to-do either in the form of charitable gifts or as tuition paid on behalf of their offspring. . . . [Hence, for a long time] since attendance involved both expense and ability to defer earning a living [schools] were enclaves for individuals of much better than average income. . . . So while educators on occasion admitted inferiority, and more often simply assumed it, many also professed the goals that they held to be intellectually more demanding or aesthetically more refined than the pecuniary preoccupations of the entrepreneur. . . . A very large amount of legislation or policy regarded as highly inimical by the entrepreneurial enterprise received its initial impetus from the academic community. Laws against monopoly, regulating access to the capital markets, in support of a wide range of welfare measures, in support of progressive taxation owed much to such origins.

During the years of burgeoning industrial development, the academic community—indigent, subordinate and weak—has invariably been pictured by historians in its relation to business as the aggrieved party. On the record this is not so certain. In consequence of its capacity for social invention, it may well have given more than it received. This has been obscured partly by the fact that members of the academic community have written the history, no minor source of power in itself, and also by the different ways in which influence manifests itself. Pecuniary power expresses itself in highly unsubtle form; it offers financial reward for conformity or threatens financial damage for dissent. Proposals for reform, by contrast, begin as seemingly eccentric and implausible suggestions. Gradually they gain adherents; in time they emerge as grave needs; and then they become fundamental human rights. It is not so easy to attribute power to those who set this process in motion.

[Yet the] power that is associated with capacity for social innovation is . . . [so important that with] the rise of the technostructure, relations between those associated with the economic enterprise and the educational and scientific estate undergo a radical transformation. . . . At this stage, the educational and scientific estate is no longer small; on the contrary, it is very large. It is no longer dependent on private income and wealth for its support; most of its sustenance is provided by the state. . . .

Meanwhile the technostructure has become deeply dependent on the educational and scientific estate for its supply of trained manpower. It needs also to maintain a close relation with the scientific sector of this estate to insure that it is safely abreast of scientific and technological innovation. And, unlike the enterpreneurial corporation, the mature corporation is much less troubled by the social inventiveness of the educational and scientific estate. The costs of reform legislation—improvements in medical care, guaranteed incomes for the poor, regeneration of slums—can be passed forward to customers or back to stockholders. . . . The burden of regulation like that of taxation is appreciably lessened by having it fall on someone else. . . .

As might be expected, the new dependence of the technostructure on the educational and scientific estate is reflected in the relation between the two. The business executive no longer sits on the college board as a source of worldly knowledge and guardian against social heresy. Rather it is because he is accorded a traditional obeisance. And his presence provides him with an opportunity to maintain closer liaison with sources of talent or to keep more closely abreast of scientific and technological innovation. While the corporation president has become increasingly a traditional or ceremonial figure in his association with education, the modern scholar of science, mathematics, information systems or communications theory is ever more in demand to guide the mature corporation through its besetting problems of science, technology and computerization. The name of a famous banker on a board of directors once advertised to the world that the corporation had access to the full capital resources of the economy. Now, the name of a scientist or, at a minimum, a college president is displayed, along with those of former Air Force generals, to show that the firm is attuned to the very latest in technological advance. . . . [As a] member of the technostructure [today's scholar] is strongly inhibited in his political role. He cannot divest himself of the organization which gives him being. And he cannot carry it with him into political life. On the other hand, he wields great public influence as, in effect, an extended arm of the bureaucracy. . . .

EDUCATION AND EMANCIPATION

[Education is], among other things, an apparatus for affecting belief and inducing more critical belief. The industrial system, by making trained and educated manpower the decisive factor of production, requires a highly developed educational system. If the educational system serves generally the beliefs of the industrial system, the influence and monolithic character of the latter will be enhanced. By the same token, should it be superior to and independent of the industrial system, it can be the necessary force for skepticism, emancipation and pluralism. . . .

[Today's] business and engineering schools are valued for their reassuring aspect of utility as are the scientists and mathematicians for their association with pregnant and often alarming change. But the service of the university to the aesthetic, cultural and intellectual enjoyments of the individual is still asserted. Indeed, such assertion comprises, by a wide margin, the largest part of the ceremonial literature of modern higher education. No university president is inaugurated, few speak, only rarely is a commencement address given, no anniversary is celebrated, and no great educator is retired without a reference to the continuing importance of liberal education for its own sake. . . . To transfer actual funds from engineering to fine arts would be more difficult. Yet even the oratory, however vacuous, suggests the problem. The industrial system has induced an enormous expansion in education. This can only be welcomed. But unless its tendencies are clearly foreseen and strongly resisted, it will place a preclusive emphasis on education that most serves the needs, but least questions the goals, of that system.

The proper course of action is clear. The college and university community must retain paramount authority for the education it provides and for the research it undertakes. The needs of the industrial system must always be secondary to the cultivation of general understanding and perception. . . . [Even so, we persist in believing] that education and research must be subordinate to the needs of the industrial system. But they need not be subordinate if it is realized that the educator is a figure of power in this context. He is the source of the factor of production on which industrial success depends; he must realize this and exert his power, not on behalf of the industrial system but on behalf of the entire human personality. . . .

In the distribution of educational resources it ought to be the rule that the student preparing for a career in personnel management, television advertising or computer programming as a servant of the industrial system, will find the requisite educational facilities and have access to the needed financial support. Concern for a remunerative career will insure an adequate number of applicants. But the individual whose concern is with poetry or painting and but slightly with his financial prospects will have equal opportunity including equal chance for a scholarship. Similarly with provision for research and scholarly effort. The price that the industrial system must pay for the education of *its* people and the conduct of *its* research is the support of general enlightenment. . . . Colleges and universities can train the people and cultivate the goals of the industrial system. They can train the people and cultivate the attitudes which insure technological advance, allow of effective planning and insure acquiescence in the management of consumer and public demand. . . . Or colleges and universities can strongly assert the values and goals of educated men—those that serve not the production of goods and associated planning but the intellectual and artistic development of man. . . .

The educational and scientific estate has the power to exercise its option. It holds the critical cards. For in committing itself to technology, planning and organization, the industrial system has made itself deeply dependent on the manpower which these require. The banker, in the days when capital was decisive, was not unaware of his bargaining power. The educator should not be more innocent today. . . .

The needed changes, including those in the images by which military and foreign policy are shaped, all involve the sensibilities and concerns of the mind. Their natural, although by no means exclusive, interest therefore is to those who are called intellectuals. The largest number of intellectuals with an occupational identification are those in the educational and scientific estate. It is to the educational and scientific estate, accordingly, that we must turn for the requisite political initiative. The initiative cannot come from the industrial system, although support can be recruited from individuals therein. Nor will it come from the trade unions. Apart from their declining numbers and power, they are under no particular compulsion to question the goals of the industrial system or the tendency to make all social purpose identical with those goals.

This is written at a time of much rather incoherent and unfocused dissent by younger people. Much of this dissent reflects a dissatisfaction with the goals so self-confidently asserted by the industrial system and its spokesmen. It will be highly responsive to leadership. It will be unfocused and ineffective until this leadership is supplied. . . .

[Unfortunately], both the educational and scientific estate and the intellectual community are handicapped by the belief that their role is professionally passive—that it is to feel and think but not to act. Righteousness, as well as convenience, defends this passivity. Politics is not the business of the intellectual or the artist. Nor of the educator nor of the scientist. Theirs is the purer domain of the spirit and the mind. This can only be sullied by concern for practical affairs. In the last milli-second before the ultimate nuclear fusion, a scientist will be heard to observe that the issue of nuclear control and military security is really one for politicians and their military and diplomatic advisers. And as the last horizon is lost behind the smoke, gas, neon lights and detritus of the industrial civilization, men of self-confessed artistic sensitivity will be heard to observe that, unfortunately, none of this is the business of the true artist. In fact, no intellectual, no artist, no educator, no scientist can allow himself the convenience of doubting his responsibility. For the goals that are now important there are no other saviors. In a scientifically exacting world scientists must assume responsibility for the consequences of science and technology. For custody of the aesthetic dimension of life there is no substitute for the artist. The individual member of the educational and scientific estate may wish to avoid responsibility; but he cannot justify it by the claim of higher commitment.[7] . . . [For in today's world] redirection of the weapons competition, social control of environment, a wider range of choice by the individual, emancipation of education—require some form of political action. . . .

[Progress toward these larger goals of life] will be much less measurable than that which associates all progress with percentage increases in Gross National Product or percentage levels of unemployment. It is because the goals of the industrial system are so narrow that they lend themselves to precise statistical assessment. But life is meant to be complex. . . . [The aesthetic dimensions of life furnish an example of the contrasting values at stake.] The aesthetic dimension being beyond the ready reach of the industrial system, members of that system are led naturally to assert its unimportance. Juveniles who do not like Latin, economists who do not like mathematics and men who do not like women manifest precisely the same tendency.

But this is not all. Cultivation of the aesthetic dimension accords a new and important role to the state and one to which, by virtue of its handicaps, the industrial system is unrelated. . . . Only the state can defend the landscape against power lines, advertisers, lumbermen, coal miners, and, on frequent occasions, its own highwaymen. Only it can rule that some patterns of consumption—the automobile in the downtown areas of the modern city is a prominent possibility—are inconsistent with aesthetic

[7] Editor's Note: For a different viewpoint on this issue, read Albert Wohlstetter, "Scientists, Seers and Strategy," *Foreign Affairs*, 41: 466–478, April 1963.

goals. The state alone can protect radio and television from contrived dissonance—or provide alternatives that are exempt. And were aesthetic priority asserted, the state would be required to come to its defense not, as now, episodically and in response to some exceptional outrage of aesthetic sensibilities. It would have to do so normally and naturally as the defender of goals in which aesthetic considerations were consistently important. Such goals, it must be added, will not occasionally but usually be achieved at some cost to industrial expansion—to economic growth. That one must pause to affirm that beauty is worth the sacrifice of some increase in the Gross National Product shows how effectively our beliefs have been accommodated to the needs of the industrial system.

But the role of the state on the aesthetic dimension is not merely protective; it is also affirmative. While art is an expression of individual personality, important branches of the arts can only flourish within a framework of order. . . . In the case of architecture and urban and environmental design, its role is decisive. Art is one manifestation of order. And it is the first casualty of disorder. Florence, Seville, Bloomsbury and Georgetown are beautiful because each part is in orderly relation to the whole. The modern commercial highway, the sprawling fringe of any city, the route into town from any airport is hideous because no part is related to a larger design. This order is rarely if ever achieved permissively; it must always be imposed by the state or by social pressure. . . . It is worth hoping that the educational and scientific estate, as it grows in power, will encourage and enforce more exacting aesthetic standards. Nothing would more justify its intrusion on public life.

Tomorrow's Agenda

6.10 INTRODUCTION: WIDER VISTAS FOR TOMORROW'S WORLD

A farmer who had never been further from home than his small rural village once got on a train to go to New York City. On his return home he reported about the many new and wonderful things he had seen—but it turned out that he had not once been outside of Grand Central Station.

Many contemporary students are like this farmer. They leave home to get a university education—to get some notion about the scope of the universe and of their place in it. But they spend so much of their time in one college, or sometimes even in one department of a college, that they remain almost completely unaware of the scope of today's universe, or how they can find a meaningful place in it.

The ideal of liberal education "to know everything about something, and something about everything" is difficult to achieve in an age of explosive change. Within a few decades we have moved into an age of extreme specialization, into the atomic age, the age of jet propulsion, the age of instantaneous communication—an age where each of us is living, so to speak, in everyone else's back yard. The harsh fact remains, that

> . . . with few exceptions, little has been done to educate American students about the cultures of Asia, Africa, and the Near East—areas with two-thirds of the world's population. The average college student knows something about Plato, Shakespeare, the French Revolution, Beethoven, and the Treaty of Versailles. But his mind is apt to be blank about the Bhagavad-Gita, the Lord Buddha, Suleiman the Magnificent, the Manchu Dynasty, and the Meiji Restoration. . . . It is up to our colleges and universities to try to adjust their curricula—particularly on the undergraduate level—to erase the abysmal ignorance of even educated Americans about the traditions, institutions, and aspirations of non-Western peoples.[8]

[8] Henry T. Heald, "American Education's New Dimension," *School and Society* 88: 173–177, April 9, 1960.

The educational problem is intimately bound up with many diverse areas of human endeavor—economic, political, cultural, social, and religious. Certainly our ability to understand the many diverse languages (and their accompanying thought patterns) and the tremendous varieties of cultural and religious traditions (and their accompanying rites, rituals, and emotional attitudes) is woefully lacking. Yet American youth may have some advantages toward the solution of such problems.

Fifty years ago Woodrow Wilson led our nation into World War I with the slogan "To Make the World Safe for Democracy." Today, we need an equally persuasive slogan—"To Make the World Safe for Diversity." Fortunately, there is no conflict between these two slogans. Indeed, our national motto, *E pluribus unum,* should remind us that we will "make the world safe for democracy" to the extent that we are able "to make the world safe for diversity." This is a formidable task. In Chapter 2, on "Race, Poverty, and Segregation" the question may have been asked: How can we have genuine education for world-mindedness until we learn how to communicate better with some of the subcultures within our own society? But perhaps the question could also be asked: Will we not learn how to communicate better with the subcultures in our slums if we learn more about the languages, the thought patterns, and the traditions of non-Western cultures? While striving for "One World," we may gain new knowledge to assist us in achieving unity amid diversity within our own nation.

In the search for a type of liberal education appropriate to the modern age, perhaps the key ingredient is a spirit of tolerance and openmindedness. Indeed, most of the issues in this anthology, and many of the difficult decisions of our courts, may be viewed as analogous to skirmishes, or battles, in the larger warfare between intolerance and tolerance. The onward march of democracy may be defined as movement from cult to culture, from dogma to dialogue, from nationalism to world-mindedness, from force to persuasion.

6.11 TEACHING FOR INTERNATIONAL UNDERSTANDING*

Harold R. W. Benjamin

What are the critical questions to ask when we examine the topic of teaching for international understanding? I see two of them. First, what do we mean by *international understanding*? And second, what do we mean by *teaching* in this connection?

The timeworn and war-torn concepts of international understanding are relatively useless. Their fundamental feature is erudition. One of these types we may call the Military Intelligence type, using the symbol M.I. for it. The goal of the M.I. type is information needed in manipulating the behavior of people in other lands. We may want some day to sell them our goods. Or perhaps, in that final arbitrament of force to which all nationalisms are inclined to revert when the going gets really tough, we may have to meet them in battle and bend their wills to our own international political patterns.

A simpler kind of international understanding is exemplified by the views of foreign lands acquired by such international students as Cousin Charlie, Uncle Bill, and Aunt Mary. They have stared at the paintings in the Louvre, they have visited the Roman Forum with their cameras at the ready. They know how to say "How much?" in seven languages. The goal of this Aunt Mary type of understanding—A.M. for short—is much more innocent in its appearance than the M.I. type, but sometimes more devastating in its effect. It is the prevalance of this A.M. erudition among the voters and even in the halls of Congress that has made possible some of the worst features of our United States foreign policy. Indeed, Aunt Mary herself would hardly have continued giving massive foreign aid to dictators thumbing their noses at the United States and encouraging their followers to desecrate the United States flag. To achieve such levels of international understanding apparently requires a special mentality found only behind State Department desks and in Senate committee rooms.

The third kind of international understanding is very different. It is designed to help the people of this planet, not just some of them but all of them regardless of nationality, religion, race, or economic status, to

* Harold R. W. Benjamin, in *Notes and Abstracts in the Social Foundations of American and International Education*, Ann Arbor, Michigan: School of Education, University of Michigan 19: 1–8, Spring 1967; condensed in the *Education Digest* 33: 24–26, October 1967. By permission.

Harold Benjamin is Distinguished Service Professor of Education at New Jersey State College, Glassboro.

change their ways under their own command in the direction of a world order in which all men will need to study war no more, in which women will not face the horrors of pressing starving babies to their emaciated, milkless breasts, and in which little children can walk confidently into futures where personal dignity and significance will have replaced the degradation and meaninglessness that now engulfs them. Let us call this third type of international understanding the W.O. type—W.O. for World Order.

Now, what do we mean by *teaching* international understanding in this connection? How can we teach the W.O. type of understanding? Emphatically, we do not mean any ordinary concept of instruction, with one person pouring facts and skills into another person's armory of knowledge and abilities. The M.I. type of international understanding can be taught that way to some degree. The A.M. type can be inculcated effectively in that fashion. But the W.O. type calls for the learner to educate himself. This kind of international understanding demands a personal involvement that cannot possibly be acquired except under the direction of the learner himself.

In a study, let us say, of modern Mexico, the M.I. type of international understanding is well served by instruction in the Spanish language and the history and economics of Mexico. The A.M. type can be served by camera studies of the pyramid at Teotihuacan, and in lively stories of Francisco Villa and Don Emiliano Zapata on his white horse. But the W.O. type of learning has to start very soberly with the learner asking himself such questions as: What do these Mexicans need in order to elevate their ways of living to the levels which a great world order will require? What are they now attempting to do in effecting the desired changes? The learner is personally involved in these problems when he works out answers for himself. This is not to imply that the W.O. type of learning should not be assisted at every possible step by teachers. It is merely to emphasize that the pupil must figure out his own answers, and he must be involved himself in the goal of this learning. When he is not thus involved, the W.O. type drops back to the A.M. or the M.I. kind of learning.

This kind of teaching, difficult though it is, can and often does occur in the elementary grades. . . . The little children in the second grade can be instructed in A.M. fashion concerning serapes, donkeys, and peons sleeping against the cathedral wall. They can learn to say *buenos dias*, and *muchas gracias*. Or they can be taught on an M.I. level that the Mexicans are still largely an agricultural people with a few small industries. But when they begin asking such questions as "Do the Mexican farmers raise enough corn and beans to feed all the Mexican children?" "Are there enough doctors and nurses to treat the sick children of the country?" they

are moving up to the W.O. level. Once they approach that level, at whatever age, the facts and skills which the M.I. and A.M. modes of instruction regard as central in their curriculums come naturally and inevitably into the total learning complex. This is why many Peace Corps members learn the language, the history, and the cultural problems of the areas where they work, with a speed, a precision, and a dedication that astonishes the ordinary observer.

The central feature of learning the W.O. type of understanding is not whether the learner is able to travel abroad. The central feature is the learner's involvement with the questions of the needs, the desires, the attempts, and results which the people of other lands exhibit. An understanding of these questions is not necessarily a matter of physical travel—it is rather, necessarily, a travel of the spirit. . . .

Of course, all of us who ever had occasion to travel in foreign lands, to use foreign languages, and to adjust to foreign ways, are in some degree bearers of Military Intelligence and Aunt Mary types of international understanding. But we who are professional teachers are well aware that it is the third kind of international understanding which by the rules of our craft we are vowed to achieve.

6.12 THE SECULARIZATION OF CULTURE*

M. M. Thomas

All over the world, the necessity of modernization of traditional societies, and the search for the higher reaches of development by modernized societies, have led to the breakdown of the traditional integration between religion, society and state and to the assertion of the autonomy of culture from religious control. Not only the structures of Christendom have broken down—that happened long ago—but even the idea of Christendom lies in ruins today. Other religious cultures in the world are in various stages

* M. M. Thomas, "Ecumenism and the Cultural Revolution," *Religious Education* 42: 93–97, March–April 1967. Used by permission of the publisher, the Religious Education Association, New York City.

M. M. Thomas is Director, Christian Institute for the Study of Religion and Society, Bangelore, India. He was Henry W. Luce Visiting Professor of World Christianity at Union Theological Seminary, New York, 1966–1967.

See also Talcott Parsons, "The Nature of American Pluralism," in the excellent anthology *Religion and Public Education*, Theodore R. Sizer, ed., Boston: Houghton Mifflin Company, 1967.

of disintegration. And people are seeking a re-integration of the totality of life in new forms of culture. The modern ecumenical Christian reformation, other renascent religions, secular ideologies and militant secular faiths are seeking to give shape to this new culture. But it is clear beyond doubt that the societies which are today emerging everywhere are secular, technical, and pluralistic, in their main features; and broadly speaking, the role of religions has to be exercised at the level of inspiring and moulding the mind and spirit of men and cultural institutions, without controlling them. At least this is the direction in which all societies seem to be moving. . . .

I would like to affirm that through the revolutions of our time, men are seeking a fuller and richer human life, a greater fulfillment of their humanity. We may discern this struggle of men for their fuller humanity at four levels.

First, there is everywhere the search for human freedom understood as creativity. Men want the freedom to create new things, new societies, new cultures and new purposes. In fact if we look at the last three to four hundred years of modern history, men have revolted against religions primarily because in the name of a fixed divinely ordained order they prevented men's creativity in science, arts, and morality. In fact, many doctrines of the creator-God have been so defined as to give no room for the creativity of men, so that men had to revolt against God himself to affirm human creativity. In a sense, the process of secularization in the modern world and a good deal even of militant secularism have been primarily an affirmation of man's humanity as essentially creative.

Secondly, today everywhere there is the search for freedom as the awareness of a responsible selfhood. Self-determination, self-development and self-identity are phrases charged with great meaning in the life of individuals as well as groups in the modern world. Men and women ask for their fundamental rights of responsibility as human persons. Nations and races and cultures are in the struggle for their self-identity and for the power and responsibility to exercise their selfhood.

Thirdly, there is among all people the search for a love which is different from paternalism. Paternalism is a form of love, no doubt. But today, it appears to men and women in all situations to be lacking in true reverence for the dignity of the person. Young people revolt against paternalism in the family; and there is revolt against paternalism of caste, class and race. In fact we shall misinterpret even the struggle of the poorer classes, races and nations against poverty, if it is seen only as a search for bread to satisfy hunger. Of course it is that, but it is the search for bread as the expression of justice to man's manhood.

Fourthly, men everywhere have become conscious of a sense of history.

On the one hand, there is the awareness of a universal history of mankind, and on the other every nation, race and group is becoming conscious of its own historical mission and vocation in the world, and is struggling to define it.

In this seeking for creativity, selfhood, love and historical mission, men are driven in the deepest levels of their spirit by the vision of new dimensions of human existence; and this new humanism is the spiritual ferment within the cultural revolutions of our contemporary world.

6.13 TOMORROW'S AGENDA*

Zbigniew Brzezinski

Each generation, it is often said, fights the wars of the preceding generation without knowing it. During the nineteenth century men died believing in the cause of royalty or republicanism. In reality, much of their sacrifice was rendered on the altar of the new nationalism. During the twentieth century men fought on behalf of nationalism. Yet the wars they fought were also engendered by dislocations in world markets and by social revolution stimulated by the coming of the industrial age.

Today, many Americans—and certainly most Communists—tend to see international conflict primarily in terms of the cold-war struggle between democracy and Communism. Inadvertently, some Americans thus accept, and project on the international scene, the basic Marxist-Leninist assumption that the decisive conflict of our age concerns the internal character of property relationships and the political organization of society, viewed in terms of the initial impact of the industrial revolution.

Yet these are no longer the basic issues facing mankind. The fundamental dilemmas to which we must respond are quite different and they cannot be analyzed properly in terms of the widely-accepted dichotomy of Western democracy versus totalitarian Communism. In the second half of the twentieth century the developed nations, given new scientific and social developments, will face a real threat to the continued existence of man as

* Zbigniew Brzezinski, "Tomorrow's Agenda," excerpted by special permission from *Foreign Affairs* 44: 661–670, July 1966. Copyright by the Council on Foreign Relations, Inc., New York.

Zbigniew Brzezinski is Director of the Research Institute on Communist Affairs, Columbia University, and author of *Ideology and Power in Soviet Politics, Alternatives to Partition,* and other works.

a spontaneous, instinctive, rather autonomous and even somewhat mysterious being; the less developed countries, because of overpopulation, economic backwardness and potential political disorder, will be challenged by a fundamental crisis of survival of organized society. Responding to these twin challenges will require a basic reordering of our perspectives.

This is not to say that the cold war no longer exists, or that the United States should opt out of it. [But the cold war is gradually diminishing in importance, and will soon be overshadowed by other factors.]. . . .

The new issues that constitute the underlying reality of international politics today stem from a fundamental revolution in the more advanced countries of man's relationship to society (both social and political) and from a basic reordering of the international system into states that are developed and underdeveloped, increasingly affluent and impoverished, overwhelmingly powerful and relatively impotent. The first poses a challenge to the individual being; the second, to the survival of organized society. It would be disastrous if in the nuclear age statesmen responded to these twin challenges in terms of old conflicts that are no longer relevant.

The social revolution already in progress in the more developed states—above all in America—is likely to be shaped by the widespread adoption of automation and cybernation for social and economic purposes, and by the application of specialized sciences such as biochemistry and molecular biology to the genetic and personal development of man. Man's environment and man himself will more and more be subject to purposive control and manipulation. The consequence will be a fundamental transformation of our society. . . .

In some ways even more far-reaching will be the changes affecting the individual himself. How will we preserve the integrity and freedom of man as an individual? As a physical being he will become more malleable, given the trends in medical sciences. As a personality, he will become increasingly subject to external manipulation, capable eventually of altering his behavior, his intelligence, his psychological state, his sexual life—in effect, himself. As man approaches the stage where he can "program" himself as he now programs his computer, he may find himself increasingly denatured. The simultaneous weakening of religious belief may create both stress and emptiness. In some respects the alienated anti-Viet Nam war demonstrators are a portent of things to come. Their attitude as well as their personal behavior are a manifestation of a psychological crisis inherent in modern society. Viet Nam provides an outlet for basic cravings and fears, and if that issue did not exist, some other one would provide an excuse for the expression of personal and political alienation.

Cumulatively, these social and individual changes—many of which will make for a better life—may present a potent challenge to the relevancy and effective operation of our democratic processes. Our institutions are based on the belief that man can and should govern himself. Yet the problems that are likely to dominate our lives in the decades to come may creep upon us without attracting sufficient advance notice and may not fit into the established modes of our political dialogue. The issues that should increasingly agitate the citizen will have little in common with variants of welfare democracy or dictatorial Communism. Rather, the concerned citizen will have to take a stand on such questions as the form, organization and degree of permissible social control in providing for mass leisure; the character of education for a society in which a great many will not need their education for employment because much of the labor will be taken over by machines; the scope of social welfare in conditions which increasingly assume relative well-being for all; the psychological consequences of seemingly purposeless lives, with the consequent possibility of widespread individual and social malaise; the source of ultimate decision concerning the sex, personality and even the intelligence of one's own offspring; the integration on a national and even international basis of weather and climate controls.

These issues, to be sure, will still involve and perhaps even give new urgency to the old dilemmas of large versus small-scale social organization, of central versus local government, or of a proper balance between social responsibility and individual autonomy. The point, however, is that the discussion of them will require an entirely new frame of reference and perhaps even major changes in the political structure of our society. Neither the discussion nor the possible reforms—if they are to have meaning—can have much in common with the traditional concepts that still shape our domestic and external perspectives. . . .

Our democratic process traditionally has involved a response to crises. Many of our governmental agencies—for example, the urban and welfare departments—developed because social needs belatedly made themselves obvious to all. Increasingly, the emphasis should be on anticipating needs and thus on the development of institutions capable of dealing with rapid social change and mitigating its consequences. This may require major reorientation in the average citizen's perception of the world around him. Finally, it would be desirable to stimulate a broad public discussion on the role and character of the individual in the scientific age about to set upon us and perhaps even to subsume us. In doing so, new and more relevant issues will come to the fore, replacing the repetitive cant of outmoded ideological conflict.

Our success or failure in adapting our democratic institutions to these new conditions, while safeguarding the individual personality, may in large measure determine the role this country will be playing in the world by the end of this century.

6.14 A CONCLUDING WORD TO STUDENTS*

O. Meredith Wilson

Fellow students: Today, each of you receives from the University of Minnesota a diploma. Like any other form of currency, your diploma is a promissory note not in itself possessed of value. In this case, the support for the promise is neither bullion at Fort Knox nor the pledged authority and guarantee of a government. The true value, of which the diploma is the promise, is in your mind, or better yet, is your mind now honed and prepared by education.

The value of the diploma is a symbolic one. At the gates of industry, church, finance, or graduate school, it may serve as a passport. If so, the acceptance of yours will depend upon the knowledge generally current about all universities and their diplomas, and upon a particular knowledge and respect for the University of Minnesota. It is true that the diploma from "X" University may be somewhat better regarded than that from "Y," but the fact that each will be accepted gives credence to Professor Kenneth Boulding's remark that "Every university is the same university. Each is but a local congregation of a world church."

Yet the use of a church as an analogue is unsatisfactory in a specific sense. It is my own perception that the function of a church is to know the truth, while the function of a university is to seek the truth. It is possible to defend dogma in the church as the salty epitome of fixed truth, whether revealed or derived.

In a university, any dogma is anathema; every assumed truth is subject to analysis; all established authority is properly questioned. The protests and demonstrations that have occurred on university campuses in recent years have not troubled me because of their challenge to authority. Yet they have troubled me because the protagonists seem so sure of themselves.

I am prepared for certainty among the knights of the Children's Crusade. One should not expect signs of doubt or the spirit of open inquiry among the soldiers of Cromwell; conviction and uncompromising conformity are appropriate to the age of Torquemada in the Spanish Inquisition, or in the angry responses of the Dutch Protestants to His Most Catholic Majesty, the King of Spain.

But at a university every proposition, however generally accepted, is only

---

* O. Meredith Wilson, "Charge to the Graduating Class," Commencement Address, University of Minnesota, Minneapolis, June 10, 1967. By permission.

O. Meredith Wilson was President of the University of Minnesota from 1960 to 1967, and is now Director, Center for Advanced Study in the Behavioral Sciences, Stanford, California.

the best formulation available until now. The university spirit tells us that we act on the basis of the best knowledge now extant, fully prepared to have new evidence unsettle today's certainties. In such an environment, pluralism is the natural consequence, and tolerance is not merely a desirable good, but a necessary condition for the intellectual life. The university's existence is a promise not only that old dogmas will be challenged, but also that the instrument of attack will be reason; the method will be inquiry; the climate of the conversation will be open and clear.

My reservations about the crusading campus dissenters may best be stated by quoting one of my predecessors, Lotus Delta Coffman:

> A university studies politics, but it will not advocate fascism or communism. A university studies military tactics, but it will not promote war. A university studies peace, but it will not promote crusades of pacifism. It will study every question that affects human welfare, but it will not carry a banner in a crusade for anything except freedom of learning.[9]

Perhaps I can serve you best in your final University pregraduation appointment by stating in staccato my conceptions of this and any great university:

1. A university is the place where tomorrow is made. True, it was founded to preserve our best tradition, to codify what we know of the laws of nature and of man, to evaluate the art, the music, the civilizing forces of our culture. But this concern about the past is prompted by the faith that, if men are warned and informed by the historical record, they can more successfully wrest the secrets of the universe from obscurity and can more confidently make a tomorrow into which men may hopefully and willingly walk.

2. A university would not exist except in a culture affected by a spirit of active optimism. We are aware of imperfections and problems, but believe that reason, however slow, is inexorable and that the most difficult problems will yield to importunate inquiry. Only men who believe in themselves and in the future would postpone today's satisfactions, turning aside from living today to prepare for a better life tomorrow. Registration at a university is an act of faith. Study is a form of personal capital formation. Formal education would not exist unless men believed that by deferring immediate satisfactions they might achieve them later richly intensified.

3. A university not only threatens all forms of authority, but also challenges our personal convictions. Some of our convictions are confirmed by inquiry. Others are revealed as prejudice rather than truth. Since error is the chief enemy of progress in knowledge, the university does us each great

---

[9] *Journal of American Association of University Women,* January 1936.

personal service when, by application of the laws of knowledge, it discovers our personal mistakes. To discover our own error should be the source of great celebration, for by correcting the error we are assured of a better tomorrow. (It is a tragic commentary on our human weakness that the sounds of joy we emit when we are discovered to be in error are so muted.)

4. A university does have its own catechism. It begins and ends with the question: Does the generalization which you claim to be truth accord with all the available evidence and respect to the laws of parsimony? A university, as it sponsors the search for truth, embodies its own canons of honesty and provides automatic enforcement of its moral code. If the scholar, to protect his own bias, tries to warp or constrain the evidence, he at once destroys his bridge to a higher order of truth, and renders himself ridiculous in the eyes of his fellow scholars. He is exposed as both dishonest and foolish.

5. The university is also a place of planting and of harvest. It is the garden in which the scholar plants his hope of continuous renewal. Today our faculty learns afresh the lesson of springtime: "As a man soweth, so also shall he reap." You are the harvest. Just as to your parents, you are the extension of your family's genetic chain, so also you are to this faculty its assurance of a strong intellectual succession.

6. A university should make you aware of what you really are: a thinking being, for whom the power to reason is the first good and the use of reason the highest obligation. One can set no bounds to thought once set in motion; neither nations nor creeds can confine it. Just as the laws of knowledge enforce their own morality, so also the boundlessness of thought breeds universality. And the diffusion of the gifts of reason among all men teaches, if not a common brotherhood, at least a common manhood. A university by its nature presses toward one world and a unity among men.

7. A university is also, and first of all, a place of preparation. It must adjust its objectives and its competence to the problems we face now, and it must temper its instruction to the educational sophistication of the men and women it has engaged to prepare. John Adams, after a trip to Paris, in 1787, wrote to his wife, Abigail:

> The mechanic arts are those for which we have occasion in a young country as yet simple and not far advanced in luxury. I must study politics and war, that my sons may have liberty to study mathematics, philosophy, geography, natural history, naval architecture, navigation, commerce and agriculture, in order to give their children a right to study painting, poetry, music, architecture, statuary, tapestry and porcelain.

John Adams had the active optimism that characterizes the university man. He confidently expected that although there were stages in the development of any young country, we would successfully pass through each stage and reach at last a gracious era in which men might enjoy music, art, and philosophy. We are his great-grandchildren. We have seen, and are the beneficiaries of, the successes he predicted. Yet we too must learn of mechanic arts and war, of politics and philosophy, of poetry and music—and all at the same time; for today, survival, development, and the good life are interwoven rather than separable opportunities.

And so I charge you, Class of 1967, to honor your parental and intellectual heritage; to accept the implications of universality embedded in the life of the mind; and . . . to fashion a good tomorrow.

TOPICS FOR FURTHER STUDY

CENSORSHIP IN THE CLASSROOM: PROS AND CONS

A. Teachers who are paid out of public funds . . . have no right . . . to believe in . . . changes in the state or national government.[10]

B. We Americans know that if freedom means anything, it means the right to think. And the right to think means the right to read—anything, written anywhere, by any man, at any time.[11]

C. In such a [Catholic parochial] school, in harmony with the Church and Christian family, the various branches of secular learning will not enter into conflict with religious instruction to the manifest detriment of education. And if, when occasion arises, it be deemed necessary to have the students read authors propounding false doctrine, for the purpose of refuting it, this will be done after due preparation and with such an antidote of sound doctrine, that it will not only do no harm, but will be an aid to the Christian formation of youth.[12]

D. Jefferson's vision, often politically compromised but never personally forfeited, was "that a free society flourished with the freely flowing intelligence of its citizens," and he knew earlier than most that religion impeded the free flow of intelligence. Education, to be sure, needed a guardian of its freedom; Jefferson tried to mature the child by removing it from its religious parent and by placing it under public protection. . . .

"Not that Jefferson was antireligious . . . . Jefferson noted and valued a profound alliance between true Christianity as he understood it and the cultivation of knowledge under the principle of the freedom of the mind. His famous personal oath of "eternal hostility against every form of tyranny over the mind of man" was profoundly religious in its intensity and was "sworn upon the altar of God." Jefferson earnestly believed "that the Christian religion, when divested of the rags" thrown around it by "the clergy, who had got a smell of union between Church and State," and when "brought in the original purity and simplicity of its benevolent institutor, is a religion of all others most friendly to liberty, science, and the freest expansion of the human mind." Just so; perverted Christianity

---

[10] Clayton W. Lusk, New York State Senator, cited by David Fellman in "Academic Freedom in American Law," 1961 *Wisconsin Law Review* 3–46, January 1961.

[11] Ex-Presidents Herbert Hoover and Harry S Truman, joint statement cited in *Censorship Bulletin* 2: 12, New York: American Book Publishers Council, Inc., April 1958.

[12] Pope Pius XI, Encyclical Letter, *Divini Illius Magistri* ("On the Christian Education of Youth"), December 31, 1929, New York: The American Press, 1936; reprinted in full in *Philosophy of Education*, H. W. Burns and C. J. Brauner, eds., New York: The Ronald Press Company, 1962, pp. 264–288.

tended to mold the mind; Jefferson measured Christianity's truth and worth by the rod of intellectual freedom.[13]

E. The issues in school library censorship include the centuries-old question of freedom of information and expression, but they are more complicated than is the problem of adult freedom to read. . . . The schools legally act *in loco parentis*, and supervision of their pupils' reading is only a part of the supervision that is assumed necessary as youngsters approach the magical age of 21. If parents have the duty to screen their daughters' boy friends and to indicate (hopefully) what time their daughters are expected home from dates, the librarian also has a duty to screen books for these daughters—and their boy friends.

In selecting books the school librarian must balance two factors: (1) a work of obvious intrinsic literary merit should not be rejected because of a few sex references or taboo words which, in context, help to create the book's merit; and (2) the adolescent's lack of experience, both of sex and of literature, sometimes makes him take sexual and taboo references out of context.

Librarians know that when a book is furtively passed to a friend with a note, "See page 161," it is not being read as a piece of literature. And yet they cannot deny good reading to the whole school because of the prurience of a few. The balancing of these two factors makes the task of selection extremely difficult and often frustrating.[14]

TEACHER MILITANCY (NEA VERSUS AFT): PROS AND CONS

Discuss the NEA and the AFT approaches to collective negotiations. The following subtopics may serve to focus attention on a few of the many facets of this problem.[15]

A. *Paternalism versus Participation.* Although the AFT and the NEA negotiate somewhat differently, both organizations believe teachers' work is professional, and they are, therefore, interested in making certain that the children have the best opportunity to learn. . . . The current era is one of participation, and a superintendent who wants to survive and get the

[13] Walter A. Clebsch, *From Sacred to Profane America: The Role of Religion in American History*, New York: Harper & Row, Publishers, 1968, pp. 111–112.

See also Paul Tillich, *My Search for Absolutes*, New York: Simon & Schuster, Inc., 1967, pp. 132 f.

[14] Samuel Withers, "The Library, The Child and the Censor," *New York Times Magazine*, April 8, 1962. See also Thorwald Esbensen, "How Far Have the Book Burners Gone?" *School Executive* 76: 69–71, May 1957; Robert F. Hogan, "Book Selection and Censorship," *National Association of Secondary School Principals Bulletin* 51: 67–77, May 1957; Jack Nelson and Gene Roberts, *The Censors and the Schools*, Boston: Little, Brown & Company, 1963; ACLU *Handbook on Academic Freedom and Tenure*, American Civil Liberties Union, 170 Fifth Avenue, New York, 1968.

[15] Quotations A–G are all taken from Edward B. Shils and C. Taylor Whittier, *Teachers, Administrators, and Collective Bargaining*, New York: Thomas Y. Crowell Company, 1968, pp. 91–92, 175, 213, 215, 402, 423, 434, 486, 502, 532, and 548–549. By permission.

job done must appreciate the growing bargaining position of teacher organizations. Despite their professionalism, the same demand for participation is occurring among nurses, social workers, engineers, physicians, and other specialized public employees.

[Both NEA and AFT agree that] class size, number of classes taught, curriculum, hiring standards, textbooks and supplies, extracurricular activities, in fact, anything having to do with the operation of the school is a matter for professional concern, and it should thus be subject to collective bargaining.

B. *Susceptibility of Women to Union Organization.* [Typically,] young female teachers get married, have children, and leave the teaching ranks. These women definitely return to the active teaching ranks when salary schedules improve. It is estimated that a reserve of over 500,000 inactive teachers exists, with over 90 percent of this group female. According to NEA more than half the female teachers have had one major interruption to their teaching careers.

Unions have never had spectacular success in organizing female college graduates. A vast majority of all teachers are female (70 percent) and the majority of all female teachers are married with husbands living and employed. As a second wage earner, and not so nearly dependent upon job security as male teachers, they are more difficult to sign up on the "strict union approach." However, when the AFT shows a concern for pupil achievement and improving the schools, the female teachers are less likely to react with fear and suspicion.

C. *Strikes and Work Stoppages.* Dr. George W. Taylor, the Chairman of the Special Rockefeller Commission studying [teachers' strikes] . . . wrote:

> I suggest that distinction should be drawn between work stoppages as an expression of a civil protest against patently unfair treatment and their adoption as a regular way of life. . . .
>
> Ours is a meeting-of-minds society grounded upon the conviction that after a negotiation confrontation, opposing interests can and will be accommodated by agreement. The future of our way of life is largely dependent, I believe, upon the institutional forms which are created to channel conflict to make a confrontation of opposing interest possible, and to facilitate the reconciliation of those interests by agreement. In these terms, the current demand by public school teachers for a more effective participation is in the established American tradition. . . .

D. *Negotiation Techniques.* The teachers' demands can be put on a priority basis, and serious bargaining can actually take place in which the teams trade this for that, the procedure known as *quid pro quo*. In a typical *quid pro quo* situation, the board's team bargains for a three-year contract and agrees to offer in exchange two or three built-in wage increases. . . .

A built-in wage increase in the second or third year of the contract will be cheaper in the long run than having the teachers back every year with new demands. . . .

Board members feel that if a contract results in a tangible improvement in the education of the children the cost of the contract is not out of line. A school board might well negotiate with the union to review at the end of the year whether the quality of education and productivity has been increased as a result of the agreement. Heightening the educational requirements for a position in order to qualify for improved salary benefits is a logical use of the *quid pro quo*. . . .

The best technique to utilize during impasse in bargaining is to keep bargaining . . . [rather than to call in] third party neutrals. . . .

E. *Exclusive Bargaining Rights*. Both the NEA and the AFT were late comers with their announcements that they favored exclusive recognition. AFT's announcement came in . . . 1964 . . . and NEA's . . . in August 1965. . . .

[In 1965] The National Association of Secondary School Principals [expressed what now seems to be the prevailing viewpoint on this issue]:

> Whenever two or more groups claim to represent teachers, experience has shown that confusion is best avoided and the negotiative process most effective if that group which represents the majority of the teachers serves as the exclusive spokesman for all the teachers. The selection of such a spokesman must always be a free choice of teachers by means of carefully regulated elections rather than a determination of a school board as to which group it believes represents the majority of its teachers. However, the recognition of one organization as the exclusive negotiating unit must never deny the right of other groups or individuals to present their problems and requests, even though they do not sit at the negotiating table.

F. *Merit Ratings*. Generally speaking, teachers detest performance evaluation. . . .[16] [whereas] School board members remain ardent advocates of merit plans. . . .

G. *Problems of Sovereign Prerogative*. According to Klaus, "A principle holds that those charged with the duty and responsibility of administering a particular governmental function may and must exercise that function themselves, and in the public interest."

Whether it be fire-fighting or education, the governmental function is delegated to an elected or appointed official who must perform for the welfare of the citizens, which [writes Klaus] raises an interesting question:

> In the context of the collective bargaining relationship, the practical issue will be how much of an area can or will government open up to the joint decision-making process of collective bargaining? May or should any of the policy aspects of government management not directly involving working conditions be determined through collective bargaining? Employee organizations will push toward opening up these areas to joint decision-making as labor has done in private industry. Government will want to stand on prerogative.

---

[16] Editor's Note: For an attempt to deal with this problem read John D. McNeil, "Antidote for School Scandal," *Educational Forum* 31: 69–77, November 1966.

Several school districts are now lending their support to achieving greater participation by teacher representatives in the development of educational policies and plans. They do this through joint committees which are discussive and which rely on consultation and communication rather than bargaining. As Ida Klaus says, the "problem is one of containment."

Open Book Exam

1. Briefly trace the successive development of the American teacher training institution from
   a. the normal school, to
   b. the teachers college, to
   c. the multipurpose state college or university with
      (1) undergraduate programs for the preparation of teachers, and
      (2) graduate programs for the continuing education of teachers and school administrators.[17]
2. Make a list of the relative merits and demerits of (a) merit pay and of (b) fixed salary increments. Include in your analysis the problem of dismissing incompetent teachers (and the related problem of raising standards for teacher-training institutions).
3. To what extent are current patterns and procedures of certification overly professionalized, legalistic, and narrowly technical—as is frequently claimed?
   Discuss the merits and demerits of a more widespread use of the so-called "Einstein clause" (a provision allowing persons of outstanding merit to teach, even though they lack the formal requirements in courses in education).
   Do the answers to these questions, to some extent at least, hinge on the question (a) whether the teaching is one in a special subject-centered area (for example, electronics), or (b) whether the teaching is more general (for example, the elementary school, or "reading" as compared with "art" or "music")?
4. What should constitute the substance of the teacher's continuing, advanced education? For the elementary teacher, for example, how should a master's program be designed? For a high school or college teacher, should the advanced study be concentrated in the field he is to teach, or should it be designed to broaden the teacher's understanding of related fields, or even of fields quite remote from his own special training?
5. Should the general (liberal) education of teachers be approximately the same as it is for other professions? Or should it be built around courses such as "philosophy of education" (rather than "philosophy"), "methods of teaching social science" rather than "history," "geography," "sociology," and so forth?

---

[17] For a short history of teacher education in the United States, read Paul Woodring, "A Century of Teacher Education," *School and Society* 90: 236–242, May 5, 1962.

6. Examine the character and operations of various existing teacher's organizations, for example, the National Education Association, the teacher's association in your state or city, the American Federation of Teachers, the American Association of University Professors, and some subject-area organization (e.g., of music teachers or biology teachers). What needs are served by these organizations? What needs are not adequately served?
7. Consider the merits and demerits of each of the following two analogies:
   a. The education profession should be organized in a manner analogous to that of the American Medical Association or the American Bar Association.
   b. The teacher should become organized in a manner analogous to American Federation of Labor (AFL).
8. Under what circumstances, if any, do teachers have a right to strike?
9. Discuss the relative merits of the NEA and the AFT (a) in some specific school system (for example, New York, Michigan, Florida), (b) more generally, in terms of the changing social and political structure of our society.
10. Under what circumstances, if any, do teachers have a right and a duty to apply sanctions, for example, (a) the attempt on the part of the NEA or other influential organizations to dissuade teachers from entering a school system which has treated teachers "unfairly"; or (b) the mass refusal on the part of teachers in a school system to renew their contracts.
11. The AFT maintains that principals must be placed in a separate category from teachers. Can a school function effectively without teachers and the principal working as a team? If so, explain the position of the principal.
12. Do most teachers enter the teaching profession with a sense of mission or merely as job-seekers? Your answer to this question will very likely determine how you will react to the following quotation.

> One thing only, said Mr. Crantit, prevents our established system of education from crumbling into the dust and ashes of the minds which devised it, and that is the stubborn virtue of individual teachers. Teachers who, under-paid and over-worked in a revolting environment—breathing daily the inspissated odours of boyhood and unclean clothes—stand like missionary saints against the hypocrisy of their present employment and the barbarism of tomorrow!
>
> —Eric Linklater, *Laxdale Hall*, cited on the Frontispiece of George N. Allen, *Undercover Teacher*, New York: Doubleday & Company, Inc., 1960.

Index of Names

Boldface page numbers indicate that the author cited is quoted in the text.

Index of Subjects